Essentials of Metaheuristics

A Set of Undergraduate Lecture Notes by

Sean Luke
Department of Computer Science
George Mason University

Second Edition
Online Version 2.0
June, 2013

Figure 0 The Mona Lisa, estimated with the $(5+1)$ Evolution Strategy. The objective is to find a set of fifty polygons which most closely approximates the original image. After Roger Alsing.

Copyright 2009–2013 by Sean Luke. ISBN: 978-1-300-54962-8

Thanks to Carlotta Domeniconi, Kenneth De Jong, John Grefenstette, Christopher Vo, Joseph Harrison, Keith Sullivan, Brian Hrolenok, Bill Langdon, R. Paul Wiegand, Brian Absetz, Jason Branly, Jack Compton, Stephen Donnelly, William Haddon, Beenish Jamil, Eric Kangas, James O'Beirne, Peshal Rupakheti, Nicholas Payette, Lee Spector, "Markus", Don Miner, Brian Ross, Mike Fadock, Ken Oksanen, Asger Ottar Alstrup, Joerg Heitkoetter, Don Sofge, Akhil Shashidhar, Jeff Bassett, Guillermo Calderón-Meza, Hans-Paul Schwefel, Pablo Moscato, Mark Coletti, Yuri Tsoy, Faisal Abidi, Ivan Krasilnikov, Yow Tzu Lim, Uday Kamath, Murilo Pontes, Rasmus Fonseca, Ian Barfield, Forrest Stonedahl, Muhammad Iqbal, Gabriel Catalin Balan, Joseph Zelibor, Daniel Carrera, Maximilian Ernestus, Arcadio Rubio Garcia, Kevin Molloy, Petr Pošík, Brian Olson, Matthew Molineaux, Bill Barksdale, Adam Szkoda, Daniel Rothman, Khaled Ahsan Talukder, Len Matsuyama, Andrew Reeves, Liang Liu, Pier Luca Lanzi, and Vittorio Ziparo.

Get the latest version of this document or suggest improvements here:

http://cs.gmu.edu/~sean/book/metaheuristics/

Cite this document as:

Sean Luke, 2013, *Essentials of Metaheuristics*, Lulu, second edition, available at http://cs.gmu.edu/~sean/book/metaheuristics/

Always include the URL, as this book is primarily found online. Do *not* include the online version numbers unless you must, as Citeseer and Google Scholar may treat each (oft-changing) version as a different book.

BibTeX: @Book{ Luke2013Metaheuristics,
              author =   { Sean Luke },
              title =   { Essentials of Metaheuristics},
              edition =   { second },
              year =   { 2013 },
              publisher = { Lulu },
              note =   { Available for free at http:/cs.gmu.edu/$\sim$sean/book/metaheuristics/ }
            }

This document is licensed under the **Creative Commons Attribution-No Derivative Works 3.0 United States License,** except for those portions of the work licensed differently as described in the next section. To view a copy of this license, visit http://creativecommons.org/licenses/by-nd/3.0/us/ or send a letter to Creative Commons, 171 Second Street, Suite 300, San Francisco, California, 94105, USA. A summary:

- You are free to redistribute this document.
- **You may not** modify, transform, translate, or build upon the document except for personal use.
- You must maintain the author's attribution with the document at all times.
- You may not use the attribution to imply that the author endorses you or your document use.

This summary is just informational: if there is any conflict in interpretation between the summary and the actual license, the actual license always takes precedence.

Certain art and text is not mine. Figure 43 is copyright 2008 by Oskar Sigvardsson, and is distributed under the Creative Commons Attribution 3.0 License. Figure 33 is by Wikipedia User "Solkoll" and is in the public domain. The top Mona Lisa (in Figure 0) is from Wikipedia and is in the public domain. The bottom Mona Lisa is mine but is inspired by Roger Alsing's method (see http://rogeralsing.com/2008/12/07/genetic-programming-evolution-of-mona-lisa/). Note to Roger: it's not Genetic Programming. The data in Table 4 is from the *NIST/SEMATECH e-Handbook of Statistical Methods*, http://itl.nist.gov/div898/handbook/ and is in the public domain.

Cover art for the second print edition is a time plot of the paths of particles in Particle Swarm Optimization working their way towards the optimum of the Rastrigin problem.

Contents

List of Algorithms		**4**
0	**Introduction**	**9**
	0.1 What is a Metaheuristic?	9
	0.2 Algorithms	10
	0.3 Notation	11
1	**Gradient-based Optimization**	**13**
2	**Single-State Methods** Depends on Section 1	**17**
	2.1 Hill-Climbing	17
	2.1.1 The Meaning of Tweak	19
	2.2 Single-State Global Optimization Algorithms	20
	2.3 Adjusting the Modification Procedure: (1+1), (1+λ), and (1, λ)	23
	2.4 Simulated Annealing	25
	2.5 Tabu Search	26
	2.6 Iterated Local Search	28
3	**Population Methods** Depends on Section 2	**31**
	3.1 Evolution Strategies	33
	3.1.1 Mutation and Evolutionary Programming	35
	3.2 The Genetic Algorithm	36
	3.2.1 Crossover and Mutation	37
	3.2.2 More Recombination	41
	3.2.3 Selection	43
	3.3 Exploitative Variations	46
	3.3.1 Elitism	46
	3.3.2 The Steady-State Genetic Algorithm	47
	3.3.3 The Tree-Style Genetic Programming Pipeline	48
	3.3.4 Hybrid Optimization Algorithms	49
	3.3.5 Scatter Search	52
	3.4 Differential Evolution	54
	3.5 Particle Swarm Optimization	55
4	**Representation** Depends on Sections 2 and 3	**59**
	4.1 Vectors	61
	4.1.1 Initialization and Bias	62
	4.1.2 Mutation	63
	4.1.3 Recombination	64
	4.1.4 Heterogeneous Vectors	65
	4.1.5 Phenotype-Specific Mutation or Crossover	66

	4.2	Direct Encoded Graphs 66

    4.2 Direct Encoded Graphs 66
        4.2.1 Initialization 68
        4.2.2 Mutation 70
        4.2.3 Recombination 70
    4.3 Trees and Genetic Programming 73
        4.3.1 Initialization 75
        4.3.2 Recombination 77
        4.3.3 Mutation 78
        4.3.4 Forests and Automatically Defined Functions 79
        4.3.5 Strongly-Typed Genetic Programming 80
        4.3.6 Cellular Encoding 81
        4.3.7 Stack Languages 82
    4.4 Lists 83
        4.4.1 Initialization 86
        4.4.2 Mutation 86
        4.4.3 Recombination 87
    4.5 Rulesets 89
        4.5.1 State-Action Rules 90
        4.5.2 Production Rules 91
        4.5.3 Initialization 93
        4.5.4 Mutation 94
        4.5.5 Recombination 95
    4.6 Bloat 95

5 Parallel Methods   Depends on Section 3   99
    5.1 Multiple Threads 101
    5.2 Island Models 103
    5.3 Master-Slave Fitness Assessment 105
    5.4 Spatially Embedded Models 107

6 Coevolution   Depends on Section 3   109
    6.1 1-Population Competitive Coevolution 111
        6.1.1 Relative Internal Fitness Assessment 113
    6.2 2-Population Competitive Coevolution 117
    6.3 N-Population Cooperative Coevolution 122
    6.4 Niching 127
        6.4.1 Fitness Sharing 128
        6.4.2 Crowding 130

7 Multiobjective Optimization   Depends on Section 3   133
    7.1 Naive Methods 134
    7.2 Non-Dominated Sorting 137
    7.3 Pareto Strength 141

8 Combinatorial Optimization — Depends on Sections 2 and 3 — 147
- 8.1 General-Purpose Optimization and Hard Constraints 148
- 8.2 Greedy Randomized Adaptive Search Procedures 151
- 8.3 Ant Colony Optimization 152
  - 8.3.1 The Ant System 153
  - 8.3.2 The Ant Colony System 156
- 8.4 Guided Local Search 158

9 Optimization by Model Fitting — Depends on Sections 3 and 4 — 161
- 9.1 Model Fitting by Classification 161
- 9.2 Model Fitting with a Distribution 164
  - 9.2.1 Univariate Estimation of Distribution Algorithms 167
  - 9.2.2 Multivariate Estimation of Distribution Algorithms 171

10 Policy Optimization — Depends on Sections 1, 3, and 4 — 173
- 10.1 Reinforcement Learning: Dense Policy Optimization 173
  - 10.1.1 Q-Learning 175
- 10.2 Sparse Stochastic Policy Optimization 182
  - 10.2.1 Rule Representation 183
- 10.3 Pitt Approach Rule Systems 186
- 10.4 Michigan Approach Learning Classifier Systems 191
- 10.5 Regression with the Michigan Approach 200
- 10.6 Is this Genetic Programming? 204

11 Miscellany — Depends on Section 4 — 205
- 11.1 Experimental Methodology 205
  - 11.1.1 Random Number Generators, Replicability, and Duplicability 205
  - 11.1.2 Comparing Techniques 206
- 11.2 Simple Test Problems 213
  - 11.2.1 Boolean Vector Problems 213
  - 11.2.2 Real-Valued Vector Problems 214
  - 11.2.3 Multiobjective Problems 218
  - 11.2.4 Genetic Programming Problems 220
- 11.3 Where to Go Next 224
  - 11.3.1 Bibliographies, Surveys, and Websites 224
  - 11.3.2 Publications 226
  - 11.3.3 Tools 227
  - 11.3.4 Conferences 229
  - 11.3.5 Journals 231
  - 11.3.6 Email Lists 231
- 11.4 Example Course Syllabi for the Text 232

Index 233

List of Algorithms

0	Bubble Sort	11
1	Gradient Ascent	13
2	Newton's Method (Adapted for Optima Finding)	14
3	Gradient Ascent with Restarts	15
4	Hill-Climbing	17
5	Steepest Ascent Hill-Climbing	18
6	Steepest Ascent Hill-Climbing With Replacement	18
7	Generate a Random Real-Valued Vector	19
8	Bounded Uniform Convolution	19
9	Random Search	20
10	Hill-Climbing with Random Restarts	21
11	Gaussian Convolution	23
12	Sample from the Gaussian Distribution (Box-Muller-Marsaglia Polar Method)	24
13	Simulated Annealing	25
14	Tabu Search	26
15	Feature-based Tabu Search	27
16	Iterated Local Search (ILS) with Random Restarts	29
17	An Abstract Generational Evolutionary Algorithm (EA)	32
18	The (μ, λ) Evolution Strategy	33
19	The $(\mu + \lambda)$ Evolution Strategy	34
20	The Genetic Algorithm (GA)	37
21	Generate a Random Bit-Vector	37
22	Bit-Flip Mutation	38
23	One-Point Crossover	38
24	Two-Point Crossover	39
25	Uniform Crossover	39
26	Randomly Shuffle a Vector	41
27	Uniform Crossover among K Vectors	41
28	Line Recombination	42
29	Intermediate Recombination	42
30	Fitness-Proportionate Selection	43
31	Stochastic Universal Sampling	44
32	Tournament Selection	45
33	The Genetic Algorithm with Elitism	46
34	The Steady-State Genetic Algorithm	47
35	The Genetic Algorithm (Tree-Style Genetic Programming Pipeline)	49
36	An Abstract Hybrid Evolutionary and Hill-Climbing Algorithm	50
37	A Simplified Scatter Search with Path Relinking	53
38	Differential Evolution (DE)	55
39	Particle Swarm Optimization (PSO)	57
40	A Gray Coding	61
41	Integer Randomization Mutation	63
42	Random Walk Mutation	63
43	Line Recombination for Integers	64

44	Intermediate Recombination for Integers	65
45	Gaussian Convolution Respecting Zeros	67
46	Sample from the Geometric Distribution	68
47	Build A Simple Graph	69
48	Build a Simple Directed Acyclic Graph	69
49	Select a Subset	70
50	Select a Subset (Second Technique)	71
51	Select a Subgraph	71
52	Randomly Merge One Graph Into Another	72
53	The Grow Algorithm	75
54	The Full Algorithm	76
55	The Ramped Half-and-Half Algorithm	76
56	The PTC2 Algorithm	77
57	Subtree Selection	78
58	Random Walk	87
59	One-Point List Crossover	88
60	Two-Point List Crossover	88
61	Duplicate Removal	89
62	Simple Production Ruleset Generation	94
63	Lexicographic Tournament Selection	96
64	Double Tournament Selection	97
65	Thread Pool Functions	100
66	Fine-Grained Parallel Fitness Assessment	101
67	Simple Parallel Fitness Assessment	101
68	Simple Parallel Genetic Algorithm-style Breeding	102
69	Fine-Grained Parallel Genetic Algorithm-style Breeding	102
70	An Abstract Generational Evolutionary Algorithm With Island Model Messaging	104
71	Fine-Grained Master-Side Fitness Assessment	105
72	Threadsafe Collection Functions	106
73	Asynchronous Evolution	107
74	Spatial Breeding	108
75	Random Walk Selection	108
76	An Abstract Generational 1-Population Competitive Coevolutionary Algorithm	113
77	Pairwise Relative Fitness Assessment	114
78	Complete Relative Fitness Assessment	114
79	*K*-fold Relative Fitness Assessment	115
80	More Precise *K*-fold Relative Fitness Assessment	115
81	Single-Elimination Tournament Relative Fitness Assessment	116
82	An Abstract Sequential 2-Population Competitive Coevolutionary Algorithm	118
83	*K*-fold Relative Fitness Assessment with an Alternative Population	119
84	An Abstract Parallel 2-Population Competitive Coevolutionary Algorithm	119
85	*K*-fold Relative Joint Fitness Assessment with an Alternative Population	120
86	An Abstract Parallel Previous 2-Population Competitive Coevolutionary Algorithm	121
87	*K*-fold Relative Fitness Assessment with the Fittest of an Alternative Population	121
88	An Abstract Sequential *N*-Population Cooperative Coevolutionary Algorithm (CCEA)	124

89	*K*-fold Joint Fitness Assessment with $N-1$ Collaborating Populations	124
90	An Abstract Parallel *N*-Population Cooperative Coevolutionary Algorithm	125
91	*K*-fold Joint Fitness Assessment of *N* Populations	125
92	Implicit Fitness Sharing	129
93	Deterministic Crowding	131
94	Multiobjective Lexicographic Tournament Selection	135
95	Multiobjective Ratio Tournament Selection	136
96	Multiobjective Majority Tournament Selection	136
97	Multiple Tournament Selection	137
98	Pareto Domination	137
99	Pareto Domination Binary Tournament Selection	138
100	Computing a Pareto Non-Dominated Front	138
101	Front Rank Assignment by Non-Dominated Sorting	139
102	Multiobjective Sparsity Assignment	140
103	Non-Dominated Sorting Lexicographic Tournament Selection With Sparsity	140
104	An Abstract Version of the Non-Dominated Sorting Genetic Algorithm II (NSGA-II)	141
105	Compute the Distance of the *K*th Closest Individual	143
106	SPEA2 Archive Construction	144
107	An Abstract Version of the Strength Pareto Evolutionary Algorithm 2 (SPEA2)	144
108	Greedy Randomized Adaptive Search Procedures (GRASP)	151
109	An Abstract Ant Colony Optimization Algorithm (ACO)	152
110	The Ant System (AS)	154
111	Pheromone Updating with a Learning Rate	155
112	The Ant Colony System (ACS)	157
113	Guided Local Search (GLS) with Random Updates	160
114	An Abstract Version of the Learnable Evolution Model (LEM)	162
115	Simple Rejection Sampling	163
116	Region-based Sampling	163
117	Weighted Rejection Sampling	164
118	An Abstract Estimation of Distribution Algorithm (EDA)	165
119	Population-Based Incremental Learning (PBIL)	168
120	The Compact Genetic Algorithm (cGA)	169
121	An Abstract Version of the Bayesian Optimization Algorithm (BOA)	172
122	*Q*-Learning with a Model	178
123	Model-Free *Q*-Learning	179
124	SAMUEL Fitness Assessment	188
125	Zeroth Classifier System Fitness Updating	193
126	Zeroth Classifier System Fitness Redistribution	193
127	The Zeroth Level Classifier System (ZCS)	194
128	XCS Fitness-Weighted Utility of an Action	196
129	XCS Best Action Determination	196
130	XCS Action Selection	196
131	XCS Fitness Updating	197
132	XCS Fitness Redistribution	198
133	XCS Fitness Updating (Extended)	199

- 134 XCSF Fitness-Weighted Collective Prediction 201
- 135 XCSF Fitness Updating 202
- 136 The XCSF Algorithm 203
- 137 Create a Uniform Orthonormal Matrix 217

0 Introduction

This is a set of lecture notes for an undergraduate class on **metaheuristics**. They were constructed for a course I taught in Spring of 2009, and I wrote them because, well, there's a lack of undergraduate texts on the topic. As these are *lecture notes* for an *undergraduate* class on the topic, which is unusual, these notes have certain traits. First, they're informal and contain a number of my own personal biases and misinformation. Second, they are light on theory and examples: they're mostly descriptions of algorithms and handwavy, intuitive explanations about why and where you'd want to use them. Third, they're chock full of algorithms great and small. I think these notes would best serve as a complement to a textbook, but can also stand alone as rapid introduction to the field.

I make **no guarantees whatsoever** about the correctness of the algorithms or text in these notes. Indeed, they're likely to have a lot of errors. *Please* tell me of any errors you find (and correct!). Some complex algorithms have been presented in simplified versions. In those cases I've noted it.

0.1 What is a Metaheuristic?

Metaheuristics is a rather unfortunate[1] term often used to describe a major subfield, indeed the primary subfield, of **stochastic optimization**. Stochastic optimization is the general class of algorithms and techniques which employ some degree of randomness to find optimal (or as optimal as possible) solutions to hard problems. Metaheuristics are the most general of these kinds of algorithms, and are applied to a very wide range of problems.

What kinds of problems? In *Jacobellis v. Ohio* (1964, regarding obscenity), the United States Supreme Court Justice Potter Stewart famously wrote,

> I shall not today attempt further to define the kinds of material I understand to be embraced within that shorthand description; and perhaps I could never succeed in intelligibly doing so. **But I know it when I see it**, and the motion picture involved in this case is not that.

Metaheuristics are applied to *I know it when I see it* problems. They're algorithms used to find answers to problems when you have very little to help you: you don't know beforehand what the optimal solution looks like, you don't know how to go about finding it in a principled way, you have very little heuristic information to go on, and brute-force search is out of the question because the space is too large. *But* if you're given a candidate solution to your problem, you *can* test it and assess how good it is. That is, you know a good one when you see it.

For example: imagine if you're trying to find an optimal set of robot behaviors for a soccer goalie robot. You have a simulator for the robot and can test any given robot behavior set and assign it a quality (you know a good one when you see it). And you've come up with a definition for what robot behavior sets look like in general. But you have no idea what the optimal behavior set is, nor even how to go about finding it.

---

[1] Ordinarily I'd call the subfield *stochastic optimization*. But that's too general a term; it includes important algorithms like **Markov Chain Monte Carlo (MCMC)** or **Gibbs Sampling**, which are *not* in this category. Metaheuristics has lately been the term of use, but I think it's profoundly misleading and weird. When I hear "metadiscussion" I think: *a discussion about discussions*. Likewise when I hear "metaheuristic" I think: *a heuristic about (or for) heuristics*. That's not at all what these algorithms are about! Perhaps the lesser-used term **black box optimization** would be better, though it too comes with some additional baggage. **Weak methods** is also too broad a term: it doesn't imply stochasticity. Sometimes the term **stochastic search** is used: but I usually define "search" problems as all-or-nothing: either you find the solution or you don't. We're not doing search; we're doing optimization.

The simplest thing you could do in this situation is **Random Search**: just try random behavior sets as long as you have time, and return the best one you discovered. But before you give up and start doing random search, consider the following alternative, known as **Hill-Climbing**. Start with a random behavior set. Then make a small, random modification to it and try the new version. If the new version is better, throw the old one away. Else throw the new version away. Now make another small, random modification to your current version (which ever one you didn't throw away). If this newest version is better, throw away your current version, else throw away the newest version. Repeat as long as you can.

Hill-climbing is a simple metaheuristic algorithm. It exploits a heuristic belief about your space of candidate solutions which is usually true for many problems: that similar solutions tend to behave similarly (and tend to have similar quality), so small modifications will generally result in small, well-behaved changes in quality, allowing us to "climb the hill" of quality up to good solutions. This heuristic belief is one of the **central defining features of metaheuristics**: indeed, nearly all metaheuristics are essentially elaborate combinations of hill-climbing and random search.

The "I know it when I see it" problems tackled by metaheuristics are a subclass of **inverse problems**. An inverse problem is one in which you have a test function f which takes a candidate solution and produces an assessment of it, but in which it's difficult or impossible to construct the inverse function f^{-1} which takes an assessment and returns a candidate solution which would have had that assessment.[2] In our example, our robot simulator and test procedure is f. But what we *really* want is an inverse function f^{-1} which takes an assessment and returns a robot behavior set. That way, if we were lucky, we could plug in the optimal assessment value into f^{-1} and get the optimal robot behavior set.

Optimization methods (such as metheuristics) are designed to overcome inverse problems. But many classic optimization techniques, such as **Gradient Ascent** (Algorithm 1) make strong assumptions about the nature of f: for example, that we also know its first derivative f'. Metaheuristics make far looser assumptions, and sometimes make none at all. This means that metaheuristics are very general, but also means that they're often best thought of as last-ditch methods, used when *no other known technique works*. As it so happens, that's the case for an enormous, important, and growing collection of problems.

0.2 Algorithms

The lecture notes have a lot of algorithms, great and small. Everything from large evolutionary computation algorithms to things as simple as "how to shuffle an array". Algorithms appear for even the most trivial and obvious of tasks. I strove to be pedantic in case anyone had any questions.

Algorithms in this book are written peculiarly. If an algorithm takes parameters, they will appear first followed by a blank line. If there are no parameters, the algorithm begins immediately. In some cases the algorithm is actually several functions, each labelled **procedure**. Sometimes certain shared, static global variables are defined which appear at the beginning and are labelled **global**. In a few cases, different parts of the algorithm are meant to be performed at different times or rates. In this case you may see some parts labelled, for example, **perform once per generation** or **perform every n iterations**, versus **perform each time**. Here is an example of a simple algorithm:

---

[2]Inverse problems are also notable in that f^{-1} may not be a valid function at all. f^{-1} may be **overspecified**, meaning that there are multiple candidate solutions which all yield a given assessment (which should be returned?). And f^{-1} may also be **underspecified**, meaning that some assessments have *no* candidate solution at all which have them (what should be returned then?).

Algorithm 0 *Bubble Sort*
1: $\vec{v} \leftarrow \langle v_1, ..., v_l \rangle$ vector to sort ▷ User-provided parameters to the algorithm appear here
  ▷ Then a blank space
2: **repeat** ▷ Algorithm begins here
3:   *swapped* $\leftarrow$ false ▷ $\leftarrow$ always means "is set to"
4:   **for** i from 1 to $l-1$ **do** ▷ Note that l is defined by v_l in Line 1
5:     **if** $v_i > v_{i+1}$ **then**
6:       Swap v_i and v_{i+1}
7:       *swapped* $\leftarrow$ true
8: **until** *swapped* = false ▷ = means "is equal to"
9: **return** $\vec{v}$ ▷ Some algorithms return nothing, so there is no **return** statement

Note that the parameters to the function are only loosely specified: and sometimes when we call a function, we don't explicitly state the parameters, if it's obvious what needs to be provided. Yeah, I could have been more formal in a lot of places. So sue me.[3]

0.3 Notation[3]

There's little special here. But just to dot our i's and cross our t's:

- **Numbers** and **booleans** are denoted with lower-case letters, greek symbols, or words (n, λ, *min*, *popsize*). The default "empty" or **"null" element** is denoted with $\square$. **Ranges** of numbers are described like this: from 1 to n inclusive. Ranges can be of integers or real values. The symbol $\leftarrow$ always means "is set to", and the symbol = usually means "equals".

- **Candidate solutions** (sometimes called **individuals, particles,** or **trails**) are indicated with upper-case letters or words (*Best, S, P_i*). Some candidate solutions are actually vectors and are described like vectors below. Others consist of a number of **components**, often designated $C_1, ..., C_j$. Candidate solutions may be associated with some kind of **quality** (**fitness**), usually via a function like Quality(S) or Fitness(P_i). Quality can be set as well. Usually quality is a single number; but can in some cases (for multiobjective optimization) be a group of numbers called **objectives**. The value of objective O_j, assigned to individual P_i, is accessed via a function like ObjectiveValue(O_j, P_i). In certain cases various other attributes may be assigned to individuals or to other objects.

- **Collections** (or bags, or groups, or pools, or lists, or multisets) are groups of objects where the objects usually don't have to be unique. In fact, the lecture notes rarely use sets, and abundantly use collections. A collection is denoted with a capital letter like P and contains some number of elements in braces $\{P_1, ..., P_n\}$. The size of P is $||P||$ or (in this case) n. Membership (or lack thereof) is indicated with $\in$ or $\notin$. Usually there is an implicit order in a collection, so you can refer to its elements uniquely (P_4 or P_i) and can scan through it like this (**for** each element $P_i \in P$ **do** ... P_i) or this (**for** i from 1 to n **do** ... P_i). Collections are generally read-only, though their elements may allow internal modification.

---
[3]Don't sue me. Thanks.
[3]This is *always* the most boring part of a book! Why are you reading this?

The union operator ($\cup$) is abused to indicate concatenating collections (like $P \leftarrow P \cup Q$). This is often used to add an element to a collection like $P \leftarrow P \cup \{R_j\}$. The minus sign is abused to indicate removing all elements that are in another collection, as in $P - M$, or removing a specific element from a collection ($P \leftarrow P - \{P_2\}$). In all these cases, presume that the new collection retains the implicit order from the old collection or collections.

The most common collections are the ones used for **populations**. Usually I denote populations with P or Q. Occasionally we need to have a collection of populations, denoted like this: $P^{(1)}, ..., P^{(n)}$. An individual numbered j in population $P^{(i)}$ would be $P^{(i)}_j$.

Sometimes children will be denoted C_a and C_b, etc. This doesn't imply the existence of a collection called C (though it's generally harmless to do so).

- **First-in, First-out Queues** are treated like collections, with the additional ability to add to the end of them and remove elements from the front or from an arbitrary location.

- **Vectors** are denoted with an over-arrow ($\vec{x}, \overrightarrow{Best}$) and contain some number of elements in angle brackets $\langle x_1, ..., x_n \rangle$. Unlike collections, vectors are modifiable. An element in a vector can be replaced with another object at the same location. Slots may not be simply deleted from a vector, but vectors can be extended by adding elements to the end of them. I use vectors instead of collections when we must explicitly change elements in certain locations.

- **Tuples** are vectors with named slots like $\vec{t} \leftarrow \langle t_{\text{lock}}, t_{\text{data}} \rangle$, rather than numbered slots.

- Two-dimensional **Arrays** or **Matrices** are denoted with capital letters (A) and their elements can be referred to in the usual manner: $A_{i,j}$. Like vectors, array elements can be replaced.

- **Probability Distributions** and other **Models** are denoted with a capital letter like T. Distributions and Models are constructed or updated; then we select random numbers under them. Along those lines, variances are denoted with σ^2, standard deviations with σ, and means are often denoted with μ.

- When passed around as data, **Functions** are in lower-case, as in f or $f(node)$.

1 Gradient-based Optimization

Before we get into metaheuristics, let's start with a traditional mathematical method for finding the maximum of a function: **Gradient Ascent**.[4] The idea is to identify the slope and move up it. Simple! The function we're going to maximize is $f(x)$. This method doesn't require us to compute or even know $f(x)$, but it *does* assume we can compute the slope of x, that is, we have $f'(x)$.

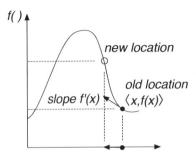

Figure 1 Gradient Ascent with a negative slope. x is decreasing.

The technique is very simple. We start with an arbitrary value for x. We then repeatedly add to it a small portion of its slope, that is, $x \leftarrow x + \alpha f'(x)$, where α is a very small positive value. If the slope is positive, x will increase. If the slope is negative, x will decrease. Figure 1 roughly illustrates this. Ultimately x will move up the function until it is at the peak, at which point the slope is zero and x won't change any more.

We're usually not interested in simple one-dimensional functions like this: more generally, we'd like to find the maximum of a multidimensional function. To do this we replace x with the vector $\vec{x}$, and replace the slope $f'(x)$ with the *gradient* of $\vec{x}$, $\nabla f(\vec{x})$. As a reminder: the gradient is simply a vector where each element is the slope of $\vec{x}$ in that dimension, that is, $\langle \frac{\partial f}{\partial x_1}, \frac{\partial f}{\partial x_2}, ..., \frac{\partial f}{\partial x_n} \rangle$. So basically we're going up the slope in all dimensions at once. Here's the Gradient Ascent algorithm in its full five-line glory:

Algorithm 1 *Gradient Ascent*

1: $\vec{x} \leftarrow$ random initial vector
2: **repeat**
3: $\quad \vec{x} \leftarrow \vec{x} + \alpha \nabla f(\vec{x})$ $\qquad\qquad\qquad\qquad\qquad$ ▷ In one dimension: $x \leftarrow x + \alpha f'(x)$
4: **until** $\vec{x}$ is the ideal solution or we have run out of time
5: **return** $\vec{x}$

Note that the algorithm runs until we've found "the ideal solution" or "we have run out of time". How do we know that we've got the ideal solution? Typically when the slope is 0. However there are points besides **maxima** where this is the case: the **minima** of functions (of course) and also **saddle points** such as in Figure 2.

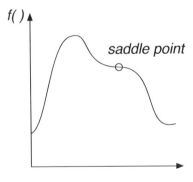

Figure 2 A saddle point.

One issue with Gradient Ascent is **convergence time**. As we get close to the maximum of the function, Gradient Ascent will *overshoot* the top and land on the other side of the hill. It may overshoot the top many times, bouncing back and forth as it moves closer to the maximum. Figure 3 shows this situation.

One of the reasons for this is that the size of the jumps Gradient Ascent makes is entirely based on the current slope. If the slope is very steep the jump will be large even if it's not warranted. One

---

[4]Actually, the method is usually called **Gradient Descent** because it's used to find the *minimum* of a function. To do that, we just *subtract* the gradient or slope rather than *add* it, that is, Algorithm 1 has its line changed to $\vec{x} \leftarrow \vec{x} - \alpha \nabla f(\vec{x})$. But in our later examples we're always finding maxima, so we're going to be consistent here.

way to deal with this is to tune Gradient Ascent for your problem, by adjusting the value of α. A very small value of α and Gradient Ascent won't overshoot hills but it may take a long time to march up the hills and converge to the top. But a very big value of α will cause Gradient Ascent to constantly overshoot the hills which *also* causes it to take a long time to converge to the maximum, if at all. We're looking for a value of α which is "just right".

We could also modify the algorithm to consider other factors. For example, if we could compute not only $f'(x)$ but also $f''(x)$, we could use **Newton's Method**.[5] This variation on Gradient Ascent includes an additional $\frac{-1}{f''(x)}$ like so: $x \leftarrow x - \alpha \frac{f'(x)}{f''(x)}$. This modification dampens α as we approach a zero slope. Additionally Newton's method no longer converges to just maxima: because of the second derivative, it'll head towards any kind of zero-slope point (maxima, minima, or saddle points).

And the multidimensional situation is not as simple as in Gradient Ascent. The multidimensional version of a first derivative $f'(x)$ is the gradient $\nabla f(\vec{x})$. But the multidimensional version of a *second* derivative $f''(x)$ is a complex matrix called a **Hessian** $H_f(\vec{x})$ consisting of partial second derivatives along each dimension. The Hessian is shown in Figure 4.

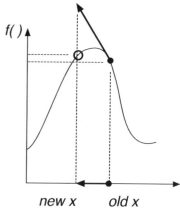

Figure 3 Gradient Ascent overshooting the maximum.

To make matters worse, we're *dividing* by the second derivative, which in the multidimensional case involves finding the inverse of this matrix. Overall, the method looks like this:

Algorithm 2 *Newton's Method (Adapted for Optima Finding)*
1: $\vec{x} \leftarrow$ random initial vector
2: **repeat**
3: $\quad \vec{x} \leftarrow \vec{x} - \alpha [H_f(\vec{x})]^{-1} \nabla f(\vec{x})$ $\qquad \triangleright$ In one dimension: $x \leftarrow x - \alpha \frac{f'(x)}{f''(x)}$
4: **until** $\vec{x}$ is the ideal solution or we have run out of time
5: **return** $\vec{x}$

Because it employs the second derivative, Newton's Method generally converges faster than regular Gradient Ascent, and it also gives us the information to determine if we're at the top of a local maximum (as opposed to a minimum or saddle point) because at a maximum, $f'(x)$ is zero and $f''(x)$ is negative.

But even so, this doesn't get around the *real* problem with these methods: they get caught in **local optima**. Local optima of a function are the optima (in our case, maxima) of a local region. **Global optima** are the optima of the entire function. Figure 5 shows the trace of Gradient Ascent getting caught in a local optimum. Gradient Ascent and Newton's Method are **local optimization algorithms**.

$$H_f(\vec{x}) = \begin{bmatrix} \frac{\partial}{\partial x_1} \frac{\partial f}{\partial x_1} & \frac{\partial}{\partial x_1} \frac{\partial f}{\partial x_2} & \cdots & \frac{\partial}{\partial x_1} \frac{\partial f}{\partial x_n} \\ \frac{\partial}{\partial x_2} \frac{\partial f}{\partial x_1} & \frac{\partial}{\partial x_2} \frac{\partial f}{\partial x_2} & \cdots & \frac{\partial}{\partial x_2} \frac{\partial f}{\partial x_n} \\ \vdots & \vdots & \ddots & \vdots \\ \frac{\partial}{\partial x_n} \frac{\partial f}{\partial x_1} & \frac{\partial}{\partial x_n} \frac{\partial f}{\partial x_2} & \cdots & \frac{\partial}{\partial x_n} \frac{\partial f}{\partial x_n} \end{bmatrix}$$

Figure 4 The Hessian $H_f(\vec{x})$.

---

[5] As in *Sir Isaac* Newton, 1642–1727. This method is normally used to find the zeros (roots) of functions, but it's easily modified to hunt for optima, as we've done here.

How do you escape local optima? With the tools we have so far, there's really only one way: change α to a sufficiently large value that the algorithm potentially overshoots not only the top of its hill but actually lands on the *next hill*.

Alternatively, we could put Gradient Ascent in a big loop: each time we start with a random starting point, and end when we've reached a local optimum. We keep trying over and over again, and eventually return the best solution discovered. To determine what the "best solution discovered" is, we need to be able to compute $f(x)$ (something we've not required up till now) so we can compare results. Assuming we have that, we can now construct a **global optimization algorithm**.

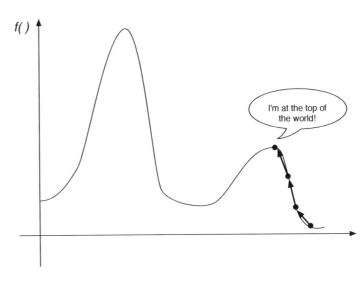

Figure 5 Gradient Ascent stuck in a local optimum.

Algorithm 3 *Gradient Ascent with Restarts*
1: $\vec{x} \leftarrow$ random initial value
2: $\vec{x}^* \leftarrow \vec{x}$ ▷ $\vec{x}^*$ will hold our best discovery so far
3: **repeat**
4:     **repeat**
5:         $\vec{x} \leftarrow \vec{x} + \alpha \nabla f(\vec{x})$ ▷ In one dimension: $x \leftarrow x + \alpha f'(x)$
6:     **until** $||\nabla f(\vec{x})|| = 0$ ▷ In one dimension: **until** $f'(x) = 0$
7:     **if** $f(\vec{x}) > f(\vec{x}^*)$ **then**   ▷ Found a new best result!
8:         $\vec{x}^* \leftarrow \vec{x}$
9:     $\vec{x} \leftarrow$ random value
10: **until** we have run out of time
11: **return** $\vec{x}^*$

A global optimization algorithm is guaranteed to find the global optimum if it runs long enough. The above algorithm is really global only in theory: we'll likely never have $f'(x)$ *precisely equal to* 0. So we'll have to fudge it: if $-\epsilon < f'(x) < \epsilon$ for some very small value of ϵ, we'll consider that "close enough to zero".[6]

---

[6]There is a gotcha with the algorithms described here: what happens when part of the function is totally flat? There's no gradient to ascend, which leads to some problems. Let's say you're in a perfectly flat valley (a local minimum) of the function. All around you the slope is 0, so Gradient Ascent won't move at all. It's stuck. Even worse: the second derivative is 0 as well, so for Newton's Method, $\frac{f'(x)}{f''(x)} = \frac{0}{0}$. Eesh. And to top it off, $f'(x) = f''(x) = 0$ for flat minima, flat saddle points, *and* flat maxima. Perhaps adding a bit of randomness might help in some of these situations: but that's for the next section....

2 Single-State Methods

Gradient-based optimization makes a big assumption: that you can compute the first (or even the second) derivative. That's a *big* assumption. If you are optimizing a well-formed, well-understood mathematical function, it's reasonable. But in most cases, you can't compute the gradient of the function *because you don't even know what the function is*. All you have is a way of creating or modifying inputs to the function, testing them, and assessing their quality.

For example, imagine that you have a humanoid robot simulator, and you're trying to find an optimal loop of timed operations to keep the robot walking forward without falling over. You have some n different operations, and your candidate solutions are arbitrary-length strings of these operations. You can plug a string in the simulator and get a quality out (how far the robot moved forward before it fell over). How do you find a good solution?

All you're given is a black box (in this case, the robot simulator) describing a **problem** that you'd like to optimize. The box has a slot where you can submit a **candidate solution** to the problem (here, a string of timed robot operations). Then you press the big red button and out comes the assessed **quality** of that candidate solution. You have no idea what kind of surface the quality assessment function looks like when plotted. Your candidate solution doesn't even have to be a vector of numbers: it could be a graph structure, or a tree, or a set of rules, or a string of robot operations! Whatever is appropriate for the problem.

To optimize a candidate solution in this scenario, you need to be able to do four things:

- Provide one or more initial candidate solutions. This is known as the **initialization procedure**.
- Assess the Quality of a candidate solution. This is known as the **assessment procedure**.
- Make a Copy of a candidate solution.
- Tweak a candidate solution, which produces a *randomly slightly different* candidate solution. This, plus the Copy operation, are collectively known as the **modification procedure**.

To this the algorithm will typically provide a **selection procedure** that decides which candidate solutions to retain and which to reject as it wanders through the space of possible solutions to the problem.

2.1 Hill-Climbing

Let's begin with a simple technique, **Hill-Climbing**. This technique is related to gradient ascent, but it doesn't require you to know the strength of the gradient or even its direction: you just iteratively test new candidate solutions in the region of your current candidate, and adopt the new ones if they're better. This enables you to climb up the hill until you reach a local optimum.

Algorithm 4 *Hill-Climbing*
1: $S \leftarrow$ some initial candidate solution $\qquad \triangleright$ The Initialization Procedure
2: **repeat**
3: $\quad R \leftarrow$ Tweak(Copy(S)) $\qquad \triangleright$ The Modification Procedure
4: $\quad$ **if** Quality(R) > Quality(S) **then** $\qquad \triangleright$ The Assessment and Selection Procedures
5: $\quad\quad S \leftarrow R$
6: **until** S is the ideal solution or we have run out of time
7: **return** S

Notice the strong resemblance between Hill-Climbing and Gradient Ascent. The only real difference is that Hill-Climbing's more general Tweak operation must instead rely on a **stochastic** (partially random) approach to hunting around for better candidate solutions. Sometimes it finds worse ones nearby, sometimes it finds better ones.

We can make this algorithm a little more aggressive: create n "tweaks" to a candidate solution all at one time, and then possibly adopt the best one. This modified algorithm is called **Steepest Ascent Hill-Climbing**, because by sampling all around the original candidate solution and then picking the best, we're essentially sampling the gradient and marching straight up it.

Algorithm 5 *Steepest Ascent Hill-Climbing*
1: $n \leftarrow$ number of tweaks desired to sample the gradient

2: $S \leftarrow$ some initial candidate solution
3: **repeat**
4:     $R \leftarrow$ Tweak(Copy(S))
5:     **for** $n - 1$ times **do**
6:        $W \leftarrow$ Tweak(Copy(S))
7:        **if** Quality(W) $>$ Quality(R) **then**
8:           $R \leftarrow W$
9:     **if** Quality(R) $>$ Quality(S) **then**
10:        $S \leftarrow R$
11: **until** S is the ideal solution or we have run out of time
12: **return** S

A popular variation, which I dub **Steepest Ascent Hill-Climbing with Replacement**, is to not bother comparing R to S: instead, we just replace S directly with R. Of course, this runs the risk of losing our best solution of the run, so we'll augment the algorithm to keep the best-discovered-so-far solution stashed away, in a reserve variable called *Best*. At the end of the run, we return *Best*. In nearly all future algorithms we'll use the store-in-*Best* theme, so get used to seeing it!

Algorithm 6 *Steepest Ascent Hill-Climbing With Replacement*
1: $n \leftarrow$ number of tweaks desired to sample the gradient

2: $S \leftarrow$ some initial candidate solution
3: *Best* $\leftarrow S$
4: **repeat**
5:     $R \leftarrow$ Tweak(Copy(S))
6:     **for** $n - 1$ times **do**
7:        $W \leftarrow$ Tweak(Copy(S))
8:        **if** Quality(W) $>$ Quality(R) **then**
9:           $R \leftarrow W$
10:     $S \leftarrow R$
11:     **if** Quality(S) $>$ Quality(*Best*) **then**
12:        *Best* $\leftarrow S$
13: **until** *Best* is the ideal solution or we have run out of time
14: **return** *Best*

2.1.1 The Meaning of Tweak

The initialization, Copy, Tweak, and (to a lesser extent) fitness assessment functions collectively define the **representation** of your candidate solution. Together they stipulate what your candidate solution is made up of and how it operates.

What might a candidate solution look like? It could be a vector; or an arbitrary-length list of objects; or an unordered set or collection of objects; or a tree; or a graph. Or any combination of these. Whatever seems to be appropriate to your problem. If you can create the four functions above in a reasonable fashion, you're in business.

One simple and common representation for candidate solutions, which we'll stick to for now, is the same as the one used in the gradient methods: a **fixed-length vector of real-valued numbers**. Creating a random such vector is easy: just pick random numbers within your chosen bounds. If the bounds are *min* and *max* inclusive, and the vector length is l, we could do this:

Algorithm 7 *Generate a Random Real-Valued Vector*
1:   *min* ← minimum desired vector element value
2:   *max* ← maximum desired vector element value

3:   $\vec{v}$ ← a new vector $\langle v_1, v_2, ... v_l \rangle$
4:   **for** i from 1 to l **do**
5:       v_i ← random number chosen uniformly between *min* and *max* inclusive
6:   **return** $\vec{v}$

To Tweak a vector we might (as one of many possibilities) add a small amount of random noise to each number: in keeping with our present definition of Tweak, let's assume **for now** that this noise is no larger than a small value. Here's a simple way of adding bounded, uniformly distributed random noise to a vector. For each slot in the vector, if a coin-flip of probability p comes up heads, we find some bounded uniform random noise to add to the number in that slot. In most cases we keep $p = 1$.

Algorithm 8 *Bounded Uniform Convolution*
1:   $\vec{v}$ ← vector $\langle v_1, v_2, ... v_l \rangle$ to be convolved
2:   p ← probability of adding noise to an element in the vector   ▷ Often $p = 1$
3:   r ← half-range of uniform noise
4:   *min* ← minimum desired vector element value
5:   *max* ← maximum desired vector element value

6:   **for** i from 1 to l **do**
7:       **if** $p \geq$ random number chosen uniformly from 0.0 to 1.0 **then**
8:           **repeat**
9:               n ← random number chosen uniformly from $-r$ to r inclusive
10:          **until** $min \leq v_i + n \leq max$
11:          $v_i \leftarrow v_i + n$
12:   **return** $\vec{v}$

We now have a knob we can turn: r, the size of the bound on Tweak. If the size is very small, then Hill-Climbing will march right up a local hill and be unable to make the jump to the next hill because the bound is too small for it to jump that far. Once it's on the top of a hill, everywhere it jumps will be worse than where it is presently, so it stays put. Further, the rate at which it climbs the hill will be bounded by its small size. On the other hand, if the size is large, then Hill-Climbing will bounce around a lot. Importantly, when it is near the top of a hill, it will have a difficult time converging to the peak, as most of its moves will be so large as to overshoot the peak.

Thus small sizes of the bound move slowly and get caught in local optima; and large sizes on the bound bounce around too frenetically and cannot converge rapidly to finesse the very top of peaks. Notice how similar this is to α used in Gradient Ascent. This knob is one way of controlling the degree of **Exploration versus Exploitation** in our Hill-Climber. Optimization algorithms which make largely local improvements are *exploiting* the local gradient, and algorithms which mostly wander about randomly are thought to *explore* the space. As a rule of thumb: you'd *like* to use a highly exploitative algorithm (it's fastest), but the "uglier" the space, the more you will have no choice but to use a more explorative algorithm.

2.2 Single-State Global Optimization Algorithms

A **global optimization algorithm** is one which, if we run it long enough, will *eventually* find the global optimum. Almost always, the way this is done is by guaranteeing that, at the limit, every location in the search space will be visited. The single-state algorithms we've seen so far cannot guarantee this. This is because of our definition (for the moment) of Tweak: to "make a small, bounded, but random change". Tweak wouldn't ever make big changes. If we're stuck in a sufficiently broad local optimum, Tweak may not be strong enough to get us out of it. Thus the algorithms so far have been **local optimization algorithms**.

There are many ways to construct a global optimization algorithm instead. Let's start with the simplest one possible: **Random Search**.

Algorithm 9 *Random Search*
1: *Best* ← some initial random candidate solution
2: **repeat**
3:     S ← a random candidate solution
4:     **if** Quality(S) > Quality(*Best*) **then**
5:         *Best* ← S
6: **until** *Best* is the ideal solution or we have run out of time
7: **return** *Best*

Random Search is the extreme in exploration (and global optimization); in contrast, Hill-Climbing (Algorithm 4), with Tweak set to just make very small changes and never make large ones, may be viewed as the extreme in exploitation (and local optimization). But there are ways to achieve reasonable exploitation and still have a global algorithm. Consider the following popular technique, called **Hill-Climbing with Random Restarts**, half-way between the two. We do Hill-Climbing for a certain random amount of time. Then when time is up, we start over with a new random location and do Hill-Climbing again for a different random amount of time.[7] And so on. The algorithm:

---

[7]Compare to Gradient Ascent with Restarts (Algorithm 3) and consider why we're doing random restarts now rather than gradient-based restarts. How do we know we're on the top of a hill now?

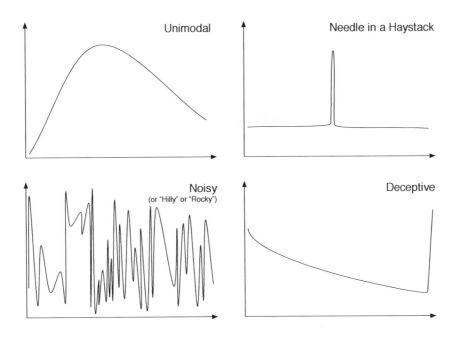

Figure 6 Four example quality functions.

Algorithm 10 *Hill-Climbing with Random Restarts*
1: $T \leftarrow$ distribution of possible time intervals

2: $S \leftarrow$ some initial random candidate solution
3: $Best \leftarrow S$
4: **repeat**
5:     $time \leftarrow$ random time in the near future, chosen from T
6:     **repeat**
7:         $R \leftarrow \mathsf{Tweak}(\mathsf{Copy}(S))$
8:         **if** $\mathsf{Quality}(R) > \mathsf{Quality}(S)$ **then**
9:             $S \leftarrow R$
10:     **until** S is the ideal solution, or *time* is up, or we have run out of total time
11:     **if** $\mathsf{Quality}(S) > \mathsf{Quality}(Best)$ **then**
12:         $Best \leftarrow S$
13:     $S \leftarrow$ some random candidate solution
14: **until** $Best$ is the ideal solution or we have run out of total time
15: **return** $Best$

If the randomly-chosen time intervals are generally extremely long, this algorithm is basically one big Hill-Climber. Likewise, if the intervals are very short, we're basically doing random search (by resetting to random new locations each time). Moderate interval lengths run the gamut between the two. That's good, right?

It depends. Consider Figure 6. The first figure, labeled *Unimodal*, is a situation where Hill-Climbing is close to optimal, and where Random Search is a very bad pick. But for the figure labelled *Noisy*, Hill-Climbing is quite bad; and in fact Random Search is expected to be about as good as you can do (not knowing anything about the functions beforehand). The difference is that in *Unimodal* there is a strong relationship between the distance (along the *x* axis) of two candidate solutions and their relationship in quality: similar solutions are generally similar in quality, and dissimilar solutions don't have any relationship per se. In the *Noisy* situation, there's no relationship like this: even similar solutions are very dissimilar in quality. This is often known as the **smoothness** criterion for local search to be effective.

This isn't sufficient though. Consider the figure labeled *Needle in a Haystack*, for which Random Search is the only real way to go, and Hill-Climbing is quite poor. What's the difference between this and *Unimodal*? After all, *Needle in a Haystack* is pretty smooth. For local search to be effective there must be an **informative gradient** which generally leads towards the best solutions. In fact, you can make highly *uninformative* gradients for which Hill-Climbing is spectacularly bad! In the figure labeled *Deceptive*, Hill-Climbing not only will not easily find the optimum, but it is actively *let away from the optimum*.

Thus there are some kinds of problems where making small local greedy changes does best; and other problems where making large, almost random changes does best. Global search algorithms run this gamut, and we've seen it before: **Exploration versus Exploitation**. Once again, as a rule of thumb: you'd *like* to use a highly exploitative algorithm (it's fastest), but the "uglier" the space, the more you will have no choice but to use a more explorative algorithm.

Here are some ways to create a global search algorithm, plus approaches to tweaking exploration vs. exploitation within that algorithm:

- **Adjust the Modification procedure** Tweak occasionally makes large, random changes.

   Why this is Global If you run the algorithm long enough, this randomness will cause Tweak to eventually try every possible solution.

   Exploration vs. Exploitation The more large, random changes, the more exploration.

- **Adjust the Selection procedure** Change the algorithm so that you can go down hills at least some of the time.

   Why this is Global If you run the algorithm long enough, you'll go down enough hills that you'll eventually find the right hill to go up.

   Exploration vs. Exploitation The more often you go down hills, the more exploration.

- **Jump to Something New** Every once in a while start from a new location.

   Why this is Global If you try enough new locations, eventually you'll hit a hill which has the highest peak.

   Exploration vs. Exploitation The more frequently you restart, the more exploration.

- **Use a Large Sample** Try many candidate solutions in parallel.

   Why this is Global With enough parallel candidate solutions, one of them is bound to be on the highest peak.

   Exploration vs. Exploitation More parallel candidate solutions, more exploration.

Let's look at some additional global optimizers. We'll focus on what I'm calling *single-state* optimizers which only keep around one candidate solution at a time. That is: no large sample.

2.3 Adjusting the Modification Procedure: (1+1), (1+λ), and (1, λ)

These three oddly named algorithms are forms of our Hill-Climbing procedures with variations of the Tweak operation to guarantee global optimization. They're actually degenerate cases of the more general (μ, λ) and $(\mu + \lambda)$ evolutionary algorithms discussed later (in Section 3.1).

The goal is simple: construct a Tweak operation which *tends* to tweak in small ways but *occasionally* makes larger changes, and *can* make any possible change. We'll mostly hill-climb, but also have the ability to, occasionally, jump far enough to land on other peaks. And there is a chance, however small, that the Hill-Climber will get lucky and Tweak will land right on the optimum.

For example, imagine that we're back to representing solutions in the form of fixed-length vectors of real numbers. Previously our approach to Tweaking vectors was Bounded Uniform Convolution (Algorithm 8). The key word is *bounded*: it required you to choose between being small enough to finesse local peaks and being large enough to escape local optima. But a **Gaussian**[8] (or **Normal**, or bell curve) distribution $N(\mu, \sigma^2)$ lets you do both: usually it makes small numbers but sometimes it makes large numbers. Unless bounded, a Gaussian distribution will *occasionally* make very large numbers indeed. The distribution requires two parameters: the mean μ (usually 0) and variance σ^2. The degree to which we emphasize small numbers over large ones can be controlled by simply changing the variance σ^2 of the distribution.

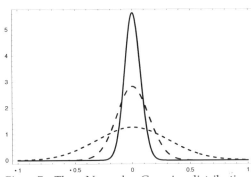

Figure 7 Three Normal or Gaussian distributions $N(\mu, \sigma^2)$ with the mean $\mu = 0$ and the variance σ^2 set to $\sigma^2 = 0.005$: ——, $\sigma^2 = 0.02$: – – –, and $\sigma^2 = 0.1$: - - - -.

We can do this by adding to each number in the vector some random noise under a Gaussian distribution with a mean $\mu = 0$. This is called **Gaussian convolution**.[9] Most noise will be near 0, so the vector values won't change much. But occasional values could be quite large.

Algorithm 11 *Gaussian Convolution*

1: $\vec{v} \leftarrow$ vector $\langle v_1, v_2, ...v_l \rangle$ to be convolved
2: $p \leftarrow$ probability of adding noise to an element in the vector   ▷ Often $p = 1$
3: $\sigma^2 \leftarrow$ variance of Normal distribution to convolve with   ▷ Normal = Gaussian
4: *min* $\leftarrow$ minimum desired vector element value
5: *max* $\leftarrow$ maximum desired vector element value

6: **for** i from 1 to l **do**
7:   **if** $p \geq$ random number chosen uniformly from 0.0 to 1.0 **then**
8:     **repeat**
9:       $n \leftarrow$ random number chosen from the Normal distribution $N(0, \sigma^2)$
10:    **until** $min \leq v_i + n \leq max$
11:    $v_i \leftarrow v_i + n$
12: **return** $\vec{v}$

---

[8] Karl Friedrich Gauss, 1777–1855, kid genius, physicist, and possibly the single most important mathematician ever.
[9] A popular competitor with Gaussian convolution is **polynomial mutation**, from Kalyanmoy Deb and Samir Agrawal, 1999, A niched-penalty approach for constraint handling in genetic algorithms, in *Proceedings of the International Conference on Artificial Neural Networks and Genetic Algorithms*, pages 235–243, Springer. Warning: polynomial mutation has many variants. A popular one is from Kalyanmoy Deb, 2001, *Multi-objective Optimization Using Evolutionary Algorithms*, Wiley.

(1+1) is the name we give to basic Hill-Climbing (Algorithm 4) with this probabilistic-modified Tweak. **(1+λ)** is the name we give to a similarly modified Steepest Ascent Hill-Climbing (Algorithm 5). And **(1, λ)** is the name we give to the modified Steepest Ascent Hill-Climbing with Replacement (Algorithm 6). These names may seem cryptic now but will make more sense later (in Section 3.1).

As it turns out, Gaussian Convolution doesn't give us just one new knob (σ^2) to adjust exploration vs. exploitation, but *two* knobs. Consider the Steepest Ascent Hill-Climbing with Replacement algorithm (Algorithm 6), where the value n specified how many children are generated from the parent candidate solution through Tweak. In the "global" version of this algorithm, $(1, \lambda)$, the value of n interacts with σ^2 in an important way: if σ^2 is large (noisy), then the algorithm will search crazier locations: but a high value of n will aggressively weed out the poor candidates discovered at those locations. This is because if n is low, a poor quality candidate may still be the best of the n examined; but if n is high, this is much less likely. Thus while σ^2 is pushing for more exploration (at the extreme: random search), a high value of n is pushing for more exploitation. n is an example of what will later be called **selection pressure**. Table 1 summarizes this interaction.

		Noise in Tweak	
		Low	High
Samples	Few		Explorative ↗
	Many	Exploitative	

Table 1 Simplistic description of the interaction of two factors and their effect on exploration versus exploitation. The factors are: degree of noise in the Tweak operation; and the samples taken before adopting a new candidate solution.

Many random number generators provide facilities for selecting random numbers under Normal (Gaussian) distributions. But if yours doesn't, you can make two Gaussian random numbers at a time using the **Box-Muller-Marsaglia Polar Method**.[10]

Algorithm 12 *Sample from the Gaussian Distribution (Box-Muller-Marsaglia Polar Method)*
1: $\mu \leftarrow$ desired mean of the Normal distribution ▷ Normal = Gaussian
2: $\sigma^2 \leftarrow$ desired variance of the Normal distribution

3: **repeat**
4:     $x \leftarrow$ random number chosen uniformly from -1.0 to 1.0
5:     $y \leftarrow$ random number chosen uniformly from -1.0 to 1.0   ▷ x and y should be independent
6:     $w \leftarrow x^2 + y^2$
7: **until** $0 < w < 1$ ▷ Else we could divide by zero or take the square root of a negative number!
8: $g \leftarrow \mu + x\sigma\sqrt{-2\frac{\ln w}{w}}$ ▷ It's σ, that is, $\sqrt{\sigma^2}$. Also, note that ln is $\log_e$
9: $h \leftarrow \mu + y\sigma\sqrt{-2\frac{\ln w}{w}}$ ▷ Likewise.
10: **return** g and h ▷ This method generates two random numbers at once. If you like, just use one.

Some random number generators (such as java.util.Random) only provide Gaussian random numbers from the **standard normal distribution** $N(0,1)$. You can convert these numbers to a Gaussian distribution for any mean μ and variance σ^2 or standard deviation σ you like very simply:

$$N(\mu, \sigma^2) = \mu + \sqrt{\sigma^2} N(0,1) = \mu + \sigma N(0,1)$$

---

[10] The method was first described in George Edward Pelham Box and Mervin Muller, 1958, A note on the generation of random normal deviates, *The Annals of Mathematical Statistics*, 29(2), 610–611. However the polar form of the method, as shown here, is usually ascribed to the mathematician George Marsaglia. There is a faster, but not simpler, method with a great, and apt, name: the **Ziggurat Method**.

2.4 Simulated Annealing

Simulated Annealing was developed by various researchers in the mid 1980s, but it has a famous lineage, being derived from the **Metropolis Algorithm**, developed by the ex-Manhattan Project scientists Nicholas Metropolis, Arianna and Marshall Rosenbluth, and Augusta and Edward Teller in 1953.[11] The algorithm varies from Hill-Climbing (Algorithm 4) in its decision of when to replace S, the original candidate solution, with R, its newly tweaked child. Specifically: if R is better than S, we'll always replace S with R as usual. But if R is worse than S, we may *still* replace S with R with a certain probability $P(t, R, S)$:

$$P(t, R, S) = e^{\frac{\text{Quality}(R) - \text{Quality}(S)}{t}}$$

where $t \geq 0$. That is, the algorithm sometimes goes down hills. This equation is interesting in two ways. Note that the fraction is negative because R is worse than S. First, if R is much worse than S, the fraction is larger, and so the probability is close to 0. If R is very close to S, the probability is close to 1. Thus if R isn't *much* worse than S, we'll still select R with a reasonable probability.

Second, we have a tunable parameter t. If t is close to 0, the fraction is again a large number, and so the probability is close to 0. If t is high, the probability is close to 1. The idea is to initially set t to a high number, which causes the algorithm to move to every newly-created solution regardless of how good it is. We're doing a **random walk** in the space. Then t decreases slowly, eventually to 0, at which point the algorithm is doing nothing more than plain Hill-Climbing.

Algorithm 13 *Simulated Annealing*
1: $t \leftarrow$ temperature, initially a high number
2: $S \leftarrow$ some initial candidate solution
3: $Best \leftarrow S$
4: **repeat**
5:     $R \leftarrow \text{Tweak}(\text{Copy}(S))$
6:     **if** Quality(R) > Quality(S) or if a random number chosen from 0 to $1 < e^{\frac{\text{Quality}(R) - \text{Quality}(S)}{t}}$ **then**
7:         $S \leftarrow R$
8:     Decrease t
9:     **if** Quality(S) > Quality($Best$) **then**
10:         $Best \leftarrow S$
11: **until** $Best$ is the ideal solution, we have run out of time, or $t \leq 0$
12: **return** $Best$

The rate at which we decrease t is called the algorithm's **schedule**. The longer we stretch out the schedule, the longer the algorithm resembles a random walk and the more exploration it does.

---

[11]Nicholas Metropolis, Arianna Rosenbluth, Marshall Rosenbluth, Augusta Teller, and Edward Teller, 1953, Equation of state calculations by fast computing machines, *Journal of Chemical Physics*, 21, 1087–1091. And yes, Arianna and Marshall were married, as were Augusta and Edward. Now *that's* a paper! This gang also developed the **Monte Carlo Method** widely used in simulation. Edward Teller later became a major advocate for nuclear testing and is believed to be one of the inspirations for Dr. Strangelove. To make this Gordion knot even more convoluted, Augusta and Edward's grandson Eric Teller, who goes by Astro Teller, did a fair bit of early work in Genetic Programming (Section 4.3)! Astro also developed the graph-structured Neural Programming: see Footnote 55.

A later paper on Simulated Annealing which established it as a real optimization algorithm is Scott Kirkpatrick, Charles Daniel Gelatt Jr., and Mario Vecchi, 1983, Optimization by simulated annealing, *Science*, 220(4598), 671–680.

Simulated Annealing gets its name from **annealing**, a process of cooling molten metal. If you let metal cool rapidly, its atoms aren't given a chance to settle into a tight lattice and are frozen in a random configuration, resulting in brittle metal. If we decrease the temperature very slowly, the atoms are given enough time to settle into a strong crystal. Not surprisingly, t means **temperature**.

2.5 Tabu Search

Tabu Search, by Fred Glover,[12] employs a different approach to doing exploration: it keeps around a history of recently considered candidate solutions (known as the *tabu list*) and refuses to return to those candidate solutions until they're sufficiently far in the past. Thus if we wander up a hill, we have no choice but to wander back down the other side because we're not permitted to stay at or return to the top of the hill.

The simplest approach to Tabu Search is to maintain a **tabu list** L, of some maximum length l, of candidate solutions we've seen so far. Whenever we adopt a new candidate solution, it goes in the tabu list. If the tabu list is too large, we remove the oldest candidate solution and it's no longer taboo to reconsider. Tabu Search is usually implemented as a variation on Steepest Ascent with Replacement (Algorithm 6). In the version below, we generate n tweaked children, but only consider the ones which aren't presently taboo. This requires a few little subtle checks:

Algorithm 14 *Tabu Search*
1: $l \leftarrow$ Desired maximum tabu list length
2: $n \leftarrow$ number of tweaks desired to sample the gradient

3: $S \leftarrow$ some initial candidate solution
4: $Best \leftarrow S$
5: $L \leftarrow \{\}$ a tabu list of maximum length l ▷ Implemented as first in, first-out queue
6: Enqueue S into L
7: **repeat**
8:     **if** Length(L) $> l$ **then**
9:         Remove oldest element from L
10:     $R \leftarrow$ Tweak(Copy(S))
11:     **for** $n - 1$ times **do**
12:         $W \leftarrow$ Tweak(Copy(S))
13:         **if** $W \notin L$ and (Quality(W) $>$ Quality(R) or $R \in L$) **then**
14:             $R \leftarrow W$
15:     **if** $R \notin L$ and Quality(R) $>$ Quality(S) **then**
16:         $S \leftarrow R$
17:         Enqueue R into L
18:     **if** Quality(S) $>$ Quality($Best$) **then**
19:         $Best \leftarrow S$
20: **until** $Best$ is the ideal solution or we have run out of time
21: **return** $Best$

---

[12]"Tabu" is an alternate spelling for "taboo". Glover also coined the word "metaheuristics", and developed Scatter Search with Path Relinking (Section 3.3.5). Tabu Search showed up first in Fred Glover, 1986, Future paths for integer programming and links to artificial intelligence, *Computers and Operations Research*, 5, 533–549.

Tabu Search really only works in discrete spaces. What if your search space is real-valued numbers? Only in truly exceptional situations will you visit the same real-valued point in space twice, making the tabu list worthless. In this situation, one approach is to consider a solution to be a member of a list if it is "sufficiently similar" to an existing member of the list. The similarity distance measure will be up to you. See Section 6.4 for some ideas.

Even so, the big problem with Tabu Search is that if your search space is very large, and particularly if it's of high dimensionality, it's easy to stay around in the same neighborhood, indeed on the same hill, even if you have a very large tabu list. There may be just too many locations. An alternative approach is to create a tabu list not of candidate solutions you've considered before, but of *changes you've made recently to certain features*. For example, imagine if you're finding a solution to a graph problem like the Traveling Salesman Problem (see Section 8). You tweak a candidate solution to create a new one, by deleting edge A and adding edges B and C, and decide to adopt the new solution. Instead of placing the solution into the tabu list, you place the *changes you made* into the list. A, B, and C each go into the list. Now for a while, while you're thinking about new tweaks, you're not allowed to even consider adding or deleting A, B, or C. They're taboo for now.

To implement this, the big change we'll need to make is in the nature of the queue acting as our tabu list. No longer can the queue be a simple first-in first-out queue because variable numbers of things will enter the queue at any time step. Instead we'll implement it as a set of tuples $\langle X, d \rangle$ where X is a feature we changed (for example "Edge A"), and d is the timestamp of when we made the change. Also, we can no longer simply test for membership in the queue. Instead, we'll have to hand the queue to the Tweak operation, so it knows which changes it's not allowed to make. Thus our revised version: Tweak(Copy(...), L). I call the new algorithm **Feature-based Tabu Search**.

Algorithm 15 *Feature-based Tabu Search*

1: $l \leftarrow$ desired queue length
2: $n \leftarrow$ number of tweaks desired to sample the gradient

3: $S \leftarrow$ some initial candidate solution
4: $Best \leftarrow S$
5: $L \leftarrow \{\}$ ▷ L will hold tuples of the form $\langle X, d \rangle$ where X is a feature and d is a timestamp
6: $c \leftarrow 0$
7: **repeat**
8: $\quad c \leftarrow c + 1$
9: $\quad$ Remove from L all tuples of the form $\langle X, d \rangle$ where $c - d > l$ ▷ The "old" ones
10: $\quad R \leftarrow$ Tweak(Copy(S), L) ▷ Tweak will not shift to a feature in L
11: $\quad$ **for** $n - 1$ times **do**
12: $\quad\quad W \leftarrow$ Tweak(Copy(S), L)
13: $\quad\quad$ **if** Quality(W) > Quality(R) **then**
14: $\quad\quad\quad R \leftarrow W$
15: $\quad S \leftarrow R$
16: $\quad$ **for** each feature X modified by Tweak to produce R from S **do**
17: $\quad\quad L \leftarrow L \cup \{\langle X, c \rangle\}$
18: $\quad$ **if** Quality(S) > Quality($Best$) **then**
19: $\quad\quad Best \leftarrow S$
20: **until** *Best* is the ideal solution or we have run out of time
21: **return** *Best*

Feature-based Tabu Search is somewhat different from the other techniques described here in that it relies on the identifiability and separability of *features* found in candidate solutions, rather than considering each candidate solution as an atomic element except for Tweak purposes. We'll see this notion put to more heavy use in Combinatorial Optimization (Section 8).

2.6 Iterated Local Search

This is the present name for a concept which has been around, in many guises, since at least the 1980s.[13] It's essentially a more clever version of Hill-Climbing with Random Restarts. Each time you do a random restart, the hill-climber then winds up in some (possibly new) local optimum. Thus we can think of Hill-Climbing with Random Restarts as doing a sort of random search through the *space of local optima*. We find a random local optimum, then another, then another, and so on, and eventually return the best optimum we ever discovered (ideally, it's a global optimum!)

Iterated Local Search (ILS) tries to search through this space of local optima in a more intelligent fashion: it tries to *stochastically hill-climb in the space of local optima*. That is, ILS finds a local optimum, then looks for a "nearby" local optimum and possibly adopts that one instead, then finds a new "nearby" local optimum, and so on. The heuristic here is that you can often find better local optima near to the one you're presently in, and walking from local optimum to local optimum in this way often outperforms just trying new locations entirely at random.

ILS pulls this off with two tricks. First, ILS doesn't pick new restart locations entirely at random. Rather, it maintains a "home base" local optimum of sorts, and selects new restart locations that are *somewhat*, though not *excessively*, in the vicinity of the "home base" local optimum. We want to restart far enough away from our current home base to wind up in a new local optimum, but not so far as to be picking new restart locations essentially at random. We want to be doing a walk rather than a random search.

Second, when ILS discovers a new local optimum, it decides whether to retain the current "home base" local optimum, or to adopt the new local optimum as the "home base". If we always pick the new local optimum, we're doing a random walk (a sort of meta-exploration). If we only pick the new local optimum if it's better than our current one, we're doing hill-climbing (a sort of meta-exploitation). ILS often picks something in-between the two, as discussed later.

If you abstract these two tricks, ILS is very simple. The only complexity lies in determining when a local optimum has been discovered. Since this is often difficult, I will instead employ the same approach here as was used in random restarts: to set a timer. Hill-climb for a while, and then when timer goes off, it's time to restart. This obviously doesn't guarantee that we've found the local optimum while hill-climbing, but if the timer is long enough, we're likely to be in the vicinity.

The algorithm is very straightforward: do hill-climbing for a while; then (when time is up) determine whether to adopt the newly discovered local optimum or to retain the current "home base" one (the NewHomeBase[14] function); then from our new home base, make a very big Tweak (the Perturb function), which is ideally *just* large enough to likely jump to a new hill. The algorithm looks like this:

---

[13] A good current summary of the technique can be found in Helena Lourenço, Olivier Martin, and Thomas Stützle, 2003, Iterated local search, in Fred Glover and Gary Kochenberger, editors, *Handbook of Metaheuristics*, pages 320–353, Springer. They trace the technique back as far as John Baxter, 1981, Local optima avoidance in depot location, *Journal of the Operational Research Society*, 32, 815–819.

[14] I made up that name.

Algorithm 16 *Iterated Local Search (ILS) with Random Restarts*
1: $T \leftarrow$ distribution of possible time intervals
2: $S \leftarrow$ some initial random candidate solution
3: $H \leftarrow S$ ▷ The current "home base" local optimum
4: $Best \leftarrow S$
5: **repeat**
6: $time \leftarrow$ random time in the near future, chosen from T
7: **repeat**
8:   $R \leftarrow \mathsf{Tweak}(\mathsf{Copy}(S))$
9:   **if** $\mathsf{Quality}(R) > \mathsf{Quality}(S)$ **then**
10:    $S \leftarrow R$
11: **until** S is the ideal solution, or *time* is up, or we have run out of total time
12: **if** $\mathsf{Quality}(S) > \mathsf{Quality}(Best)$ **then**
13:    $Best \leftarrow S$
14: $H \leftarrow \mathsf{NewHomeBase}(H, S)$
15: $S \leftarrow \mathsf{Perturb}(H)$
16: **until** *Best* is the ideal solution or we have run out of total time
17: **return** *Best*

Much of the thinking behind the choices of Perturb and NewHomeBase functions is a black art, determined largely by the nature of the particular problem being tackled. Here are some hints.

The goal of the Perturb function is to make a very large Tweak, big enough to likely escape the current local optimum, but not so large as to be essentially a randomization. Remember that we'd like to fall onto a *nearby* hill. The meaning of "big enough" varies wildly from problem to problem.

The goal of the NewHomeBase function is to intelligently pick new starting locations. Just as global optimization algorithms in general lie between the extremes of exploration (random search and random walks) and exploitation (hill-climbing), the NewHomeBase should lie somewhere between these extremes when considering among *local optima*.[15] At one extreme, the algorithm could always adopt the new local optimum, that is,

$$\mathsf{NewHomeBase}(H, S) = S$$

This results in essentially a random walk from local optimum to local optimum. At the other extreme, the algorithm could only use the new local optimum if it's of equal or higher quality than the old one, that is,

$$\mathsf{NewHomeBase}(H, S) = \begin{cases} S & \text{if } \mathsf{Quality}(S) \geq \mathsf{Quality}(H) \\ H & \text{otherwise} \end{cases}$$

This results, more or less, in a kind of hill-climbing among the local optima. Most ILS heuristics try to strike a middle-ground between the two. For example, ILS might hill-climb unless it hasn't seen a new *and* better solution in a while, at which point it starts doing random walks for a bit. There are other options of course: we could apply a Simulated Annealing approach to NewHomeBase, or a Tabu Search procedure of sorts.

---

[15]Thus this function truly is a *meta*-heuristic. Finally a valid use of the term!

Mixing and Matching The algorithms described in this section are not set in stone. There are lots of ways to mix and match them, or develop other approaches entirely. For example, it's not unreasonable to use Hill-Climbing with Random Restarts mixed with a $(1+1)$-style Tweak operation. You could also construct Steepest Ascent versions of Random Restarts. Tabu Search could be done in $(1, \lambda)$ style. Or construct a Tweak procedure which slowly decreases Gaussian convolution's σ^2 according to a Simulated Annealing-style temperature. And so on. Be imaginative.

3 Population Methods

Population-based methods differ from the previous methods in that they keep around a *sample* of candidate solutions rather than a single candidate solution. Each of the solutions is involved in tweaking and quality assessment, but what prevents this from being just a parallel hill-climber is that candidate solutions affect *how* other candidates will hill-climb in the quality function. This could happen either by good solutions causing poor solutions to be rejected and new ones created, or by causing them to be Tweaked in the direction of the better solutions.

It may not be surprising that most population-based methods steal concepts from biology. One particularly popular set of techniques, collectively known as **Evolutionary Computation (EC)**, borrows liberally from population biology, genetics, and evolution. An algorithm chosen from this collection is known as an **Evolutionary Algorithm (EA)**. Most EAs may be divided into **generational** algorithms, which update the entire sample once per iteration, and **steady-state** algorithms, which update the sample a few candidate solutions at a time. Common EAs include the **Genetic Algorithm (GA)** and **Evolution Strategies (ES)**; and there are both generational and steady-state versions of each. There are quite a few more alphabet soup subalgorithms.

Because they are inspired by biology, EC methods tend to use (and abuse) terms from genetics and evolution. Because the terms are so prevalent, we'll use them in this and most further sections.

Definition 1 *Common Terms Used in Evolutionary Computation*

individual	a candidate solution
child and parent	a *child* is the Tweaked copy of a candidate solution (its *parent*)
population	set of candidate solutions
fitness	quality
fitness landscape	quality function
fitness assessment or evaluation	computing the fitness of an individual
selection	picking individuals based on their fitness
mutation	plain Tweaking. This is often thought as "asexual" breeding.
recombination or crossover	a special Tweak which takes two parents, swaps sections of them, and (usually) produces two children. This is often thought as "sexual" breeding.
breeding	producing one or more children from a population of parents through an iterated process of selection and Tweaking (typically mutation or recombination)
genotype or genome	an individual's data structure, as used during breeding
chromosome	a genotype in the form of a fixed-length vector
gene	a particular slot position in a chromosome
allele	a particular setting of a gene
phenotype	how the individual operates during fitness assessment
generation	one cycle of fitness assessment, breeding, and population re-assembly; or the population produced each such cycle

Evolutionary Computation techniques are generally **resampling techniques**: new samples (populations) are generated or revised based on the results from older ones. In contrast, **Particle Swarm Optimization**, in Section 3.5, is an example of a **directed mutation** method, where candidate solutions in the population are modified, but no resampling occurs per se.

The basic generational evolutionary computation algorithm first constructs an initial population, then iterates through three procedures. First, it **assesses the fitness** of all the individuals in the population. Second, it uses this fitness information to **breed** a new population of children. Third, it **joins** the parents and children in some fashion to form a new next-generation population, and the cycle continues.

Algorithm 17 *An Abstract Generational Evolutionary Algorithm (EA)*

1: $P \leftarrow$ Build Initial Population
2: $Best \leftarrow \square$ ▷ $\square$ means "nobody yet"
3: **repeat**
4:     AssessFitness(P)
5:     **for** each individual $P_i \in P$ **do**
6:         **if** $Best = \square$ or Fitness(P_i) > Fitness($Best$) **then** ▷ Remember, Fitness is just Quality
7:             $Best \leftarrow P_i$
8:     $P \leftarrow$ Join(P, Breed(P))
9: **until** *Best* is the ideal solution or we have run out of time
10: **return** *Best*

Notice that, unlike the Single-State methods, we now have a separate AssessFitness function. This is because typically we need all the fitness values of our individuals before we can Breed them. So we have a certain location in the algorithm where their fitnesses are computed.

Evolutionary algorithms differ from one another largely in how they perform the Breed and Join operations. The Breed operation usually has two parts: **Selecting** parents from the old population, then Tweaking them (usually **Mutating** or **Recombining** them in some way) to make children. The Join operation usually either completely replaces the parents with the children, or includes fit parents along with their children to form the next generation.[16]

Population Initialization All the algorithms described here basically use the same initialization procedures, so it's worthwhile giving some tips. Initialization is typically just creating some n individuals at random. However, if you know something about the likely initial "good" regions of the space, you could **bias** the random generation to *tend* to generate individuals in those regions. In fact, you could **seed** the initial population partly with individuals of your own design. Be careful about such techniques: often though you *think* you know where the good areas are, there's a good chance you don't. Don't put all your eggs in one basket: include a significant degree of uniform randomness in your initialization. More on this later on when we talk about representations (in Section 4.1.1).

It's also worthwhile to enforce diversity by guaranteeing that every individual in the initial population is unique. Each time you make a new individual, don't scan through the whole population to see if that individual's already been created: that's $O(n^2)$ and foolish. Instead, create a hash table which stores individuals as keys and anything arbitrary as values. Each time you make an individual, check to see if it's already in the hash table as a key. If it is, throw it away and make another one. Else, add the individual to the population, and hash it in the hash table. That's $O(n)$.

---

[16]Though it's usually simpler than this, the Join operation can be thought of as kind of selection procedure, choosing from among the children and the parents to form the next generation. This general view of the Join operation is often called **survival selection**, while the selection portion of the Breed operation is often called **parent selection**.

3.1 Evolution Strategies

The family of algorithms known as **Evolution Strategies (ES)** were developed by Ingo Rechenberg and Hans-Paul Schwefel at the Technical University of Berlin in the mid 1960s.[17] ES employ a simple procedure for selecting individuals called **Truncation Selection**, and (usually) only uses mutation as the Tweak operator.

Among the simplest ES algorithms is the (μ, λ) algorithm. We begin with a population of (typically) λ number of individuals, generated randomly. We then iterate as follows. First we assess the fitness of all the individuals. Then we delete from the population all but the μ fittest ones (this is all there's to Truncation Selection). Each of the μ fittest individuals gets to produce λ/μ children through an ordinary Mutation. All told we've created λ new children. Our Join operation is simple: the children just replace the parents, who are discarded. The iteration continues anew.

In short, μ is the number of parents which survive, and λ is the number of kids that the μ parents make in total. Notice that λ should be a multiple of μ. ES practitioners usually refer to their algorithm by the choice of μ and λ. For example, if $\mu = 5$ and $\lambda = 20$, then we have a "(5, 20) Evolution Strategy". Here's the algorithm pseudocode:

Algorithm 18 *The (μ, λ) Evolution Strategy*

1: $\mu \leftarrow$ number of parents selected
2: $\lambda \leftarrow$ number of children generated by the parents

3: $P \leftarrow \{\}$
4: **for** λ times **do** ▷ Build Initial Population
5:     $P \leftarrow P \cup \{\text{new random individual}\}$
6: $Best \leftarrow \square$
7: **repeat**
8:     **for** each individual $P_i \in P$ **do**
9:         AssessFitness(P_i)
10:         **if** $Best = \square$ or Fitness(P_i) > Fitness($Best$) **then**
11:             $Best \leftarrow P_i$
12:     $Q \leftarrow$ the μ individuals in P whose Fitness( ) are greatest ▷ Truncation Selection
13:     $P \leftarrow \{\}$ ▷ Join is done by just replacing P with the children
14:     **for** each individual $Q_j \in Q$ **do**
15:         **for** λ/μ times **do**
16:             $P \leftarrow P \cup \{\text{Mutate(Copy}(Q_j))\}$
17: **until** $Best$ is the ideal solution or we have run out of time
18: **return** $Best$

Note the use of the function Mutate instead of Tweak. Recall that population-based methods have a variety of ways to perform the Tweak operation. The big two are **mutation**, which is just like the Tweaks we've seen before: convert a single individual into a new individual through a (usually small) random change; and **recombination** or **crossover**, in which multiple (typically two) individuals are mixed and matched to form children. **We'll be using these terms in the algorithms from now on out** to indicate the Tweak performed.

---

[17]Ingo Rechenberg, 1973, *Evolutionsstrategie: Optimierung technischer Systeme nach Prinzipien der biologischen Evolution*, Fromman-Holzbook, Stuttgart, Germany. In German!

The (μ, λ) algorithm has three knobs with which we may adjust exploration versus exploitation. Figure 8 shows the effect of variations with these operations.

- The size of λ. This essentially controls the sample size for each population, and is basically the same thing as the n variable in Steepest-Ascent Hill Climbing With Replacement. At the extreme, as λ approaches ∞, the algorithm approaches exploration (random search).

- The size of μ. This controls how *selective* the algorithm is; low values of μ with respect to λ push the algorithm more towards exploitative search as only the best individuals survive.

- The degree to which Mutation is performed. If Mutate has a lot of noise, then new children fall far from the tree and are fairly random regardless of the selectivity of μ.

The second Evolution Strategy algorithm is called $(\mu + \lambda)$. It differs from (μ, λ) in only one respect: the Join operation. Recall that in (μ, λ) the parents are simply replaced with the children in the next generation. But in $(\mu + \lambda)$, the next generation consists of the μ parents plus the λ new children. That is, the parents compete with the kids next time around. Thus the next and all successive generations are $\mu + \lambda$ in size. The algorithm looks like this:

Algorithm 19 *The $(\mu + \lambda)$ Evolution Strategy*
1: $\mu \leftarrow$ number of parents selected
2: $\lambda \leftarrow$ number of children generated by the parents

3: $P \leftarrow \{\}$
4: **for** λ times **do**
5: $\quad P \leftarrow P \cup \{\text{new random individual}\}$
6: $Best \leftarrow \square$
7: **repeat**
8: $\quad$ **for** each individual $P_i \in P$ **do**
9: $\quad\quad$ AssessFitness(P_i)
10: $\quad\quad$ **if** $Best = \square$ or Fitness(P_i) > Fitness($Best$) **then**
11: $\quad\quad\quad Best \leftarrow P_i$
12: $\quad Q \leftarrow$ the μ individuals in P whose Fitness( ) are greatest
13: $\quad P \leftarrow Q$ $\quad\quad\quad\quad\quad\quad\quad\quad\quad\quad\quad\quad\quad\quad$ ▷ The Join operation is the only difference with (μ, λ)
14: $\quad$ **for** each individual $Q_j \in Q$ **do**
15: $\quad\quad$ **for** λ/μ times **do**
16: $\quad\quad\quad P \leftarrow P \cup \{\text{Mutate(Copy}(Q_j))\}$
17: **until** $Best$ is the ideal solution or we have run out of time
18: **return** $Best$

Generally speaking, $(\mu + \lambda)$ may be more exploitative than (μ, λ) because high-fitness parents persist to compete with the children. This has risks: a sufficiently fit parent may defeat other population members over and over again, eventually causing the entire population to **prematurely converge** to immediate descendants of that parent, at which point the whole population has been trapped in the local optimum surrounding the parent.

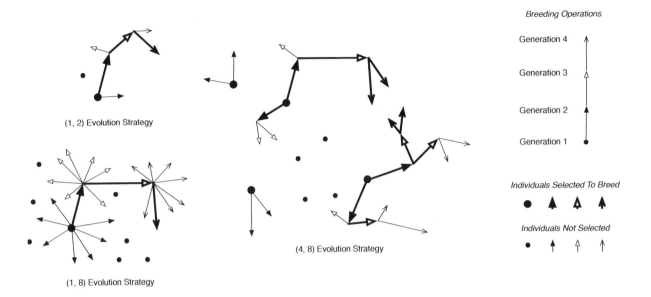

Figure 8 Three (μ, λ) Evolution Strategy variations. Each generation, μ individuals are selected to breed, and each gets to create λ/μ children, resulting in λ children in total.

If you think about it, $(\mu + \lambda)$ resembles Steepest Ascent Hill-Climbing in that both of them allow the parent to compete against the children for supremacy in the next iteration. Whereas (μ, λ) resembles Steepest Ascent Hill-Climbing with Replacement in that the parents are replaced with the best children. This is more than a coincidence: the hill-climbers are essentially degenerate cases of the ES algorithms. Recall that with the right Tweak operator, plain Hill-Climbing becomes the $(1+1)$ algorithm, Steepest Ascent Hill-Climbing with Replacement becomes $(1, \lambda)$, and Steepest Ascent Hill-Climbing becomes $(1 + \lambda)$. Armed with the explanation of the algorithms above, it should be a bit clearer why this is.

3.1.1 Mutation and Evolutionary Programming

Evolution Strategies historically employ a representation in the form of a fixed-length vector of real-valued numbers. Typically such vectors are initialized using something along the lines of Algorithm 7. Mutation is typically performed using Gassian Convolution (Algorithm 11).

Gaussian Convolution is controlled largely by the distribution variance σ^2. The value of σ^2 is known as the **mutation rate** of an ES, and determines the noise in the Mutate operation. How do you pick a value for σ^2? You might pre-select its value; or perhaps you might slowly decrease the value; or you could try to adaptively change σ^2 based on the current statistics of the system. If the system seems to be too exploitative, you could increase σ^2 to force some more exploration (or likewise decrease it to produce more exploitation). This notion of changing σ^2 is known as an **adaptive mutation rate**. In general, such **adaptive** breeding operators adjust themselves over time, in response to statistics gleaned from the optimization run.[18]

---

[18]Evolution Strategies have also long been associated with **self-adaptive operators** which are stochastically optimized along with individuals. For example, individuals might contain their own mutation procedures which can themselves be mutated along with the individual.

One old rule for changing σ^2 adaptively is known as the **One-Fifth Rule**, by Ingo Rechenberg,[19] and it goes like this:

- If more than $\frac{1}{5}$ children are fitter than their parents, then we're exploiting local optima too much, and we should increase σ^2.

- If less than $\frac{1}{5}$ children are fitter than their parents, then we're exploring too much, and we should decrease σ^2.

- If exactly $\frac{1}{5}$ children are fitter than their parents, don't change anything.

This rule was derived from the results of experiments with the $(1+1)$ ES on certain simple test problems. It may not be optimal for more complex situations: but it's a good starting point.

You don't have to do ES just with vectors. In fact, a little earlier than ES, an almost identical approach was developed by Larry Fogel at the National Science Foundation (Washington DC) and later developed in San Diego.[20] The technique, called **Evolutionary Programming (EP)**, differs from ES in two respects. First, it historically only used a $(\mu + \lambda)$ strategy with $\mu = \lambda$. That is, half the population was eliminated, and that half was then filled in with children. Second, EP was applied to most any representation. From the very start Fogel was interested in evolving graph structures (specifically finite state automata, hence the "programming"). Thus the Mutate operation took the form of adding or deleting an edge, adding or deleting a node, relabeling an edge or a node, etc.

Such operations are reasonable as long as they have two features. First, to guarantee that the algorithm remains global, we must guarantee that, with some small probability, a parent can produce *any* child. Second, we ought to retain the feature that *usually* we make *small* changes likely to not deviate significantly in fitness; and only occasionally make *large* changes to the individual. The degree to which we tend to make small changes could be adjustable, like σ^2 was. We'll get to such representational issues for candidate solutions in detail in Section 4.

3.2 The Genetic Algorithm

The **Genetic Algorithm (GA)**, often referred to as *genetic algorithms*, was invented by John Holland at the University of Michigan in the 1970s.[21] It is similar to a (μ, λ) Evolution Strategy in many respects: it iterates through fitness assessment, selection and breeding, and population reassembly. The primary difference is in how selection and breeding take place: whereas Evolution Strategies select the parents and *then* creates the children, the Genetic Algorithm little-by-little selects a few parents and generates children until enough children have been created.

To breed, we begin with an empty population of children. We then select two parents from the original population, copy them, cross them over with one another, and mutate the results. This forms two children, which we then add to the child population. We repeat this process until the child population is entirely filled. Here's the algorithm in pseudocode.

---

[19] Also in his evolution strategies text (see Footnote 17, p. 33).

[20] Larry Fogel's dissertation was undoubtedly the first such thesis, if not the first major work, in the field of evolutionary computation. Lawrence Fogel, 1964, *On the Organization of Intellect*, Ph.D. thesis, University of California, Los Angeles.

[21] Holland's book is one of the more famous in the field: John Holland, 1975, *Adaptation in Natural and Artificial Systems*, University of Michigan Press.

Algorithm 20 *The Genetic Algorithm (GA)*
1: *popsize* ← desired population size   ▷ This is basically λ. Make it even.
2: $P \leftarrow \{\}$
3: **for** *popsize* times **do**
4:     $P \leftarrow P \cup \{$new random individual$\}$
5: *Best* ← □
6: **repeat**
7:     **for** each individual $P_i \in P$ **do**
8:         AssessFitness(P_i)
9:         **if** *Best* = □ or Fitness(P_i) > Fitness(*Best*) **then**
10:             *Best* ← P_i
11:     $Q \leftarrow \{\}$ ▷ Here's where we begin to deviate from (μ, λ)
12:     **for** *popsize*/2 times **do**
13:         Parent $P_a \leftarrow$ SelectWithReplacement(P)
14:         Parent $P_b \leftarrow$ SelectWithReplacement(P)
15:         Children $C_a, C_b \leftarrow$ Crossover(Copy(P_a), Copy(P_b))
16:         $Q \leftarrow Q \cup \{$Mutate(C_a), Mutate(C_b)$\}$
17:     $P \leftarrow Q$ ▷ End of deviation
18: **until** *Best* is the ideal solution or we have run out of time
19: **return** *Best*

Though it can be applied to any kind of vector (and indeed many representations) the GA classically operated over fixed-length vectors of *boolean values*, just like ES often were applied to ones of *floating-point values*. For a moment, let's be pedantic about generation of new individuals. If the individual is a vector of floating-point values, creating a new random vector could be done just like in ES (that is, via Algorithm 7). If our representation is a boolean vector, we could do this:

Algorithm 21 *Generate a Random Bit-Vector*
1: $\vec{v} \leftarrow$ a new vector $\langle v_1, v_2, ... v_l \rangle$
2: **for** i from 1 to l **do**
3:     **if** 0.5 > a random number chosen uniformly between 0.0 and 1.0 inclusive **then**
4:         $v_i \leftarrow$ true
5:     **else**
6:         $v_i \leftarrow$ false
7: **return** $\vec{v}$

3.2.1 Crossover and Mutation

Note how similar the Genetic Algorithm is to (μ, λ), except during the breeding phase. To perform breeding, we need two new functions we've not seen before: SelectWithReplacement and Crossover; plus of course Mutate. We'll start with Mutate. Mutating a real-valued vector could be done with Gaussian Convolution (Algorithm 11). How might you Mutate a boolean vector? One simple way is **bit-flip mutation**: march down the vector, and flip a coin of a certain probability (often $1/l$, where l is the length of the vector). Each time the coin comes up heads, flip the bit:

Algorithm 22 *Bit-Flip Mutation*

1: $p \leftarrow$ probability of flipping a bit ▷ Often p is set to $1/l$
2: $\vec{v} \leftarrow$ boolean vector $\langle v_1, v_2, ... v_l \rangle$ to be mutated

3: **for** i from 1 to l **do**
4:     **if** $p \geq$ random number chosen uniformly from 0.0 to 1.0 inclusive **then**
5:         $v_i \leftarrow \neg(v_i)$
6: **return** $\vec{v}$

Crossover is the Genetic Algorithm's distinguishing feature.[22] It involves mixing and matching parts of two parents to form children. How you do that mixing and matching depends on the representation of the individuals. There are three classic ways of doing crossover in vectors: **One-Point**, **Two-Point**, and **Uniform Crossover**.

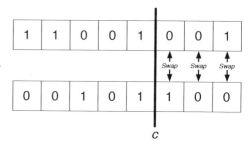

Figure 9 One-Point Crossover.

Let's say the vector is of length l. One-point crossover picks a number c between 1 and l, inclusive, and swaps all the indexes $< c$, as shown in Figure 9. The algorithm:

Algorithm 23 *One-Point Crossover*

1: $\vec{v} \leftarrow$ first vector $\langle v_1, v_2, ... v_l \rangle$ to be crossed over
2: $\vec{w} \leftarrow$ second vector $\langle w_1, w_2, ... w_l \rangle$ to be crossed over

3: $c \leftarrow$ random integer chosen uniformly from 1 to l inclusive
4: **if** $c \neq 1$ **then**
5:     **for** i from 1 to $c - 1$ **do**
6:         Swap the values of v_i and w_i
7: **return** $\vec{v}$ and $\vec{w}$

If $c = 1$ no crossover happens. This empty crossover occurs with $\frac{1}{l}$ probability. If you'd like to instead control this probability, you can pick c from between 2 to l inclusive and decide on your own when crossover will occur.

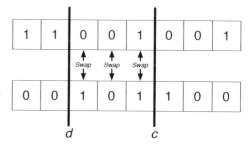

Figure 10 Two-Point Crossover.

The problem with one-point crossover lies in the possible **linkage** (also called **epistasis**) among the elements in the vector. Notice that the probability is high that v_1 and v_l will be broken up due to crossover, as almost any choice of c will do it. Similarly, the probability that v_1 and v_2 will be broken up is quite small, as c must be equal to 2. If the organization of your vector was such that elements v_1 and v_l had to work well in tandem in order to get a high fitness, you'd be constantly breaking up good pairs that the system discovered. Two-point crossover is one way to clean up the linkage problem: just pick *two* numbers c and d, and swap the indexes between them. Figure 10 gives the general idea, and the pseudocode is below:

---

[22] Though it's long since been used in various ways with Evolution Strategies as well.

Algorithm 24 *Two-Point Crossover*

1: $\vec{v} \leftarrow$ first vector $\langle v_1, v_2, ...v_l \rangle$ to be crossed over
2: $\vec{w} \leftarrow$ second vector $\langle w_1, w_2, ...w_l \rangle$ to be crossed over

3: $c \leftarrow$ random integer chosen uniformly from 1 to l inclusive
4: $d \leftarrow$ random integer chosen uniformly from 1 to l inclusive
5: **if** $c > d$ **then**
6:     Swap c and d
7: **if** $c \neq d$ **then**
8:     **for** i from c to $d - 1$ **do**
9:         Swap the values of v_i and w_i
10: **return** $\vec{v}$ and $\vec{w}$

As was the case for one-point crossover, when $c = d$ you get an empty crossover (with $\frac{1}{l}$ probability). If you'd like to control the probability of this yourself, just force d to be different from c, and decide on your own when crossover happens.

It's not immediately obvious two-point crossover would help things. But think of the vectors not as vectors but as *rings* (that is, v_l is right next to v_1). Two-point crossover breaks the rings at two spots and trades pieces. Since v_l is right next to v_1, the only way they'd break up is if c or d sliced right between them. The same situation as v_1 and v_2.[23]

Even so, there's still a further linkage problem. v_1 and v_l are now being treated fairly, but how about v_1 and $v_{l/2}$? Long distances like that are still more likely to be broken up than short distances like v_1 and v_2 (or indeed v_1 and v_l). We can treat all genes fairly with respect to linkage by crossing over each point independently of one another, using Uniform crossover. Here we simply march down the vectors, and swap individual indexes if a coin toss comes up heads with probability p.[24]

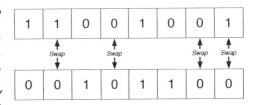

Figure 11 Uniform Crossover.

Algorithm 25 *Uniform Crossover*

1: $p \leftarrow$ probability of swapping an index   ▷ Often p is set to $1/l$. At any rate, $p \leq 0.5$
2: $\vec{v} \leftarrow$ first vector $\langle v_1, v_2, ...v_l \rangle$ to be crossed over
3: $\vec{w} \leftarrow$ second vector $\langle w_1, w_2, ...w_l \rangle$ to be crossed over

4: **for** i from 1 to l **do**
5:     **if** $p \geq$ random number chosen uniformly from 0.0 to 1.0 inclusive **then**
6:         Swap the values of v_i and w_i
7: **return** $\vec{v}$ and $\vec{w}$

---

[23]We can generalize two-point crossover into a **Multi-Point Crossover**: pick n random points and sort them smallest first: $c_1, c_2, ..., c_n$. Now swap indexes in the region between c_1 and c_2, and between c_3 and c_4, and likewise c_5 and c_6, etc.

[24]The original uniform crossover assumed $p = 1/2$, and was first proposed in David Ackley, 1987, *A Connectionist Machine for Genetic Hillclimbing*, Kluwer Academic Publishers. The more general form, for arbitrary p, is sometimes called *parameterized* uniform crossover.

Crossover is not a global mutation. If you cross over two vectors you can't get every conceivable vector out of it. Imagine your vectors were points in space. Now imagine the hypercube formed with those points at its extreme corners. For example, if your vectors were 3-dimensional, they'd form the corners of a cube (or box) in space, as shown in Figure 12. All the crossovers so far are very constrained: they will result in new vectors which lie at some other corner of the hypercube.

By extension, imagine an entire population P as points in space (such as the three-dimensional space in Figure 12). Crossover done on P can only produce children inside the bounding box surrounding P in space. Thus P's bounding box can never increase: you're doomed to only search inside it.

As we repeatedly perform crossover and selection on a population, it may reach the situation where certain alleles (values for certain positions in the vector) have been eliminated, and the bounding box will collapse in that dimension. Eventually the population will **converge**, and often (unfortunately) **prematurely converge**, to copies of the same individual. At this stage there's no escape: when an individual crosses over with itself, nothing new is generated.[25] Thus to make the Genetic Algorithm global, you also need to have a Mutate operation.

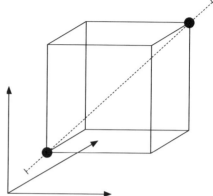

Figure 12 A box in space formed by two three-dimensional vectors (black circles). The dashed line connects the two vectors.

What's the point of crossover then? Crossover was originally based on the premise that highly fit individuals often share certain traits, called **building blocks**, in common. For fixed-length vector individuals a building block was often defined as a collection of genes set to certain alleles. For example, in the boolean individual 10110101, perhaps ***101*1 might be a building block (where the * positions aren't part of the building block). In many problems for which crossover was helpful, the fitness of a given individual is often at least partly correlated to the degree to which it contains various of these building blocks, and so crossover works by spreading building blocks quickly throughout the population. Building blocks were the focus of much early genetic algorithm analysis, formalized in an area known as **schema theory**.

That's the idea anyway. But, hand-in-hand with this building-block hypothesis, Crossover methods also assume that there is some degree of **linkage**[26] between genes on the chromosome: that is, settings for certain genes in groups are strongly correlated to fitness improvement. For example, genes A and B might contribute to fitness only when they're *both* set to 1: if either is set to 0, then the fact that the other is set to 1 doesn't do anything. One- and Two-point Crossover also make the even more tenuous assumption that your vector is structured such that highly linked genes are located near to one another on the vector: because such crossovers are unlikely to break apart closely-located gene groups. Unless you have carefully organized your vector, this assumption is probably a bug, not a feature. Uniform Crossover also makes some linkage assumptions but does not have this linkage-location bias. Is the general linkage assumption true for your problem? Or are your genes essentially independent of one another? For most problems of interest, it's the former: but it's dicey. Be careful.

---

[25]Crossovers which don't make anything new when an individual crosses over with itself are called **homologous**.

[26]One special kind of linkage effect has its own term stolen straight from biology: **epistasis**. Here, genes A and B are linked because gene B has an *effect* on the expression of gene A (on the other hand, A may not affect B). The term "epistasis" can also be used more generally as a synonym for linkage.

In theory, you could perform uniform crossover with several vectors at once to produce children which are the combination of all of them.[27] To avoid sheer randomization, probably you'd want only a bit of mixing to occur, so the probability of swapping any given index shouldn't be spectacularly high. Something like this is very rare in practice though. To do it, we first need to define how to uniformly randomly shuffle a vector. Surprisingly, it's not as obvious as you'd think.

Algorithm 26 *Randomly Shuffle a Vector*
1: $\vec{p} \leftarrow$ elements to shuffle $\langle p_1, ..., p_l \rangle$

2: **for** i from l down to 2 **do**   ▷ Note we don't go to 1
3:     $j \leftarrow$ integer chosen at random from 1 to i inclusive
4:     Swap p_i and p_j

Armed with a random shuffler (we'll use it in future algorithms too), we can now cross over k vectors at a time, trading pieces with one another, and producing k children as a result.

Algorithm 27 *Uniform Crossover among K Vectors*
1: $p \leftarrow$ probability of swapping an index   ▷ Ought to be very small
2: $W \leftarrow \{W_1, ..., W_k\}$ vectors to cross over, each of length l

3: $\vec{v} \leftarrow$ vector $\langle v_1, ..., v_k \rangle$
4: **for** i from 1 to l **do**
5:     **if** $p \geq$ random number chosen uniformly from 0.0 to 1.0 inclusive **then**
6:        **for** j from 1 to k **do**   ▷ Load $\vec{v}$ with the ith elements from each vector in W
7:           $\vec{w} \leftarrow W_j$
8:           $v_j \leftarrow w_i$
9:     Randomly Shuffle $\vec{v}$
10:     **for** j from 1 to k **do**   ▷ Put back the elements, all mixed up
11:          $\vec{w} \leftarrow W_j$
12:          $w_i \leftarrow v_j$
13:          $W_j \leftarrow \vec{w}$
14: **return** W

3.2.2 More Recombination

So far we've been doing crossovers that are just swaps: but if the vectors are of floating-point values, our recombination could be something fuzzier, like averaging the two values rather than swapping them. Imagine if our two vectors were points in space. We draw a line between the two points and choose two new points between them. We could extend this line somewhat beyond the points as well, as shown in the dashed line in Figure 12, and pick along the line. This algorithm, known as **Line Recombination**, here presented in the form given by Heinz Mühlenbein and Dirk Schlierkamp-Voosen, depends on a variable p which determines how far out along the line we'll allow children to be. If $p = 0$ then the children will be located along the line within the hypercube (that is, between the two points). If $p > 0$ then the children may be located anywhere on the line, even somewhat outside of the hypercube.

---

[27]There's nothing new under the sun: this was one of the early ES approaches tried by Hans-Paul Schwefel.

Algorithm 28 *Line Recombination*
1: $p \leftarrow$ positive value which determines how far long the line a child can be located   ▷ Try 0.25
2: $\vec{v} \leftarrow$ first vector $\langle v_1, v_2, ...v_l \rangle$ to be crossed over
3: $\vec{w} \leftarrow$ second vector $\langle w_1, w_2, ...w_l \rangle$ to be crossed over

4: $\alpha \leftarrow$ random value from $-p$ to $1+p$ inclusive
5: $\beta \leftarrow$ random value from $-p$ to $1+p$ inclusive
6: **for** i from 1 to l **do**
7:     $t \leftarrow \alpha v_i + (1-\alpha) w_i$
8:     $s \leftarrow \beta w_i + (1-\beta) v_i$
9:     **if** t and s are within bounds **then**
10:         $v_i \leftarrow t$
11:         $w_i \leftarrow s$
12: **return** $\vec{v}$ and $\vec{w}$

We could extend this further by picking random α and β values for each position in the vector. This would result in children that are located within the hypercube or (if $p > 0$) slightly outside of it. Mühlenbein and Schlierkamp-Voosen call this **Intermediate Recombination**.[28]

Algorithm 29 *Intermediate Recombination*
1: $p \leftarrow$ positive value which determines how far long the line a child can be located   ▷ Try 0.25
2: $\vec{v} \leftarrow$ first vector $\langle v_1, v_2, ...v_l \rangle$ to be crossed over
3: $\vec{w} \leftarrow$ second vector $\langle w_1, w_2, ...w_l \rangle$ to be crossed over

4: **for** i from 1 to l **do**
5:     **repeat**
6:         $\alpha \leftarrow$ random value from $-p$ to $1+p$ inclusive   ▷ We just moved these two lines!
7:         $\beta \leftarrow$ random value from $-p$ to $1+p$ inclusive
8:         $t \leftarrow \alpha v_i + (1-\alpha) w_i$
9:         $s \leftarrow \beta w_i + (1-\beta) v_i$
10:    **until** t and s are within bounds
11:    $v_i \leftarrow t$
12:    $w_i \leftarrow s$
13: **return** $\vec{v}$ and $\vec{w}$

Since we're using different values of α and β for each element, instead of rejecting recombination if the elements go out of bounds, we can now just repeatedly pick a new α and β.

Why bother with values of $p > 0$? Imagine that you have no Mutate operation, and are just doing Intermediate or Line Recombination. Each time you select parents and generate a child,

---
[28]Okay, they called them *Extended* Line and *Extended* Intermediate Recombination, in Heinz Mühlenbein and Dirk Schlierkamp-Voosen, 1993, Predictive models for the breeder genetic algorithm: I. continuous parameter optimization, *Evolutionary Computation*, 1(1). These methods have long been in evolutionary computation, but the terms are hardly standardized: notably Hans-Paul Schwefel's original Evolutionary Strategies work used (among others) line recombination with $p = -0.5$, but he called it *intermediate recombination*, as do others. Schwefel also tried a different variation: for each gene of the child, two parents were chosen at random, and their gene values at that gene were averaged.

that child is located somewhere within the cube formed by the parents (recall Figure 12). Thus it's impossible to generate a child *outside the bounding box of the population*. If you want to explore in those unknown regions, you need a way to generate children further out than your parents are.

Other Representations So far we've focused on vectors. In Section 4 we'll get to other representations. For now, remember that if you can come up with a reasonable notion of Mutate, any representation is plausible. How might we do graph structures? Sets? Arbitrary-length lists? Trees?

3.2.3 Selection

In Evolution Strategies, we just lopped off all but the μ best individuals, a procedure known as **Truncation Selection**. Because the Genetic Algorithm performs iterative selection, crossover, and mutation while breeding, we have more options. Unlike Truncation Selection, the GA's SelectWithReplacement procedure can (by chance) pick certain Individuals over and over again, and it also can (by chance) occasionally select some low-fitness Individuals. In an ES an individual is the parent of a fixed and predefined number of children, but not so in a GA.

The original SelectWithReplacement technique for GAs was called **Fitness-Proportionate Selection**, sometimes known as **Roulette Selection**. In this algorithm, we select individuals in proportion to their fitness: if an individual has a higher fitness, it's selected more often.[29] To do this we "size" the individuals according to their fitness as shown in Figure 13.[30] Let $s = \sum_i f_i$ be the sum fitness of all the individuals. A random number from 0 to s falls within the range of some individual, which is then selected.

Figure 13 Array of individual ranges in Fitness Proportionate Selection.

Algorithm 30 *Fitness-Proportionate Selection*
1: **perform once per** generation
2:     **global** $\vec{p} \leftarrow$ population copied into a vector of individuals $\langle p_1, p_2, ..., p_l \rangle$
3:     **global** $\vec{f} \leftarrow \langle f_1, f_2, ..., f_l \rangle$ fitnesses of individuals in $\vec{p}$ in the same order as $\vec{p}$ ▷ Must all be ≥ 0
4:     **if** $\vec{f}$ is all 0.0s **then**   ▷ Deal with all 0 fitnesses gracefully
5:         Convert $\vec{f}$ to all 1.0s
6:     **for** i from 2 to l **do**   ▷ Convert $\vec{f}$ to a CDF. This will also cause $f_l = s$, the sum of fitnesses
7:         $f_i \leftarrow f_i + f_{i-1}$
8: **perform each time**
9:     $n \leftarrow$ random number from 0 to f_l inclusive
10:     **for** i from 2 to l **do**   ▷ This could be done more efficiently with binary search
11:         **if** $f_{i-1} < n \leq f_i$ **then**
12:             **return** p_i
13:     **return** p_1

---

[29] We presume here that fitnesses are ≥ 0. As usual, higher is better.
[30] Also due to John Holland. See Footnote 21, p. 36.

Notice that Fitness-Proportionate Selection has a preprocessing step: converting all the fitnesses (or really copies of them) into a cumulative distribution. This only needs to be done once per generation. Additionally, though the code searches linearly through the fitness array to find the one we want, it'd be smarter to do that in $O(\lg n)$ time by doing a binary search instead.

One variant on Fitness-Proportionate Selection is called **Stochastic Universal Sampling** (or **SUS**), by James Baker. In SUS, we select in a fitness-proportionate way but biased so that fit individuals always get picked at least once. This is known as a *low variance resampling* algorithm and I include it here because it is now popular in other venues than just evolutionary computation (most famously, **Particle Filters**).[31]

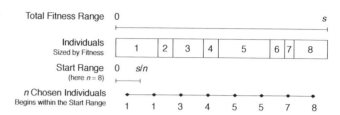

Figure 14 Array of individual ranges, start range, and chosen points in Stochastic Universal Sampling.

SUS selects n individuals at a time (typically n is the size of the next generation, so in our case $n = l$). To begin, we build our fitness array as before. Then we select a random position from 0 to s/n. We then select the individual which straddles that position. We then increment the position by s/n and repeat (up to n times total). Each increment, we select the individual in whose fitness region we landed. This is shown in Figure 14. The algorithm is:

Algorithm 31 *Stochastic Universal Sampling*
1: **perform once per** n individuals produced   ▷ Usually $n = l$, that is, once per generation
2:    **global** $\vec{p} \leftarrow$ copy of vector of individuals (our population) $\langle p_1, p_2, ..., p_l \rangle$, shuffled randomly
          ▷ To shuffle a vector randomly, see Algorithm 26
3:    **global** $\vec{f} \leftarrow \langle f_1, f_2, ..., f_l \rangle$ fitnesses of individuals in $\vec{p}$ in the same order as $\vec{p}$ ▷ Must all be ≥ 0
4:    **global** *index* $\leftarrow 0$
5:    **if** $\vec{f}$ is all 0.0s **then**
6:        Convert $\vec{f}$ to all 1.0s
7:    **for** i from 2 to l **do**   ▷ Convert $\vec{f}$ to a CDF. This will also cause $f_l = s$, the sum of fitnesses.
8:        $f_i \leftarrow f_i + f_{i-1}$
9:    **global** *value* $\leftarrow$ random number from 0 to f_l/n inclusive
10: **perform each time**
11:    **while** $f_{index} < value$ **do**
12:        $index \leftarrow index + 1$
13:    $value \leftarrow value + f_l/n$
14:    **return** p_{index}

There are basically two advantages to SUS. First, it's $O(n)$ to select n individuals, rather than $O(n \lg n)$ for Fitness-Proportionate Selection. That used to be a big deal but it isn't any more, since the lion's share of time in most optimization algorithms is spent in assessing the fitness of individuals, not in the selection or breeding processes. Second and more interesting, SUS

---

[31] And they never seem to cite him. Here it is: James Edward Baker, 1987, Reducing bias and inefficiency in the selection algorithm, in John Grefenstette, editor, *Genetic Algorithms and Their Applications: Proceedings of the Second International Conference on Genetic Algorithms (ICGA)*, pages 14–21, Lawrence Erlbaum Associates, Hillsdale.

guarantees that if an individual is fairly fit (over s/n in size), it'll get chosen for sure, sometimes multiple times. In Fitness-Proportionate Selection even the fittest individual may never be selected.

There is a big problem with the methods described so far: they presume that the actual fitness *value* of an individual really means something important. But often we choose a fitness function such that higher ones are "better" than smaller ones, and don't mean to imply anything else. Even if the fitness function was carefully chosen, consider the following situation, where a fitness function goes from 0 to 10. Near the end of a run, all the individuals have values like 9.97, 9.98, 9.99, etc. We want to finesse the peak of the fitness function, and so we *want* to pick the 9.99-fitness individual. But to Fitness-Proportionate Selection (and to SUS), all these individuals will be selected with nearly identical probability. The system has converged to just doing random selection.

To fix this we could **scale** the fitness function to be more sensitive to the values at the top end of the function. But to really remedy the situation we need to adopt a **non-parametric** selection algorithm which throws away the notion that fitness values mean anything other than bigger is better, and just considers their rank ordering. Truncation Selection does this, but the most popular technique by far is **Tournament Selection**,[32] an astonishingly simple algorithm:

Algorithm 32 *Tournament Selection*
1: $P \leftarrow$ population
2: $t \leftarrow$ tournament size, $t \geq 1$

3: *Best* $\leftarrow$ individual picked at random from P with replacement
4: **for** i from 2 to t **do**
5:     *Next* $\leftarrow$ individual picked at random from P with replacement
6:     **if** Fitness(*Next*) > Fitness(*Best*) **then**
7:         *Best* $\leftarrow$ *Next*
8: **return** *Best*

We return the fittest individual of some t individuals picked at random, with replacement, from the population. That's it! Tournament Selection has become the **primary selection technique used for the Genetic Algorithm** and many related methods, for several reasons. First, it's not sensitive to the particulars of the fitness function. Second, it's dead simple, requires no preprocessing, and works well with parallel algorithms. Third, it's tunable: by setting the **tournament size** t, you can change how selective the technique is. At the extremes, if $t = 1$, this is just random search. If t is very large (much larger than the population size itself), then the probability that the fittest individual in the population will appear in the tournament approaches 1.0, and so Tournament Selection just picks the fittest individual each time (put another way, it approaches Truncation Selection with $\mu = 1$).

In the Genetic Algorithm, the most popular setting is $t = 2$. For certain representations (such as those in Genetic Programming, discussed later in Section 4.3), it's common to be more selective ($t = 7$). To be *less* selective than $t = 2$, but not be totally random, we'd need some kind of trick. One way I do it is to also allow real-numbered values of t from 1.0 to 2.0. In this range, with probability $t - 1.0$, we do a tournament selection of size $t = 2$, else we select an individual at random ($t = 1$).[33]

---

[32]Tournament Selection may be a folk algorithm: but the earliest usage I'm aware of is Anne Brindle, 1981, *Genetic Algorithms for Function Optimization*, Ph.D. thesis, University of Alberta. She used binary tournament selection ($t = 2$).
[33]You could generalize this to any real-valued $t \geq 1.0$: with probability $t - \lfloor t \rfloor$ select with size $\lceil t \rceil$, else with size $\lfloor t \rfloor$.

3.3 Exploitative Variations

It seems the trend in new algorithms is to be more exploitative. Some variations such as **Elitism**, the **Steady-State Genetic Algorithm** (and **Generation Gap** methods), and the Genetic Algorithm with a **Tree-Style Genetic Programming Pipeline**, are exploitative because highly-fit parents can linger in the population and compete with their children, like $(\mu + \lambda)$. Other variations are exploitative because they directly augment evolution with hill-climbing: for example, certain kinds of **Hybrid Optimization Algorithms**, and a method called **Scatter Search with Path Relinking**. We discuss all these next.

3.3.1 Elitism

Elitism is simple: we augment the Genetic Algorithm to directly inject into the next population the fittest individual or individuals from the previous population.[34] These individuals are called the **elites**. By keeping the best individual (or individuals) around in future populations, this algorithm begins to resemble $(\mu + \lambda)$, and has similar exploitation properties. This exploitation can cause premature convergence if not kept in check: perhaps by increasing the mutation and crossover noise, or weakening the selection pressure, or reducing how many elites are being stored.

A minor catch. If you want to maintain a population size of *popsize*, and you're doing crossover, you'll need to have *popsize*, minus the number of elites, be divisible by two, as in this algorithm:

Algorithm 33 *The Genetic Algorithm with Elitism*
1: *popsize* ← desired population size
2: n ← desired number of elite individuals   ▷ *popsize* − n should be even

3: $P \leftarrow \{\}$
4: **for** *popsize* times **do**
5:      $P \leftarrow P \cup \{\text{new random individual}\}$
6: *Best* ← □
7: **repeat**
8:      **for** each individual $P_i \in P$ **do**
9:          AssessFitness(P_i)
10:          **if** *Best* = □ or Fitness(P_i) > Fitness(*Best*) **then**
11:              *Best* ← P_i
12:      $Q \leftarrow \{\text{the } n \text{ fittest individuals in } P, \text{ breaking ties at random}\}$
13:      **for** $(popsize - n)/2$ times **do**
14:          Parent $P_a \leftarrow$ SelectWithReplacement(P)
15:          Parent $P_b \leftarrow$ SelectWithReplacement(P)
16:          Children $C_a, C_b \leftarrow$ Crossover(Copy(P_a), Copy(P_b))
17:          $Q \leftarrow Q \cup \{\text{Mutate}(C_a), \text{Mutate}(C_b)\}$
18:      $P \leftarrow Q$
19: **until** *Best* is the ideal solution or we have run out of time
20: **return** *Best*

---

[34] Elitism was coined by Ken De Jong in his thesis (see Footnote 36, p. 48.).

Or you can just throw away an extra crossed-over child if it'd put you over the population size, as is done in The Genetic Algorithm (Tree-style Genetic Programming Pipeline) (Algorithm 3.3.3).

Elitism is very common. For example, most major multiobjective algorithms (Section 7) are strongly elitist. Many recent Ant Colony Optimization algorithms (ACO, Section 8.3) are also elitist. And of course anything resembling $(\mu + \lambda)$, including Scatter Search (Section 3.3.5) is heavily elitist. Even Particle Swarm Optimization (PSO, Section 3.5) has a kind of elitism in its own regard.

3.3.2 The Steady-State Genetic Algorithm

An alternative to a traditional generational approach to the Genetic Algorithm is to use a **steady-state** approach, updating the population in a piecemeal fashion rather than all at one time. This approach was popularized by the Darrell Whitley and Joan Kauth's GENITOR system. The idea is to iteratively breed a new child or two, assess their fitness, and then reintroduce them directly into the population itself, killing off some preexisting individuals to make room for them. Here's a version which uses crossover and generates two children at a time:

Algorithm 34 *The Steady-State Genetic Algorithm*
1: *popsize* ← desired population size
2: $P \leftarrow \{\}$
3: **for** *popsize* times **do**
4:     $P \leftarrow P \cup \{$new random individual$\}$
5: *Best* ← □
6: **for** each individual $P_i \in P$ **do**
7:     AssessFitness(P_i)
8:     **if** *Best* = □ or Fitness(P_i) > Fitness(*Best*) **then**
9:         *Best* ← P_i
10: **repeat**
11:     Parent P_a ← SelectWithReplacement(P)   ▷ We first breed two children C_a and C_b
12:     Parent P_b ← SelectWithReplacement(P)
13:     Children C_a, C_b ← Crossover(Copy(P_a), Copy(P_b))
14:     C_a ← Mutate(C_a)
15:     C_b ← Mutate(C_b)
16:     AssessFitness(C_a)   ▷ We next assess the fitness of C_a and C_b
17:     **if** Fitness(C_a) > Fitness(*Best*) **then**
18:         *Best* ← C_a
19:     AssessFitness(C_b)
20:     **if** Fitness(C_b) > Fitness(*Best*) **then**
21:         *Best* ← C_b
22:     Individual P_d ← SelectForDeath(P)
23:     Individual P_e ← SelectForDeath(P)   ▷ P_d must be $\neq P_e$
24:     $P \leftarrow P - \{P_d, P_e\}$ ▷ We then delete P_d and P_e from the population
25:     $P \leftarrow P \cup \{C_a, C_b\}$ ▷ Finally we add C_a and C_b to the population
26: **until** *Best* is the ideal solution or we have run out of time
27: **return** *Best*

The Steady-State Genetic Algorithm has two important features. First, it uses half the memory of a traditional genetic algorithm because there is only one population at a time (no Q, only P). Second, it is fairly exploitative compared to a generational approach: the parents stay around in the population, potentially for a very long time, and thus, like $\mu + \lambda$ and Elitism, this runs the risk of causing the system to prematurely converge to largely copies of a few highly fit individuals. This may be exaggerated by how we decide to SelectForDeath. If we tend to select *unfit* individuals for death (using, for example, a Tournament Selection based on the *least fit* in the tournament), this can push diversity out of the population even faster. More commonly, we might simply select individuals at random for death. Thus the fit culprits in premature convergence can eventually be shoved out of the population.[35] If we want less exploitation, we may do the standard tricks: use a relatively unselective operator for SelectWithReplacement, and make Crossover and Mutate noisy.

We could of course generalize this algorithm to replace not just two individuals but some n individuals all at once. Methods using large values of n (perhaps 50% of the total population size or more) are often known as **Generation Gap Algorithms**,[36] after Ken De Jong. As n approaches 100%, we get closer and closer to a plain generational algorithm.

3.3.3 The Tree-Style Genetic Programming Pipeline

Genetic Programming (discussed in Section 4.3) is a community interested in using metaheuristics to find highly fit *computer programs*. The most common form of Genetic Programming, **Tree-Style Genetic Programming**, uses trees as its representation. When doing Tree-Style Genetic Programming it's traditional, but hardly required, to use a variant of The Genetic Algorithm with a special breeding technique due to John Koza.[37] Rather than performing crossover and then mutation, this algorithm first flips a coin. With 90% probability it selects two parents and performs only crossover. Otherwise, it selects one parent and directly copies the parent into the new population. It's this direct copying which makes this a strongly exploitative variant.

A few items of note. First, there's no mutation: this is not a global algorithm. However the peculiar version of crossover used in Tree-Style Genetic Programming is so mutative that in practice mutation is rarely needed. Second, this algorithm could produce one more child than is needed: just discard it. Third, traditionally the selection procedure is one that is highly selective: Genetic Programming usually employs Tournament Selection with a tournament size $t = 7$. Here we go:

---

[35] An interesting question to ask: assuming we have enough memory, why bother deleting individuals at all?

[36] There's a lot of history here. Early ES work employed the now-disused $(\mu + 1)$ evolution strategy, where μ parents (the population) work together to create one new child (see Footnote 17, p. 33). Ken De Jong did early studies of generation gap methods in Kenneth De Jong, 1975, *An Analysis of the Behaviour of a Class of Genetic Adaptive Systems*, Ph.D. thesis, University of Michigan. GENITOR later popularized the notion of steady-state algorithms. Darrell Whitley and Joan Kauth, 1988, GENITOR: A different genetic algorithm, Technical Report CS-88-101, Colorado State University.

[37] John R. Koza, 1992, *Genetic Programming: On the Programming of Computers by Means of Natural Selection*, MIT Press.

Algorithm 35 *The Genetic Algorithm (Tree-Style Genetic Programming Pipeline)*
1: *popsize* ← desired population size
2: *r* ← probability of performing direct reproduction ▷ Usually $r = 0.1$

3: $P \leftarrow \{\}$
4: **for** *popsize* times **do**
5: $\quad P \leftarrow P \cup \{\text{new random individual}\}$
6: *Best* ← □
7: **repeat**
8: $\quad$ **for** each individual $P_i \in P$ **do**
9: $\quad\quad$ AssessFitness(P_i)
10: $\quad\quad$ **if** *Best* = □ or Fitness(P_i) > Fitness(*Best*) **then**
11: $\quad\quad\quad$ *Best* ← P_i
12: $\quad Q \leftarrow \{\}$
13: $\quad$ **repeat** ▷ Here's where we begin to deviate from The Genetic Algorithm
14: $\quad\quad$ **if** $r \geq$ a random number chosen uniformly from 0.0 to 1.0 inclusive **then**
15: $\quad\quad\quad$ Parent $P_i \leftarrow$ SelectWithReplacement(P)
16: $\quad\quad\quad$ $Q \leftarrow Q \cup \{\text{Copy}(P_i)\}$
17: $\quad\quad$ **else**
18: $\quad\quad\quad$ Parent $P_a \leftarrow$ SelectWithReplacement(P)
19: $\quad\quad\quad$ Parent $P_b \leftarrow$ SelectWithReplacement(P)
20: $\quad\quad\quad$ Children $C_a, C_b \leftarrow$ Crossover(Copy(P_a), Copy(P_b))
21: $\quad\quad\quad$ $Q \leftarrow Q \cup \{C_a\}$
22: $\quad\quad\quad$ **if** $||Q|| <$ *popsize* **then**
23: $\quad\quad\quad\quad$ $Q \leftarrow Q \cup \{C_b\}$
24: $\quad$ **until** $||Q|| =$ *popsize* ▷ End Deviation
25: $\quad P \leftarrow Q$
26: **until** *Best* is the ideal solution or we have run out of time
27: **return** *Best*

3.3.4 Hybrid Optimization Algorithms

There are many *many* ways in which we can create hybrids of various metaheuristics algorithms, but perhaps the most popular approach is a hybrid of evolutionary computation and a local improver such as hill-climbing.

The EA could go in the inner loop and the hill-climber outside: for example, we could extend Iterated Local Search (ILS, Section 2.6) to use a population method in its inner loop, rather than a hill-climber, but retain the "Perturb" hill-climber in the outer loop.

But by far the most common approach is the other way around: augment an EA with some hill-climbing during the fitness assessment phase to revise each individual as it is being assessed. The revised individual replaces the original one in the population. Any EA can be so augmented: below is the abstract EA from Algorithm 17 converted into a Hybrid Algorithm.

Algorithm 36 *An Abstract Hybrid Evolutionary and Hill-Climbing Algorithm*
1: $t \leftarrow$ number of iterations to Hill-Climb

2: $P \leftarrow$ Build Initial Population
3: $Best \leftarrow \square$
4: **repeat**
5:     AssessFitness(P)
6:     **for** each individual $P_i \in P$ **do**
7:         $P_i \leftarrow$ Hill-Climb(P_i) for t iterations   ▷ Replace P_i in P
8:         **if** $Best = \square$ or Fitness(P_i) > Fitness($Best$) **then**
9:             $Best \leftarrow P_i$
10:    $P \leftarrow$ Join(P, Breed(P))
11: **until** $Best$ is the ideal solution or we have run out of time
12: **return** $Best$

The length of t, of course, is a knob that adjusts the degree of exploitation in the algorithm. If t is very long, then we're doing more hill-climbing and thus more exploiting; whereas if t is very short, then we're spending more time in the outer algorithm and thus doing more exploring.

There are many other ways to mix an exploitative (and likely local) algorithm with an explorative (usually global) algorithm. We've already seen one example: Hill-Climbing with Random Restarts (Algorithm 10), which combines a local searching algorithm (Hill-Climbing) with a global algorithm (Random Search). Another hybrid: Iterated Local Search (Algorithm 16), places Hill-Climbing inside another, more explorative Hill-Climber. Indeed, the local-improvement algorithm doesn't even have to be a metaheuristic: it could be a machine learning or heuristic algorithm, for example. In general, the overall family of algorithms that combines *some* kind of global optimization algorithm with *some* kind of local improvement algorithm in *some* way... is often saddled with an ill-considered name: **Memetic Algorithms**.[38] Though this term encompasses a fairly broad category of stuff, the lion's share of memetic algorithms in the literature have been hybrids of global search (often evolutionary computation) and hill-climbing: and that's usually how it's thought of I think.

Perhaps a better term we might use to describe such algorithms could be **"Lamarckian Algorithms"**. Jean-Baptiste Lamarck was a French biologist around the time of the American revolution who proposed an early but mistaken notion of evolution. His idea was that after individuals improved themselves during their lifetimes, they then passed those traits genetically to their offspring. For example, horse-like animals in Africa might strain to reach fruit in trees, stretching their necks. These slightly longer necks were then passed to their offspring. After several generations of stretching, behold the giraffe. Similarly, these kinds of hybrid algorithms often work by individuals improving themselves during fitness assessment and then passing on their improvements

---

[38]In my opinion, Memetic Algorithms have little to do with *memes*, a Richard Dawkins notion which means *ideas* that replicate by causing their recipients to forward them to others. Examples include everything from religions to email chain letters. The term *memetic algorithms* was notionally justified because memetic algorithm individuals are improved locally, just as memes might be "improved" by humans before passing them on. But I think the distinguishing feature of memes isn't local improvement: it's replication, even parasitic replication. Nothing in memetic algorithms gets at this.

Richard Dawkins first coined the term *meme* in Richard Dawkins, 1976, *The Selfish Gene*, Oxford University Press. The term *memetic algorithms* was coined in Pablo Moscato, 1989, On evolution, search, optimization, genetic algorithms and martial arts: Towards memetic algorithms, Technical Report 158–79, Caltech Concurrent Computation Program, California Institute of Technology.

to their children. Another reasonable name would be a **"Baldwin Effect Algorithm"**, named after a more plausible variation of Lamarckianism that has found its place in real evolutionary theory. Much later on we'll see another example of a Lamarckian algorithm in SAMUEL, an algorithm for optimizing policies in Section 10.3 with special local-improvement operators.

Another approach to hybridization is to alternate between two disjoint algorithms. For example, the **Learnable Evolution Model (LEM)**, discussed later in Section 9.1, alternates between evolution and a machine-learning classification technique.

Still another kind of hybrid algorithm — perhaps less aimed at exploitation — is to have one metaheuristic optimize the *runtime parameters of another metaheuristic*. For example, we could use a genetic algorithm to search for the optimal mutation rate, crossover type, etc., for a *second* genetic algorithm running on a problem of interest.[39] These methods were originally studied under the name **Meta-Genetic Algorithms**,[40] or more generally **Meta-Optimization**, techniques in the oddly-named family of **Hyperheuristics**.[41] Some hyperheuristics focus not just on optimizing parameters for another optimization procedure, but on optimizing *which* optimization procedure should be used in the first place.

If you're thinking that hyperheuristics are absurdly expensive, you'd be right. The original thinking behind these techniques was that researchers nearly always do some optimization by hand anyway: if you're going to do a whole lot of runs using a genetic algorithm and a particular problem family, you're likely to play around with the settings up front to get the genetic algorithm tuned well for those kinds of problems. And if this is the case, why not automate the process?

This thinking suggests that the end product of a hyperheuristic would be a set of parameter settings which you can then use later on. But in some limited situations it might make sense to apply a hyperheuristic to obtain an optimal end solution. For example, suppose you had a moderate number of computers available to you and were planning on running a great many optimization runs on them and then returning the best result you discover. You don't know the best settings for these runs. But if you're going to do all those runs anyway, perhaps you might consider a meta-evolutionary run: create an initial population of individuals in the form of parameter settings, try each on a different computer a few times, then evolve and repeat.[42]

---

[39] An interesting question: what are the parameter settings for your hyperheuristic, and can you optimize those with *another* algorithm? How far down the rabbit hole do you go?

[40] The earliest notion of the idea that I am aware of is Daniel Joseph Cavicchio Jr., 1970, *Adaptive Search Using Simulated Evolution*, Ph.D. thesis, Computer and Communication Sciences Department, University of Michigan. This was then expanded on significantly in Robert Ernest Mercer and Jeffrey R. Sampson, 1978, Adaptive search using a reproductive meta-plan, *Kybernetes*, 7(3), 215–228. The most famous early presentation of the concept is John Grefenstette, 1986, Optimization of control parameters for genetic algorithms, *IEEE Transactions on Systems, Man, and Cybernetics*, SMC-16(1), 122–128. Grefenstette also coined the term (he called it a "meta-level GA").

[41] What an ill-conceived name: *hyper* is simply the wrong word. Metaheuristics, Hyperheuristics, Memetic Algorithms: we have a lot of unfortunate terms.

[42] Parallelizing these runs is probably best done by using a combination of hyperheuristics and Master-Slave Fitness Assessment (see Section 5.3). Also: if you were testing each parameter-setting individual with a single run, perhaps its fitness would be set to the best fitness discovered in that run. But since metaheuristics are stochastic, such a fitness would be very noisy of course. To get a better handle on the true quality of a parameter-setting individual, you might need to run multiple times with those parameter settings, and use the mean best fitness of the runs.

This stuff can get complicated fast.

3.3.5 Scatter Search

Fred Glover's **Scatter Search with Path Relinking**[43] combines a hybrid evolutionary and hill-climbing algorithm, line recombination, $(\mu + \lambda)$, and an explicit procedure to inject some diversity (exploration) into the mix! Standard Scatter Search with Path Relinking is complex and baroque, but we can describe a simplified version here. The algorithm combines exploitative mechanisms (hybrid methods, steady-state evolution) with an explicit attempt to force diversity (and hopefully exploration) into the system. The algorithm starts with a set of initial seeded individuals provided by you. Then the algorithm tries to produce a large number of random individuals that are very different from one another and from the seeds. These, plus the seeds, form the population. Then we do some hill-climbing on each of the individuals to improve them.

We then do the following loop. First, we truncate the population to a small size consisting of some very fit individuals and some very diverse individuals (to force diversity). Then we perform some kind of pairing up and crossover (usually using line recombination) on that smaller population: in our version, we do line recombination on every pair of individuals in the population, plus some mutating for good measure. Then we do hill-climbing on these new individuals to improve them, add them to the population, and repeat the loop.

To do the ProduceDiverseIndividual function and the procedure to determine the most diverse individuals in Q (line 17), you'll need a distance measure among individuals: for example, if two individuals were real-valued vectors $\vec{v}$ and $\vec{u}$, use Euclidian distance, that is, $\sqrt{\sum_i (v_i - u_i)^2}$. These are often metric distances (discussed later in Niching, Section 6.4). From there you could define the diversity of an individual as its sum distance from everyone else, that is for Population P, the diversity of P_i is $\sum_j \text{distance}(P_i, P_j)$.

Now we have a way to select based on who's the "most diverse". But *producing* a "diverse" individual is mostly ad-hoc: I'd generate a lot of individuals, then select a subset of them using a tournament selection based on maximum diversity from the seeds. Or you could find gene values uncommon among the seeds and build an individual with them. The simplified algorithm:

---

[43]Glover also invented Tabu Search (Section 2.5). And coined the term "metaheuristics". It's tough to pin down the first papers in Scatter Search. But a good later tutorial is Fred Glover, Manuel Laguna, and Rafael Martí, 2003, Scatter search, in Ashish Ghosh and Shigeyoshi Tsutsui, editors, *Advances in Evolutionary Computing: Theory and Applications*, pages 519–538, Springer. Glover also attempted a full, detailed template of the process in Fred Glover, 1998, A template for scatter search and path relinking, in *Proceedings of the Third European Conference on Artificial Evolution*, pages 1–51, Springer. The algorithm shown here is approximately derived from these papers.

Algorithm 37 *A Simplified Scatter Search with Path Relinking*
1: *Seeds* ← initial collection of individuals, defined by you
2: *initsize* ← initial sample size   ▷ The size of the initial population before truncation
3: t ← number of iterations to Hill-Climb
4: n ← number of individuals to be selected based on fitness
5: m ← number of individuals to be selected based on diversity

6: $P \leftarrow Seeds$
7: **for** $initsize - ||Seeds||$ times **do**
8:     $P \leftarrow P \cup \{\text{ProduceDiverseIndividual}(P)\}$ ▷ Make an individual very different from what's in P
9: $Best \leftarrow \square$
10: **for** each individual $P_i \in P$ **do**   ▷ Do some hill-climbing
11:     $P_i \leftarrow \text{Hill-Climb}(P_i)$ for t iterations   ▷ Replace P_i in P
12:     AssessFitness(P_i)
13:     **if** $Best = \square$ or Fitness(P_i) > Fitness($Best$) **then**
14:         $Best \leftarrow P_i$
15: **repeat**   ▷ The main loop
16:     $B \leftarrow$ the fittest n individuals in P
17:     $D \leftarrow$ the most diverse m individuals in P ▷ Those as far from others in the space as possible
18:     $P \leftarrow B \cup D$
19:     $Q \leftarrow \{\}$
20:     **for** each individual $P_i \in P$ **do**
21:         **for** each individual $P_j \in P$ where $j \neq i$ **do**
22:             Children $C_a, C_b \leftarrow$ Crossover(Copy(P_i), Copy(P_j))   ▷ Line Recombination, Algorithm 28
23:             $C_a \leftarrow$ Mutate(C_a)   ▷ Scatter Search wouldn't do this normally: but I would
24:             $C_b \leftarrow$ Mutate(C_b)   ▷ Likewise
25:             $C_a \leftarrow$ Hill-Climb(C_a) for t iterations
26:             $C_b \leftarrow$ Hill-Climb(C_b) for t iterations
27:             AssessFitness(C_a)   ▷ We next assess the fitness of C_a and C_b
28:             **if** Fitness(C_a) > Fitness($Best$) **then**
29:                 $Best \leftarrow C_a$
30:             AssessFitness(C_b)
31:             **if** Fitness(C_b) > Fitness($Best$) **then**
32:                 $Best \leftarrow C_b$
33:             $Q \leftarrow Q \cup \{C_a, C_b\}$
34:     $P \leftarrow Q \cup P$
35: **until** *Best* is the ideal solution or we have run out of time
36: **return** *Best*

3.4 Differential Evolution

Differential Evolution (DE) determines the size of Mutates largely based on the current variance in the population. If the population is spread out, Mutate will make major changes. If the population is condensed in a certain region, Mutates will be small. It's an adaptive mutation algorithm (like the one-fifth rule in Evolution Strategies). DE was developed by Kenneth Price and Rainer Storn.[44]

DE's mutation operators employ vector addition and subtraction, so it really only works in metric vector spaces (booleans, metric integer spaces, reals). DE has a variety of mutation operators, but the early one described here is common and easy to describe. For each member i of the population, we generate a new child by picking three individuals from the population and performing some vector additions and subtractions among them. The idea is to mutate away from one of the three individuals ($\vec{a}$) by adding a vector to it. This vector is created from the difference between the other two individuals $\vec{b} - \vec{c}$. If the population is spread out, $\vec{b}$ and $\vec{c}$ are likely to be far from one another and this mutation vector is large, else it is small. This way, if the population is spread throughout the space, mutations will be much bigger than when the algorithm has later converged on fit regions of the space. The child is then crossed over with $\vec{i}$. (Differential Evolution has lots of other mutation variations not shown here).

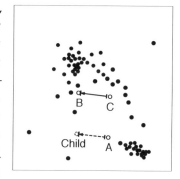

Figure 15 Differential Evolution's primary mutation operator. A copy of individual A is mutated by adding to it the vector between two other individuals B and C, producing a child.

Finally, after we have built up a new group of children, we compare each child with the parent which created it (each parent created a single child). If the child is better than the parent, it replaces the parent in the original population.

The new locations of children are entirely based on the existing parents and which combinations we can make of adding and subtracting them. This means that this algorithm isn't global in the sense that any point in the space is possible: though through successive choices of individuals, and mutating them, we can hone in on certain spots in the space. Also oddly this algorithm traditionally mutates each individual in turn. Perhaps better would be either to mutate all of them in parallel (in a generational fashion) or to pick i at random each time (steady-state style).

It's crucial to note that Differential Evolution "selects" individuals in a way quite different from what we've seen so far. A child is created by mutating existing individuals largely picked *at random* from the population. So where's the selection? It comes *after* generating a child, when it competes for survival with a specific individual already in the population. If the child is fitter, it replaces that individual, else the child is thrown away. This hill-climbing-ish approach to selection is a variation of **survival selection** (as opposed to **parent selection**).[45]

Below we show one simple implementation of Differential Evolution, as described above. Note that in this code we will treat the population as a vector, not a collection: this is to make the pseudocode a bit more clear. Also, note that since Differential Evolution always uses vector representations for individuals, we'll treat individuals both as individuals (such as Q_i and as vectors (such as $\vec{a}$) interchangeably. Here we go:

---

[44]DE grew out of a series of papers as it evolved, but one of its better known papers, if not the earliest, is Rainer Storn and Kenneth Price, 1997, Differential evolution: A simple and efficient heuristic for global optimization over continuous spaces, *Journal of Global Optimization*, 11(4), 341–359. Price, Storn, and Jouni Lampinen later wrote a pretty big book on the subject: Kenneth Price, Rainer Storn, and Journi Lampinen, 2005, *Differential Evolution: A Practical Approach to Global Optimization*, Springer.

[45]See footnote 16.

Algorithm 38 *Differential Evolution (DE)*
1: $\alpha \leftarrow$ mutation rate ▷ Commonly between 0.5 and 1.0, higher is more explorative
2: *popsize* $\leftarrow$ desired population size

3: $P \leftarrow \langle \rangle$ ▷ Empty population (it's convenient here to treat it as a vector), of length *popsize*
4: $Q \leftarrow \square$ ▷ The parents. Each parent Q_i was responsible for creating the child P_i
5: **for** i from 1 to *popsize* **do**
6:    $P_i \leftarrow$ new random individual
7: $Best \leftarrow \square$
8: **repeat**
9:    **for** each individual $P_i \in P$ **do**
10:      AssessFitness(P_i)
11:      **if** $Q \neq \square$ and Fitness(Q_i) > Fitness(P_i) **then**
12:         $P_i \leftarrow Q_i$ ▷ Retain the parent, throw away the kid
13:      **if** $Best = \square$ or Fitness(P_i) > Fitness($Best$) **then**
14:         $Best \leftarrow P_i$
15:    $Q \leftarrow P$
16:    **for** each individual $Q_i \in Q$ **do** ▷ We treat individuals as vectors below
17:      $\vec{a} \leftarrow$ a copy of an individual other than Q_i, chosen at random with replacement from Q
18:      $\vec{b} \leftarrow$ a copy of an individual other than Q_i or $\vec{a}$, chosen at random with replacement from Q
19:      $\vec{c} \leftarrow$ a copy of an individual other than Q_i, $\vec{a}$, or $\vec{b}$, chosen at random with replacement from Q
20:      $\vec{d} \leftarrow \vec{a} + \alpha(\vec{b} - \vec{c})$ ▷ Mutation is just vector arithmetic
21:      $P_i \leftarrow$ one child from Crossover($\vec{d}$, Copy(Q_i))
22: **until** $Best$ is the ideal solution or we ran out of time
23: **return** $Best$

Crossover can be anything: but one common approach is to do a uniform crossover (Algorithm 25), but guarantee that at least one gene from Q_i (the gene is chosen at random) survives in P_i.

3.5 Particle Swarm Optimization

Particle Swarm Optimization (PSO) is a stochastic optimization technique somewhat similar to evolutionary algorithms but different in an important way. It's modeled not after evolution per se, but after swarming and flocking behaviors in animals. Unlike other population-based methods, PSO does not resample populations to produce new ones: it has no selection *of any kind*. Instead, PSO maintains a single static population whose members are Tweaked in response to new discoveries about the space. The method is essentially a form of **directed mutation**. The technique was developed by James Kennedy and Russell Eberhart in the mid-1990s.[46]

---

[46]Among the earliest papers on PSO is James Kennedy and Russell Eberhart, 1995, Particle swarm optimization, in *Proceedings of IEEE International Conference on Neural Networks*, pages 1942–1948. Eberhart, Kennedy, and Yuhui Shi later wrote a book on the topic: James Kennedy, Russell Eberhart, and Yuhui Shi, 2001, *Swarm Intelligence*, Morgan Kaufmann.

Like Differential Evolution, PSO operates almost exclusively in multidimensional metric, and usually real-valued, spaces. This is because PSO's candidate solutions are Mutated *towards* the best discovered solutions so far, which really necessitates a metric space (it's nontrivial to Mutate, say, a tree "towards" another tree in a formal, rigorous fashion).

Because of its use in real-valued spaces, and because PSO is inspired by flocks and swarms, PSO practitioners tend to refer to candidate solutions not as a population of individuals but as a **swarm** of **particles**. These particles never die (there is no selection). Instead, the directed mutation moves the particles about in the space. A particle consists of two parts:

- The particle's location in space, $\vec{x} = \langle x_1, x_2, ...\rangle$. This is the equivalent, in evolutionary algorithms, of the individual's genotype.

- The particle's velocity, $\vec{v} = \langle v_1, v_2, ...\rangle$. This is the speed and direction at which the particle is traveling each timestep. Put another way, if $\vec{x}^{(t-1)}$ and $\vec{x}^{(t)}$ are the locations in space of the particle at times $t-1$ and t respectively, then at time t, $\vec{v} = \vec{x}^{(t)} - \vec{x}^{(t-1)}$.

Each particle starts at a random location and with a random velocity vector, often computed by choosing two random points in the space and using half the vector from one to the other (other options are a small random vector or a zero vector). We must also keep track of a few other things:

- The fittest known location $\vec{x}^*$ that $\vec{x}$ has discovered so far.

- The fittest known location $\vec{x}^+$ that any of the **informants** of $\vec{x}$ have discovered so far. In early versions of the algorithm, particles were assigned "grid neighbors" which would inform them about known best-so-far locations. Nowadays the informants of $\vec{x}$ are commonly a small set of particles chosen randomly each iteration. $\vec{x}$ is always one of its own informants.

- The fittest known location $\vec{x}^!$ that has been discovered by *anyone* so far.

Each timestep we perform the following operations:

1. Assess the fitness of each particle and update the best-discovered locations if necessary.

2. Determine how to Mutate. For each particle $\vec{x}$, we update its velocity vector $\vec{v}$ by adding in, to some degree, a vector pointing towards $\vec{x}^*$, a vector pointing towards $\vec{x}^+$, and a vector pointing towards $\vec{x}^!$. These are augmented by a bit of random noise (different random values for each dimension).

3. Mutate each particle by moving it along its velocity vector.

The algorithm looks like this:

Algorithm 39 *Particle Swarm Optimization (PSO)*
1: *swarmsize* ← desired swarm size
2: α ← proportion of velocity to be retained
3: β ← proportion of personal best to be retained
4: γ ← proportion of the informants' best to be retained
5: δ ← proportion of global best to be retained
6: ϵ ← jump size of a particle

7: $P \leftarrow \{\}$
8: **for** *swarmsize* times **do**
9:     $P \leftarrow P \cup \{$new random particle $\vec{x}$ with a random initial velocity $\vec{v}\}$
10: $\overrightarrow{Best} \leftarrow \square$
11: **repeat**
12:     **for** each particle $\vec{x} \in P$ with velocity $\vec{v}$ **do**
13:         AssessFitness($\vec{x}$)
14:         **if** $\overrightarrow{Best} = \square$ or Fitness($\vec{x}$) > Fitness($\overrightarrow{Best}$) **then**
15:             $\overrightarrow{Best} \leftarrow \vec{x}$
16:     **for** each particle $\vec{x} \in P$ with velocity $\vec{v}$ **do**   ▷ Determine how to Mutate
17:         $\vec{x}^* \leftarrow$ previous fittest location of $\vec{x}$
18:         $\vec{x}^+ \leftarrow$ previous fittest location of informants of $\vec{x}$ ▷ (including $\vec{x}$ itself)
19:         $\vec{x}^! \leftarrow$ previous fittest location any particle
20:         **for** each dimension i **do**
21:             $b \leftarrow$ random number from 0.0 to β inclusive
22:             $c \leftarrow$ random number from 0.0 to γ inclusive
23:             $d \leftarrow$ random number from 0.0 to δ inclusive
24:             $v_i \leftarrow \alpha v_i + b(x_i^* - x_i) + c(x_i^+ - x_i) + d(x_i^! - x_i)$
25:     **for** each particle $\vec{x} \in P$ with velocity $\vec{v}$ **do**   ▷ Mutate
26:         $\vec{x} \leftarrow \vec{x} + \epsilon \vec{v}$
27: **until** $\overrightarrow{Best}$ is the ideal solution or we have run out of time
28: **return** $\overrightarrow{Best}$

This implementation of the algorithm relies on five parameters:

- α: how much of the original velocity is retained.

- β: how much of the personal best is mixed in. If β is large, particles tend to move more towards their own personal bests rather than towards global bests. This breaks the swarm into a lot of separate hill-climbers rather than a joint searcher.

- γ: how much of the informants' best is mixed in. The effect here may be a mid-ground between β and δ. The *number* of informants is also a factor (assuming they're picked at random): more informants is more like the global best and less like the particle's local best.

- δ: how much of the global best is mixed in. If δ is large, particles tend to move more towards the best known region. This converts the algorithm into one large hill-climber rather than separate hill-climbers. Perhaps because this threatens to make the system highly exploitative, δ is often set to 0 in modern implementations.

- ϵ: how fast the particle moves. If ϵ is large, the particles make big jumps towards the better areas — and can jump over them by accident. Thus a big ϵ allows the system to move quickly to best-known regions, but makes it hard to do fine-grained optimization. Just like in hill-climbing. Most commonly, ϵ is set to 1.

4 Representation

Most techniques discussed later are typically done with population-based algorithms. So from now on we will usually use Evolutionary Computation versions of terms: *individual* instead of *candidate solution*; *fitness* instead of *quality*, etc.

The **representation** of an individual is the approach you take to constructing, tweaking, and presenting the individual for fitness assessment. Although often we'll refer to the representation as the data structure used to define the individual (a vector, a tree, etc.) it's useful to think of the representation not as the data type but instead simply as two functions:

- The **initialization** function used to generate a random individual.
- The **Tweak** function, which takes one individual (or more) and slightly modifies it.

To this we might add...

- The **fitness assessment** function.
- The **Copy** function.

These functions are the only places where many optimization algorithms deal with the internals of individuals. Otherwise the algorithms treat individuals as black boxes. By handling these functions specially, we can separate the entire concept of representation from the system.

Much of the success or failure of a metaheuristic lies in the design of the representation of the individuals, because their representation, and particularly how they Tweak, has such a strong impact on the trajectory of the optimization procedure as it marches through the fitness landscape (that is, the quality function). A lot of the black magic involved in constructing an appropriate representation lies in finding one which improves (or at least doesn't *worsen*) the **smoothness** of the landscape. As mentioned earlier, the smoothness criterion was approximately defined as: individuals which are similar to each other tend to behave similarly (and thus tend to have similar fitness), whereas individuals dissimilar from one another make no such promise.

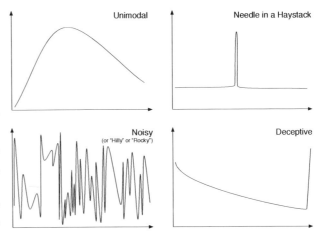

Figure 16 Four fitness landscapes. Repeats Figure 6.

The smoother a landscape, the fewer hills it has and the more it begins to resemble a unimodal landscape, as shown in Figure 16. Recall that this isn't a *sufficient* criterion though, as **needle-in-a-haystack** or (worse) **deceptive** environments are highly smooth, yet can be extremely challenging for an optimization algorithm.

When we refer to individuals *being similar*, we mean that they have similar **genotypes**, and when we refer to individuals as *behaving similarly*, we mean that they have similar **phenotypes**.[47] What do we mean by *similar* genotypes? Generally genotype A is similar to genotype B if the probability is high that Tweaking

---

[47] Recall that, in evolutionary computation at least, the phrase "genotype" refers to how the individual appears to the genetic operators (perhaps it's a vector, or a tree), and the phrase "phenotype" refers to *how* (not *how well*) the individual *performs* when evaluated for fitness assessment.

59

A will result in *B* (or vice versa). Thus things are similar not because their genotypes *look* similar, but because they are near each other in the space *with respect to your choice of the Tweak operation*.

It's tempting to think of a stochastic optimization system as largely working in genotype space, then translating the genotypes to phenotypes for purposes of evaluation. But when thinking about the effect of representations, it's better to consider the other way around: an individual's natural arrangement is its phenotype, and when the algorithm needs to make a new individual, it translates the phenotype to a genotype, Tweaks it, then translates back to the phenotype. Commonly we refer to phenotype→genotype translation as **encoding**, and the reverse as **decoding**. Thus we can think of this process as:

Parent Phenotype ⟶ Encode ⟶ Tweak ⟶ Decode ⟶ *Child Phenotype*

This view helps us see the perils of poor encoding choices. Imagine that your individuals take the phenotypical form, for some reason, of Rubik's Cube configurations. You'd like that Tweak operator to make small changes like rotating a side, etc. If you used a genotype in the form of a Rubik's Cube, you're all set: the Tweak operator already does exactly what you want. But imagine if your encoding operation was as follows:

Parent ⟶ Do 20 specific unusual moves ⟶ Tweak ⟶ Undo those 20 moves ⟶ *Child*

You can imagine that after doing the twenty moves, a single twist of one side (the Tweak) will have *huge* consequences after you undo those twenty moves. It causes almost total randomization from parent to child. Lesson: you want an encoding/decoding mechanism which doesn't cause your carefully-selected, smooth Tweak operations to cause the phenotype space to go haywire.

This isn't just of academic concern. In the past, Genetic Algorithm folks used to encode *everything* as a binary vector of fixed length. The reasoning was: if there's only one genotype, we could develop a canonical Genetic Algorithm as a library function, and the only differences of significance would be the encoding procedure. As it turns out, this wasn't all that good of an idea. Consider the situation where an individual consists of a single integer from 0 to 15. We'd represent it as a vector of 4 bits. The fitness function is shown at right. Notice that it increases until 8, and then "falls off the cliff" at 9. This fitness function abuses a bad feature in the genotype: what is known in the Genetic Algorithm community as a **Hamming cliff**, located at the jump from 7 to 8. A Hamming cliff is where, to make a *small* change in the phenotype or fitness, you must make a very *large* change in the genotype. For example, to mutate 7 (0111) into 8 (1000), you have to make four bit-flips in succession. The function at right is hard to optimize because to get to 8, notionally you could approach from 7 (requiring four lucky mutations) or you could approach from 9 or 10 (which aren't often going to be selected, because of bad fitness).

Phenotype	Genotype	Gray Code	Fitness
0	0000	0000	0
1	0001	0001	1
2	0010	0011	2
3	0011	0010	3
4	0100	0110	4
5	0101	0111	5
6	0110	0101	6
7	0111	0100	7
8	1000	1100	8
9	1001	1101	0
10	1010	1111	0
11	1011	1110	0
12	1100	1010	0
13	1101	1011	0
14	1110	1001	0
15	1111	1000	0

Table 2 A fitness function that exploits a Hamming Cliff.

Now consider instead representing the individual not by the binary encoding genotype shown above but rather its **Gray code**[48] encoding shown next to it. This encoding has an interesting property: each successive number differs from its previous number by only one bit flip. And 15 differs from 0 by only one bit flip. Thus if we're at 7 (Gray code 0100) we can easily mutate to 8 (Gray code 1100). Hamming cliff problem solved. By the way, Gray-coding is easy to do:

Algorithm 40 *A Gray Coding*
1: $\vec{v} \leftarrow$ boolean vector encoding a standard binary number $\langle v_1, v_2, ...v_l \rangle$ to be converted to Gray code

2: $\vec{w} \leftarrow \text{Copy}(\vec{v})$
3: **for** i from 2 to l **do**
4:     **if** v_{i-1} is true **then**
5:         $w_i \leftarrow \neg(v_i)$
6: **return** $\vec{w}$

The point of this exercise is *not* to convince you to use Gray codes: indeed, we can construct nasty fitness functions which cause problems for Gray codes as well, and Gray coding is somewhat old fashioned now. The point is to illustrate the notion of smoothness and its value. **If you encode your individual such that small changes in the genotype (like one bit flip) are** *somewhat more* **likely to result in small changes in the fitness, you can help your optimizer.**

One heuristic approach to smooth fitness landscapes is to make the genotype as similar to the phenotype as possible: if your phenotype is a graph structure, let the genotype be a graph structure as well. That way your fitness function may still be hilly but at least you're not making it *even hillier* by running it through an unfortunate encoding. But remember that this is thinking of the representation as if it's a data structure, when it's not. It's largely two functions: the initialization function and the Tweak function.

Much of Representation Is an Art, Not a Science How are you going to Tweak a graph structure in a smooth way? No, seriously. Certain representations (notably fixed-length vectors of booleans or of floating-point values) are very well understood and there's a bunch of good theory around them. But many representations are still basically ad-hoc. Many of the algorithms and ideas in this section should not be taken as *directions*, or even *recommendations*, but *suggestions* of one particular possible way to do representations that maintain smoothness properties. We'll first take care of the easy, well-understood one that we've seen before a lot: vectors.

4.1 Vectors

Just to be clear, by *vectors* we mean fixed-length one-dimensional arrays. We'll get to arbitrary-length lists in Section 4.4. Vectors usually come in three flavors: boolean, real-valued, and integer.[49] The first two — boolean and real-valued vectors — we've seen a lot so far. As a result we've built up several initialization, mutation, and crossover algorithms for them. In summary:

---

[48] After Frank Gray, who developed it in 1947 at Bell Labs to reduce errors in the output of phone system switches.
[49] There's no reason you couldn't have a vector of trees, or a vector of rules, or a vector where some elements were reals and others were booleans, etc. (In fact, we'll see vectors of trees and rules later on in Section 4.3.4!) You just need to be more careful with your mutation and initialization mechanisms.

Boolean Vectors
   Initialization
      Generate a Random Bit-Vector   Algorithm 21   Page 37
   Mutation
      Bit-Flip Mutation   Algorithm 22   Page 38

Floating-Point Vectors
   Initialization
      Generate a Random Real-Valued Vector   Algorithm 7   Page 19
   Mutation
      Bounded Uniform Convolution   Algorithm 8   Page 19
      Gaussian Convolution   Algorithm 11   Page 23
   Floating-Point-Specific Crossover
      Line Recombination   Algorithm 28   Page 42
      Intermediate Recombination   Algorithm 29   Page 42

Vector Crossover *(applies to any vector type)*
   One-Point Crossover   Algorithm 23   Page 38
   Two-Point Crossover   Algorithm 24   Page 39
   Uniform Crossover   Algorithm 25   Page 39
   Uniform Crossover among *K* Vectors   Algorithm 27   Page 41

Integer Vectors We've not seen integer vectors yet: and integer vectors have a twist to consider. What do the integers in your vector represent? Do they define a set of unordered objects (1=China, 2=England, 3=France, ...) or do they form a metric space (IQ scores, or street addresses, or final course grades) where the *distance* between, say, 4 and 5 is greater than the distance between 1 and 5? Mutation decisions often center on whether the space is a metric space.

The remainder of this section will focus on integer vectors, but it also gives some discussion relevant to initialization and mutation of all vector types.

4.1.1 Initialization and Bias

Creating random initial vectors is usually just a matter of picking each vector position v_i uniformly among all possible values. If you have some knowledge about your problem, however, you could **bias** the system by tending to pick values in certain regions of the space. For example, if you believe that better solutions usually lie in the regions where $v_1 = v_2 \times v_3$, you could emphasize generating vectors in those regions.

Another way to bias the initial configuration of your population is to **seed** the initial population with pre-chosen individuals of your own design. For example, my students were trying to optimize vectors which defined how a bipedal robot walked, kicked, etc. These vectors translated into joint angles and movements for the many motors on the robot. Rather than start with random values, the vast majority of which were nonsense, they instead chose to wire a student up to a 3D tracker and have him perform the motions. They then converted the resulting data into joint angle movements, which they used to seed the initial population.

Some suggestions. First, biasing is dangerous. You may *think* you know where the best solutions are, but you probably don't. So if you bias the initial configuration, you may actually make it harder for the system to find the right answer. Know what you're getting into. Second, even if you choose to bias the system, it may be wise to start with values that aren't *all* or *exactly* based on your heuristic bias. Diversity is useful, particularly early on.

4.1.2 Mutation

It's rare that you'd mutate floating-point vectors with anything other than Guassian convolution (or some similar distribution-based noise procedure). Likewise, bit-vectors are typically mutated using bit-flip mutation. For integer vectors, it depends. If your representation treats integers as members of a set (for example, red=1, blue=2, ...), the best you may be able to do is randomize each slot with a given probability:

Algorithm 41 *Integer Randomization Mutation*
1: $\vec{v} \leftarrow$ integer vector $\langle v_1, v_2, ...v_l \rangle$ to be mutated
2: $p \leftarrow$ probability of randomizing an integer   ▷ Perhaps you might set p to $1/l$ or lower

3: **for** i from 1 to l **do**
4:     **if** $p \geq$ random number chosen uniformly from 0.0 to 1.0 inclusive **then**
5:         $v_i \leftarrow$ new random legal integer
6: **return** $\vec{v}$

If instead your integers represent a metric space, you might wish to mutate them in a manner similar to gaussian convolution, so that the changes to integers tends to be small. One of a great many ways to do this is to keep flipping a coin until it comes up heads, and do a random walk of that length.[50] This creates noise centered around the original value, and is global.

Algorithm 42 *Random Walk Mutation*
1: $\vec{v} \leftarrow$ integer vector $\langle v_1, v_2, ...v_l \rangle$ to be mutated
2: $p \leftarrow$ probability of randomizing an integer   ▷ Perhaps you might set p to $1/l$ or lower
3: $b \leftarrow$ coin-flip probability   ▷ Make b bigger if you have many legal integer values so the random walks are longer

4: **for** i from 1 to l **do**
5:     **if** $p \geq$ random number chosen uniformly from 0.0 to 1.0 inclusive **then**
6:         **repeat**
7:             $n \leftarrow$ either a 1 or -1, chosen at random
8:             **if** $v_i + n$ is within bounds for legal integer values **then**
9:                 $v_i \leftarrow v_i + n$
10:            **else if** $v_i - n$ is within bounds for legal integer values **then**
11:                 $v_i \leftarrow v_i - n$
12:         **until** $b <$ random number chosen uniformly from 0.0 to 1.0 inclusive
13: **return** $\vec{v}$

Point Mutation The mutation methods discussed so far all have the same property: *every* gene in the genome has an independent probability of being mutated. Perhaps you may have thought

---
[50]Note: I just made up this mutator, but it's probably not bad. And someone else probably already invented it.

of a different approach: pick a single random gene, then mutate that gene, and you're done. (Or perhaps pick *n* genes at random and mutate them). Such **point mutation** methods are sometimes useful but are often dangerous.

First the useful part: there exist some problems where you can make progress through the space by changing a single gene, but if you change several genes at a time, even by a small amount, it's tougher to make progress. The Mona Lisa picture on the front page is an example of this: the genome consists of some *m* polygons with random colors. Change one polygon at a time, by a fair bit, and you can eventually eek out a Mona Lisa. Change *n* polygons (or even all *m* polygons) at one time, even through small perturbation, and it turns out to be quite difficult to get a better child.

But beware: it's very easy to construct problems where point mutation is quite bad indeed. Consider simple boolean individuals of the form $\langle x, y \rangle$, where x and y can each be 1 or 0, and we're doing a simple hill-climber (or (1 + 1) if you will). The problem uses the fitness function shown in Table 3, and our intrepid initial candidate solution starts at $\langle 0, 0 \rangle$, which at present has a fitness of 5. Our mutation function flips a single gene. If we flipped gene x, we'd wind up in $\langle 1, 0 \rangle$, with a fitness of -100, which would get promptly rejected. On the other hand, if we flipped gene y, we'd wind up in $\langle 0, 1 \rangle$, also with a fitness of -100. There's no way to get to the optimum $\langle 1, 1 \rangle$ without flipping *both genes* at the same time. But our mutation operator won't allow that. The issue is that point mutation is *not a global operator*: it can only make horizontal moves through the space, and so cannot reach all possible points in one jump. In summary: point mutation can sometimes be useful, but know what you're getting into.

	x	
	0	1
y 0	5	-100
1	-100	10

Table 3 A trivial boolean fitness function which is hostile to point mutation.

4.1.3 Recombination

So far we've seen three kinds of general-purpose vector recombination: **One-** and **Two-point Crossover**, and **Uniform Crossover**. Additionally we've seen two kinds of recombination designed for real-valued number recombination: **Line Recombination** and **Intermediate Recombination**. Of course you could do a similar thing as these last two algorithms with metric-space integers:

Algorithm 43 *Line Recombination for Integers*
1: $\vec{v} \leftarrow$ first vector $\langle v_1, v_2, ... v_l \rangle$ to be crossed over
2: $\vec{w} \leftarrow$ second vector $\langle w_1, w_2, ... w_l \rangle$ to be crossed over
3: $p \leftarrow$ positive value which determines how far along the line a child can be located

4: $\alpha \leftarrow$ random value from $-p$ to $1 + p$ inclusive
5: $\beta \leftarrow$ random value from $-p$ to $1 + p$ inclusive
6: **for** i from 1 to l **do**
7:     **repeat**
8:         $t \leftarrow \alpha v_i + (1 - \alpha) w_i$
9:         $s \leftarrow \beta w_i + (1 - \beta) v_i$
10:     **until** $\lfloor t + 1/2 \rfloor$ and $\lfloor s + 1/2 \rfloor$ are within bounds   ▷ The $\lfloor ... + 1/2 \rfloor$ bit is rounding
11:     $v_i \leftarrow \lfloor t + 1/2 \rfloor$
12:     $w_i \leftarrow \lfloor s + 1/2 \rfloor$
13: **return** $\vec{v}$ and $\vec{w}$

Algorithm 44 *Intermediate Recombination for Integers*

1: $\vec{v} \leftarrow$ first vector $\langle v_1, v_2, ...v_l \rangle$ to be crossed over
2: $\vec{w} \leftarrow$ second vector $\langle w_1, w_2, ...w_l \rangle$ to be crossed over
3: $p \leftarrow$ positive value which determines how far long the line a child can be located

4: **for** i from 1 to l **do**
5:    **repeat**
6:       $\alpha \leftarrow$ random value from $-p$ to $1 + p$ inclusive
7:       $\beta \leftarrow$ random value from $-p$ to $1 + p$ inclusive
8:       $t \leftarrow \alpha v_i + (1 - \alpha) w_i$
9:       $s \leftarrow \beta w_i + (1 - \beta) v_i$
10:    **until** $\lfloor t + 1/2 \rfloor$ and $\lfloor s + 1/2 \rfloor$ are within bounds
11:    $v_i \leftarrow \lfloor t + 1/2 \rfloor$
12:    $w_i \leftarrow \lfloor s + 1/2 \rfloor$
13: **return** $\vec{v}$ and $\vec{w}$

4.1.4 Heterogeneous Vectors

A vector doesn't have to be all real values or all integer values or all booleans. It could be a mixture of stuff. For example, the first ten genes might be booleans, the next twenty genes might be integers, and so on. The naive way to handle this would be to make everything real-valued numbers and then just interpret each gene appropriately at evaluation time. But if certain genes are to be interpreted as integers or booleans, you'll want to make mutation and initialization procedures appropriate to them. It may be unwise to rely on standard real-valued mutation methods.

For example, imagine if a gene has three values *red*, *blue*, and *green*, and you've decided to map these to 1.0, 2.0, and 3.0. You're using Gaussian Convolution (Algorithm 11) for mutation. This will produce numbers like 1.6 — is this a 2.0, that is, blue? Let's presume that during evaluation you're rounding to the nearest integer to deal with that issue. Now you're faced with more subtle problems: applying Gaussian Convolution to a value of 1.0 (red) is more likely to produce something near to 2.0 (blue) than it is to produce something near to 3.0 (green). Do you really want mutation from red to more likely be blue than green? Probably not! Along the same vein, if you don't pick an appropriate variance, a whole lot of mutations from 1.0 (red) will be things like 1.001 or 1.02, which of course will still be red.

This kind of nonsense arises from shoehorning integers, or unordered sets (red, green, blue), into real-valued metric spaces. Instead it's probably smarter to just permit each gene to have its own mutation and initialization procedure. You could still have them all be real-valued numbers, but the per-gene mutators and initializers would understand how to properly handle a real-valued number that's "actually" an integer, or "actually" a boolean.

Using a real-valued vector, plus per-gene initializers and mutators, probably works fine if your genes are all interpreted as reals, integers, set members (red, green, blue), and booleans.[51] But if some of your genes need to be, say, trees or strings, then you'll probably have no choice but to make a vector of "objects" rather than real numbers, and do everything in a custom fashion.

---

[51]You do need to keep an eye on crossover. Most crossover methods will work fine, but some crossover methods, such as Line Recombination (Algorithm 28) or Intermediate Recombination (Algorithm 29), assume that your genes operate as real numbers. It'd probably make things easier if you avoided them.

4.1.5 Phenotype-Specific Mutation or Crossover

Last but not least, you might try instead to perform mutation or crossover on your representations in a manner that makes sense with regard to their *phenotype*. For example, what if your phenotype is a **matrix**, and you're using vectors to represent those matrices? Perhaps your recombination operators should take into consideration the two-dimensional nature of the phenotype. You might design an operator which does two one-point crossovers to slice out a rectangular region:

$$\begin{bmatrix} 1 & 4 & 7 \\ 9 & 2 & 3 \\ 8 & 5 & 6 \end{bmatrix} \text{ crossed over with } \begin{bmatrix} 21 & 99 & 46 \\ 31 & 42 & 84 \\ 23 & 67 & 98 \end{bmatrix} \longrightarrow \begin{bmatrix} 1 & 4 & 46 \\ 9 & 2 & 84 \\ 23 & 67 & 98 \end{bmatrix}$$

This leads us to using representations more apropos to your problem: so on to more complex representations. Remember all that talk about the value of smoothness? Hold onto your hat because when you get to nastier representations, guaranteeing smoothness becomes very hard indeed.

4.2 Direct Encoded Graphs

Graphs are just about the *most complex* of various representations, but it's useful to discuss them next. Why would you want to come up with an optimal graph structure? Graphs are used to represent many things: neural networks, finite-state automata or Petri nets or other simple computational devices, electrical circuits, relationships among people, etc. Correspondingly, there are lots of kinds of graph structures, such as directed graphs, undirected graphs, graphs with labels on the edges or nodes, graphs with weights (numbers) on the edges rather than labels, recurrent graphs, feed-forward (non-recurrent) graphs, sparse or dense graphs, planar graphs, etc. It depends on your problem. A lot of the decisions with regard to Tweaking must work within the constraints of the graph structure you've decided on.

First note that you don't need a special representation if your graph structure is fixed and you're just finding weights or labels. For example, if you're developing a neural network with a fixed collection of edges, there's no need to discover the structure of this network (it's fixed!). Just discover the weights of the edges. If you have 100 edges, just optimize a vector of 100 real-valued numbers, one per edge weight, and you're done. Thus most "graph representations" of interest here are really **arbitrary-structured graph representations**. Such structures have been around for a very long time. Larry Fogel developed Evolutionary Programming, probably the earliest evolutionary algorithm, specifically to discover graph structures in the form of finite-state automata.[52]

There are generally two approaches to developing graph structures (and certain other complex structures): **direct encoding** and **indirect** (or **developmental**) **encoding**. Direct encoding stores the exact edge-for-edge, node-for-node description of the graph structure in the representation itself. Indirect encoding has the representation define a small program or set of rules of some kind which, when executed, "grow" a graph structure.

Why would you do an indirect encoding? Perhaps when you wish to cross over certain traits in your graph structure described by subsets of those rules which are bundled together. Or perhaps if your rules recursively cause other rules to fire, you may view certain sets of rules as *functions* or *modules* which always produce the same subgraph. Thus if your optimal graph structures are highly repetitive, you can take advantage of this by evolving a single function which produces that repetitive element rather than having to rediscover the subgraph over and over again during the search process. If the graph has little repetition in it (for example, neural network weights tend to

---
[52]For Fogel's thesis, in which these ideas were advanced, see Footnote 20, p. 36.

have little repetition among them) and is very dense, a direct encoding might be a better choice. Because indirect encodings represent the graph in a non-graph way (as a tree, or a set of rules, or a list of instructions to build the graph, etc.), we'll discuss them later (in Sections 4.3.6 and 4.5). For now, we consider direct encodings.

The simplest direct encoding is a **full adjacency matrix**. Here we have settled on an absolute maximum size for our graph. Let's say we need to create a recurrent directed graph structure and have decided that our graph will contain no more than 5 nodes and have no more than one edge between any two nodes. Let's also say that self-edges are allowed, and we need to find weights for the edges. We could simply represent the graph structure as a 5×5 adjacency matrix describing the edges from every node to every other node:

$$\begin{bmatrix} 0.5 & 0.7 & -0.1 & 0.2 & \text{Off} \\ \text{Off} & -0.5 & -0.8 & 0.4 & \text{Off} \\ 0.6 & 0.7 & 0.8 & \text{Off} & -0.4 \\ -0.1 & \text{Off} & \text{Off} & 0.2 & \text{Off} \\ 0.2 & \text{Off} & -0.7 & \text{Off} & \text{Off} \end{bmatrix}$$

"Off" in position $\langle i, j \rangle$ means "there is no edge connecting j to i". If we want fewer than 5 nodes, we could just assign *all* the weights going in or out of a node to be "Off". We could represent this matrix in many ways. Here are two. First, we might have a single vector of length 25 which stores all the weights, with "Off" being represented as 0.0. Or we could represent the matrix as *two* vectors, a real-valued one which stores all the weights, and a boolean one which stores whether or not an edge is "On" or "Off". Either way, we could use standard crossover and mutation operators, though we might want to be careful about changing "Off" values. If we used the two-vector version, that's done for us for free. If we just use a single real-valued vector, we could create a modified Gaussian Convolution algorithm which only *sometimes* turns edges on or off:

Algorithm 45 *Gaussian Convolution Respecting Zeros*

1: $\vec{v} \leftarrow$ vector $\langle v_1, v_2, ... v_l \rangle$ to be convolved
2: $p \leftarrow$ probability of changing an edge from "On" to "Off" or vice versa
3: $\sigma^2 \leftarrow$ variance of gaussian distribution to convolve with
4: $min \leftarrow$ minimum desired vector element value
5: $max \leftarrow$ maximum desired vector element value

6: **for** i from 1 to l **do**
7:     **if** $p \geq$ random number chosen uniformly from 0.0 to 1.0 inclusive **then**
8:         **if** $v_i = 0.0$ **then**   ▷ Turn "On": pick a random edge weighting
9:             $v_i \leftarrow$ random number chosen uniformly from 0.0 to 1.0 inclusive
10:         **else**   ▷ Turn "Off"
11:             $v_i \leftarrow 0.0$
12:     **else if** $v_i \neq 0.0$ **then**   ▷ Mutate an existing "On" weight
13:         **repeat**
14:             $n \leftarrow$ random number chosen from the Normal distribution $N(0, \sigma^2)$ ▷ See Algorithm 12
15:         **until** $min \leq v_i + n \leq max$
16:         $v_i \leftarrow v_i + n$
17: **return** $\vec{v}$

The disadvantage of this approach is that once an edge is turned "Off", when it's turned back "On", its previously carefully-optimized weight is lost. Perhaps the two-vector approach might yield better results.

If we don't have a maximum size for our graph, we might need to use an **arbitrary directed graph structure**, an approach done very early on (in EP) but popularized by Peter Angeline, Greg Saunders, and Jordan Pollack's **GNARL**.[53] Here our representation isn't a vector: it's an actual graph, stored however we like. To do this, we need to create custom initialization and mutation or crossover operators to add and delete nodes, add and delete edges, relabel nodes and edges, etc.

A similar approach is taken in **NEAT**,[54] Ken Stanley and Risto Miikkulainen's method for optimizing feed-forward neural networks. NEAT represents a graph as two sets, one of nodes and one of vectors. Each node is simply a node *number* and a declaration of the purpose of the node (in neural network parlance: an input, output, or hidden unit). Edges are more interesting: each edge contains, among other things, the nodes the edge connected (by number), the weight of the edge, and the *birthday* of the edge: a unique counter value indicating when the edge had been created. The birthday turns out to be useful in keeping track of which edges should merge during crossover, as discussed in Section 4.2.3.

4.2.1 Initialization

Creating an initial graph structure is mostly informed by the kind of graphs you think you need. First, we might decide on how many nodes and edges we want. We could pick these from some distribution—perhaps a uniform distribution from 1 to some large value. Or we might choose a them from a distribution which heavily favors small numbers, such as the Geometric Distribution. This distribution is formed by repeatedly flipping a coin with probability p until it comes up heads:

Algorithm 46 *Sample from the Geometric Distribution*
1: $p \leftarrow$ probability of picking a bigger number
2: $m \leftarrow$ minimum legal number

3: $n \leftarrow m - 1$
4: **repeat**
5:     $n \leftarrow n + 1$
6: **until** $p <$ random number chosen uniformly from 0.0 to 1.0 inclusive
7: **return** n

The larger the value of p, the larger the value of n on average, using the equation $E(n) = m + p/(1-p)$. For example, if $m = 0$ and $p = 3/4$, then n will be 3 on average, while if $p = 19/20$, then n will be 19 on average. Beware that this distribution has a strong tendency to make lots of small values. It's easy to compute, but may wish to use a less skewed distribution.

Once we have our node and edge counts, we can build a graph by laying out the nodes first, then filling in the edges:

---

[53] Peter J. Angeline, Gregory M. Saunders, and Jordan P. Pollack, 1994, An evolutionary algorithm that constructs recurrent neural networks, *IEEE Transactions on Neural Networks*, 5(1), 54–65.

[54] Kenneth O. Stanley and Risto Miikkulainen, 2002, Evolving neural networks through augmenting topologies, *Evolutionary Computation*, 10(2), 99–127.

Algorithm 47 *Build A Simple Graph*

1: $n \leftarrow$ chosen number of nodes
2: $e \leftarrow$ chosen number of edges
3: $f(j, k, Nodes, Edges) \leftarrow$ function which returns 'true' if an edge from j to k is allowed

4: set of nodes $N \leftarrow \{N_1, ... N_n\}$ ▷ Brand new nodes
5: set of edges $E \leftarrow \{\}$
6: **for** each node $N_i \in N$ **do**
7:     ProcessNode(N_i) ▷ Label it, etc., whatever
8: **for** i from 1 to e **do**
9:     **repeat**
10:         $j \leftarrow$ random number chosen uniformly from 1 to n inclusive
11:         $k \leftarrow$ random number chosen uniformly from 1 to n inclusive
12:     **until** $f(j, k, N, E)$ returns 'true'
13:     $g \leftarrow$ new edge from N_j to N_k
14:     ProcessEdge(g) ▷ Label it, weight it, undirect it, whatever
15:     $E \leftarrow E \cup \{g\}$
16: **return** N, E

Note the ProcessNode and ProcessEdge functions, which give you a place to label and weight edges and nodes. A difficulty with this approach is that we could wind up with a disjoint graph: you may need to adjust this algorithm to guarantee connectedness. Another very common graph representation is a **directed acyclic graph**, where all edges go from later nodes to earlier ones:

Algorithm 48 *Build a Simple Directed Acyclic Graph*

1: $n \leftarrow$ chosen number of nodes
2: $D(m) \leftarrow$ probability distribution of the number of edges out of a node, given number of in-nodes m
3: $f(j, k, Nodes, Edges) \leftarrow$ function which returns 'true' if an edge from j to k is allowed

4: set of nodes $N \leftarrow \{N_1, ... N_n\}$ ▷ Brand new nodes
5: set of edges $E \leftarrow \{\}$
6: **for** each node $N_i \in N$ **do**
7:     ProcessNode(N_i) ▷ Label it, etc., whatever
8: **for** i from 2 to n **do**
9:     $p \leftarrow$ random integer ≥ 1 chosen using $D(i-1)$
10:     **for** j from 1 to p **do**
11:         **repeat**
12:             $k \leftarrow$ random number chosen uniformly from 1 to $i-1$ inclusive
13:         **until** $f(i, k, N, E)$ returns 'true'
14:         $g \leftarrow$ new edge from N_i to N_k
15:         ProcessEdge(g)
16:         $E \leftarrow E \cup \{g\}$
17: **return** N, E

This representation is connected but of course there are no loops. Anyway, these algorithms are only to give you ideas: definitely don't rely on them! Do it right. There are tons of (much better) randomized graph-building algorithms: consult any general algorithms text.

4.2.2 Mutation

One of many ways to mutate an arbitrary graph is to pick some number n of mutations, then n times do any of:

- With α_1 probability, delete a random edge.
- With α_2 probability, add a random edge (if using NEAT, this edge would get a brand new birthday number; see Section 4.2.3 next).
- With α_3 probability, delete a node and all its edges (yeesh!)
- With α_4 probability, add a node
- With α_5 probability, relabel a node
- With α_6 probability, relabel an edge   ... etc. ...

... where $\sum_i \alpha_i = 1.0$. Obviously some of these operations are very mutative, and thus perhaps should have a smaller probability. Keep in mind that small, common changes should result in small fitness changes, that is, more mutative operations should be done less often. Last, how do we pick a value for n? Perhaps we might pick uniformly between some values $1...M$. Or we might choose a value from the Geometric Distribution again.

4.2.3 Recombination

Crossover in graphs is such a mess that many people don't do it at all. How do you cross over graphs in a meaningful way? That is, transferring essential and useful elements from individual to individual without having crossover basically be randomization?

To cross over nodes and edges we often need to get subsets of such things. To select a subset:

Algorithm 49 *Select a Subset*
1: $S \leftarrow$ original set
2: $p \leftarrow$ probability of being a member of the subset

3: subset $S' \leftarrow \{\}$
4: **for** each element $S_i \in S$ **do**
5:     **if** $p \geq$ random number chosen uniformly from 0.0 to 1.0 inclusive **then**
6:         $S' \leftarrow S' \cup \{S_i\}$
7: **return** S'

This is basically the same general notion as was used in Uniform Crossover or Bit-flip Mutation. But you might not like this distribution of subsets. An alternative would be to pick a random number under some distribution of your choosing and select a subset of that size:

Algorithm 50 *Select a Subset (Second Technique)*
1: $S \leftarrow$ original set
2: $n \leftarrow$ number of elements in the subset

3: subset $S' \leftarrow \{\}$
4: **for** i from 1 to n **do**
5: $\quad S' \leftarrow S' \cup \{$random element from S chosen *without* replacement$\}$
6: **return** S'

Note that unlike most situations here, we're picking *without* replacement—that is, an element can't be picked more than once.

So back to crossover. One naive approach might be to pick some subset of nodes and subset of edges in each graph, and exchange subsets. But what if graph A hands graph B an edge $i \rightarrow j$ but B doesn't have i or j among its nodes? Back to the drawing board. An alternative might be to swap nodes, then swap edges with the constraint that an edge can only be swapped to the other graph if the other graph received the relevant nodes as well. The difficulty here is, of course, that the swapped-in subgraph will be disjoint with the existing nodes in that individual's graph. And you might miss some important edges that connected the nodes in the original graph.

A third choice is to pick whole subgraphs and swap them. To pick a subgraph, here is one of a great many possible algorithms:

Algorithm 51 *Select a Subgraph*
1: $N \leftarrow$ nodes in the original graph
2: $E \leftarrow$ edges in the original graph

3: $N' \subseteq N \leftarrow$ nodes in the subgraph (chosen with a subset selection operation)
4: subset $E' \leftarrow \{\}$
5: **for** each edge $E_i \in E$ **do**
6: $\quad j, k \leftarrow$ nodes connected by E_i
7: $\quad$ **if** $j \in N'$ and $k \in N'$ **then**
8: $\quad\quad E' \leftarrow E' \cup \{E_i\}$
9: **return** N', E'

Again, the problem is that the swapped-in subgraph is disjoint with the graph that's already there. At this point you may need to *merge* some nodes in the original graph with those in the newly-swapped in subgraph. As nodes get merged together, certain edges need to be renamed since they're pointing to things that don't exist any more. It's still possible that the two graphs will be disjoint but unlikely. We can force at least one node to merge, thus guaranteeing that the graphs won't be disjoint. The algorithm would then look something like this:

Algorithm 52 *Randomly Merge One Graph Into Another*

1: $N \leftarrow$ nodes in the first graph, shuffled randomly ▷ To shuffle an array randomly, see Algorithm 26
2: $N' \leftarrow$ nodes in the second graph
3: $E \leftarrow$ edges in the first graph
4: $E' \leftarrow$ edges in the second graph
5: $p \leftarrow$ probability of merging a given node from N into a node from N'

6: **for** l from 1 to $||N||$ **do**
7:    **if** $l = 1$ or $p \geq$ random number chosen uniformly from 0.0 to 1.0 inclusive **then**
8:       $n' \leftarrow$ random node chosen uniformly from N' ▷ We'll merge N_l with n'
9:       **for** i from 1 to $||E||$ **do**
10:          $j, k \leftarrow$ nodes connected by E_i
11:          **if** $j = N_l$ **then**
12:             Change j to n' in E_i
13:          **if** $k = N_l$ **then**
14:             Change k to n' in E_i
15:    **else** ▷ No merge, just add N_l into the new graph directly
16:       $N' \leftarrow N' \cup \{N_l\}$
17: $E' \leftarrow E' \cup E$
18: **return** N', E'

Another strategy, used in the NEAT algorithm, merges *all* the edges of two parents into one child. But if edges have the same birthday (that is, originally they were the same edge), NEAT throws one of them out. Thus subgraphs don't just get arbitrarily merged during crossover: they're merged back in the way they used to be. The idea is to retain subgraph structures and reduce the randomness of crossover.

Sometimes you might be able to use internal running statistics to guess which subgraphs would be good to cross over or mutate. For example, Astro Teller's **Neural Programming (NP)** was direct graph encoding for computer programs in which graph nodes were functions connected by directed edges. In the first timestep, each node emitted a certain value. Thereafter in timestep t each node would read (via incoming edges) the emitted values of other nodes at $t - 1$, then use those values as arguments to the node's function, and emit the result. Figure 17 shows a simple example from Teller's thesis[55] which computes the Fibonacci Sequence. NP was notable for its use of internal reinforcement to determine the degree to which various

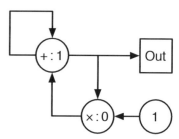

Figure 17 Neural Programming encoding of the Fibonacci Sequence (1, 1, 2, 3, 5, 8, 13, 21, 34, 55, 89, 144, 233, 377, 610, 987, *etc.*). See if you can work it out. The node "1" always emits a 1. The node "+ : 1" emits a 1 on the first timestep, then later emits the sum of its inputs. The node "× : 0" emits a 0 on the first timestep, then later emits the product of its inputs. The sequence is read at the node "Out".

---

[55]Though it's best lumped in with other genetic programming methods (notably Cartesian Genetic Programming, see Section 4.4), I include NP here because it's a true direct graph encoding with an interesting approach to dealing with the mess of graph crossover and mutation. For more hints on how to interpret and evaluate individuals of this kinds, see Sections 4.3 and 4.4. Probably the best place to learn about NP and its internal reinforcement strategy is Astro Teller's thesis: Astro Teller, 1998, *Algorithm Evolution with Internal Reinforcement for Signal Understanding*, Ph.D. thesis, School of Computer Science, Carnegie Mellon University, Technical Report Number CMU-CS-98-132. As it so happens, Astro Teller is related to Edward Teller, of the Metropolis Algorithm (see Footnote 11).

nodes and edges were beneficial to program. NP would then make it more likely that less desirable nodes or edges were more likely to be swapped out via crossover, or to be mutated.

We've not even gotten to how to make sure that your particular graph constraint needs (no self-loops, no multiple edges, etc.) are kept consistent over crossover or mutation. What a mess. As a representation, graphs usually involve an awful lot of ad-hoc hacks and domain specificity. The complete opposite of vectors.

4.3 Trees and Genetic Programming

Genetic Programming (GP) is a research community more than a technique per se. The community focuses on how to use stochastic methods to search for and optimize small *computer programs* or other computational devices. Note that to *optimize* a computer program, we must allow for the notion of *suboptimal* programs rather than programs which are simply right or wrong.[56] GP is thus generally interested in the space where there are *lots* of possible programs (usually small ones) but it's not clear which ones outperform the others and to what degree. For example, finding team soccer robot behaviors, or fitting arbitrary mathematical equations to data sets, or finding finite-state automata which match a given language.

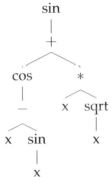

Because computer programs are variable in size, the representations used by this community are also variable in size, mostly **lists** and **trees**. In GP, such lists and trees are typically formed from basic functions or CPU operations (like + or *if* or *kick-towards-goal*). Some of these operations cannot be performed in the context of other operations. For example, 4 + *kick-towards-goal*() makes no sense unless *kick-towards-goal* returns a number. In a similar vein, certain nodes may be restricted to having a certain *number* of children: for example, if a node is *matrix-multiply*, it might be expecting exactly two children, representing the matrices to multiply together. For this reason, GP's initialization and Tweaking operators are particularly concerned with maintaining **closure**, that is, producing *valid* individuals from previous ones.

Figure 18 A Symbolic Regression parse tree.

One of the nifty things about optimizing computer programs is how you assess their fitness: run them and see how they do! This means that the *data* used to store the genotypes of the individuals might be made to conveniently correspond to the *code* of the phenotypes when run. It's not surprising that the early implementations of GP all employed a language in which code and data were closely related: Lisp.

The most common form of GP employs **trees** as its representation, and was first proposed by Nichael Cramer,[57] but much of the work discussed here was invented by John Koza, to whom a lot of credit is due.[58]

---

[56]John Koza proposed exactly this notion in his book *Genetic Programming*: "...you probably assumed I was talking about writing a *correct* computer program to solve this problem.... In fact, this book, focuses almost entirely on *incorrect* programs. In particular, I want to develop the notion that there are gradations in performance among computer programs. Some incorrect programs are very poor; some are better than others; some are approximately correct; occasionally, one may be 100% correct." (p. 130 of John R. Koza, 1992, *Genetic Programming: On the Programming of Computers by Means of Natural Selection*, MIT Press.)

[57]In a single paper Cramer proposed both tree-based GP and a list-based GP similar to that discussed in Section 4.4. He called the list-based version the JB Language, and the tree-based version the TB Language. Nichael Lynn Cramer, 1985, A representation for the adaptive generation of simple sequential programs, in John J. Grefenstette, editor, *Proceedings of an International Conference on Genetic Algorithms and the Applications*, pages 183–187.

[58]Except as noted, the material in Section 4.3 is all due to John Koza. For the primary work, see Footnote 56.

Consider the tree in Figure 18, containing the mathematical expression $\sin(\cos(x - \sin x) + x\sqrt{x})$. This is the *parse tree* of a simple program which performs this expression. In a parse tree, a node is a function or if statement etc., and the children of a node are the arguments to that function. If we used only functions and no operators (for example, using a function subtract(x, y) instead of $x - y$), we might write this in pseudo-C-ish syntax such as:

```
sin(
    add(
        cos(subtract(x, sin(x))),
        multiply(x, sqrt(x))));
```

The Lisp family of languages is particularly adept at this. In Lisp, the function names are tucked *inside* the parentheses, and commas are removed, so the function foo(bar, baz(quux)) appears as (foo bar (baz quux)). In Lisp objects of the form (...) are actually singly-linked lists, so Lisp can manipulate code as if it were data. Perfect for tree-based GP. In Lisp, Figure 18 is:

```
(sin
    (+
        (cos (− x (sin x)))
        (∗ x (sqrt x))))
```

How might we evaluate the fitness of the individual in Figure 18? Perhaps this expression is meant to fit some data as closely as possible. Let's say the data is twenty pairs of the form $\langle x_i, f(x_i) \rangle$. We could test this tree against a given pair i by setting the return value of the x operator to be x_i, then executing the tree, getting the value v_i it evaluates to, and computing the some squared error from $f(x_i)$, that is, $\delta_i = (v_i - f(x_i))^2$. The fitness of an individual might be the square root of the total error, $\sqrt{\delta_1 + \delta_2 + ... + \delta_n}$. The family of GP problems like this, where the objective is to fit an arbitrarily complex curve to a set of data, is called **symbolic regression**.

Programs don't have to be equations: they can actually *do* things rather than simply *return values*. An example is the tree shown in Figure 19, which represents a short program to move an ant about a field strewn with food. The operator if-food-ahead takes two children, the one to evaluate if there is food straight ahead, and the one to evaluate if there isn't. The do operator takes two children and evaluates the left one, then the right one. The left and right operators turn the ant 90° to the left or right, forward moves the ant forward one step, consuming any food directly in front. Given a grid strewn with food, the objective is to find a program which, when executed (perhaps multiple times), eats as much food as possible. The fitness is simply the amount of food eaten. This is actually a common test problem called the **artificial ant**.

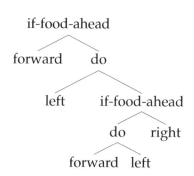

Figure 19 An Artificial Ant tree.

The code for Figure 19 in a pseudo-Lisp and C would look something like:

Pseudo-Lisp:
```
(if-food-ahead
    forward
    (do
        left
        (if-food-ahead
            (do forward left)
            right)))
```

Pseudo-C:
```
if (foodAhead) forward();
else {
    left();
    if (foodAhead) {
        forward();
        left();
    }
    else right();
}
```

Tree-style GP can be used with any optimization algorithm of course. But for no particular reason it has its own traditional algorithm, which was described earlier in Section 3.3.3.

4.3.1 Initialization

GP builds new trees by repeatedly selecting from a **function set** (the collection of items which may appear as nodes in a tree) and stringing them together. In the Artificial Ant example, the function set might consist of if-food-ahead, do, forward, left, and right. In the Symbolic Regression example, the function set might consist of $+$, $-$, $*$, sin, cos, sqrt, x, and various other mathematical operators. Note that the functions in the function set each have an **arity**, meaning, a pre-defined number of children. sin takes one child. do and $+$ take two children. x and forward take no children. Nodes with a zero arity (taking no children) are considered to be *leaf nodes* in the function set, and nodes with an arity ≥ 1 are *nonleaf nodes*. Algorithms which string nodes together generally need to respect these conventions in order to build a valid tree.

One common algorithm is the **Grow** algorithm, which builds random trees depth-first up to a certain depth:

Algorithm 53 *The Grow Algorithm*
1: $max \leftarrow$ maximum legal depth
2: $FunctionSet \leftarrow$ function set

3: **return** DoGrow(1, *max, FunctionSet*)

4: **procedure** DoGrow(*depth, max, FunctionSet*)
5:     **if** $depth \geq max$ **then**
6:         **return** Copy(a randomly-chosen leaf node from *FunctionSet*)
7:     **else**
8:         $n \leftarrow$ Copy(a randomly-chosen node from the *FunctionSet*)
9:         $l \leftarrow$ number of child nodes expected for n
10:        **for** i from 1 to l **do**
11:            Child i of $n \leftarrow$ DoGrow(*depth* + 1, *max, FunctionSet*)
12:        **return** n

The **Full** algorithm is a slight modification of the Grow algorithm which forces full trees up to the maximum depth. It only differs in a single line:

Algorithm 54 *The Full Algorithm*
1: *max* ← maximum legal depth
2: *FunctionSet* ← function set

3: **return** DoFull(1, *max*, *FunctionSet*)

4: **procedure** DoFull(*depth*, *max*, *FunctionSet*)
5:     **if** *depth* ≥ *max* **then**
6:         **return** Copy(a randomly-chosen leaf node from *FunctionSet*)
7:     **else**
8:         n ← Copy(a randomly-chosen non-leaf node from *FunctionSet*)   ▷ The only difference!
9:         l ← number of child nodes expected for n
10:        **for** i from 1 to l **do**
11:           Child i of n ← DoFull(*depth* + 1, *max*, *FunctionSet*)
12:        **return** n

GP originally built each new tree by picking either of these algorithms half the time, with a max depth selected randomly from 2 to 6. This procedure was called **Ramped Half-and-Half**.

Algorithm 55 *The Ramped Half-and-Half Algorithm*
1: *minMax* ← minimum allowed maximum depth
2: *maxMax* ← maximum allowed maximum depth   ▷ ... if that name makes any sense at all...
3: *FunctionSet* ← function set

4: d ← random integer chosen uniformly from *minMax* to *maxMax* inclusive
5: **if** 0.5 < a random real value chosen uniformly from 0.0 to 1.0 **then**
6:     **return** DoGrow(1, d, *FunctionSet*)
7: **else**
8:     **return** DoFull(1, d, *FunctionSet*)

The problem with these algorithms is that they provide no control over the size of the trees: and indeed tend to produce a fairly odd distribution of trees. There are quite a number of algorithms with better control.[59] Here's a one of my own design, **PTC2**,[60] which produces a tree of a desired size, or up to the size plus the maximum number of children to any given nonleaf node. It's easy to describe. We randomly extend the horizon of a tree with nonleaf nodes until the number of nonleaf nodes, plus the remaining spots, is greater than or equal to the desired size. We then populate the remaining slots with leaf nodes:

---

[59]Liviu Panait and I did a survey of the topic in Sean Luke and Liviu Panait, 2001, A survey and comparison of tree generation algorithms, in Lee Spector, *et al.*, editors, *Proceedings of the Genetic and Evolutionary Computation Conference (GECCO-2001)*, pages 81–88, Morgan Kaufmann, San Francisco, California, USA.

[60]PTC2 was proposed in Sean Luke, 2000, Two fast tree-creation algorithms for genetic programming, *IEEE Transactions on Evolutionary Computation*, 4(3), 274–283. It's an obvious enough algorithm that it's been no doubt used many times prior in other computer science contexts.

Algorithm 56 *The PTC2 Algorithm*
1: $s \leftarrow$ desired tree size
2: $FunctionSet \leftarrow$ function set

3: **if** $s = 1$ **then**
4:     **return** Copy(a randomly-chosen leaf node from *FunctionSet*)
5: **else**
6:     $Q \leftarrow \{\}$
7:     $r \leftarrow$ Copy(a randomly-chosen non-leaf node from *FunctionSet*)
8:     $c \leftarrow 1$
9:     **for** each child argument slot b of r **do**
10:         $Q \leftarrow Q \cup \{b\}$
11:     **while** $c + ||Q|| < s$ **do**
12:         $a \leftarrow$ an argument slot removed at random from Q
13:         $m \leftarrow$ Copy(a randomly-chosen non-leaf node from *FunctionSet*)
14:         $c \leftarrow c + 1$
15:         Fill slot a with m
16:         **for** each child argument slot b of m **do**
17:             $Q \leftarrow Q \cup \{b\}$
18:     **for** each argument slot $q \in Q$ **do**
19:         $m \leftarrow$ Copy(a randomly-chosen leaf node from *FunctionSet*)
20:         Fill slot q with m
21:     **return** r

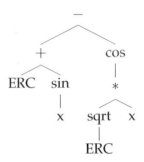

Figure 20 A tree with ERC placeholders inserted. See Figure 21.

Ephemeral Random Constants It's often useful to include in the function set a potentially infinite number of constants (like 0.2462 or $\langle 0.9, -2.34, 3.14 \rangle$ or 2924056792 or "s%&e:m") which get sprinkled into your trees. For example, in the Symbolic Regression problem, it might be nice to include in the equations constants such as -2.3129. How can we do this? Well, function sets don't have to be fixed in size if you're careful. Instead you might include in the function set a special node (often a leaf node) called an **ephemeral random constant** (or **ERC**). Whenever an ERC is selected from the function set and inserted into the tree, it automatically transforms itself into a randomly-generated constant of your choosing. From then on, that particular constant never changes its value again (unless mutated by a special mutation operator). Figure 20 shows ERCs inserted into the tree, and Figure 21 shows their conversion to constants.

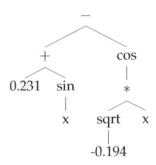

Figure 21 The tree in Figure 20 with ERC placeholders replaced with permanent constants.

4.3.2 Recombination

GP usually does recombination using **subtree crossover**. The idea is straightforward: in each individual, select a random subtree (which can possibly be the root). Then swap those two subtrees. It's common, but hardly necessary, to select random subtrees by picking leaf nodes 10% of the time and non-leaf nodes 90% of the time. Algorithm 57 shows how select a subtree of a given type.

Algorithm 57 *Subtree Selection*
1: $r \leftarrow$ root node of tree
2: $f(node) \leftarrow$ a function which returns true if the node is of the desired type

3: **global** $c \leftarrow 0$
4: CountNodes(r, f)
5: **if** $c = 0$ **then** ▷ Uh oh, no nodes were of the desired type!
6:     **return** □ ▷ "null" or "failure" or something
7: **else**
8:     $a \leftarrow$ random integer from 1 to c inclusive
9:     $c \leftarrow 0$
10:     **return** PickNode(r, a, f)

11: **procedure** CountNodes(r, f) ▷ This is just depth-first search
12:     **if** $f(r)$ is true **then**
13:         $c \leftarrow c + 1$
14:     **for** each child i of r **do**
15:         CountNodes(i, f)

16: **procedure** PickNode(r, a, f) ▷ More depth-first search!
17:     **if** $f(r)$ is true **then**
18:         $c \leftarrow c + 1$
19:         **if** $c \geq a$ **then**
20:             **return** r
21:     **for** each child i of r **do**
22:         $v \leftarrow$ PickNode(i, a, f)
23:         **if** $v \neq$ □ **then**
24:             **return** v
25:     **return** □ ▷ You shouldn't be able to reach here

4.3.3 Mutation

GP doesn't often do mutation, because the crossover operator is **non-homologous**[61] and is highly mutative. Even so, there are many possibilities for mutation. Here are just a few:

- **Subtree mutation**: pick a random subtree and replace it with a randomly-generated subtree using the algorithms above. Commonly Grow is used with a max-depth of 5. Again, leaf nodes are often picked 10% of the time and non-leaf nodes 90% of the time.

- Replace a random non-leaf node with one of its subtrees.

---
[61] Recall that with homologous crossover, an individual crossing over with itself will just make copies of itself.

- Pick a random non-leaf node and swap its subtrees.

- If nodes in the trees are ephemeral random constants, mutate them with some noise.

- Select two subtrees in the individual such that neither is contained within the other, and swap them with one another.

Again, we can use Algorithm 57 to select subtrees for use in these techniques. Algorithm 57 is called **subtree selection** but it could have just as well been called *node selection*: we're just picking a node. First we count all the nodes of a desired type in the tree: perhaps we want to just select a leaf node for example. Then we pick a random number a less than the number of nodes counted. Then we go back into the tree and do a depth-first traversal, counting off each node of the desired type, until we reach a. That's our node.

4.3.4 Forests and Automatically Defined Functions

Genetic Programming isn't constrained to a single tree: it's perfectly reasonable to have a genotype in the form of a vector of trees (commonly known as a **forest**). For example, I once developed simple soccer robot team programs where an individual was an entire robot team. Each robot program was two trees: a tree called when the robot was far from the ball (it returned a vector indicating where to run), and another tree called when the robot was close enough to a ball to kick it (it would return a vector indicating the direction to kick). The individual consisted of some n of these tree pairs, perhaps one per robot, or one per robot class (goalies, forwards, etc.), or one for every robot to use (a homogeneous team). So a soccer individual might have from 2 to 22 trees!

Trees can also be used to define **automatically defined functions (ADFs)**[62] which can be called by a primary tree. The heuristic here is one of **modularity**. Modularity lets us search very large spaces if we know that good solutions in them are likely to be repetitive: instead of requiring the individual to contain all of the repetitions perfectly (having all its ducks in order) — a very unlikely result — we can make it easier on the individual by breaking the individuals into *modules* with an overarching section of the genotype define how those modules are arranged.

In the case of ADFs, if we notice that ideal solutions are likely to be large trees with often-repeated subtrees within them, we'd prefer that the individual consist of one or two *subfunctions* which are then called repeatedly from a main tree. We do that by adding to the individual a second tree (the ADF) and including special nodes in the original parent tree's function set[63] which are just function calls to that second tree. We can add further ADFs if needed.

For purposes of illustration, let's say that a good GP solution to our problem will likely need to develop a certain subfunction of two arguments. We don't know what it will look like but we believe this to be the case. We could apply this heuristic belief by using a GP individual representation consisting of two trees: the main tree and a two-argument ADF tree called, say, ADF1.

We add a new non-leaf node to its function set: ADF1(*child1, child2*). The ADF1 tree can have whatever function set we think is appropriate to let GP build this subelement. But it will need to have two additional leaf-node functions added to the main tree's function set as well. Let's call them ARG1 and ARG2.

---

[62]Automatically Defined Functions are also due to John Koza, but are found in his second book, John R. Koza, 1994, *Genetic Programming II: Automatic Discovery of Reusable Programs*, MIT Press.

[63]Every tree has its own, possibly unique, function set.

Figure 22 shows an example individual. Here's how it works. We first evaluate the main tree. When it's time to call an ADF1 node, we first call its two children and store away their results (call them *result1* and *result2*). We then call the ADF1 tree. When its ARG1 function is called, it automatically returns *result1*. Likewise ARG2 automatically returns *result2*. When the ADF1 tree is finished, we store away its return value (let's call it *final*). We then return to the Main tree: the ADF1 node returns the value *final*, and we continue execution where we left off in the Main tree.

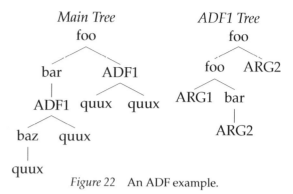

Figure 22 An ADF example.

Note that you could have more than one ADF tree. And you can have ADF trees which call other ADF trees! There's no reason you can't have nested function calls, right? In theory you *could* have recursive calls, that is, ADF trees which call each other. But your individuals won't be smart enough to build a base case automatically, so to keep the system from going into an infinite recursive loop, you'll need to have some maximum call depth built in.

One last variation: **automatically defined macros (ADMs)**, due to Lee Spector.[64] Here, when the ADF1 node is called, we jump immediately to the ADF1 tree without bothering to call the children to the ADF1 node first. Instead, whenever ARG1 is called, we jump back to the main tree for a second, call the first child, get its result, come back to the ADF1 tree, and have ARG1 return that value. This happens each time ARG1 is called. Likewise for ARG2. The idea is that this gives us a limited ability to selectively, or repeatedly, call children, in a manner similar to if-then constructs, while-loops, etc. (Lisp implements these as *macros*, hence the name).

4.3.5 Strongly-Typed Genetic Programming

Strongly-Typed Genetic Programming is a variant of Genetic Programming initially by David Montana.[65] Recall that in the examples shown earlier, each node returns the same kind of thing (for example, in symbolic regression, all nodes return floating-point values). But in more complex programs, this isn't really an option. For example, what if we wanted to add to symbolic regression a special operator, If, which takes three arguments: a boolean *test*, the *then-value* to return if the test is true, and the *else-value* to return if the test is false. If returns floating-point values like the other nodes, but it requires a node which returns a boolean value. This means we'll need to add some nodes which return only boolean values; both leaf nodes and perhaps some non-leaf node operators like And or Not.

The problem here is that in order to maintain closure, we can no longer just build trees, cross them over, or mutate them, without paying attention to the which nodes are permitted to be children of which other nodes and where. What happens, for example, if we try to multiply $\sin(x)$ by "false"? Instead, we need to assign **type constraints** to nodes to specify which nodes are permitted to hook up with which others and in what way.

---

[64]Lee Spector, 1996, Simultaneous evolution of programs and their control structures, in Peter J. Angeline and K. E. Kinnear, Jr., editors, *Advances in Genetic Programming 2*, chapter 7, pages 137–154, MIT Press.

[65]David Montana, 1995, Strongly typed genetic programming, *Evolutionary Computation*, 3(2), 199–230.

There are a variety of approaches to typing. In the simplest approach, **atomic typing**, each type is just a symbol or integer. The return value of each node, the expected child types for each node, and the expected return type for the tree as a whole, each get assigned one of these types. A node may attach as the child of another, or act as the root node of the tree, only if the types match. In **set typing**, the types aren't simple symbols but are *sets* of symbols. Two types would match if their intersections are nonempty. Set typing can be used to provide sufficient typing information for a lot of things, including the class hierarchies found in object-oriented programming.

But even this may not be enough. Atomic and set typing presume a finite number of symbols. How would we handle the situation where nodes operate over matrices? For example, consider a *matrix-multiply* node which takes two children (providing matrices) and multiplies them, returning a new matrix. The dimensions of the returned matrix are functions of the two children matrices. What if we change one of the children to a subtree which returns a new, differently-sized matrix? It's possible to do this if we can reconcile it by changing the return type of the parent. This may trigger a cascade of changes to return types, or to the types of children, as the tree readjusts itself. Such typing is commonly known as **polymorphic typing** and relies on type resolution algorithms similar those found in polymorphic typing programming languages like Haskell or ML. It's complex.

4.3.6 Cellular Encoding

Trees can also be used as short programs to instruct an interpreter how to create a *second* data structure (usually a graph). This second data structure is then used as the phenotype. This technique is commonly known as **Cellular Encoding** (by Frédéric Gruau).[66] The general idea is to take a *seed* (perhaps a graph consisting of a single node or a single edge) and hand it to the root of the tree. The root operator modifies and expands the graph, then hands certain expanded elements off to its children. They then expand the graph further, handing expanded pieces to *their children*, and so on, until the tree is exhausted. The fully expanded graph is then used as the phenotype.

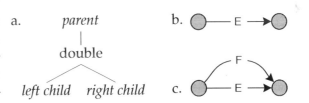

Figure 23 The double Edge Encoding operator.

Gruau's original formulation, which was used mostly for neural networks, operated on graph *nodes*, which requires a fairly complicated mechanism. An alternative would be to operate on graph *edges*, which doesn't allow all possible graphs, but is fairly useful for sparse or planar graphs such as are often found in electrical circuits or finite-state automata. Early on, Lee Spector and I dubbed this **Edge Encoding**.[67] Edge Encoding is easier to describe, so that's what I'll show off here.

---

[66] Frédéric Gruau, 1992, Genetic synthesis of boolean neural networks with a cell rewriting developmental process, in J. D. Schaffer and D. Whitley, editors, *Proceedings of the Workshop on Combinations of Genetic Algorithms and Neural Networks (COGANN92)*, pages 55–74, IEEE Computer Society Press.

[67] Lee Spector and I wrote an early paper on which named it Edge Encoding: Sean Luke and Lee Spector, 1996, Evolving graphs and networks with edge encoding: Preliminary report, in John R. Koza, editor, *Late Breaking Papers at the Genetic Programming 1996 Conference*, pages 117–124, Stanford Bookstore. But I doubt we're the inventors: when the paper came out, John Koza, Forrest Bennett, David Andre, and Martin Keane were already using a related representation to evolve computer circuits. See John R. Koza, Forrest H Bennett III, David Andre, and Martin A. Keane, 1996, Automated WYWIWYG design of both the topology and component values of electrical circuits using genetic programming, in John R. Koza, *et al.*, editors, *Genetic Programming 1996: Proceedings of the First Annual Conference*, pages 123–131, MIT Press.

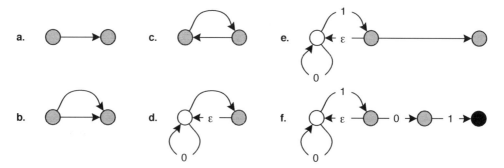

Figure 25 Expansion of a finite-state automaton using the Edge Encoding in Figure 24. (a) The initial edge. (b) After applying double. (c) After applying reverse. (d) After applying loop, ϵ, start, and 0. The white circle is a starting state. (e) After applying bud and 1. (f) After applying split, 0, accept, and 1. The black circle is an accepting state.

Edge and Cellular Encoding tree nodes work differently from, say, the ones used for Symbolic Regression: they take things from parents, operate on them, and then hand them to their children. As an example, Figure 23 shows an Edge Encoding operator called double. It takes an edge handed to it by its parent (Edge E in Figure 23b), and creates a duplicate edge connecting the same two nodes (Edge F in Figure 23c). It then hands one edge each to its two children.

Figure 24 shows an edge encoding tree which will construct a finite-state automaton. Besides double, the main operators are: reverse, which reverses an edge; loop, which creates a self-loop edge on the head node of loop's edge; bud, which creates a new node and then a new edge from the head node of bud's edge out to the new node; split, which splits its edge into an edge from split's tail node out to a new node, and then another edge back to split's head node. Other finite-state automaton-specific operators ($\epsilon, 1, 0$) label their edge or (start, accept) label the head node of their edge.

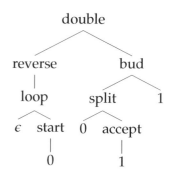

Figure 24 An Edge Encoding.

Confused at this point? I would be! Perhaps this will help. Figure 25 shows the expansion of Figure 24, starting with a single edge, and eventually growing into a full finite-state automaton which interprets the regular language $(1|0)^*01$.

Cellular and Edge encoding are examples of an **indirect** or **developmental encoding**: a representation which contains a set of rules to develop a secondary data structure which is then used as the phenotype. Indirect encodings are a popular research topic for two reasons. First there's the biological attraction: DNA is an indirect encoding, as it creates RNA and protein which then go on to do the heavy lifting in living organisms. Second, there's the notion of **compactness** and **modularity** discussed earlier: many indirect encoding rules make repeated calls to sub-rules of some form. In Cellular and Edge encoding there's no modularity, but you can add it trivially by including some Automatically Defined Functions. Likewise, unless you use an ADF, there's little compactness: Edge Encoding trees will have at least as many nodes as the graph has edges!

4.3.7 Stack Languages

An alternative to Lisp are **stack languages** in which code takes the form of a stream of instructions, usually in postfix notation. Real-world stack languages include FORTH and PostScript. These languages assume the presence of a stack onto which temporary variables, and in some cases chunks of code, can be pushed and popped. Rather than say $5 \times (3 + 4)$, a stack language might say 5 3 4 + ×. This pushes 5, 3, and 4 on the stack; then pops the last two numbers (4 and 3) off the stack, adds them, and pushes the result (7) on the stack; then pops off of the stack the remaining two numbers (7 and 5), multiplies them, and pushes the result (35) back on.

Stack languages often create subroutines by pushing chunks of code onto the stack, then executing them from the stack multiple times. For example, we might generalize the procedure above — $a \times (b + c)$ — into a subroutine by wrapping its operators in parentheses and subjecting them to a special code-pushing operator like this: push (+×). Given another special operator do, which pops a subroutine off the stack, executes it n times, and pushes it back on the stack, we can do stuff like 5 7 9 2 4 3 6 5 9 push (+×) 4 do, which computes $5 \times (7+9) \times (2+4) \times (3+6) \times (5+9)$.

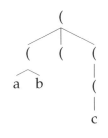

Figure 26 The expression ((a b) ( ) ((c))) as rooted parentheses.

Stack languages have long been used in genetic programming. Among the most well-known is Lee Spector's GP stack language, **Push**.[68] Push maintains multiple stacks, one for each data type, allowing code to operate over different kinds of data cleanly. Push also includes special stacks for storing, modifying, and executing code. This allows Push programs to modify their own code *as they are executing it*. This makes possible, for example, the automatic creation of **self-adaptive** breeding operators.

The use of stack languages in optimization presents some representational decisions. If the language simply forms a stream of symbols with no constraints, just use a list representation (see the next Section, 4.4). But most stack languages at least require that the parentheses used to delimit code must be paired. There are many ways to guarantee this constraint. In some stack languages a left parenthesis must always be followed by a non-parenthesis. This is easy to do: it's exactly like the earlier Lisp expressions (see Figures 18 and 19). If instead your language allows parentheses immediately after left parentheses, as in ((a b) ( ) ((c))), you could just use the left parenthesis as the root node of a subtree and the elements inside the parentheses as the children of that node, as shown in

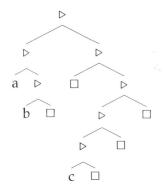

Figure 27 The expression ((a b) ( ) ((c))) in cons cells.

Figure 26. Both approaches will require that tree nodes have arbitrary arity. Or, as is the case for Push, you could use the traditional internal format of Lisp: nested linked lists. Each parenthesized expression (like (a b)) forms one linked list, and elements in the expression can be other linked lists. Nodes in each linked list node are called **cons cells**, represented in Figure 27 as ▷. The left child of a cons cell holds a list element, and the right child points to the next cons cell in the list, or to □, indicating the end of the list.

4.4 Lists

Parse trees aren't the only way to represent programs: they could also be represented as arbitrary-length **lists** (or **strings**) of machine language instructions. Individuals are evaluated by converting the lists into functions and executing them. This is known as **Linear Genetic Programming**, and

---

[68]The basics: Lee Spector and Alan Robinson, 2002, Genetic programming and autoconstructive evolution with the push programming language, *Genetic Programming and Evolvable Machines*, 3(1), 7–40. Then for the latest version of the language, check out: Lee Spector, Jon Klein, and Martin Keijzer, 2005, The Push3 execution stack and the evolution of control, in *Proceedings of the Genetic and Evolutionary Conference (GECCO 2005)*, pages 1689–1696, Springer.

Grammar			An Arbitrary Individual
tree	→	$n+n$ | $n-n$	
n	→	$n*m$ | $\sin m$	false false true true false true false true true false false
m	→	1 | 2	

Figure 28 A Grammatical Evolution grammar, and an individual with a list representation.

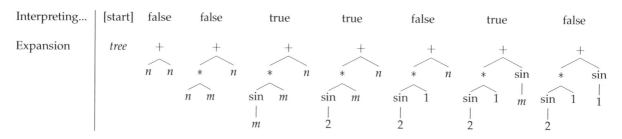

Figure 29 Expansion of the individual shown in Figure 28.

the most well-known practitioners of this approach are Wolfgang Banzhaf, Peter Nordin, Robert Keller, and Frank Francone. They sell a GP system called Discipulus based on this notion, and also wrote a well-regarded book on both tree-based and linear Genetic Programming.[69]

Executing arbitrary machine code strings can be dangerous if closure isn't maintained. But how to maintain closure in such a situation? Certainly your individual wouldn't be just a bit-string, because that would allow all sorts of machine language instructions, even undesirable ones or nonsense ones.[70] Clearly it'd have to be a list of instructions chosen from a carefully-selected set.

If the instruction set is finite in length, we could just assign a unique integer to each instruction and represent a genotype as a list of integers. Usually schemes employ a finite set of registers as well: this allows the machine code lists to operate essentially like directed acyclic graphs (DAGs), with early instructions affecting instructions much further down in the list due to their shared register. Additionally we might find it desirable to include some special instructions that operate on constants (Add 2, etc.).

Stack languages bear a strong resemblance to machine code, so it shouldn't be too terribly surprising that, as mentioned in Section 4.3.7, some stack languages are straightforwardly applied to list representations, particularly if the language has no particular syntactic constraints.

Lists can be used to generate trees as well: consider **Grammatical Evolution (GE)**, invented by Conor Ryan, J. J. Collins, and Michael O'Neill.[71] Grammatical Evolution's representation is a list of integers or boolean values. It then uses this list as the decision points in a pre-defined tree grammar to build a GP Tree. The tree is then evaluated in GP style to assess fitness. This somewhat complex approach is yet another example of an indirect encoding, and though it doesn't have the modularity common in many indirect encodings, it does have a method to its madness: it can straightforwardly define *any tree* for *any desired language*.

As an example, consider the ridiculous grammar and an individual represented as a list, shown in Figure 28. To interpret this, we start with *tree*, and use the first element in the list to decide how

---

[69] Wolfgang Banzhaf, Peter Nordin, Robert E. Keller, and Frank D. Francone, 1998, *Genetic Programming: An Introduction*, Morgan Kaufmann.

[70] You probably don't want to call the infamous HCF ("Halt and Catch Fire") instruction. Look for it on Wikipedia.

[71] Conor Ryan, J. J. Collins, and Michael O'Neill, 1998, Grammatical evolution: Evolving programs for an arbitrary language, in *EuroGP 1998*, pages 83–96.

Node	2	3	4	5	6	7	8	9	10	11 (F_1)	12 (F_2)	13 (F_3)
Gene	510*	101	611*	002	223	203	055	026	473*	5	9	10

Gene	Function
0	+
1	−
2	×
3	/
4	sin
5	cos
6	sqrt

$$F_1 = x + \cos(y) \qquad F_2 = \cos(y) + \cos(y) \times (x - y) \qquad F_3 = \sin(x \times (x - y))$$

Figure 30 A Cartesian Genetic Programming example. Note that node 13 (F_3) has a single gene value (10), and not two gene values 1 and 0. In all other cases genes are single-digit. See text for interpretation of this figure.

to expand that (we'll assume that *false* expands to the first item, and *true* expands to the second item). Once we expand, we expand the remaining undefined variables in a depth-first fashion. Figure 29 shows the expansion of the Individual in Figure 28.

Now we have a tree we can evaluate! Notice that we wound up not using the last 4 bits in the individual (*true true false false*). What if the list is too short and we don't have enough decision points? Typically one just wraps around to the beginning of the list again. It's not a great solution but it's workable.[72] GE is clever in that it allows us to construct *any* valid tree for a given grammar, which is a lot more flexible than standard Tree-based GP: indeed it negates the need to even bother with strong typing. The downside is that this representation is naturally un-smooth in certain places: tiny changes early in the list result in gigantic changes in the tree. This can be a problem.

I include one final encoding here: **Cartesian Genetic Programming (CGP)** by Julian Miller.[73] Consider Figure 30, with a fixed-length vector of 30 numbers, found in the row labeled *Gene*.(Note that the final gene is a 10 and not two genes 1 and 0.) Cartesian Genetic Programming will interpret the genes in this vector to build a graph of function nodes similar to those in genetic programming. These nodes come in three categories: input nodes, output nodes, and hidden (function) nodes. The experimenter pre-defines how many of each of these nodes there are, and their layout, as appropriate to his problem. In Figure 30 there are two input nodes (x and y), nine hidden nodes, and three output nodes F_1, F_2, and F_3.

Each node has a unique number, which is shown inside a diamond at that node. Notice that genes are grouped together with a certain *Node*. These genes are responsible for defining the inputs to that node and its function label. For example, the first group, 510, is responsible for node 2.

Some genes are bunched together into groups. The size of the group is the maximum number of arguments to any function in the function set, plus one. In our function set, the functions $+ - \times /$ all take two arguments, so the group size is 3. The first gene a group defines the function the node

---

[72]I don't like that approach: instead, I'd bypass evaluation and just assign the individual the worst possible fitness.
[73]Note that this encoding is *not* a list encoding, but more properly a fixed-length vector encoding. I include it here because it's more at home with the other list-style GP methods.

will be assigned: for example, the 5 in 510 refers to the function *cos*. The remaining genes in the group specify the nodes from which there are incoming edges. For example, the 1 in 510 indicates that there is an incoming edge from node 1 (the y). The final gene, 0, is marked with an asterisk (*) to indicate that it's unused (because the function *cos* only needs one incoming edge).

The nodes 11 (F_1), 12 (F_2), and 13 (F_3) have only a single gene each, which indicates the node from which there is an incoming edge. For example, node 11 (F_1) has an incoming edge from node 5. Nodes 0 (x) and 1 (y) do not have any associated gene values. Also, you'll need to restrict the possible values each gene as appropriate. In this example, the genes defining functions are restricted to 0–6, and the genes defining connections are restricted to refer only to node numbers less than their node. CGP traditionally does the second bit using a constraint that requires that connection-genes for a given node can only refer to nodes at most some M columns prior.

After defining the graph, we can now run it, just like a genetic programming individual: in this case, we have a symbolic-regression solution, so we provide values for x and y, and feed values through edges to function nodes, finally reading the results at F_1, F_2, and F_3. Unlike in tree-based genetic programming, CGP is capable of defining multiple functions at once. The three functions that have been defined by this graph are shown at the bottom of Figure 30. Note that nodes 4 and 8 don't contribute to the final solution at all. These are examples of **introns**, a term we'll get to in Section 4.6.

There are obviously other reasons why you might want to use a list as a representation, besides alternative genetic programming techniques. For example, lists could be used to represent sets or collections, or other direct graph encodings, or strings.

Warning Lists aren't particularly compatible with heterogeneous genomes (Section 4.1.4), where each gene has its own mutation and initialization mechanisms. This is because list crossover and mutation methods not only change the value of genes but their location.

4.4.1 Initialization

How new lists are generated largely depends on the domain-specific needs of the method involved. But generally speaking there are two issues: specifying the length of the list, and populating it. One simple way to do the former is to sample a length from the geometric distribution (Algorithm 46, perhaps with the minimum list size being 1). Beware again that the distribution will have a very high number of small lists: you may wish to use a flatter distribution.

To populate the list, just march through the list and set each of its values to something random but appropriate. Remember that for some problems this isn't sufficient, as there may be constraints on which elements may appear after other elements, so you'll need to be more clever there.

4.4.2 Mutation

Like initialization, mutation in lists has two parts: changing the size of the list, and changing the contents of the list. Contents may be changed in exactly the same way that you do for fixed-length vectors: using a bit-flip mutation or integer randomization, etc. Remember that you may not be able to change some elements without changing others due to certain constraints among the elements.

Changing the length likewise depends on the problem: for example, some problems prefer to only add to the end of a list. One simple approach is to sample from some distribution, then add (or subtract, if it so happens) that amount to the list length. For example, we could do a random walk starting at 0, flipping a coin until it comes up tails. The number we arrive at is what you add to (or delete from, if it's negative) the end of the list. This should look familiar:

Algorithm 58 *Random Walk*
1: $b \leftarrow$ coin-flip probability $\quad\triangleright$ Make b bigger to make the random walks longer and more diffuse

2: $m \leftarrow 0$
3: **if** $p \geq$ random number chosen uniformly from 0.0 to 1.0 inclusive **then**
4: $\quad$ **repeat**
5: $\quad\quad n \leftarrow$ either a 1 or -1, chosen at random
6: $\quad\quad$ **if** $m + n$ is an acceptable amount **then**
7: $\quad\quad\quad m \leftarrow m + n$
8: $\quad\quad$ **else if** $m - n$ is an acceptable amount **then**
9: $\quad\quad\quad m \leftarrow m - n$
10: $\quad$ **until** $b <$ random number chosen uniformly from 0.0 to 1.0 inclusive
11: **return** m

Don't confuse this with Algorithm 42 (Random Walk Mutation), which uses a similar random walk to determine the noise with which to mutate. Beware that because lists can't be any smaller than 1, but can be arbitrarily large, a random walk like this may cause the individual lists to become fairly large: you may need to add some countering force to keep your population from growing simply due to your mutation operator (see the **bloat** discussion below for other reasons for growth).

Warning In some list-representation problems, such as Grammatical Evolution, the early elements in the list are *far* more important than the later elements. In GE this is because the early elements determine the early choices in the tree grammar, and changing them radically changes the tree; whereas the later elements only change small subtrees or individual elements (or if the list is too long, they don't change anything at all!) This has a huge effect on the smoothness of the landscape, and you want to make sure your mutation procedure reflects this. For example, you might only *occasionally* change the elements at the beginning of the list, and much more often change the elements near the end of the list. Linear GP may or may not have this property depending on the nature of your problem, and in fact it can actually can have the opposite situation if the final machine code elements in the list get to make the last and most important changes.

4.4.3 Recombination

Like mutation, crossover also may depend on constraints, but ignoring that, there are various ways you could do crossover among variable-length lists. Two easy ones are **one-point** and **two-point list crossover**, variations on the standard one- and two-point vector crossovers. In one-point list crossover, shown in Figure 31, we pick a (possibly different) point in each list, then cross over the segments to the right of the points. The segments can be non-zero in length. The algorithm should look eerily familiar:

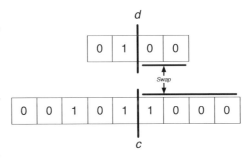

Figure 31 One-point List Crossover.

Algorithm 59 *One-Point List Crossover*
1: $\vec{v} \leftarrow$ first list $\langle v_1, v_2, ... v_l \rangle$ to be crossed over
2: $\vec{w} \leftarrow$ second list $\langle w_1, w_2, ... w_k \rangle$ to be crossed over

3: $c \leftarrow$ random integer chosen uniformly from 1 to l inclusive
4: $d \leftarrow$ random integer chosen uniformly from 1 to k inclusive
5: $\vec{x} \leftarrow$ snip out v_c through v_l from $\vec{v}$
6: $\vec{y} \leftarrow$ snip out w_d through w_k from $\vec{w}$
7: Insert $\vec{y}$ into $\vec{v}$ where $\vec{x}$ was snipped out
8: Insert $\vec{x}$ into $\vec{w}$ where $\vec{y}$ was snipped out
9: **return** $\vec{v}$ and $\vec{w}$

Two-point list crossover, shown in Figure 32, is similar: we pick *two* points in each individual and swap the midsections. Again, note that the points don't have to be the same. Think carefully about your list representation to determine if one- or two-point list crossover make sense. They have quite different dynamics. Is your representation reliant to the particulars of what's going on in the middle, and sensitive to disruption there, for example?

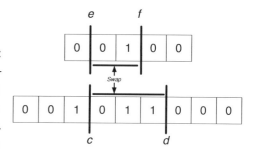

Figure 32 Two-point List Crossover.

Another Warning Just as mentioned for mutation, certain elements of the list may be more important than others and more sensitive to being messed up via crossover. So in Grammatical Evolution for example you might want to consider picking two-point crossover points near to the end of the list more often than ones near the front. Or stick with one-point crossover.

The two-point list crossover algorithm should likewise feel familiar to you:

Algorithm 60 *Two-Point List Crossover*
1: $\vec{v} \leftarrow$ first list $\langle v_1, v_2, ... v_l \rangle$ to be crossed over
2: $\vec{w} \leftarrow$ second list $\langle w_1, w_2, ... w_k \rangle$ to be crossed over

3: $c \leftarrow$ random integer chosen uniformly from 1 to l inclusive
4: $d \leftarrow$ random integer chosen uniformly from 1 to l inclusive
5: $e \leftarrow$ random integer chosen uniformly from 1 to k inclusive
6: $f \leftarrow$ random integer chosen uniformly from 1 to k inclusive
7: **if** $c > d$ **then**
8:     Swap c and d
9: **if** $e > f$ **then**
10:     Swap e and f
11: $\vec{x} \leftarrow$ snip out v_c through v_d from $\vec{v}$
12: $\vec{y} \leftarrow$ snip out w_e through w_f from $\vec{w}$
13: Insert $\vec{y}$ into $\vec{v}$ where $\vec{x}$ was snipped out
14: Insert $\vec{x}$ into $\vec{w}$ where $\vec{y}$ was snipped out
15: **return** $\vec{v}$ and $\vec{w}$

4.5 Rulesets

A set is, of course, a collection of objects, possibly empty, where all the objects are different. Sets can be used for all sorts of stuff, but the big item seems to be sets of *rules* which either form a computer program of sorts (perhaps to direct a robot about in a simulated environment) or which define an indirect encoding which grows a graph structure from a simple initial seed.

Rules in rulesets usually take a form which looks like *if*→*then*. The *if* part is commonly called the **body** of the rule and the *then* part is commonly called the **head** of the rule. There are two common kinds of rulesets, which I will call **state-action** and **production** rulesets. State-action rules are designed to perform some action (the *then*) when some situation or event has occurred in the world (the *if*). For example, a robot's sensors might trigger a rule which causes the robot to turn left. Production rules are different in that some rules' *then* actions trigger other rules' *if* portions. For example, if a rule $a \to b$ fires, it would then cause some other rule $b \to c$ to fire. Production rules are mostly used to construct indirect encodings which grow graph structures etc. The interconnection among the rules in production rulesets means that they bear more than a passing resemblance, representation-wise, to directed graph structures.

The first question is: what data structure would you use to hold a set of objects? We could use a variable-sized vector structure like a list. Or we could use a hash table which stores the elements as keys and arbitrary things as values. In my experience, most people implement sets with lists.

The basic closure constraint in a set is its uniqueness property: often you have to make sure that when you create sets, mutate them, or cross them over, the rules remain all different. Unless you have a mutation or crossover operation which does this naturally, you may need to go back into the set after the fact and remove duplicates. This is a trivial procedure:

Algorithm 61 *Duplicate Removal*
1: $\vec{v} \leftarrow$ collection of elements converted into a vector $\langle v_1, v_2, ...v_l \rangle$
2: $h \leftarrow \{\}$ ▷ Represent h with a hash table, it's faster
3: $l' \leftarrow l$
4: **for** i from l down to 1 **do**
5:     **if** $v_i \in h$ **then** ▷ A duplicate!
6:         Swap v_i and $v_{l'}$
7:         $l' \leftarrow l' - 1$
8:     **else** ▷ Not a duplicate!
9:         $h \leftarrow h \cup \{v_i\}$
10: $\vec{v}' \leftarrow$ blank vector $\langle v'_1, v'_2, ...v'_{l'} \rangle$
11: **for** i from 1 to l' **do**
12:     $v'_i \leftarrow v_i$
13: **return** $\vec{v}'$ converted back into a collection

Note that this modifies the order of the original list $\vec{v}$. You can represent h with a hash table easily: to add an element to h, you just add it as the key to the hash table (the value can be anything: for example, the element itself). To test to see if $v_i \in h$, you just check to see if v_i is a key in the hash table already. Piece of cake.

4.5.1 State-Action Rules

An **agent** is an autonomous computational entity, that is, one which manipulates the world on its own, in response to feedback it receives from the world. Agents include autonomous robots, game agents, entities in simulations, etc. One common kind of program an agent might follow is a **policy**: a collection of simple rules to tell the agent what to do in each possible situation it may find itself in. These rules are often called **state-action rules**. Here are some state-action rules for an agent to get around in a city: are you downtown? Then get on the train. Are you on the train? Then take the train to the wharf. Did you miss your stop? Then get off the train and get on the return train. Etc.

State-action rules take on various guises, but a typical form is $a \wedge b \wedge ... \wedge y \rightarrow z$, where the $a, b, ..., y$ are *state descriptions* and z is an *action* or *class*. A state description is some feature about the current world that might or might not be true. An action is what we should do if that feature is true. For example, a robot might have rules like:

$$\text{Left Sonar Value} > 3.2 \quad \wedge \quad \text{Forward Sonar Value} \leq 5.0 \quad \longrightarrow \quad \text{Turn Left to } 50°$$

We might test our ruleset by plopping a simulated robot down in an environment and using these rules to guide it. Each time the robot gets sensor information, it gathers the rules whose bodies are true given its current sensor values. The matching rules are collectively known as the **match set**. Then the robot decides what to do based on what the heads of these rules suggest (suggest as "turn left by 50°").

One way to think of the rule bodies is as describing regions in the **state space** of the robot, and the heads as what to do in those regions. In the case of the rule above, the rule body has roped off a region that's less than 3.2 in one dimension and ≥ 5.0 in another dimension, and doesn't cut out any portions along any other dimensions.

There are two interesting issues involved here. First, what if no rules match the current condition? This is commonly known as **under-specification** of the state space: there are holes in the space which no rule covers. This is often handled by requiring a **default rule** which fires when no other rule fires. More interestingly, what if more than one rule matches the current condition, but those rules disagree in their heads in an incompatible way (one says "Turn Left" and one says "Turn Right", say)? This is known as **over-specification** of the state space. We'll need employ some kind of **arbitration scheme** to decide what to do. Most commonly, if we have lots of rules, we might have a **vote**. Another way is to pick a rule at random. And yes: a state space can be simultaneously under- and over-specified.

State-action rulesets often introduce a twist to the fitness assessment process. Specifically, as we move the agent around, we may not only assess the fitness of the individual itself but also assess the fitness of the individual rules *inside* the ruleset individual. At the very least this can be done by breaking the rules into those which fired during the course of running the individual and those which never fired (and thus aren't responsible for the wonderful/terrible outcome that resulted). We can then punish or reward only the rules which fired. Or if after turning Left the robot received an electric shock, which might penalize the series of rules whose firings which led up to that shock, but not penalize later rules. We might be more inclined to mutate or eliminate (by crossover) the more-penalized rules.

Metaheuristics designed for optimizing policies using state-action rules, **Michigan-Approach Learning Classifier Systems** and **Pitt-Approach Rule Systems**, are discussed in Section 10.

4.5.2 Production Rules

Production rules are similar to state-action rules except that the "actions" are used to trigger the states of other rules. Production rules are sort of backwards looking: they tend to look like this: $a \to b \wedge c \wedge ... \wedge z$. This is because production rules are fired (typically) by a single event (triggered by some other rule usually) and then this causes them to trigger multiple downstream rules in turn. A lot of the uses for production rules is to enable *modular* indirect encodings which can describe large complex solutions with lots of repetitions, but do so in a small, compact rule space which is more easily searched. This of course assumes that good solutions will *have* lots of repetitions; this in turn depends largely on the kind of problem you're trying to solve.

Typically the symbols which appear in the heads (the right side) production rules are of two forms: **nonterminal** symbols, which may also appear in the bodies of rules, and **terminal** symbols, which often may not. Terminal symbols basically don't expand any further. Note that for most production systems, there's a fixed number of rules, one per nonterminal.

An early example of applying evolutionary computation to production rules was developed by Hiroaki Kitano to find certain optimal graph structures for recurrent neural networks and the like.[74] Imagine that you're trying to create an 8-node directed, unlabeled graph structure. Our ruleset might look like this (numbers are terminal symbols):

$$a \to \begin{bmatrix} b & c \\ c & d \end{bmatrix} \quad b \to \begin{bmatrix} 1 & 0 \\ d & c \end{bmatrix} \quad c \to \begin{bmatrix} 1 & 1 \\ 1 & 0 \end{bmatrix} \quad d \to \begin{bmatrix} 0 & 1 \\ 0 & 0 \end{bmatrix} \quad 0 \to \begin{bmatrix} 0 & 0 \\ 0 & 0 \end{bmatrix} \quad 1 \to \begin{bmatrix} 1 & 1 \\ 1 & 1 \end{bmatrix}$$

This is an indirect encoding of the graph structure, believe it or not. We start with the 1×1 matrix $[a]$. We then apply the rule which matches a, expanding the $[a]$ matrix into $\begin{bmatrix} b & c \\ c & d \end{bmatrix}$. From there we apply rules to each of the elements in *that* matrix, expanding them into their 2×2 elements, resulting in the matrix $\begin{bmatrix} 1 & 0 & 1 & 1 \\ d & c & 1 & 0 \\ 1 & 1 & 0 & 1 \\ 1 & 0 & 0 & 0 \end{bmatrix}$. From there, we expand to $\begin{bmatrix} 1 & 1 & 0 & 0 & 1 & 1 & 1 & 1 \\ 1 & 1 & 0 & 0 & 1 & 1 & 1 & 1 \\ 0 & 1 & 1 & 1 & 1 & 1 & 0 & 0 \\ 0 & 0 & 1 & 0 & 1 & 1 & 0 & 0 \\ 1 & 1 & 1 & 1 & 0 & 0 & 1 & 1 \\ 1 & 1 & 1 & 1 & 0 & 0 & 1 & 1 \\ 1 & 1 & 0 & 0 & 0 & 0 & 0 & 0 \\ 1 & 1 & 0 & 0 & 0 & 0 & 0 & 0 \end{bmatrix}$. At this point we're out of nonterminal symbols. (Since we made up "expansion rules" like $1 \to \begin{bmatrix} 1 & 1 \\ 1 & 1 \end{bmatrix}$ for our terminal symbols, we could have either expanded until we ran out of nonterminals, or expanded some number of predefined times.) This is our adjacency matrix for the graph, where a 1 at position $\langle i, j \rangle$ means "there's an edge from i to j" and a 0 means "no edge". I won't bother drawing this sucker for you!

---

[74]This paper was one of the seminal papers in indirect encodings. Hiroaki Kitano, 1990, Designing neural networks using a genetic algorithm with a graph generation system, *Complex Systems*, 4, 461–476.

A more recent example of indirect encoding with production rules is in finding optimal **Lindenmayer Systems** (or **L-Systems**). These are sets of production rules which produce a string of symbols. That string is then interpreted as a small computer program of sorts to produce some final object such as a plant or tree, fractal or pattern, or machine of some sort. L-Systems were made popular by Aristid Lindenmayer, a biologist who developed them to describe plant growth patterns.[75] A simple example of an L-System is one which creates the **Koch Curve**, a fractal pattern. The rule system consists of the single rule $F \to F + F - F - F + F$. It works like this: we start with a single F. Applying this rule, this expands to $F + F - F - F + F$. Expanding each of these F's using the rule, we get:

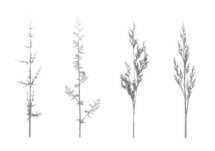

Figure 33 Plant patterns created by a Lindenmayer System.

$F + F - F - F + F + F + F - F - F + F - F + F - F - F + F - F + F - F - F + F + F + F - F - F + F$

Expanding yet again, we get:

$F + F - F - F + F + F + F - F - F + F - F + F - F - F + F - F + F - F - F + F + F + F - F - F + F +$
$F + F - F - F + F + F + F - F - F + F - F + F - F - F + F - F + F - F - F + F + F + F - F - F + F -$
$F + F - F - F + F + F + F - F - F + F - F + F - F - F + F - F + F - F - F + F + F + F - F - F + F -$
$F + F - F - F + F + F + F - F - F + F - F + F - F - F + F - F + F - F - F + F + F + F - F - F + F +$
$F + F - F - F + F + F + F - F - F + F - F + F - F - F + F - F + F - F - F + F + F + F - F - F + F$

The + and − are terminal symbols. What do you do with such a string? Well, if you interpreted the F as "draw a line forward" and + and − as "turn left" and "turn right" respectively, you would wind up with the Koch Curve shown in Figure 34. Further expansions create more complex patterns.

These rules can get really complicated. Figure 35 shows an actual L-System used by biologists to describe the branching pattern of the red seaweed *Bostrychia radicans*.[76]

One interesting use of L-Systems with evolutionary computation, by Greg Hornby, was in discovering useful designs such as novel chairs or tables. Hornby also applied L-Systems together with Edge Encoding to discover animal body forms and finite-state automata-like graph structures.[77] The L-System ruleset expanded into a string, which was then interpreted as a series of Edge Encoding instructions (double, split, etc.) to produce the final graph.

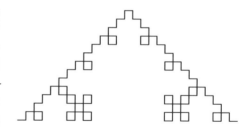

Figure 34 A Quadratic Koch Curve.

---

[75]Przemyslaw Prusinkiewicz and Aristid Lindenmayer produced a beautiful book on L-Systems: Przemyslaw Prusinkiewicz and Aristid Lindenmayer, 1990, *The Algorithmic Beauty of Plants*, Springer. It's out of print but available online now, at http://algorithmicbotany.org/papers/#abop

[76]From Ligia Collado-Vides, Guillermo Gómez-Alcaraz, Gerardo Rivas-Lechuga, and Vinicio Gómez-Gutierrez, 1997, Simulation of the clonal growth of Bostrychia radicans (Ceramiales-Rhodophyta) using Lindenmayer systems, *Biosystems*, 42(1), 19–27.

[77]Greg gave what I consider the best paper presentation *ever* at GECCO. He did a regular presentation on using L-systems to evolve walking creatures. But at the end of the presentation he dumped out of a canvas sack a mass of tinkertoys and servos. He pressed a button, and it came to life and began to walk across the table. It was a tinkertoy version of his best-fitness-of-run individual. For more information on Greg's work, his thesis is a good pick: Gregory Hornby, 2003, *Generative Representations for Evolutionary Design Automation*, Ph.D. thesis, Brandeis University.

4.5.3 Initialization

Like direct-enoded graph structures, building rulesets is mostly a matter of determining how many elements you want, and then creating them. We begin by picking a desired ruleset size n, using some distribution (the Geometric Distribution, Algorithm 46, is probably fine). We then create a ruleset out n of randomly-generated elements.

When doing production rules, there are some additional constraints. Specifically, the various **symbols** which appear in the heads of the rules need to match symbols in the bodies of the rules. Otherwise, how would you match up an event triggered by a rule with the follow-on rule which is fired as a result? Likewise, you probably won't want two rules that have the same body, that is, two production rules of the form $a \to b, c$ and $a \to d, e, f$. Which one should fire? Arbitration doesn't make much sense in production rules, unlike state-action rules, unless perhaps your production rules are probabilistic.

O	→	FGD
D	→	G[+++FGFGRG][-GF]GFGA
A	→	FGFGFGFG[+++FGR][-GF]GFGB
B	→	FGFGFGFG[+++FGR][-GF]GFGC
C	→	FGFGFGFG[+++FGR][-GF]GFGK
R	→	FG[+FGFGU]GFGFGE
E	→	[-FGFGX]GFGFGH
H	→	[+FGFGW]GFGFGZFG
K	→	FGFGFG[+++FGR][-FGA]GFGL
L	→	FGFGFG[+++FGR][-GF]GFGP
P	→	FGFGFG[+++FGR][-GF]GFGQ
Q	→	FGFGFGT
T	→	FGFGFG[+++FGR][+FGA]GFGA
U	→	[+FGFGF]GFG
X	→	[-FGFGF]GFG
W	→	[+FGFGF]GFG
Z	→	[-FGFGF]GFG

Figure 35 Another L-System.

In some production rule systems, the number of rules is fixed to the size of the nonterminal set. In other rule systems you might have a variable number of symbols. In the second case you will need to make sure that all the symbols in rule heads have a corresponding rule with that symbol in the body. And rules with symbols in their bodies but appearing nowhere in any other rule's heads are essentially orphans (this can happen in the fixed-case as well). Additionally, you may or may not allow recursion among your rules: can rule A trigger rule B, which then triggers rule A again? For example, imagine if letters are our expansion variable symbols and numbers are our terminals. Here's a ruleset with some potential problems:

a	→	b, c	*There's no c rule! What gets triggered from the c event?*
b	→	d, 0	
a	→	d, b	*Um, do we want duplicate rule bodies?*
d	→	b	*Is recursion allowed in this ruleset?*
e	→	1	*There's nothing that will ever trigger this rule! It's just junk!*

During initialization you'll need to handle some of these situations. You could generate rules at random and then try to "fix" things. Or you could create some n nonterminal symbols and then construct rules for each of them. Here's an algorithm along those lines: it's not particularly uniform, but it does let you choose whether to allow recursive rules or not, and whether or not to permit disconnected rules (that is, ones never triggered). It should get you the general idea: but if you used this, you'd probably need to heavily modify it for your purposes.

Algorithm 62 *Simple Production Ruleset Generation*
1: $\vec{t} \leftarrow$ pre-defined set of terminal symbols (that don't expand)
2: $p \leftarrow$ approximate probability of picking a terminal symbol
3: $r \leftarrow$ flag: true if we want to allow recursion, else false
4: $d \leftarrow$ flag: true if we want to allow disconnected rules, else false

5: $n \leftarrow$ a random integer > 0 chosen from some distribution
6: $\vec{v} \leftarrow$ vector of unique symbols $\langle v_1, ..., v_n \rangle$ ▷ The symbol in v_1 will be our "start" symbol
7: $\overrightarrow{rules} \leftarrow$ empty vector of rules $\langle rules_1, ..., rules_n \rangle$
8: **for** i from 1 to n **do** ▷ Build rules
9:     $l \leftarrow$ a random integer ≥ 1 chosen from some distribution
10:     $\vec{h} \leftarrow$ empty vector of symbols $\langle h_1, ... h_l \rangle$
11:     **for** j from 1 to l **do**
12:         **if** ($r =$ false and $i=n$) or $p <$ random value chosen uniformly from 0.0 to 1.0 inclusive **then**
13:             $h_j \leftarrow$ a randomly chosen terminal symbol from $\vec{t}$ not yet appearing in $\vec{h}$.
14:         **else if** $r =$ false **then**
15:             $h_j \leftarrow$ a randomly chosen nonterminal from $v_{i+1}, ..., v_n$ not yet appearing in $\vec{h}$
16:         **else**
17:             $h_j \leftarrow$ a randomly chosen nonterminal symbol from $\vec{v}$ not yet appearing in $\vec{h}$
18:     $rules_i \leftarrow$ rule of the form $v_i \rightarrow h_1 \wedge h_2 \wedge ... \wedge h_l$
19: **if** $d =$ false **then** ▷ Fix disconnected rules
20:     **for** i from 2 to n **do**
21:         **if** v_i does not appear in the head of any of the rules $rules_1, ..., rules_{i-1}$ **then**
22:             $l \leftarrow$ a random integer chosen uniformly from 1 to $i-1$ inclusive
23:             Change $rules_l$ from the form $v_l \rightarrow h_1 \wedge ...$ to the form $v_l \rightarrow v_i \wedge h_1 \wedge ...$
24: **return** $\overrightarrow{rules}$

4.5.4 Mutation

Mutation in sets is often similar to mutation in lists. That is, you usually have two tasks: changing the size of the ruleset (if you're allowed to), and mutating the rules in the set. The advice we have to offer here is basically the same as for lists too. For example, one way to change the size is to sample a small value from the geometric distribution, then either add or delete that number of rules from the set (you might select victims at random). Likewise, you could mutate rules in the set in the same manner as bit-flip mutation: mutate each rule with a certain independent probability.

    Production rules, as usual, have additional constraints. If you mutate the head of a rule you'll need to make sure the resultant symbols match up. You may have created orphans, and will need to decide if that's acceptable. Likewise you may want to be very careful about mutating the *body* (the primary symbol) of a production rule — you may create orphans or rulesets with more than one rule with the same symbol in the body.

4.5.5 Recombination

If you have a fixed number of rules, one per production symbol (for example), then recombination may be easy: just use uniform crossover to swap some subset of the rules. If your number of rules is arbitrary, you may need to pick a subset of rules in each individual and swap them (see Algorithm 49 to select a subset).

In any case, if you've got constraints on your rules (such as in production rules), you need to be careful about crossover: what happens if you orphan a rule? (Or do you care?) What happens if you eliminated a rule for which some other rule had an event that triggered it? Who gets triggered now? One of the biggest issues in crossing over arbitrary-length production rulesets is in merging the symbols: you may have symbols in one ruleset which don't match up with symbols in the other ruleset. As a result, the rulesets are essentially disjoint. How do you merge them? You may need to go through the rulesets and decide that certain rules in one ruleset will trigger rules in the crossed-in ruleset in certain ways. This can be a real mess. And there isn't any good guidance here: like graphs, it's fairly ad-hoc.

4.6 Bloat

Many of the representations presented here are variable-sized in nature. One of the interesting problems with variable-sized representations is that, over time, the individuals in your population may start to increase in size. This is commonly known as **bloat** (or "code bloat", or "code growth", take your pick[78]). Bloat has been studied the most in the context of Genetic Programming, where it's a real problem. Bloated individuals are slow to evaluate. They consume your memory. And worst of all, bloated individuals tend to be *very far* from the optimum, which is often not all that big. It's a deceptive problem situation.

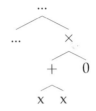

Figure 36 Inviable code example.

Early on GP researchers noticed that large, bloated trees contained a lot of subtrees which didn't do anything at all. These subtrees were dubbed **introns**, like their DNA counterparts. Figure 36 shows a particular kind of intron called **inviable code**. Here, the subtree (+ x x) is worthless because no matter what it returns, it's multiplied against zero. Early GP work assumed that these introns were the problem. The idea went like this: most Tweaks are damaging to the fitness of an individual. So in order to survive, you don't really need to improve yourself per se: you just need to be able to keep your head above water. One way to do this is to make it hard for Tweak to damage you, even if that also means preventing it from improving you. If you have a lot of introns, and particularly inviable code, then you increase the chance that the Tweaks will fall in those intron regions, where it doesn't matter what gets changed, and your fitness will stay the same. That was the idea anyway. But it turned out to not be true: if you eliminated the ability for individuals to Tweak in inviable code regions, bloat kept on going.[79]

So at this stage the reason for bloat is still up in the air. My own theory is that bloat is mostly due to individuals wanting to have deeper and deeper Tweak points because deeper areas in the tree tend to have less of an effect on the fitness of the child. Deeper points turn out to be well correlated with bigger kids. There are other theories out there too.

---

[78]Bill Langdon has been known to call it "survival of the fattest".

[79]I wrote a paper which showed this: Sean Luke, 2000, Code growth is not caused by introns, in Darrell Whitley, editor, *Late Breaking Papers at the 2000 Genetic and Evolutionary Computation Conference*, pages 228–235.

At any rate, lacking a good firm understanding of just what the heck is going on, most of the approaches to bloat control are somewhat ad-hoc. There are three common ways to keep individuals small:

- **Limit** the sizes when the individuals are Tweaked.
- **Edit** the individuals, to remove introns and the like.
- **Punish** individuals for being very large.

Genetic Programming traditionally limited individuals by placing a bound on the maximum allowable depth of an individual (to 17). But nowadays the trend is towards punishing individuals for being large by hurting their chances of being selected. This is called **parsimony pressure**.[80] The most straightforward way to do parsimony pressure is to include some portion of the individual's size as part of their fitness. For example, we might define the fitness f of an individual as $f = \alpha r - (1 - \alpha)s$ where r is the *raw* (or "actual") *fitness* of the individual, and s is the size of the individual. $0 \leq \alpha \leq 1$ is a constant to determine how much size counts and how much raw fitness counts. This concept is popularly known as **linear parsimony pressure**. The big problem with linear parsimony pressure is that you have to know how much of size is worth so much of fitness. And as discussed before, we usually design fitness functions in an arbitrary way. Even so, linear parsimony pressure is often quite good.

Another approach is to do a **non-parametric parsimony pressure** method which doesn't consider the specific fitness or fatness values of the individual and just picks based on comparing who's fitter and who's fatter. There are lots of these. For example, **lexicographic parsimony pressure** modifies Tournament selection to have individuals win if they're fitter, but if there's a tie, the individual that wins is the one that's smaller.[81]

Algorithm 63 *Lexicographic Tournament Selection*
1: $P \leftarrow$ population
2: $t \leftarrow$ tournament size, $t \geq 1$

3: *Best* $\leftarrow$ individual picked at random from P with replacement
4: **for** i from 2 to t **do**
5:    *Next* $\leftarrow$ individual picked at random from P with replacement
6:    **if** Fitness(*Next*) > Fitness(*Best*), or Fitness(*Next*) = Fitness(*Best*) and *Next* is smaller, **then**
7:       *Best* $\leftarrow$ *Next*
8: **return** *Best*

This works okay in environments where there are lots of ties. But often that's not the case. Another approach is to push for both smallness and fitness in your chosen individual. In **double**

---

[80]Liviu Panait and I did a shootout of all the parsimony pressure methods described here, and a host of other popular methods, in Sean Luke and Liviu Panait, 2006, A comparison of bloat control methods for genetic programming, *Evolutionary Computation*, 14(3), 309–344.

[81]Lexicographic parsimony pressure has been around since at least 1994, where it appeared casually in both Conor Ryan, 1994, Pygmies and civil servants, in Kenneth E. Kinnear, Jr., editor, *Advances in Genetic Programming*, chapter 11, pages 243–263, MIT Press (and) Simon Lucas, 1994, Structuring chromosomes for context-free grammar evolution, in *Proceedings of the First IEEE Conference on Evolutionary Computation*, pages 130–135, IEEE.

tournament, we do a tournament selection based on fitness. But the individuals entering the tournament aren't from the general population. Rather they were chosen from *other* tournament selection operations which were based on *smallness*.

Algorithm 64 *Double Tournament Selection*
1: $P \leftarrow$ population
2: $t_1 \leftarrow$ tournament size for fitness, $t_1 \geq 1$
3: $t_2 \leftarrow$ tournament size for smallness, $t_2 \geq 1$

4: $Best \leftarrow$ SmallnessTournament(P, t_2)
5: **for** i from 2 to t_1 **do**
6: $\quad Next \leftarrow$ SmallnessTournament(P, t_2)
7: $\quad$ **if** Fitness($Next$) $>$ Fitness($Best$) **then**
8: $\quad\quad Best \leftarrow Next$
9: **return** $Best$

10: **procedure** SmallnessTournament(P, t_2)
11: $\quad Best \leftarrow$ individual picked at random from P with replacement
12: $\quad$ **for** i from 2 to t_2 **do**
13: $\quad\quad Next \leftarrow$ individual picked at random from P with replacement
14: $\quad\quad$ **if** $Next$ is smaller than $Best$ **then**
15: $\quad\quad\quad Best \leftarrow Next$
16: $\quad$ **return** $Best$

Now we have two tournament sizes: t_1 and t_2. Assuming we keep with GP tradition and have $t_1 = 7$, a good setting for t_2 appears to be 2. Actually, the best value is around 1.4: remember that for values of t less than 2, with probability $t - 1.0$, we do a tournament selection of size $t = 2$, else we select an individual at random. You could do it the other way around too, of course: pick by fitness first, the by smallness. There are lots of choices for parsimony pressure, but these two give you the general idea (and are based on tournament selection to boot!).

5 Parallel Methods

Metaheuristics can be expensive. It's not uncommon, for example, to see over well over 100,000 assessments per run in Genetic Programming (say, a population size of 2000, run for 50 generations). And assessments can take a while to run: perhaps they're simulations, or complex chemical structure analyses. As a result, parallel methods are enticing.

I believe this is the strongest argument for parallel methods. But there are those in the community who argue that certain parallel methods (notably Island Models, discussed in Section 5.2) have a positive effect on the optimization process itself. For example, Zbigniew Skolicki[82] identified fitness functions where parallel methods are better than a single evolutionary computation population even if you discount the speedup enjoyed by multiple machines.

Lots of stochastic optimization techniques can be parallelized: but some perhaps more easily than others. Single-state methods (hill-climbing, simulated annealing, tabu search, etc.) are parallelizable but, in my opinion, only in awkward ways. Perhaps the most readily parallelizable methods are the population methods, since they already deal with many simultaneous candidate solutions which need to all be assessed. The five biggest ways to parallelize:[83]

- Do separate runs in parallel.

- Do one run which splits the fitness assessment task (and possibly also the breeding and initialization tasks) among **multiple threads** on the same machine.

- Do separate runs in parallel which occasionally hand high-quality individuals to one another (spreading the goodness). These are known as **Island Models**.

- Do one run which, when it needs to assess the fitness of individuals, farms them out to remote machines. This is known as **Master-Slave**, **Client-Server**, or **Distributed Fitness Assessment**.

- Do one run with a selection procedure which presumes that individuals are spread out in a parallel array on a vector computer (called **spatially embedded** or **fine-grained models**).

These five can also be mixed in quite a lot of ways. There's no reason you can't do an island model where each island does master-slave fitness assessment, for example.

Thread Pools Several of the following algorithms assume that the threads have spawned themselves and have inserted themselves into a *thread pool* from which we may draw them and tell them to start; when they finish they reenter the thread pool again.

---

[82]Zbigniew Skolicki, 2007, *An Analysis of Island Models in Evolutionary Computation*, Ph.D. thesis, George Mason University, Fairfax, Virginia.

[83]Though many people have contributed to the literature on methods like these, John Grefenstette's 1981 technical report on the subject was unusually prescient. His algorithm A described a multiple-thread or Master-Slave method; algorithms B and C described Asynchronous Evolution (a Master-Slave variant described later), and algorithm D described Island Models. From John Grefenstette, 1981, Parallel adaptive algorithms for function optimization, Technical Report CS-81-19, Computer Science Department, Vanderbilt Univesity.

Algorithm 65 *Thread Pool Functions*
1: **global** $l \leftarrow$ lock for the pool
2: **global** $T \leftarrow \{\ \}$ empty pool of tuples $\vec{t} = \langle t_{\text{lock}}, t_{\text{data}} \rangle$ where t_{lock} is a lock and t_{data} is any object

3: **procedure** InsertMyselfAndWait( )
4:     Acquire lock l
5:     $\vec{t} \leftarrow$ new tuple $\langle t_{\text{lock}}, t_{\text{data}} \rangle$ ▷ t_{lock} is a new lock. t_{data} can be anything for now
6:     $T \leftarrow T \cup \{t\}$
7:     Acquire lock t_{lock}
8:     Notify threads waiting on l
9:     Wait on t_{lock} ▷ This releases both locks, waits to be notified on t_{lock}, then reacquires the locks
10:     $o \leftarrow$ copy of t_{data} ▷ At this point t_{data} was set in TellThreadToStart(...)
11:     Release lock t_{lock}
12:     Release lock l
13:     **return** o

14: **procedure** ThreadIsInserted( )
15:     Acquire lock l
16:     **if** T is empty **then**
17:         Release lock l
18:         **return** false
19:     **else**
20:         Release lock l
21:         **return** true

22: **procedure** TellThreadToStart(information o)
23:     Acquire lock l
24:     **while** T is empty **do**
25:         Wait on l ▷ This releases the lock, waits to be notified on l, then reacquires the lock
26:     $t \leftarrow$ arbitrary tuple in T
27:     $T \leftarrow T - \{t\}$
28:     Acquire lock t_{lock}
29:     $t_{\text{data}} \leftarrow$ copy of o
30:     Notify threads waiting on t_{lock}
31:     Release lock t_{lock}
32:     Release lock l
33:     **return** t

34: **procedure** WaitForAllThreads(number of threads n)
35:     Acquire lock l
36:     **while** $||T|| < n$ **do**
37:         Wait on l
38:     Release lock l

This can be complicated and hard to debug. The thread pool in turn requires the ability to:

- Spawn threads.
- *Acquire* and *release locks* on a per-thread basis. If a thread tries to acquire a lock already acquired by someone else, the thread pauses until the lock is released to them.
- Have the ability to *wait* on a lock, meaning to release the lock to others and pause until someone else has *notified* you regarding that lock.
- Have the ability to *notify* threads waiting on a given lock. This causes the threads to one-by-one reacquire the lock, unpause themselves, and go on their merry way.

Basically every threading library provides this functionality. Using this, we can spawn as many threads as we want initially, and direct them to call InsertMyselfAndWait to get the next individual they're supposed to work on. This is pretty standard stuff but it's a bit complex.

5.1 Multiple Threads

To assess a population, we could hand off individuals one by one to threads as they come available. When a thread finishes an individual, it is made available for another one.

Algorithm 66 *Fine-Grained Parallel Fitness Assessment*
1: $P \leftarrow$ current population

2: **for** each individual $P_i \in P$ **do**
3:     TellThreadToStart($\{P_i\}$)   ▷ If total threads $\geq ||P||$, one will always be available
4:     WaitForAllThreads()
5: **return** P

This requires use of a thread pool. A simpler approach, which requires no locks, just breaks the population into chunks and hands each chunk to a separate newly spawned thread. Then at the end we just gather up all the threads.

Algorithm 67 *Simple Parallel Fitness Assessment*
1: $P \leftarrow$ population $\{P_1, ..., P_l\}$
2: $T \leftarrow$ set of threads $\{T_1, ...T_n\}$

3: **for** i from 1 to n **do**
4:     $a \leftarrow \lfloor l/n \rfloor \times (i-1) + 1$ ▷ Figure out the lower (a) and upper (b) boundaries for chunk i
5:     **if** $i = n$ **then**
6:         $b \leftarrow l$
7:     **else**
8:         $b \leftarrow \lfloor l/n \rfloor \times i$
9:     Spawn T_i and tell it to Assess individuals P_a through P_b
10: **for** i from 1 to n **do**
11:     Wait for T_i to exit
12: **return** P

Here we just need to be able to spawn threads and wait for them to finish (both standard functions in a thread package). You can "wait" for the threads to finish simply by "joining" with them (a standard function in parallel toolkits). The downside of this is that it's often the case that one chunk happens to have all the slow-to-assess individuals (if such things exist), and the other threads will wind up sitting around idling waiting for that last thread to finish up.

It's possible to do the same tricks to parallelize population initialization, though it's rare for it to take long to initialize a population. Still, Algorithm 66 could be used except that instead of evaluating an existing individual P_i, each thread is told to create an individual and insert it into slot i. Similarly, Algorithm 67 could be used for initialization, where instead of doing Assess($P_a...P_b$), we tell each thread to initialize $b - a + 1$ individuals and stick them in slots $a...b$.

Likewise, you could do the same tricks for breeding, but it can be complicated by choice of selection procedure if certain things need to be done offline. Tournament Selection works nicely, as it doesn't require any beforehand, offline stuff. Note that we're no longer dividing up the population P into chunks, but rather dividing up the next-generation population Q into chunks:

Algorithm 68 *Simple Parallel Genetic Algorithm-style Breeding*
1: $P \leftarrow$ current population
2: $T \leftarrow$ set of threads $\{T_1, ...T_n\}$
3: $l \leftarrow$ desired size of new population

4: $\vec{q} \leftarrow$ empty array $\langle q_1, ..., q_l \rangle$ ▷ Will hold the newly bred individuals
5: **for** i from 1 to n **do**
6: $\quad a \leftarrow \lfloor l/n \rfloor \times (i-1) + 1$
7: $\quad$ **if** $i = n$ **then**
8: $\quad\quad b \leftarrow l$
9: $\quad$ **else**
10: $\quad\quad b \leftarrow \lfloor l/n \rfloor \times i$
11: $\quad$ Spawn T_i and tell it to Breed individuals into slots q_a through q_b
12: **for** i from 1 to n **do**
13: $\quad$ Wait for T_i to exit
14: **return** $\vec{q}$ converted into a population

Algorithm 69 *Fine-Grained Parallel Genetic Algorithm-style Breeding*
1: $P \leftarrow$ current population
2: $l \leftarrow$ desired size of new population ▷ Presumably even in length

3: $\vec{q} \leftarrow$ empty array $\langle q_1, ..., q_l \rangle$
4: **for** i from 1 to l by 2 **do** ▷ We jump by 2 to allow crossover to make two kids
5: $\quad$ TellThreadToStart($\{\vec{q}, i, i+1\}$) ▷ The thread breeds from P into slots q_i and q_{i+1}
6: WaitForAllThreads(total number of threads)
7: **return** $\vec{q}$ converted into a population

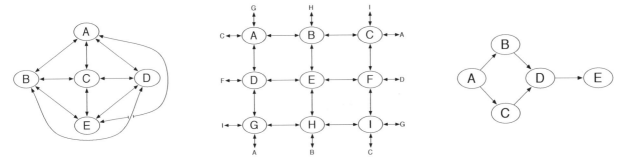

Figure 37   Fully-Connected, 2-D Toroidal Grid, and Injection Island Model topologies.

The reason these algorithms work is that breeding is a **copy-forward** procedure: we select individuals in *P*, *copy them*, then modify the *copies*. So we never need to bother locking on individuals in *P*. Other procedures might require more complexity than this.

5.2 Island Models

An island model is a group of simultaneous evolutionary optimization processes which occasionally send individuals to one another to help spread news of newly-discovered fit areas of the space. Some island models send the fittest individuals they have, or use a selection operation to pick them. Others send random individuals (which is less exploitative).

Island models are primarily meant to take advantage of computational resources, commonly by loading each of *n* computers with one process each. But they have another feature: because the population is broken into separate **subpopulations** (sometimes called **demes**), it can take longer for fit solutions to take over the whole population, which makes the whole system more diverse and explorative. Another argument made in favor of island models is that if you have a fitness function which can be broken into different components, island models might theoretically help those different components be developed in separate populations.

To set up an island model you need to define an **island topology**. Which islands will send individuals to which other islands? There are three common ones, shown in Figure 37. A **fully-connected** topology has every island talking with every other island. A **toroidal grid** topology lays out the islands in, well, an *n*-dimensional toroidal grid. In a fully-connected topology, spreading an individual from one island to any other one requires a single hop, but in a grid topology, it can take a while for an individual to wander through various populations to get to a distant population. Thus we might expect a grid to promote diversity more.

One more topology: an **injection model** is a feed-forward structure. Sometimes this is used to assist the fitness function. Let's say you are looking for a robot soccer player. The EA can't come up with everything at one time, so you've constructed a pipeline to help things by constantly upping the ante. In an early island, the fitness function is: how well can you kick? Individuals then migrate to a later island where the fitness function has changed to: how well can you pass the ball? Further individuals might migrate to another island where the objective is to keep the ball away from an opponent by kicking carefully between teammates. And so on.

Once you've settled on a topology, you'll need to modify the EA. Here's how I do it:

Algorithm 70 *An Abstract Generational Evolutionary Algorithm With Island Model Messaging*
1: $P \leftarrow$ Build Initial Population
2: $Best \leftarrow \square$
3: **repeat**
4:     AssessFitness(P)
5:     Send copies of some individuals from P to mailboxes of neighboring islands
6:     **for** each individual $P_i \in P$ **do**
7:         **if** $Best = \square$ or Fitness(P_i) > Fitness($Best$) **then**
8:             $Best \leftarrow P_i$
9:     $M \leftarrow$ extract and return all contents of my mailbox
10:    $P \leftarrow$ Join($P, M,$ Breed(P))   ▷ It's possible you may breed individuals but never use them
11: **until** *Best* is the ideal solution or we have run out of time
12: **return** *Best*

We've augmented the abstract EA with a mailbox metaphor: each island has a mailbox to which other islands may send individuals. Islands can, at their leisure, extract and return the individuals presently in their mailboxes. We've added three gizmos to the abstract algorithm using this metaphor: **sending** individuals to neighboring islands, **receiving** individuals that have shown up in our mailbox from neighboring islands, then **joining** those individuals with the population along with the others (notice that Join now takes three arguments). If you're doing an injection model, individuals arriving at your mailbox may need to have their fitnesses reassessed given your own island-specific fitness function.

It's possible that your particular approach will require a **synchronous** algorithm where the islands all wait until everyone has caught up before sending individuals to one another. But in most cases an **asynchronous** mechanism makes better use of network resources. Here individuals just get sent whenever, and pile up at the doorstep of the receiving island until it's ready to take them in. This allows some islands to be slower than others. Of course, in that situation you'll need to decide what to do if a mailbox is overflowing.

Another issue affecting network throughput is the number and kind of connections in your topology. Which machines are connected? How often do they send individuals to each other, and when? How many individuals get sent? Lots of connections, or poorly considered topologies, can stress parts of your network. In my department we have a cluster with two networks, each with its own router. The two routers are then connected together on a fast channel but not fast enough. Here, I'd probably want a network configuration where nodes on the same router talk to each other much more often. Additionally I might configure things so that each island only sends out individuals every m generations, and those islands stagger when they send individuals. When doing layouts like this, think about how to maximize throughput.

In Section 5.1 we went in detail about how to handle the locking etc. to do the parallel model. For island models we won't do this detail, but it's not super complex. You connect to your neighbor islands via sockets, then either use the UNIX select() function, or spawn a separate thread for each socket. Let's presume the latter. The thread loops, reading from the socket, locking on the mailbox, adding to the mailbox, then releasing the lock. In the main EA, to get the current contents of the mailbox and clear it, you just need to acquire the lock first, then release it afterwards. Sending individuals to neighbors is just a matter of writing to the remote socket (no threads involved).

5.3 Master-Slave Fitness Assessment

This is the most common form of parallel metaheuristics, and it's also among the most straightforward. The machines at your disposal are divided up into a **master** and some n **slaves**.[84] When you need to assess an individual, you send it off to a slave to do the job. This becomes more useful as the time cost of assessing the fitness of an individual becomes high. And for a great many optimization tasks of interest nowadays, fitness assessment time is so long that it's far and away the dominant factor in the optimization process.

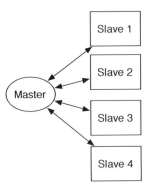

Figure 38 Master-slave fitness assessment.

So how do you set up a master-slave arrangement? Basically the same way you do multithreaded fitness assessment (Algorithms 65 and 66 — I wouldn't bother with Algorithm 67). The only real difference is that each thread registered in the thread pool is assigned to talk to a particular slave over the socket. Instead of assessing the individual (or individuals) directly in the thread, the thread sends it over a socket to get assessed remotely. You'll need to modify Algorithm 66 to allow a thread to receive multiple individuals at once, like this:

Algorithm 71 *Fine-Grained Master-Side Fitness Assessment*
1: $P \leftarrow$ current population $\{P_1, ..., P_l\}$
2: $n \leftarrow$ number of individuals to send to the slave at one time

3: **for** i from 1 to l by n **do**
4:    TellThreadToStart($\{P_i, ..., P_{\min(i+n-1,l)}\}$)   ▷ The thread will ship them off to the remote slave
5: WaitForAllThreads()
6: **return** P

This approach is also nice because it's relatively graceful with slow slaves, and with variable-length fitness assessment times, and also allows new slaves to show up. To robustly handle slaves which disappear while assessing fitness requires more complexity which we won't bother with here (though it's important!).

When is a master-slave process useful? It's all down to how much network capacity and speed you have. A master-slave approach becomes useful when you have enough capacity and speed that the time spent shipping an individual to a remote site and back is less than just assessing the fitness on your own processor. There are a couple of tricks you can employ to maximize throughput. First, compress your individuals when sending out on the socket, particularly if they're GP or other individuals with a lot of redundancy. Second, in many cases you don't need an individual sent back to you from the slave: you may just need its fitness (it depends, as we'll see in a moment). Third, many networks send in packets that incur a constant overhead: you'd like to load up that packet if you can. Sending a chunk of individuals to a slave may fill the packet nicely, but sending a single individual can waste a lot of overhead.

Here's how I see master-slave versus island models. If your throughput is low and your fitness assessment time is very short, you might pick an island model. Or you might pick an island model if you wish to optimize using a *very* large population. Otherwise I'd pick master-slave.

---
[84]Or if you like, a *client* and *servers*, or is it a *server* and *clients*?

You could mix the two as well. For example, you could have a bunch of islands, with each island assigned its own set of fitness assessment slaves. Or you could try what I call **Opportunistic Evolution**,[85] which is particularly good for grid computing scenarios. Here, you have a bunch of slaves as usual, and send some n individuals to each slave at a time. Each slave is also given a certain large time interval, big enough to justify shipping the individuals off to it. When a slave has finished assessing its individuals, and there's more time left in the interval, the slave does a little optimization (perhaps hill-climbing or evolutionary computation) with its n individuals as a mini population. When time is up, the slave returns the revised mini-population to the master rather than the original individuals. (Note that to do this you *must* send individuals back to the master, not just fitnesses).

You can also mix Master-Slave Fitness assessment with a Steady-State Genetic Algorithm in a fairly elegant way, a notion called **Asynchronous Evolution**. Whenever a slave is ready to receive individuals, we select and breed individuals right there and ship them off to the slave. Asynchronous Evolution doesn't wait for slaves to all complete — it's asynchronous — but rather whenever a slave has finished (taking as long as it likes), its individuals get Joined into the population. Different slaves can finish at different times. This approach tolerates an *extremely* wide variance in fitness assessment time: of course, long-evaluating Individuals may be at a disadvantage because they can't breed as often.

Asynchronous Evolution relies on a threadsafe collection (multiset). Whenever a thread receives completed individuals from its remote slave, the thread inserts them into the collection using the AddToCollection(...) function. The Asynchronous Evolution algorithm itself polls for new completed individuals by repeatedly calling the RetrieveAllFromColection(...) function. Trivially:

Algorithm 72 *Threadsafe Collection Functions*
1: **global** $S \leftarrow \{\}$
2: **global** $l \leftarrow$ lock for the collection S

3: **procedure** AddToCollection(T) ▷ T is a set of things
4:      Acquire lock l
5:      $S \leftarrow S \cup T$
6:      Release lock l

7: **procedure** RetrieveAllFromCollection( )
8:      Acquire lock l
9:      $T \leftarrow S$
10:      $S \leftarrow \{\}$
11:      Release lock l
12:      **return** T

Given the threadsafe collection, Asynchronous Evolution proceeds as follows.

---

[85]This notion was first suggested in a technical report: Ricardo Bianchini and Christopher Brown, 1993, Parallel genetic algorithms on distributed-memory architectures, Revised Version 436, Computer Science Department, University of Rochester, Rochester, NY 14627.

The term *Opportunistic Evolution* was coined by Steven Armentrout for a paper we wrote: Keith Sullivan, Sean Luke, Curt Larock, Sean Cier, and Steven Armentrout, 2008, Opportunistic evolution: efficient evolutionary computation on large-scale computational grids, in *GECCO '08: Proceedings of the 2008 GECCO Conference Companion on Genetic and Evolutionary Computation*, pages 2227–2232, ACM, New York, NY, USA.

Algorithm 73 *Asynchronous Evolution*

1: $P \leftarrow \{\}$
2: $n \leftarrow$ number of individuals to send to a slave at one time
3: *popsize* $\leftarrow$ desired population size

4: $Best \leftarrow \square$
5: **repeat**
6:    **if** ThreadIsInserted( ) = true **then**   ▷ Check for processors with nothing to do
7:       **if** $||P|| <$ *popsize* **then**   ▷ Still initializing population
8:          $Q \leftarrow n$ new random individuals
9:       **else**   ▷ Steady State
10:          $Q \leftarrow \{\}$
11:          **for** i from 1 to n by 2 **do**   ▷ Obviously we could do some other kind of breeding
12:             Parent $P_a \leftarrow$ SelectWithReplacement(P)
13:             Parent $P_b \leftarrow$ SelectWithReplacement(P)
14:             Children $C_a, C_b \leftarrow$ Crossover(Copy(P_a), Copy(P_b))
15:             $Q \leftarrow Q \cup \{$ Mutate(C_a), Mutate(C_b) $\}$
16:       TellThreadToStart($\{Q_1, ..., Q_n\}$)
17:    $M \leftarrow$ RetrieveAllFromCollection( ) ▷ Get all individuals who have completed fitness assessment
18:    **for** each individual $M_i \in M$ **do**
19:       **if** $Best = \square$ or Fitness(M_i) $>$ Fitness($Best$) **then**
20:          $Best \leftarrow M_i$
21:       **if** $||P|| =$ *popsize* **then**   ▷ Steady State
22:          Individual $P_d \leftarrow$ SelectForDeath(P)
23:          $P \leftarrow P - \{P_d\}$
24:       $P \leftarrow P \cup \{M_i\}$
25:    **if** ThreadIsInserted( ) = false and M is empty **then**
26:       Pause for a little while   ▷ Nothing's going in or out: give your CPU a break
27: **until** $Best$ is the ideal solution or we have run out of time
28: **return** $Best$

5.4 Spatially Embedded Models

A spatially embedded model adds to the population a notion of *physical locations* of individuals in the population. For example, the population may be laid out in a 3D grid, or a 1D ring, and each individual occupies a certain point in that space. Figure 39 shows individuals laid out in a 2D grid.

Such models are mostly used to maintain diversity in the population, and so promote exploration. Individuals are only allowed to breed with "nearby" individuals, so a highly fit individual cannot spread as rapidly through a population as it could if there were no breeding constraints. Notionally regions of the population might develop their own cultures, so to speak, similar to Island Models.

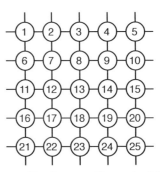

Figure 39 A spatially embedded population of individuals in a 2D grid. Individuals 1...25 shown.

Spatially embedded models are parallelizable in the multi-threaded sense. But if you have a **vector processor**, that is, a machine which performs many identical simultaneous operations at one time, there exist techniques for doing all the breeding and selection in parallel on the processor. Nowadays the most common vector processor in your possession is your graphics processing unit (GPU). Assuming we stick with the multithreaded example, we can easily do multi-threaded fitness assessment and multi-threaded breeding. We just need a modification of the breeding procedure.

Algorithm 74 *Spatial Breeding*
1: $P \leftarrow$ current population, organized spatially

2: $Q \leftarrow$ new population, organized spatially in same way as P
3: **for** each individual $P_i \in P$ **do** ▷ This can be done in parallel threads as before
4:     $N \leftarrow$ Neighbors(P_i, P)
5:     Parent $N_a \leftarrow$ SelectWithReplacement(N)
6:     Parent $N_b \leftarrow$ SelectWithReplacement(N)
7:     Children $C_a, C_b \leftarrow$ Crossover(Copy(N_a), Copy(N_b))
8:     $Q_i \leftarrow$ Mutate(C_a) ▷ C_b is discarded. C_a goes directly to spatial slot i in Q
9: **return** Q

Or if you like, we could just do mutation, no crossover. The important part is that we are specifically replacing individuals, in each slot, with children bred from neighbors in that area.

To replace an individual P_i, selection is performed not from the whole population but rather on a subset N of **neighbors** of P_i. It's up to you to define the neighborhood function. You could define neighbors of P_i as the individuals which reside within a box centered at P_i's location and of m size in each dimension. Or you could build up N by repeatedly doing random walks starting at P_i; each time you finish the walk, you add the final individual to N. Individuals selected this way are chosen roughly according to a gaussian-ish distribution centered P_i. The longer the walk, the larger the neighborhood. For example:

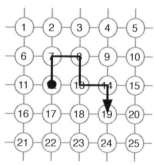

Figure 40 A random walk in the grid, starting at individual 12.

Algorithm 75 *Random Walk Selection*
1: $P \leftarrow$ current population
2: $r \leftarrow$ chosen random walk length
3: $P_i \leftarrow$ Start Individual

4: $\vec{l} \leftarrow$ location $\langle l_1...l_n \rangle$ of P_i in the space
5: **for** r times **do**
6:     **repeat**
7:         $d \leftarrow$ random integer chosen uniformly between 1 and n inclusive
8:         $j \leftarrow$ either a 1 or -1, chosen at random
9:     **until** $l_d + j$ is an acceptable value for dimension d in the space
10:     $l_d \leftarrow l_d + j$ ▷ Wrap-around as necessary if in a toroidal environment
11: **return** the individual located at $\vec{l}$ in the space

6 Coevolution

Coevolution can mean a lot of things in biology, but the classic notion is one of different species acting as foils against one another and causing one another to adapt. For example, a particular fungus might develop an antibiotic to kill a particular bacterium, and the bacterium then adapts to not be harmed by that antibiotic, forcing the fungus to construct a tougher antibiotic. Coevolution could also include symbiotic relationships: leafcutter ants and the fungus they farm for food, both co-adapting to work better as a team, so to speak.

Coevolution is also a common framework in metaheuristics, and is usually applied to population-based optimization methods. In optimization, coevolution generally refers to situations where the fitnesses of individuals in a population are affected by the presence of other individuals in the population(s). More formally, we'd say that a system exhibits coevolutionary properties if the question of whether individual A is superior to individual B is dependent on the presence or absence of some other individual or individuals C in the population. For example, let's say that the fitness of an individual is based on competing with other individuals in the population in Tic-Tac-Toe. A usually wins more games than B does, so A has a higher fitness. But whenever A plays C, A loses badly. Curiously C always loses to B! So if C is in the population and playing, then A's fitness may drop to less than B's. The fitness is context-sensitive.

Such scenarios lead to certain odd pathological conditions: and indeed there are a lot of open issues in coevolution dealing with ironing out these conditions and getting coevolutionary systems to behave more like regular optimization techniques. This is a well-motivated area of research because coevolutionary methods are promising in important ways! Coevolution can allow a system to gracefully ramp up in difficulty, to provide diversity in the system, to discover not just high-quality but *robust* solutions, and to solve complex, high-dimensional problems by breaking them along semi-decomposable lines.[86]

Here are the main kinds of coevolutionary techniques:[87]

- **1-Population Competitive Coevolution** Individuals in a single population base their fitness on games they play against one another. Commonly used to evolve good competitive strategies (for checkers or soccer, for example).

- **2-Population Competitive Coevolution** The population is broken into two **subpopulations** (or **demes**). The fitness of an individual in subpopulation 1 is based on how many individuals in subpopulation 2 it is able to defeat in some competition (and vice versa). Commonly subpopulation 1 contains the candidate solutions of interest to us, and subpopulation

---

[86]By *semi-decomposable* I mean that the problem may not be *entirely* decomposable into separate subproblems to be optimized separately, but that the linkage between those subproblems is fairly low (while within the subproblem the linkage may be high).

Coevolutionary algorithms are sometimes motivated because they're more "biological", if that matters to you from an engineering perspective (it oughtn't). I recall a biologist remarking that coevolutionary algorithms should have instead been called *evolutionary algorithms*, because the algorithms we call evolutionary algorithms really have little to do with evolution. And that's basically right. Evolutionary algorithms are more like dog breeding: you select and breed the dogs, er, algorithms based on assessments of them independent of one another. That is, you're doing a form of *artificial directed selection*. But in real *natural selection*, individuals survive based on the makeup of their particular populations (helping and/or competing with them) and the presence of certain predators or prey. It's context-sensitive.

[87]The terms *competitive* and *cooperative coevolution* come from similar notions in game theory. But a dangerous faction of theorists prefers to call them **compositional** if the objective is to put pieces together to form a complete solution (like N-Population Cooperative Coevolution) and **test-based**, if the objective is for one population to provide a foil for the other population (as is usually done in 2-Population Competitive Coevolution).

2 contains foils meant to test them. Usually used to force subpopulation 1 to find robust candidate solutions despite everything subpopulation 2 can throw at them.

- **N-Population Cooperative Coevolution**   The problem to be solved is divided into n subproblems: for example, if the problem is to find soccer strategies for a team of n robots, it's divided into subproblems, each of which is to find a strategy for one of the robots. The task of finding each of these subsolutions is given to each of n subpopulations. The fitness of an individual (in this case, a robot strategy) is assessed by selecting individuals from the other subpopulations, grouping them with the individual to form a complete n-sized solution (a complete soccer robot team), and determining the fitness of that solution. Commonly used to reduce the high dimensionality of big problems by decomposing them into multiple simpler problems.

- **Diversity Maintenance (Niching)**   Individuals in a single population are forced to spread portions of their fitness to one another, or to be grouped into competitive **niches** (or **species**), etc., to impose diversity on the population.

These are the main groups. But there are many other variations on these themes.[88] For example, in what I call **Cooperative-Competitive Coevolution**, a solution is composed of multiple subpieces as in N-Population Cooperative Coevolution. But the solution is tested by playing it against other such solutions in a game, as in 1-Population Competitive Coevolution. For example, imagine that we're looking for soccer teams consisting of a goalie, forwards, midfielders, and defenders. We have four subpopulations (goalies, forwards, etc.). An individual (a goalie, say) is assessed by selecting from these subpopulations to form a team which includes that individual. Then we select from the subpopulations to form an opposing team, and play a game of soccer.

Because coevolution is most commonly seen in population-based methods (notably Evolutionary Computation), the algorithms described here are in that context. But there is no reason why it can't be applied in limited form to single-state metaheuristics. For example, to use a hill-climber, just define your "population" as your current two individuals (parent and child). To avoid the evolution stigma, we might instead call such algorithms **co-adaptive** rather than **coevolved**.

What does Fitness Mean Now?   The fitness of individuals in a coevolutionary system is a **relative fitness** based on how they performed in the context of individuals *in the same optimization process*. For example, if the individuals were competing against one another in a game, an individual in generation 0 might have a decent fitness (because the other individuals in generation 0 are awful), but if it was magically teleported to generation 100 its fitness would be terrible (because they've improved). We no longer have an **absolute fitness**.

The appearance of relative fitness creates two gotchas. First, it mucks with the dynamics of selection and breeding, which can result in problematic operation of the system, as we'll see in a bit. Second, it's a big problem if we want to assess how well the algorithm is doing. Previously we could just sample individuals out of each generation and see their fitnesses going up and up. But

---

[88]Certain other techniques discussed later exhibit coevolutionary traits (and likely pathologies). **Ant Colony Optimization** (Section 8.3) and **Michigan-Approach Learning Classifier Systems** (Section 10.4) both have features similar to the 1-Population methods above. And **Univariate Estimation of Distribution Algorithms** (Section 9.2.1) turn out to have a very close theoretical relationship with N-Population Cooperative Coevolution. **Island Models**, discussed earlier in Section 5.2, also use subpopulations, and also have certain diversity-maintenance features, and so exhibit certain relationships with coevolutionary models.

now it's possible that the individuals will be improving, but the fitnesses will be staying roughly the same because their opponents are improving as well.

This brings up two common uses of fitness: an **internal fitness** is a measure used by the optimization system to determine selection. An **external fitness** is a measure used to examine the quality of an individual in order to gauge the progress of the algorithm. As we've seen, internal fitnesses can be either relative or absolute, but we'd like the external fitness to be absolute. We will distinguish between these using AssessInternalFitness(...) and AssessExternalFitness(...).

As it's relative, an internal fitness may change based on the tests performed in the context of other individuals in the population. Thus you may need to re-assess the fitness of all individuals each time around.

Tests Sometimes fitness assessments are done by doing a collection of **tests** on your individual; commonly the fitness is the sum or average of the test results. This might be because you have a fixed set of **test cases** (for example the Genetic Programming / Symbolic Regression example in Section 4.3 is often done by testing each individual against some m test cases). It can also be because you have a very large (often infinite) set of possible situations for which you'd like your individual to be optimal, or at least pretty good. We call an individual which is good in lots of situations, even if not optimal anywhere in particular, a **robust** individual. Such tests thus would sample a lot of places in the situation space. You might also perform multiple tests with an individual to find a location in the space where it is particularly impressive, even if it's not impressive everywhere. Last, multiple tests might be important in order to weed out noise.

Multiple-test fitness assessment shows up over and over in coevolution. It's a natural fit because if you're testing an individual against other individuals, you might as well test against a bunch of them to get a good sample. Each of the methods discussed here will employ fitness tests for different purposes, so the algorithms usually will have two stages to fitness assessment: first, gather some m tests for each individual (using Test(...)) in the context of other individuals, then assess the fitness of the individual based on those tests.

6.1 1-Population Competitive Coevolution

1-Population Competitive Coevolution is mostly used for optimizing candidate solutions designed to compete in some kind of game. For example, Kumar Chellapila and David Fogel[89] used 1-Population Competitive Coevolution to search for good-quality checkers players.[90] I also used this kind of coevolution to search for robot soccer team strategies. The idea is simple: each individual's fitness is assessed by playing that individual against other individuals in the population in the game of interest (checkers, soccer, whatnot).

The intuition behind this idea is to improve the **learning gradient** of the search space. Imagine that you're trying to find a good poker player. One way to do it would be to build a really good "guru" poker player by hand, then assess the fitness of individuals based on how many hands, out of n, in which they beat the guru. The problem is that the vast majority of random individuals are awful: they lose every single hand to the guru. Early on your population will consist entirely of these individuals and so the optimization system wouldn't be able to tell which of the individuals

---

[89]Son of Larry Fogel, of Evolutionary Programming fame. See Section 3.1.1.

[90]More specifically: they were looking for neural networks which performed the board evaluation function to be attached to standard α-β game tree algorithms for checkers. See also Footnote 92. The paper was Kumar Chellapila and David Fogel, 2001, Evolving an expert checkers playing program without using human expertise, *IEEE Transactions on Evolutionary Computation*, 5(4), 422–428.

were better than the others. The quality function would be flat until you find an individual who's *sometimes* able to beat the guru, which is rare. If you are so lucky, then it's easier going from there.

Figure 41 shows this situation. Basically your system can't get started because there's no way to differentiate among all the initial individuals because they're so bad against the guru. Until you get players who can start beating the guru *sometimes*, it's essentially a needle-in-a-haystack scenario. You could fix this by coming up with a special way of assessing fitness among the individuals who always lose against the guru: how badly did they lose? Did they do something smart somewhere? Etc. But this is often quite complicated to do. Alternatively you could create a panel of hand-built custom players, from very simple, stupid ones, all the way up to the guru. Individuals would be assessed based on how many of the custom players they beat. This would present a more gentle hill for the system to climb up. Even so, if you're smart enough to be able to construct a wide range of poker playing programs to test your individuals, why in the world would you be using stochastic optimization to find a good poker player? Don't you already know how to do that?

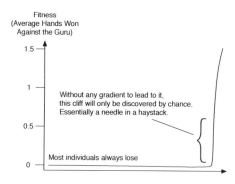

Figure 41 A tough learning gradient when playing poker with a guru.

An alternative route (1-Population Competitive Coevolution) is to have your individuals play each other. Initially, an individual is bad, but the players he's being tested against *are bad too*. Someone's got to win the poker hand, so your players won't have all zero fitness. Your optimization algorithm can tell which ones are (marginally) better. Later on, as the individuals improve, *so do the players against which they are being tested*. As your individuals get better, the problem naturally gets harder. We've created an automatically self-adjusting learning gradient.

Handling external fitness can be a problem. Some ways to compute an external fitness:

- Test against a guru or against a panel of hand-created players.

- Test against a sample of players from previous generations (assuming they're not as good).

- Test against some external system in the real world.

The first option has the same issues as was discussed before. The second option makes a big assumption: that your later players are better than your earlier individuals. Essentially your external fitness wouldn't be an absolute measure but *relative* to other players, which could create some odd results if the system's not stable.

The third option is what Chellapilla and Fogel did for their checkers player. To test the progress of their system, they occasionally collected an individual from the current generation and played it on MSN Gaming Zone[91] against real people in the site's checkers room, eventually garnering a checkers ranking. The system was improving if the ranking was going up.[92] Chellapilla and Fogel

---

[91] http://games.msn.com/

[92] This leads to a notorious anecdote. At the time, the checkers room of MSN Gaming Zone consisted largely of teenage and twentysomething males. When the evolved checkers player was losing against these people, they'd play to the end. But when it was beating them, they'd drop the game. Thus Chellapilla and Fogel couldn't collect enough positive samples to assess their program, just negative samples. This led them to adopt the fictional online persona of a 24-year-old, beautiful female PhD student who went by the username of Blondie24. The MSN Gaming Zone players,

also used the "guru" option for their external fitness, by playing against Chinook,[93] a well-regarded checkers program, and one which can be adjusted to play at different levels of difficulty.

This external fitness metric is the primary thing that distinguishes the abstract algorithm from the abstract version of a traditional evolutionary algorithm. Here's the abstract algorithm:

Algorithm 76 *An Abstract Generational 1-Population Competitive Coevolutionary Algorithm*
1: $P \leftarrow$ Build Initial Population
2: $Best \leftarrow \square$
3: **repeat**
4:     AssessInternalFitness(P)   ▷ Used for Selection (in Breeding)
5:     AssessExternalFitness(P)   ▷ Used to determine algorithm progress and *Best*
6:     **for** each individual $P_i \in P$ **do**
7:         **if** $Best = \square$ or ExternalFitness(P_i) > ExternalFitness($Best$) **then**
8:             $Best \leftarrow P_i$
9:     $P \leftarrow$ Join(P, Breed(P))
10: **until** *Best* is the ideal solution or we have run out of time
11: **return** *Best*

1-Population Competitive Coevolution could also be cast in an **asynchronous** Steady State form. As part of their work with NEAT, Ken Stanley and Risto Miikkulainen did a project involving the optimization of robot game agents in a free-for-all 2D shoot-em-up.[94] The entire population participated at the same time in the game, shooting at each other. Those individuals with better skills lasted longer; the less fit individuals, once shot, would be removed from the game and replaced with children newly bred from the remaining population. An approach like this is fairly rare, but intriguing from a biological or social modeling perspective. Perhaps a method like this might be helpful for, say, for modeling competing restaurants in a city, or competing gangs, etc.

6.1.1 Relative Internal Fitness Assessment

There are a variety of ways that one might assess the fitness of individuals by pitting them against other individuals in the population. The primary issue that you're going to face is the number of tests (evaluations) involved in order to assess the fitness of the population. Many games, competitions, or similar things are stochastic: you might win one time, lose another. For example, in poker, you might need to play a bunch of hands to determine which player is doing better.

---

thinking they were playing against a woman, would play to the very end regardless of whether they were winning or not. Fogel later wrote a book about the experience: David Fogel, 2001, *Blondie24: Playing at the Edge of AI*, Morgan Kauffman. See also Footnote 90.

[93]http://www.cs.ualberta.ca/~chinook/ Chinook was also the first program to win a the world championship in a nontrivial game. Marion Tinsley (*the* greatest human checkers player ever) wanted to play Chinook for the championship after Chinook started winning competitions. But the American and English checkers associations refused. So Tinsley forced their hand by resigning his title. They gave in, he got to play Chinook, and he won 4 to 2 with 33 ties. On the rematch four years later, after 6 ties, Tinsley withdrew because of stomach pains; and died soon thereafter of pancreatic cancer. So Chinook won, but sadly it did so by default. It's since improved to the point that Chinook likely cannot be beaten by any man or machine. But who knows if Tinsley would have won?

[94]The game environment is called NERO: Neuro-Evolving Robotic Operatives. http://nerogame.org/ Coevolution with NEAT was discussed in Kenneth O. Stanley and Risto Miikkulainen, 2004, Competitive coevolution through evolutionary complexification, *Journal of Artificial Intelligence Research*, 21, 63–100.

Even if your game isn't stochastic, it's also common that you're going to run into a major pathology in 1-Population Competitive coevolution: the presence of **cycles** among game players. That is, Individual *A* beats Individual *B*, and *B* beats *C*, but *C* beats *A*. In that case, who is better? Worse still, perhaps *A* beats *B*, but *B* beats far more individuals than *A* beats. Who's better in that situation? It depends on what you're looking for. Often the case is that you're looking for the individual which wins against the most players; or against the most "good" players, or wins by the most total points on average. In such cases it's common to require multiple tests to identify which individuals are *really* the better ones.

The tradeoff here is how many tests you need to run. If you have a fixed budget of tests, you can spend them on more precisely determining fitness; or you can spend them on searching further. How to spend that budget is yet another parameter to deal with. Different ways of assessing the fitness of individuals lie at different points along this tradeoff spectrum. One simple approach is to pair off all the players, have the pairs play each other, and use the results as fitness. We introduce a Test function which tests two individuals (plays them against each other) and stores the results, which are then used by the fitness assessment procedure. The simple approach is:

Algorithm 77 *Pairwise Relative Fitness Assessment*
1: $P \leftarrow$ population

2: $Q \leftarrow P$, shuffled randomly   ▷ To shuffle an array randomly, see Algorithm 26
3: **for** i from 1 to $||Q||$ by 2 **do**   ▷ We assume $||Q||$ is even
4:     Test(Q_i, Q_{i+1})
5:     AssessFitness(Q_i)   ▷ Using the results of the Test
6:     AssessFitness(Q_{i+1})   ▷ Using the results of the Test
7: **return** P

This has the advantage of only requiring $||P||/2$ tests to assess the fitness of individuals in the population. But each individual only gets to be tested against *one* other individual, which is probably very noisy. An alternative is to test individuals against *every other individual* in the population. The fitness is then based on the various tests the individual received, like so:

Algorithm 78 *Complete Relative Fitness Assessment*
1: $P \leftarrow$ population

2: **for** i from 1 to $||P||$ **do**
3:     **for** j from $i+1$ to $||P||$ **do**
4:         Test(P_i, P_j)
5:     AssessFitness(P_i)   ▷ Using the results of all Tests involving P_i
6: **return** P

This involves each individual in $||P|| - 1$ tests, but as a result it requires $\frac{||P|| \times (||P||-1)}{2}$ tests all told! That's a *lot* of tests. Is the tradeoff worth it? We can strike a middle ground between these two by testing each individual against some *k* other individuals in the population, chosen at random. Some individuals will ultimately get tested more than *k* times, but each individual will get at *least k* tests to assess its fitness. The algorithm looks something like this:

Algorithm 79 *K-fold Relative Fitness Assessment*
1: $P \leftarrow$ population
2: $k \leftarrow$ desired minimum number of tests per individual

3: **for** each individual $P_i \in P$ **do**
4:      $Q \leftarrow k$ unique individuals chosen at random from P, other than P_i
5:      **for** each individual $Q_j \in Q$ **do**
6:          Test(P_i, Q_j)
7:      AssessFitness(P_i)   ▷ Using the results of all Tests involving P_i
8: **return** P

This lets us adjust the number of tests via k. Each individual will be involved in at least k tests, and our total number of tests will be $k \times ||P||$. This might be too much still. If we wanted to be a little more pedantic, we could make sure that each individual had *almost exactly* k tests and the total would be some value $\leq k \times ||P||$. It needs some bookkeeping, and isn't particularly random, but:

Algorithm 80 *More Precise K-fold Relative Fitness Assessment*
1: $P \leftarrow$ population
2: $k \leftarrow$ desired minimum number of tests per individual

3: $R \leftarrow P$ ▷ Holds individuals who've not had enough tests yet
4: **for** each individual $P_i \in P$ **do**
5:      **if** $P_i \in R$ **then**
6:          $R \leftarrow R - \{P_i\}$
7:      **repeat**
8:          **if** $||R|| < k$ **then**
9:              $Q \leftarrow R \cup$ some $||R|| - k$ unique individuals chosen at random from $P - R$, other than P_i
10:         **else**
11:             $Q \leftarrow k$ unique individuals chosen at random from R
12:         **for** each individual $Q_j \in Q$ **do**
13:             Test(P_i, Q_j)
14:             **if** $Q_j \in R$ and Q_j has been involved in at least k tests **then**
15:                 $R \leftarrow R - \{Q_j\}$
16:      **until** P_i has been involved in at least k tests
17: **for** each individual $P_i \in P$ **do**
18:      AssessFitness(P_i)   ▷ Using the results of all Tests involving P_i
19: **return** P

But this still might be too many. If fitness is done simply by counting number of games *won* (as opposed to total score, etc.), another tack is to involve the entire population in a big single-elimination tournament. The fitness of an individual is how high it rises in the tournament:

Algorithm 81 *Single-Elimination Tournament Relative Fitness Assessment*
1: $P \leftarrow$ population ▷ We presume $||P||$ is a power of 2
2: $R \leftarrow P$, shuffled randomly ▷ To shuffle an array randomly, see Algorithm 26
3: **for** i from 1 to $\lg ||P||$ **do** ▷ Oh, all right. lg is $\log_2$
4: $\quad Q \leftarrow R$ ▷ Q holds the current rank of undefeated individuals
5: $\quad R \leftarrow \{\}$ ▷ R will hold the next rank of undefeated individuals
6: $\quad$ **for** j from 1 to $||Q||$ by 2 **do**
7: $\quad\quad$ Test(Q_j, Q_{j+1})
8: $\quad\quad$ **if** Q_j defeated Q_{j+1} in that last Test **then**
9: $\quad\quad\quad R \leftarrow R \cup \{Q_j\}$
10: $\quad\quad$ **else**
11: $\quad\quad\quad R \leftarrow R \cup \{Q_{j+1}\}$
12: **for** each individual $P_i \in P$ **do**
13: $\quad$ AssessFitness(P_i) ▷ Using the results of all Tests involving P_i
14: **return** P

This has exactly $||P|| - 1$ tests, and involves individuals in about 2 tests *on average*. But it has an interesting and important feature that distinguishes it from Pairwise Relative Fitness Assessment (Algorithm 77): individuals which are better *are involved in more tests*. In some sense this lets us be a bit more discerning in distinguishing among our better players (who are more likely to be selected anyway) than in distinguishing among the rabble. The disadvantage is that if the games are fairly noisy, then a good player might be accidentally lost in the rabble. However, Single-Elimination Tournament has often performed very well, *if* your desired test metric is simply based on games won or lost (rather than points).[95]

Single-Elimination and Pairwise Relative Fitness Assessment bring up one cute additional opportunity: **fitnessless selection** (a notion by Wojciech Jaśkowski, Krzysztof Krawiec, and Bartosz Wieloch). Rather than use these methods to compute fitness, we might simply use them to determine the winner in Tournament Selection without ever computing a fitness at all! For example, let's imagine we're using Tournament Selection with a tournament of size 2. We need to select an individual. To do so, we pick two individuals at random from the population and have them play a game right then and there. The winner is the one selected. More specifically, if our tournament size n is a power of 2, we could select n unique individuals at random from the population, and put them through a little single-elimination tournament. The winner of the tournament is selected. We could hash the tournament results to avoid replaying individuals in the off-chance they've played against one another before.[97]

---

[95]Yes, yes, you could construct a double-elimination tournament algorithm as well, or World-Cup soccer tournament algorithm. But for heavens' sakes, don't model it after the BCS![96]

[96]http://en.wikipedia.org/wiki/Bowl_Championship_Series

[97]In theory, this notion of lazy fitness assessment could be done for regular evolutionary computation too: only assess the fitness of individuals once they've been entered into a Tournament Selection tournament. But the number of individuals who are *never* picked, at random, for *any* tournament during the selection process, is probably pretty small, so it's not a huge advantage. Fitnessless selection was proposed in Wojciech Jaśkowski, Krzysztof Krawiec, and Bartosz Wieloch, 2008, Fitnessless coevolution, in Conor Ryan and Maarten Keijzer, editors, *Genetic and Evolutionary Computation Conference (GECCO)*, pages 355–362, ACM.

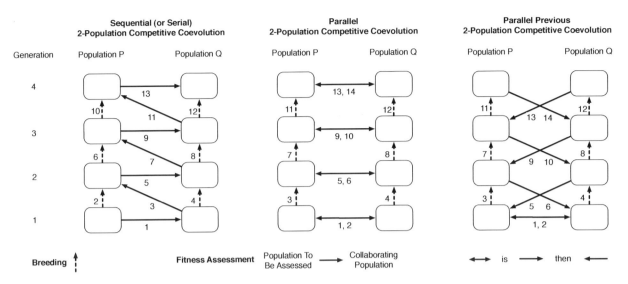

Figure 42 Three different fitness assessment and breeding strategies for 2-Population Competitive Coevolution. Shown are the two populations going through successive generations. Numbers indicate the order in which either breeding or fitness assessment takes place.

Two more items of note. First, it may be possible to improve the gradient even further by playing not against other individuals in the current generation, but against ones in, say, the previous generation. See the discussion of Algorithm 87 for more on that trick. Second, 1-Population Competitive Coevolution's nice gradient-reduction feature is hardly a panacea. It's still fairly easy for the whole population to get stuck in notorious local optima. For example, if you're looking for an optimal soccer team, your initial population might contain terrible arbitrary players, but one or two of them contain players which simply go to the ball and kick it into the goal (easy procedures). These rack up such huge scores against the terrible players that soon the entire population consists of teams of players who all go straight to the ball and try to kick it to the goal, and the population just won't budge from that local optimum, forcing you to rethink how to assess fitness.[98]

6.2 2-Population Competitive Coevolution

2-Population Competitive Coevolution finds robust solutions by simultaneously looking for good solutions while searching for the places in the space of test cases that are most challenging. The idea is simple and appealing: we construct not one but *two* populations (or if you like, subpopulations or **demes**). Population P will contain the individuals we're trying to robustify. Population Q will contain **test cases** to challenge the individuals in P. The fitness of individuals in population P will be based on how well they perform against the individuals in population Q, and likewise, the individuals in Q will be assessed based on how well they perform against the individuals in population P.

I call P the **primary population** and Q the **alternative** or **foil population**. Ultimately we're really just interested in the primary population. Thus, unlike 1-Population Competitive Coevolution, we only bother to assess the external fitness of population P, and likewise only maintain the best individuals from P. Rarely are the best of Q interesting. When we test one population in the context of the other (be it P or Q), the other population is known as the **collaborating population**.

---

[98]This happened to me.

The classic illustration of 2-Population Competitive Coevolution is Danny Hillis's[99] attempt to discover optimal **sorting networks**. A sorting network is a series of comparisons on elements in the array which, when completed, results in the array being sorted. Each comparison compares two fixed elements in the array. If the upper item is smaller than the lower item, then the two items are swapped. Some comparisons can be done in parallel, and the whole mechanism is attractive because it can be done in hardware. The objective is not only to find a *correct* sorting network, but one which has the *fewest* comparisons possible.

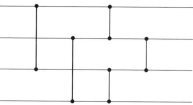

Figure 43 A sorting network for an array of four numbers. Vertical lines indicate comparisons. Progresses left to right. Two of the comparisons can be done in parallel.

The problem of finding an optimal sorting network is one which requires test cases: there are lots and lots of different arrays of numbers to test against, and you need to find a network which works properly with all of them. Hillis began with a population of sorting networks and tested each one against a random sample of test cases. However, a random sample was unlikely to provide those pathological test cases that would be particularly difficult for an individual. To deal with this, Hillis turned to 2-Population Competitive Coevolution: he coevolved a population of sorting networks against a competing population of *hard-to-sort arrays of numbers*. The fitness of a sorting network was the number of arrays it got correct; and the fitness of an array was the number of sorting networks it stumped. Thus while the sorting networks were improving themselves, the arrays were finding harder corner cases to challenge the sorting networks.

Because it has mutliple populations, 2-Population Competitive coevolution introduces new ways to interleave fitness assessment and breeding. Three are shown in Figure 42. The first way is to assess the internal fitness of P in the context of Q (and also assess P's external fitness), then breed P, then assess the internal fitness of Q in the context of the new P, then breed Q, and so forth. This is known as a **sequential** or **serial** 2-Population Competitive Coevolutionary Algorithm:

Algorithm 82 *An Abstract Sequential 2-Population Competitive Coevolutionary Algorithm*

1: $P \leftarrow$ Build Initial Population
2: $Q \leftarrow$ Build Initial Alternative Population
3: $Best \leftarrow \square$
4: **repeat**
5:     AssessInternalFitness(P, Q)
6:     AssessExternalFitness(P)   ▷ Used to determine algorithm progress and *Best*.
7:     **for** each individual $P_i \in P$ **do**
8:         **if** $Best = \square$ or ExternalFitness(P_i) > ExternalFitness($Best$) **then**
9:             $Best \leftarrow P_i$
10:    $P \leftarrow$ Join(P, Breed(P))
11:    AssessInternalFitness(Q, P)
12:    $Q \leftarrow$ Join(Q, Breed(Q))
13: **until** *Best* is the ideal solution or we have run out of time
14: **return** *Best*

---

[99]Google his name. Danny Hillis invented the coolest supercomputer ever. Hillis's coevolution paper is Daniel Hillis, 1990, Co-evolving parasites improve simulated evolution as an optimization procedure, *Physica D*, 42(1–3). It's a famous paper, but it has some oddities, including a pretty unusual **diploid** representation with two copies of each gene.

This requires some way to assess the internal fitness of a population in the context of its collaborating population. The straightforward way to do it is to sample k individuals from the collaborating population to test against:

Algorithm 83 *K-fold Relative Fitness Assessment with an Alternative Population*
1: $M \leftarrow$ population to be Tested
2: $C \leftarrow$ collaborating Population   ▷ Either one could be P or Q, depending
3: $k \leftarrow$ desired minimum number of tests per individual

4: **for** each individual $M_i \in M$ **do**
5:     $W \leftarrow k$ unique individuals chosen at random from C
6:     **for** each individual $W_j \in W$ **do**
7:        Test(M_i, W_j)
8:     AssessFitness(M_i)   ▷ Using the results of all Tests involving M_i
9: **return** M

Notice that we didn't call the two populations P and Q, but rather M and C, because either one could be P (and the other Q), depending on which population is being assessed.

Sequential 2-Population Competitive Coevolution has two downsides which make it less than attractive. First, Q must be tested against the new, improved P, always one step ahead of it. Second, the assessments are separated, which means you can't combine AssessInternalFitness(P, Q) and AssessInternalFitness(Q, P). Probably when you were testing P, you got some fitness information about individuals in Q as well. Why throw that information away? This leads to our second method: a **parallel** 2-Population Competitive Coevolutionary Algorithm. Here, each population is tested against the other, and *then* both of them breed. This solves both of these problems: neither population has a leg up on the other by design, and we can group internal fitness assessment together for both populations:

Algorithm 84 *An Abstract Parallel 2-Population Competitive Coevolutionary Algorithm*
1: $P \leftarrow$ Build Initial Population
2: $Q \leftarrow$ Build Initial Alternative Population
3: $Best \leftarrow \square$
4: **repeat**
5:     AssessInternalFitness(P, Q)   ▷ Internal fitness assessment could be done simultaneously
6:     AssessInternalFitness(Q, P)
7:     AssessExternalFitness(P)   ▷ Used to determine algorithm progress and *Best*.
8:     **for** each individual $P_i \in P$ **do**
9:        **if** $Best = \square$ or ExternalFitness(P_i) $>$ ExternalFitness($Best$) **then**
10:           $Best \leftarrow P_i$
11:     $P \leftarrow$ Join(P, Breed(P))
12:     $Q \leftarrow$ Join(Q, Breed(Q))
13: **until** *Best* is the ideal solution or we have run out of time
14: **return** *Best*

We could do the internal fitness tests separately still if we liked. But if we wished, we could test them together. For example, if the two populations were the same size, we could shuffle P, then test each individual P_i against the corresponding individual Q_i. To do further tests, we might test each P_i against Q_{i+1}, then Q_{i+2}, and so on, wrapping around as necessary. But this creates statistical dependencies among the tests: for example, individuals P_i and P_{i+1} would be tested against almost exactly the same individuals, which is probably not good. Instead we could shuffle the population P each time, but then we'd like to guarantee that in the shuffling certain individuals never get paired up again if they've been tested together before. A quick-and-dirty, not particularly elegant solution to that is to shuffle P each time, then as long as there is a pair that's already been tested before, we break up that pair. It's a hack. Here we go:

Algorithm 85 *K-fold Relative Joint Fitness Assessment with an Alternative Population*
1: $P \leftarrow$ population
2: $Q \leftarrow$ alternative Population
3: $k \leftarrow$ desired minimum number of tests per individual

4: $P' \leftarrow P$, shuffled randomly   ▷ To shuffle an array randomly, see Algorithm 26
5: **for** j from 1 to k **do**
6:    **for** i from 1 to $||P||$ **do**   ▷ We assume that $||P|| = ||Q||$
7:       Test(P'_i, Q_i)
8:    Shuffle P' randomly
9:    **while** there is a value i where P'_i and Q_i have already been tested together **do**
10:       Swap P'_i with some randomly chosen individual P'_l
11: **for** i from 1 to $||P||$ **do**
12:    AssessFitness(P'_i)   ▷ Using the results of all Tests involving P'_i
13:    AssessFitness(Q_i)   ▷ Using the results of all Tests involving Q_i
14: **return** P, Q

External fitness assessment can be a problem for both of these options (if you care about doing it). You can't test against Q per se, because Q keeps changing (and ideally improving), and so you won't get a consistent, absolute fitness metric for P. It's the same conundrum that occurs in 1-Population Competitive Coevolution. Perhaps you could create a fixed sample drawn from the test-case space and test against that; or create a guru of some sort.

One last option is to assess each population against the *previous* generation of the collaborating population. This might help improve the gradient a bit because each population is given a bit easier time. Except for the first generation, we're back to testing populations separately again. I call this the **Parallel Previous 2-Population Competitive Coevolutionary Algorithm**.[100]

---
[100]Parallel Previous brings up one interesting approach to doing external fitness assessment: report how well you defeated the previous generation. This fitness metric is essentially measuring the *slope* of your fitness improvement: if it's positive, you're making progress.

Algorithm 86 *An Abstract Parallel Previous 2-Population Competitive Coevolutionary Algorithm*
1: $P \leftarrow$ Build Initial Population
2: $Q \leftarrow$ Build Initial Alternative Population
3: $Best \leftarrow \square$
4: AssessInternalFitness(P, Q) ▷ Internal fitness assessment could be done simultaneously
5: AssessInternalFitness(Q, P)
6: AssessExternalFitness(P)
7: **for** each individual $P_i \in P$ **do**
8:     **if** $Best = \square$ or ExternalFitness(P_i) > ExternalFitness($Best$) **then**
9:         $Best \leftarrow P_i$
10: **repeat**
11:     $P' \leftarrow$ Join(P, Breed(P)) ▷ We do this to let us test against the previous generation
12:     $Q' \leftarrow$ Join(Q, Breed(Q)) ▷ Ditto
13:     AssessInternalFitness(P', Q)
14:     AssessInternalFitness(Q', P)
15:     AssessExternalFitness(P')
16:     **for** each individual $P'_i \in P'$ **do**
17:         **if** ExternalFitness(P'_i) > ExternalFitness($Best$) **then**
18:             $Best \leftarrow P'_i$
19:     $P \leftarrow P'$
20:     $Q \leftarrow Q'$
21: **until** *Best* is the ideal solution or we have run out of time
22: **return** *Best*

There is one nifty thing you can do with the Parallel Previous version: because individuals are being tested against *last generations' individuals*, we know those previous generations' individuals' fitnesses already. That means that we could choose to test not just against random individuals but against, say, the fittest individuals of the previous population. To test against the fittest individuals of a collaborating population:

Algorithm 87 *K-fold Relative Fitness Assessment with the Fittest of an Alternative Population*
1: $M \leftarrow$ population to be Tested ▷ Either P or Q could be M or C
2: $C \leftarrow$ collaborating Population ▷ Individuals in C already have their fitnesses assessed
3: $k \leftarrow$ desired minimum number of tests per individual

4: $C' \leftarrow C$ sorted by fitness, fittest individuals first
5: **for** each individual $M_i \in M$ **do**
6:     **for** j from 1 to k **do**
7:         Test(M_i, C'_j)
8:     AssessFitness(M_i) ▷ Using the results of all Tests involving M_i
9: **return** M

Of course, you could do a mix of the Parallel and Parallel Previous methods: test an individual against some *k* individuals from the current-generation collaborating population, and *also* test the individual against the *n* fittest individuals from the previous-generation collaborating population. This could also work with 1-Population Competitive Coevolution as well. In that case, *M* is the current generation of the individuals and *C* is the *previous generation* of the same individuals.

Arms Races and Loss of Gradient 2-Population Competitive Coevolution is often viewed as an abstract version of a biological **arms race**: one population learns a trick, forcing the second population to learn a new trick to beat the first one, and so on. In an ideal world, the arms race results in a natural, gradual build-up of gradient, so we're not faced with the Needle-in-a-Haystack scenario as had been shown in Figure 41.

Sadly, this is often not the case. Instead, one population may have an easier optimization task, and so it improves so rapidly that it leaves the other population in the dust. At some point all the individuals in one population (say, *Q*) are so good that they *all* defeat the individuals in *P* soundly. When this happens, all the individuals in *Q* now basically have all the same fitness, because they all beat everyone in *P*. Likewise all the individuals in *P* have the same fitness because they all lose to everyone in *Q*.

This condition is called **loss of gradient**: the selection operator no longer has anything to go on, and starts picking individuals at random. This usually causes the external fitness to start *dropping* until the populations reestablish gradient again, resulting in the maddening situation shown in Figure 44. This isn't an easy thing

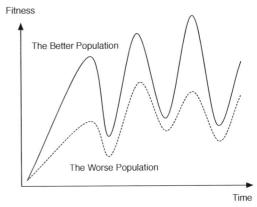

Figure 44 Loss of Gradient. One population periodically improves so much that selection starts to fail, causing a drop in fitness.

to fix, though here's one strategy: if you can somehow detect that a population is improving too rapidly and loss of gradient is seeping in, you might pause the evolution of that population until gradient is reestablished. Of course, you'd need to think about how to detect that: perhaps lower variance among the fitnesses in your populations?

You might also try using the Parallel Previous variation: I suspect (but have no evidence that) it will dampen loss of gradient a bit.

6.3 N-Population Cooperative Coevolution

Competitive coevolution tries to improve individuals by pitting them against other individuals. In contrast, cooperative coevolution, proposed by Mitchell Potter and Ken De Jong,[101] strives to find individuals who work well together. Why would you want to do that? The issue is this: some optimization spaces are high-dimensional and gigantic. Cooperative coevolution simplifies those spaces by breaking them into multiple, much simpler, subspaces for different populations to search.

---

[101] I think the earliest of their publications on the matter is Mitchell Potter and Kenneth De Jong, 1994, A cooperative coevolutionary approach to function optimization, in Yuval Davidor, Hans-Paul Schwefel, and Reinhard Manner, editors, *Proceedings of the Third Conference on Parallel Problem Solving from Nature*, pages 249–257. The two then more fully fleshed it out in Mitchell A. Potter and Kenneth A. De Jong, 2000, Cooperative coevolution: An architecture for evolving coadapted subcomponents, *Evolutionary Computation*, 8(1), 1–29.

Let's say you're looking for an optimal robot soccer team. Each team has eleven different players, all of whom you believe must have unique robot behaviors[102] There are 1000 different behaviors for each robot. As a result, you are trying to find an optimal setting in a space of 1000^{11} (or 100000000000000000000000000000000) possibilities. That's a big number.

Here's what you could do instead. For each robot, create an arbitrary set of behaviors for everyone *but* that robot. Then use an optimization method to find the optimal robot behavior given his arbitrary team of fixed collaborating robots. At the end, take the optimal robots and put them together to form a final team. This requires 11 optimization runs, each of which is over a simple space of only 1000 possibilities. However there's no guarantee that those robots will work together well at the end: after all they were not designed for one another but rather were designed to be the best robot given the arbitrary team they were forced to work with.

N-Population Cooperative Coevolution strikes a middle-ground between these two situations. We perform 11 optimization runs at one time, but individuals in each run are tested by grouping them with the current individuals *from the other runs*. We do this by creating 11 populations: a population of goalies, a population of left fullbacks, a population of right fullbacks, ... etc. Each population has its own optimization process. When an individual from a population needs to be tested as part of his fitness assessment, we group it with individuals selected from the other populations to form a complete soccer team. We then play a match, and the match results become the individual's test results.

In short, each of the populations in *N*-Population Cooperative Coevolution is finding an optimal **subsolution**: a sub-part of the complete solution. This allows us to break a search space of size n^a into n search spaces each of size a, a huge reduction in complexity. In 2-Population Cooperative Coevolution, there was one specific population of interest to us. But now all the populations are of interest to us because they are each solving a piece of the problem. We can easily construct an external fitness to gauge the system: it's the fittest collaboration we've found so far among the individuals in the various populations.

N-Population Cooperative Coevolution can be done in any of the same frameworks that were shown in Figure 42 for 2-Population Competitive Coevolution, but in truth, we only really see the Sequential and Parallel methods in practice. Whereas the Sequential method has problems for Competitive Coevolution, it's a fine technique for Cooperative Coevolution, assuming that we have the time to waste on additional tests.[103] So rather than show Internal and External fitness assessment, we'll just assess a **joint fitness**, and then store in *Best* the fittest joint *vector* of individuals, one from each population, that we've found so far.

---

[102]If you were smart about it, you might instead just have four behaviors: one for the goalie, one that all defenders use, one that all midfielders uses, and one that all attackers use. That'd be a lot simpler space to search.

[103]Sequential *N*-Population Cooperative Coevolution is an example of an **Alternating Optimization (AO)** algorithm. AO algorithms presume that you are trying to optimize a function $f(\vec{x})$ by breaking $\vec{x}$ into various smaller variables $\langle x_1, ..., x_n \rangle$. To start, you assign arbitrary values to each of the x_i. Then you optimize x_1 while holding the other x_i fixed. Once x_1 is sufficiently optimized, you fix it to its new value, and now optimize x_2 while holding all other x_i fixed. Continue this process up through x_n. Then repeat again, optimizing x_1 with the others fixed, and so on. Sound familiar? AO doesn't presume any particular optimization method for each of the x_i: it's just a framework for a variety of algorithms. If you're interested, other (famous but non-metaheuristic) algorithms which fall squarely under the AO banner are **Expectation Maximization (EM)** and its degenerate variation **k-Means Clustering**, techniques for finding clusters in data.

Algorithm 88 *An Abstract Sequential N-Population Cooperative Coevolutionary Algorithm (CCEA)*
1: $P^{(1)}, ..., P^{(n)} \leftarrow$ Build n Initial Populations
2: $\overrightarrow{Best} \leftarrow \square$
3: **repeat**
4:     **for** i from 1 to n **do**
5:         AssessJointFitness($\langle i \rangle, P^{(1)}, ..., P^{(n)}$)   ▷ Computes fitness values for only population $P^{(i)}$
6:         **for** each vector $\vec{s}$ of individuals $\langle P_a^{(1)}, ..., P_z^{(n)} \rangle : P_a^{(1)} \in P^{(1)}$, etc., assessed in Line 5 **do**
7:             **if** $\overrightarrow{Best} = \square$ or JointFitness($\vec{s}$) > JointFitness($\overrightarrow{Best}$) **then**
8:                 $\overrightarrow{Best} \leftarrow \vec{s}$
9:         $P^{(i)} \leftarrow$ Join($P^{(i)}$, Breed($P^{(i)}$))
10: **until** $\overrightarrow{Best}$ is the ideal solution or we have run out of time
11: **return** $\overrightarrow{Best}$

Note that in the For-loop we assess some joint fitnesses but only apply them to the individuals in population $P^{(i)}$. We could do that with a variant of algorithm 83 which works like this. For each individual in $P^{(i)}$ we perform some k tests by grouping that individual with randomly-chosen individuals from the other populations to form a complete solution:

Algorithm 89 *K-fold Joint Fitness Assessment with $N - 1$ Collaborating Populations*
1: $P^{(1)}, ..., P^{(n)} \leftarrow$ populations
2: $i \leftarrow$ index number of the Population to be Tested
3: $k \leftarrow$ desired minimum number of tests per individual

4: $\vec{s} \leftarrow \langle s_1, ..., s_n \rangle$ an (empty for now) complete solution   ▷ We'll fill it up with individuals
5: **for** each individual $P_j^{(i)} \in P^{(i)}$ **do**   ▷ For each individual to test...
6:     **for** w from 1 to k **do**   ▷ Do k tests...
7:         **for** l from 1 to n **do**   ▷ Build a complete solution including the individual to test
8:             **if** $l = i$ **then**   ▷ It's the individual to test
9:                 $s_l = P_j^{(l)}$
10:             **else**   ▷ Pick a random collaborator
11:                 $s_l =$ individual chosen at random from $P^{(l)}$
12:         Test($\vec{s}$)   ▷ Test the complete solution
13:     AssessFitness($P_j^{(i)}$)   ▷ Using the results of all Tests involving $P_j^{(i)}$
14: **return** $P^{(1)}, ..., P^{(n)}$

We've abandoned here any attempt of using *unique* collaborators: but you can do that if you really want to try it. I don't think it's that valuable because the space is so much larger. The Sequential approach is the original method proposed by Potter and De Jong, and it still remains popular. But, in the formulation described above, it's wasteful because we do many tests but only use them to assess the fitness of a single individual—the collaborators are forgotten about. We could fix that by keeping around the previous tests and including them when we get around to testing the collaborating individuals for *their* fitness assessment. Or we could just do the Parallel approach. Specifically, we test everyone together, then breed everyone at once:

Algorithm 90 *An Abstract Parallel N-Population Cooperative Coevolutionary Algorithm*
1: $P^{(1)}, ..., P^{(n)} \leftarrow$ Build n Initial Populations
2: $\overrightarrow{Best} \leftarrow \square$
3: **repeat**
4:     AssessJointFitness($\langle 1, ..., n \rangle, P^{(1)}, ..., P^{(n)}$)   ▷ Computes fitness values for all populations
5:     **for** each vector $\vec{s}$ of individuals $\langle P_a^{(1)}, ..., P_z^{(n)} \rangle : P_a^{(1)} \in P^{(1)}$, etc., assessed in Line 4 **do**
6:         **if** $\overrightarrow{Best} = \square$ or JointFitness($\vec{s}$) > JointFitness($\overrightarrow{Best}$) **then**
7:             $\overrightarrow{Best} \leftarrow \vec{s}$
8:     **for** i from 1 to n **do**
9:         $P^{(i)} \leftarrow$ Join($P^{(i)}$, Breed($P^{(i)}$))
10: **until** $\overrightarrow{Best}$ is the ideal solution or we have run out of time
11: **return** $\overrightarrow{Best}$

This doesn't look like a big change, but it is. Because we can group all the joint fitnesses together at one time, we can save some testing time by not doing further tests on collaborators who've been involved in a sufficient number of tests already. We could do this with a variation of Algorithm 85, but with $N > 2$ it might suffice to just pick collaborators at random, even if some by chance get tested more than others, hence:

Algorithm 91 *K-fold Joint Fitness Assessment of N Populations*
1: $P^{(1)}, ..., P^{(n)} \leftarrow$ populations
2: $k \leftarrow$ desired minimum number of tests per individual

3: $\vec{s} \leftarrow \langle s_1, ..., s_n \rangle$ an (empty for now) complete solution   ▷ We'll fill it up with individuals
4: **for** i from 1 to n **do**   ▷ For each population...
5:     **for** each individual $P_j^{(i)} \in P^{(i)}$ **do**   ▷ For each individual in that population...
6:         $m \leftarrow$ number of tests individual $P_j^{(i)}$ has been involved in so far
7:         **for** w from $m+1$ to k **do**   ▷ Do at most k tests...
8:             **for** l from 1 to n **do**   ▷ Build a complete solution including the individual to test
9:                 **if** $l = i$ **then**   ▷ It's the individual to test
10:                     $s_l = P_j^{(l)}$
11:                 **else**   ▷ Pick a random collaborator
12:                     $s_l =$ individual chosen at random from $P^{(l)}$
13:             Test($\vec{s}$)   ▷ Test the complete solution
14: **for** i from 1 to n **do**
15:     **for** each individual $P_j^{(i)} \in P^{(i)}$ **do**
16:         AssessFitness($P_j^{(i)}$)   ▷ Using the results of all Tests involving $P_j^{(i)}$
17: **return** $P^{(1)}...P^{(n)}$

Pathological Conditions in Testing So what could go wrong? For one, there's the theoretical possibility of **laziness**. If certain populations are doing impressively, other populations may just come along for the ride. For example, let's say you're trying to find an optimal team of basketball players. You've got a population of centers, of forwards, of guards, etc. Your guard population has converged largely to consist of copies of Michael Jordan. The Michael Jordans are so impressive that the population of (say) forwards doesn't need to do any work for the team to be near optimal. In essence, all the forwards' fitnesses look the same to the system: regardless of the forward selected, the team does really really well. So the system winds up selecting forwards at random and the forwards don't improve. This condition is the cooperative equivalent of the Loss of Gradient pathology discussed earlier. The basic solution to this is to change your fitness function to be more sensitive to how the forwards are doing. For example, you might apply some kind of **credit assignment** scheme to assign the fitness differently to different cooperating individuals. Be careful: the system is now likely no longer cooperative, that is, coordinating individuals no longer receive the same fitness, and this can result in unexpected dynamics.

Laziness is the tip of the iceberg though. How do you assess the fitness of a cooperative coevolutionary individual based on tests? Early on it was thought that you might base it on the *average* of the test results with various collaborators from the other population(s). Let's say that there is one optimal joint solution, but the hill leading to it is very small; whereas there's a large suboptimal peak elsewhere, as in Figure 45. If we tested individuals $A1$ and $A2$ with many individuals from Population B and took the average, $A1$ would appear fitter *on average* even though $A2$ was actually a collaborator in the optimum. $A1$ is a jack-of-all-trades-but-master-of-none individual which is never phenomenal anywhere, but most of the time it's involved in a joint solution that's better than average.

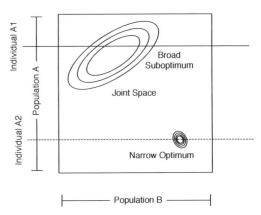

Figure 45 Relative Overgeneralization.

This situation leads to a pathological condition called **relative overgeneralization**, where the populations converge to joint solutions which are suboptimal, but involve lots of jacks-of-all-trades. Paul Wiegand discovered this unfortunate situation.[104] The way to fix this is to assess fitness as the *maximum* of the tests rather than their average. However to get good results you may need to do a **lot** of tests, perhaps even against the *entire* other population. It turns out that usually there are just a few "special" collaborators in the other population(s) which, if you tested just with them, would compute fitness orderings for your entire population in exactly the same way as testing against *everyone*. Liviu Panait, a former student of mine, developed a 2-population cooperative algorithm, **iCCEA**, which computes this **archive** of special collaborators, resulting in far fewer tests.[105]

Finally, if your fitness function has multiple global optima, or near-optima, you could also wind up victim to **miscoordination**.[106] Let's say you have two cooperating populations, A and B,

---

[104]See Paul's thesis: R. Paul Wiegand, 2004, *An Analysis of Cooperative Coevolutionary Algorithms*, Ph.D. thesis, George Mason University, Fairfax, Virginia.

[105]See his thesis: Liviu Panait, 2006, *The Analysis and Design of Concurrent Learning Algorithms for Cooperative Multiagent Systems*, Ph.D. thesis, George Mason University, Fairfax, Virginia.

[106]Miscoordination isn't a disaster: an explorative enough system will find its way out. But it's worthwhile mentioning that it *is* a disaster in a sister technique in artificial intelligence, multiagent reinforcement learning.

and two global optima, 1 and 2. The two optima are offset from one another as shown in Figure 46. Population *A* has discovered an individual *A1* who is part of global optimum 1 (yay!), and likewise Population *B* has discovered an individual *B2* who is part of global optimum 2 (yay!). But neither of these individuals will survive, because Population *A* hasn't yet discovered individual *A2* who, when collaborating with *B2*, would help *B2* shine. Likewise Population *B* hasn't yet found individual *B1* who would make *A1* look great. In the worst case, these populations are trying out *A1* and *B2* in combination, which winds up in a quite suboptimal region of the joint space. Thus, though *A1* and *B2* are optimal for their respective populations, the populations can't tell: they look bad.

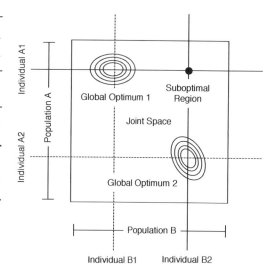

Figure 46 Miscoordination.

6.4 Niching: Diversity Maintenance Methods

To add exploration in your system, perhaps to prevent it from converging too rapidly to suboptimal solutions, there are many options available. So far we've considered:

- Increasing your sample (population) size

- Adding noise to your Tweak procedure

- Being less selective among individuals (picking less fit ones more often)

- Adding random restarts to your system

- Adding explicit separation constraints in your population (as is done in various parallel stochastic optimization approaches like Island Models or Spatially-embedded Models)

- Explicitly trying to add different individuals from the current ones in the population (as is done in Scatter Search with Path Relinking)

One approach we've not yet considered is to punish individuals in some way for being too similar to one another. For example, we might explicitly lower the fitness of individuals if they're too close to other individuals (**fitness sharing**). Or we could pick individuals to die based on how similar they are to new incoming children in a steady-state or generation-gap algorithm (**crowding**). These approaches all affect the survivability of individual *A* (versus individual *B*) based on whether or not there exists some individual *C* (which is similar to *A*), in the population already, or being introduced new to the population. Thus these methods are coevolutionary in nature.[107]

Before we examine techniques, we need to consider what *similar* means. Two individuals can be similar in at least three ways:

---

[107] One additional diversity maintenance approach we won't really discuss here — it's not coevolutionary in nature — is **incest prevention**. Here, individuals are not permitted to cross over with other individuals if they share a parent (or a grandparent, or however deep you'd like to go). There has also been a bit of work on what I call **explicit speciation**, where each individual has a small tag which indicates its "species" (the tag can be mutated), and selection or breeding is constrained in some way to be mostly within species. This usually is for other purposes than diversity maintenance.

- *Phenotypically*: they behave similarly.

- *Genotypically*: they have roughly the same makeup when it comes to breeding.

- Individuals may have similar *fitness*.

Ideally we're looking for a phenotypical similarity: but often it's not easy to determine what that is exactly — or perhaps your phenotypes and genotypes are basically identical. So often one settles on some notion of genotypical similarity. Fitness similarity makes no sense in this context: but when we get to multi-objective algorithms (which have more than one fitness measure), it will suddenly make lots of sense!

To determine how similar individuals are, we'll need some kind of **distance measure** which ideally defines a **metric distance**[108] in the phenotypical (or genotypical) space. If your individuals already reside in a metric space, you're in luck. For example, if your individuals are vectors of real-valued numbers (individual i has the genotype $\langle i_1, ..., i_n \rangle$ and individual j has the genotype $\langle j_1, ..., j_n \rangle$), and you're making the assumption that genotype distance is the same as phenotype distance, then you might use the sum squared genotype distance, that is, $d(i,j) = \sqrt{\sum_k (i_k - j_k)^2}$. For boolean vectors, you could use the **Hamming distance**, which counts the number of times that two genes are different, that is, $d(i,j) = \sum_k i_k \oplus j_k$, where $\oplus$ is the XOR (exclusive OR) operator. If your individuals are more complex — trees, say — have a lot of fun defining a distance measure among them!

6.4.1 Fitness Sharing

The idea behind **fitness sharing** is to encourage diversity in individuals by reducing their fitness for being too similar to one another.[109] The most common form of fitness sharing, proposed by David Goldberg and Jon Richardson, requires you to define a *neighborhood radius* σ. We punish a given individual's fitness if there are other individuals within that radius. The more individuals inside that radius, and the closer the individuals are to the given individual, the worse its fitness.

Given our distance function $d(i,j)$, we compute a *sharing function* s between two individuals i and j, which tells us how much punishment i will receive for j being near it:

$$s(i,j) = \begin{cases} 1 - (d(i,j)/\sigma)^\alpha & \text{if } d(i,j) < \sigma \\ 0 & \text{otherwise} \end{cases}$$

$\alpha > 0$ is a tuning parameter you can set to change the degree of punishment i receives for j being particularly close by. The size of σ is tricky: too small and the force for diversity is weak; but

---

[108] A metric space is a space where we can construct a distance measure which obeys the *triangle inequality*. More specifically, the distance function $d(i,j)$ must have the following properties. First, it should always be ≥ 0 (what's a negative distance?). Second, it should be 0 only if $i = j$. Third, the distance from i to j should be the same as the distance from j to i. And last, the triangle inequality: for any three points i, j, and k, it must always be true that $d(i,k) \leq d(i,j) + d(j,k)$. That is, going from point i to point k directly is always at least as short as taking a detour through j. Metric spaces include ordinary multi-dimensional real-valued Euclidian space and the space of boolean vectors (using Hamming distance). But what's the metric space of trees? Does one even exist?

[109] The term "fitness *sharing*" is unfortunate: they're not sharing fitness with one another. They're all just having their fitnesses reduced because they're too close to one another. The technique was first discussed, I believe, in David Goldberg and Jon Richardson, 1987, Genetic algorithms with sharing for multimodal function optimization, in John J. Grefenstette, editor, *Proceedings of the Second International Conference on Genetic Algorithms*, pages 41–49, Lawrence Erlbaum Associates.

it shouldn't be so large that multiple optima fall in the same neighborhood (or even close to that). Now we adjust the fitness as follows:

$$f_i = \frac{(r_i)^\beta}{\sum_j s(i,j)}$$

r_i is the actual (raw) fitness of individual i and f_i is the adjusted fitness we will use for the individual instead. $\beta > 1$ is a scaling factor which you'll need to tune carefully. If it's too small, individuals won't move towards optima out of fear of crowding too near one another. If it's too large, crowding will have little effect. Of course you probably don't know much about the locations of your optima (which is why you're using an optimization algorithm!), hence the problem. So there you have it, three parameters to fiddle with: α, β, and σ.

If your fitness assessment is based on testing an individual against a bank of test problems (for example, seeing which of 300 test problems it's able to solve), you have another, simpler way to do all this. Robert Smith, Stephanie Forrest, and Alan Perelson have proposed an **implicit fitness sharing**:[110] if an individual can perform well on a certain test case and few other individuals can do so, then the individual gets a big boost in fitness. The approach Smith, Forrest, and Perelson took was to repeatedly sample from the population over and over again, and base fitness on those samples. In Implicit Fitness Sharing, you must divide the spoils with everyone else who did as well as you did on a given test.

Algorithm 92 *Implicit Fitness Sharing*

1: $P \leftarrow$ population
2: $k \leftarrow$ number of times we should sample ▷ Should be much bigger than $||P||$
3: $\sigma \leftarrow$ how many individuals per sample
4: $T \leftarrow$ test problems used to assess fitness

5: $C \leftarrow ||P||$ by $||T||$ matrix, initially all zeros ▷ $C_{i,j}$ is how often individual P_i was in a sample for T_j
6: $R \leftarrow ||P||$ by $||T||$ matrix, initially all zeros ▷ $R_{i,j}$ is individual P_i's sum total reward for T_j
7: **for** each $T_j \in T$ **do**
8:     **for** k times **do**
9:         $Q \leftarrow \sigma$ unique individuals chosen at random from P
10:         **for** each individual $Q_l \in Q$ **do**
11:             $i \leftarrow$ index of Q_l in P
12:             $C_{i,j} \leftarrow C_{i,j} + 1$
13:         $S \leftarrow$ individual(s) in Q which performed best on T_j ▷ Everyone in S performed the same
14:         **for** each individual $S_l \in S$ **do**
15:             $i \leftarrow$ index of S_l in P
16:             $R_{i,j} \leftarrow R_{i,j} + 1/||S||$
17: **for** each individual P_i in P **do**
18:     Fitness(P_i) $\leftarrow \sum_j R_{i,j}/C_{i,j}$
19: **return** P

---

[110]This was part of a larger effort to develop optimization algorithms fashioned as **artificial immune systems**. The authors first suggested it in Robert Smith, Stephanie Forrest, and Alan Perelson, 1992, Population diversity in an immune system model: Implications for genetic search, in L. Darrell Whitley, editor, *Proceedings of the Second Workshop on Foundations of Genetic Algorithms*, pages 153–165, Morgan Kaufmann.

Note that it's possible that an individual will never get tested with this algorithm, especially if k is too small: you will want to check for this and include the individual in a few tests.

Believe it or not, this is quite similar to fitness sharing: the "neighborhood" of an individual is phenotypical: those individuals who solved similar test problems. You'll again need a "neighborhood radius" σ. But this time instead of defining an explicit radius in phenotype space, the "radius" is a sample size of individuals that compete for a given test problem t. You'll need to fiddle with the new σ as well, but it's likely not as sensitive. k is a parameter which should be as large as you can afford (time-wise) to get a good sample.

6.4.2 Crowding

Crowding doesn't reduce the fitness of individuals for being too similar; rather it makes them more likely to be picked for death in a steady-state system. Though steady-state evolution is usually exploitative, the diversity mechanism of crowding counters at least some of that. The original version of crowding, by Ken De Jong,[111] was similar to a steady-state mechanism: each generation we breed some n new individuals. Then one by one we insert the individuals in the population, replacing some individual already there. The individual selected to die is chosen using Tournament Selection not based on fitness but on *similarity* with the individual to insert. Note that because of the one-by-one insertion, some of the individuals chosen to die might be some of those n children; so this isn't *quite* a steady-state algorithm. But it's fine to do crowding by using a plain-old steady-state algorithm with selection for death based on similarity to the inserted child.

As it turns out, crowding doesn't perform all that well. But we can augment it further by requiring that the child only replaces the individual chosen to die if the child is fitter than that individual. This approach is called **Restricted Tournament Selection**,[112] by Georges Harik, and seems to work pretty well.

Samir Mahfoud proposed an entirely different mechanism, **Deterministic Crowding**,[113] in which we randomly pair off parents in the population, then each pair produces two children. Each child is matched with the parent to which it is most similar. If the child is fitter than its matched parent, it replaces the parent in the population. The idea here is to push children to replace individuals (in this case, their own parents) which are similar to them *and* aren't as fit as they are. Mahfoud's formulation is an entire generational evolutionary algorithm instead of simply a fitness assessment mechanism:

---

[111] From his thesis, Kenneth De Jong, 1975, *An Analysis of the Behaviour of a Class of Genetic Adaptive Systems*, Ph.D. thesis, University of Michigan. The thesis is available online at http://cs.gmu.edu/~eclab/kdj_thesis.html

[112] Georges Harik, 1995, Finding multimodal solutions using restricted tournament selection, in Larry J. Eshelman, editor, *Proceedings of the 6th International Conference on Genetic Algorithms*, pages 24–31, Morgan Kaufmann.

[113] Mahfoud first mentioned this in Samir Mahfoud, 1992, Crowding and preselection revisited, in Reinhard Männer and Bernard Manderick, editors, *Parallel Problem Solving From Nature II*, pages 27–36, North-Holland. But it actually got fleshed out in his thesis, Samir Mahfoud, 1995, *Niching Methods for Genetic Algorithms*, Ph.D. thesis, University of Illinois and Urbana-Champaign.

This is somewhat related to an early notion of niching called **preselection**, where an individual would simply replace its direct parent if it was fitter than the parent. There's no need to compute a distance or similarity measure at all: we just run on the heuristic assumption that parents are usually very similar to their children. Preselection is an old concept, dating at least from Daniel Joseph Cavicchio Jr., 1970, *Adaptive Search Using Simulated Evolution*, Ph.D. thesis, Computer and Communication Sciences Department, University of Michigan.

Algorithm 93 *Deterministic Crowding*
1: *popsize* ← desired population size
2: $P \leftarrow \{\}$
3: **for** *popsize* times **do**
4:     $P \leftarrow P \cup \{\text{new random individual}\}$
5: $Best \leftarrow \square$
6: **for** each individual $P_i \in P$ **do**
7:     AssessFitness(P_i)
8:     **if** $Best = \square$ or Fitness(P_i) > Fitness($Best$) **then**
9:         $Best \leftarrow P_i$
10: **repeat**
11:     Shuffle P randomly   ▷ To shuffle an array randomly, see Algorithm 26
12:     **for** i from 1 to $||P||$ by 2 **do**
13:         Children $C_a, C_b \leftarrow$ Crossover(Copy(P_i), Copy(P_{i+1}))
14:         $C_a \leftarrow$ Mutate(C_a)
15:         $C_b \leftarrow$ Mutate(C_b)
16:         AssessFitness(C_a)
17:         AssessFitness(C_b)
18:         **if** Fitness(C_a) > Fitness($Best$) **then**
19:             $Best \leftarrow C_a$
20:         **if** Fitness(C_b) > Fitness($Best$) **then**
21:             $Best \leftarrow C_b$
22:         **if** $d(C_a, P_i) + d(C_b, P_{i+1}) > d(C_a, P_{i+1}) + d(C_b, P_i)$ **then**
23:             Swap C_a and C_b ▷ Determine which child should compete with which parent
24:         **if** Fitness(C_a) > Fitness(P_i) **then**   ▷ Replace the parent if the child is better
25:             $P_i \leftarrow C_a$
26:         **if** Fitness(C_b) > Fitness(P_{i+1}) **then**   ▷ Replace the parent if the child is better
27:             $P_{i+1} \leftarrow C_b$
28: **until** *Best* is the ideal solution or we have run out of time
29: **return** *Best*

7 Multiobjective Optimization

It's often the case that we're not interested in optimizing a single fitness or quality function, but rather multiple functions. For example, imagine that a building engineer wants to come up with an optimal building. He wants to find buildings that are cheap, tall, resistant to earthquakes, and energy efficient. Wouldn't that be a great building? Unfortunately, it might not exist.

Each of these functions to optimize is known as an **objective**. Sometimes you can find solutions which are optimal for every objective. But more often than not, objectives are at odds with one another. Your solutions are thus often trade-offs of various objectives. The building engineer knows he can't find the perfect building: cheap, tall, strong, green. Rather, he might be interested in all the *best options* he has available. There are lots of ways of defining a set of "best options", but there's one predominant way: the **Pareto**[114] **front** of your space of candidate solutions.

Let's say you have two candidate buildings, M and N. M is said to **Pareto dominate** N if M is *at least as good as* N in all objectives, and *superior to* N in at least one objective. If this were the case, why would you ever pick N instead of M? M is at least as good everywhere and better in something. If we have just two objectives (Cheaper, More Energy Efficient) Figure 47 shows the region of space dominated by a given building solution A. The region is "nearly closed": the border is also dominated by A, except the corner (individuals identical to A in all objectives).

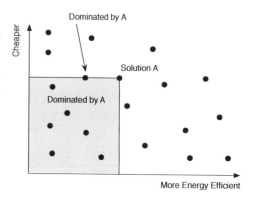

Figure 47 Region of solutions Pareto dominated by solution A, including the solution on the border. Keep in mind that this is *not a depiction of the phenotype space*, but rather results for the two objectives.

Neither M nor N dominates the other if they're identical in all objectives, or if N is better in some things but M is better in other things. In those cases, both M and N are of interest to our building engineer. So another way of saying the "best options" is the set of buildings which are dominated by *no other building*. We say that these buildings are **nondominated**. This set of buildings is the *Pareto nondominated front* (or just "Pareto front") of the space of solutions. Figure 48 at right shows the Pareto front of the possible solutions in our two-objective space. Pareto fronts

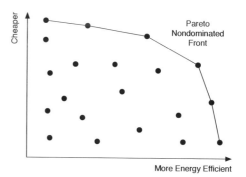

Figure 48 The Pareto front of nondominated solutions.

define outer borders. In a two-objective situation the Pareto front is often a curve demarcating that outer border. In a three-objective situation it's a skin of sorts. If you have one solution which is clearly superior to all the others (a superman, so to speak), the front collapses to that single individual.

As shown in Figure 49, Pareto fronts come in different flavors. **Convex** fronts are curved outwards towards better solutions. **Concave** fronts are curved inwards away from better solutions.

---

[114] Vilfredo Pareto (1848–1923) was an Italian economist responsible for a lot of important economics mathematics concepts, including Pareto's Law of income distribution, the 80–20 Rule (80% of events happen from only 20% of causes, so you can fix most of your problems by focusing on just a few issues), and Pareto Efficiency and Pareto Optimality, which is what we're discussing here.

Nonconvex fronts aren't entirely convex, and they include concave fronts as a subcategory. Fronts can also be **discontinuous**, meaning that there are regions along the front which are simply impossible for individuals to achieve: they'd be dominated by another solution elsewhere in the valid region of the front. There also exist **locally Pareto-optimal fronts** in the space where a given point, not on the global Pareto front, happens to be pareto-optimal to everyone near the point. This is the multiobjective optimization equivalent of local optima.

Spread It's not enough to offer our building engineer 100 points that lie on the Pareto front. What if they're all in one far corner of the front? That doesn't tell him much at all about the options he has available. More likely he wants samples that are **spread** evenly across the entire front. Thus many of the algorithms that optimize for Pareto fronts also try to force diversity measures. But interestingly, the distance measures used are rarely with regard to genotypical or phenotypical distance; rather they're distance in fitness: how far are the candidate solutions away from each other in the multi-objective space? This turns out to be much simpler to compute than genotypical or phenotypical distance.

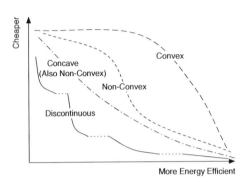

Figure 49 Four kinds of Pareto fronts.

The Problem of Too Many Objectives As the number of objectives grows, the necessary size of the populations needed to accurately sample the Pareto front grows exponentially. All the methods in this section face certain challenges when scaling to large numbers of objectives (and by "large" I mean "perhaps more than 4"). It's a difficulty stemming from the nature of the problem itself. To counter this, researchers have lately been turning to more exotic techniques, particularly ones centering around the **hypervolume** covered by the Pareto front; but these techniques are both complex and generally of high computational cost. We'll focus on the more basic methods here.

A Note on Defining Fitness It is traditional in multiobjective optimization literature to define fitness in terms of error. That is, the *lower* the objective value, the better. Thus in most Pareto optimization diagrams you come across, the front will be those individuals closer to the origin. I try to be consistent throughout this text, and so in this section we'll continue to assume that *larger* objective values are superior. Hence the organization of figures and algorithms in this chapter.

7.1 Naive Methods

Before we get to the Pareto methods, let's start with the more naive (but sometimes pretty good) methods used to shoehorn multiobjective problems into a style usable by most "traditional" metaheuristic algorithms.

The simplest way to do this is to bundle all the objectives into a single fitness using some kind of linear function. For example, maybe you feel that one unit of Cheap is worth ten units of Tall, five units of Earthquake Resistant, and four units of Energy Efficient. Thus we might define the quality of a solution as a weighted sum of how well it met various objectives:

$$\text{Fitness}(i) = \text{Cheapness}(i) + \frac{1}{10}\text{Height}(i) + \frac{1}{5}\text{EarthquakeResistance}(i) + \frac{1}{4}\text{EnergyEfficiency}(i)$$

We've seen this theme a number of times in the past so far. For example: linear parsimony pressure; and the average of various test cases. There are three problems with this. First, you're required to come up with the degree to which one objective is worth another objective. This is likely hard to do, and may be close to impossible if your objectives are nonlinear (that is, the difference between 9 and 10 height is much greater than the difference between 2 and 3 height, say). It's the same basic problem discussed regarding linear parsimony pressure in the Section 4.6 (Bloat). Second, realize that if M Pareto dominates N, it's *already* the case that Fitness(M) $\geq$ Fitness(N), assuming your weights are positive. So a Pareto method in some sense gives you some of this stuff for free already. Third, a weighted sum may not match the goal of moving towards the Pareto Front. Consider the simplest scenario, where we're adding up the objectives (that is, all weights are 1). We have two objectives, and Figure 50 shows the true Pareto front. Individual A is very close to the front, and so is the more desirable individual. But Individual B sums to a higher value, and so would be selected over A using this fitness strategy.

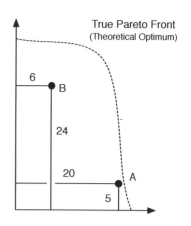

Figure 50 A may be considered superior, but B has a higher total.

To solve the first problem (having to come up with weights), we could instead abandon linear functions and simply treat the objectives as uncomparable functions. For example, perhaps we simply invent preferences among the objectives in order to perform a lexicographic ordering: M is better than N if it is superior in Height. If they're the same Height, it's better if it's superior in Cheapness. Then Earthquake Resistance. Then Energy Efficiency. We can provide a selection procedure by extending Algorithm 63 (Lexicographic Tournament Selection) to the case of more than two objectives. Basically when comparing two individuals, we run through the objectives (most important to least important) until we find one clearly superior to the other in that objective. Assuming we have an ObjectiveValue(*objective*, *individual*) function which tells us the quality of *individual* with regard to the given *objective*, we might perform a tournament selection like this:

Algorithm 94 *Multiobjective Lexicographic Tournament Selection*
1: *Best* ← individual picked at random from population with replacement
2: $O \leftarrow \{O_1, ..., O_n\}$ objectives to assess with ▷ In lexicographic order, most to least preferred.
3: $t \leftarrow$ tournament size, $t \geq 1$

4: **for** i from 2 to t **do**
5:     *Next* ← individual picked at random from population with replacement
6:     **for** j from 1 to n **do**
7:         **if** ObjectiveValue(O_j, *Next*) > ObjectiveValue(O_j, *Best*) **then** ▷ Clearly superior
8:             *Best* ← *Next*
9:             **break** from inner **for**
10:         **else if** ObjectiveValue(O_j, *Next*) < ObjectiveValue(O_j, *Best*) **then** ▷ Clearly inferior
11:             **break** from inner **for**
12: **return** *Best*

We could also pick an objective at random each time to use for fitness for this selection only:

Algorithm 95 *Multiobjective Ratio Tournament Selection*
1: $Best \leftarrow$ individual picked at random from population with replacement
2: $O \leftarrow \{O_1, ..., O_n\}$ objectives to assess with
3: $t \leftarrow$ tournament size, $t \geq 1$

4: $j \leftarrow$ random number picked uniformly from 1 to n
5: **for** i from 2 to t **do**
6:     $Next \leftarrow$ individual picked at random from population with replacement
7:     **if** ObjectiveValue(O_j, $Next$) > ObjectiveValue(O_j, $Best$) **then**
8:         $Best \leftarrow Next$
9: **return** $Best$

Or we could use voting: an individual is preferred if it is ahead in *more* objectives:

Algorithm 96 *Multiobjective Majority Tournament Selection*
1: $Best \leftarrow$ individual picked at random from population with replacement
2: $O \leftarrow \{O_1, ..., O_n\}$ objectives to assess with, more important objectives first
3: $t \leftarrow$ tournament size, $t \geq 1$

4: **for** i from 2 to t **do**
5:     $Next \leftarrow$ individual picked at random from population with replacement
6:     $c \leftarrow 0$
7:     **for** each objective $O_j \in O$ **do**
8:         **if** ObjectiveValue(O_j, $Next$) > ObjectiveValue(O_j, $Best$) **then**
9:             $c \leftarrow c + 1$
10:        **else if** ObjectiveValue(O_j, $Next$) < ObjectiveValue(O_j, $Best$) **then**
11:            $c \leftarrow c - 1$
12:     **if** $c > 0$ **then**
13:         $Best \leftarrow Next$
14: **return** $Best$

Finally, we could extend Algorithm 64 (Double Tournament Selection) to the case of more than two objectives. Here we perform a tournament based on one objective. The entrants to that tournament are selected using tournament selections on a second objective. The entrants to that tournament are selected using tournament selections on a third objective, and so on. Thus the winner is more often that not a jack-of-all-trades which is pretty good in *all* objectives.

Algorithm 97 *Multiple Tournament Selection*
1: $O \leftarrow \{O_1, ..., O_n\}$ objectives to assess with
2: $T \leftarrow \{T_1, ..., T_n\}$ tournament sizes for the objectives in O, all ≥ 1 ▷ Allows different weights

3: **return** ObjectiveTournament(O, T)

4: **procedure** ObjectiveTournament(O, T)
5:     *Best* ← individual picked at random from population with replacement
6:     $n \leftarrow ||O||$ ▷ O and T change in size. The current last elements are O_n and T_n
7:     **if** $O - \{O_n\}$ is empty **then**   ▷ O_n is the last remaining objective!
8:         *Best* ← individual picked at random from population with replacement
9:     **else**
10:         *Best* ← ObjectiveTournament($O - \{O_n\}, T - \{T_n\}$)   ▷ Delete the current objective
11:     **for** i from 2 to T_n **do**
12:         **if** $O - \{O_n\}$ is empty **then**   ▷ This is the remaining objective!
13:             *Next* ← individual picked at random from population with replacement
14:         **else**
15:             *Next* ← ObjectiveTournament($O - \{O_n\}, T - \{T_n\}$)   ▷ Delete the current objective
16:         **if** ObjectiveValue(O_n, *Next*) > ObjectiveValue(O_n, *Best*) **then**
17:             *Best* ← *Next*
18:     **return** *Best*

7.2 Non-Dominated Sorting

The previous algorithms attempt to merge objectives into one single fitness value by trading off one objective for another in some way. But a lot of current algorithms instead use notions of Pareto domination to get a little more closely at what "better" means in a multiobjective sense.

One simple way to do this is to construct a tournament selection operator based on Pareto domination. But first, let's review the definition. Individual A Pareto dominates individual B if A is at least as good as B in every objective and better than B in at least one objective. Here's an algorithm which computes that:

Algorithm 98 *Pareto Domination*
1: $A \leftarrow$ individual A   ▷ We'll determine: does A dominate B?
2: $B \leftarrow$ individual B
3: $O \leftarrow \{O_1, ..., O_n\}$ objectives to assess with

4: $a \leftarrow$ false
5: **for** each objective $O_i \in O$ **do**
6:     **if** ObjectiveValue(O_i, A) > ObjectiveValue(O_i, B) **then**
7:         $a \leftarrow$ true   ▷ A *might* dominate B
8:     **else if** ObjectiveValue(O_i, B) > ObjectiveValue(O_i, A) **then**
9:         **return** false   ▷ A definitely does not dominate B
10: **return** a

Now we can build a binary tournament selection procedure based on Pareto domination:

Algorithm 99 *Pareto Domination Binary Tournament Selection*
1: $P \leftarrow$ population

2: $P_a \leftarrow$ individual picked at random from P with replacement
3: $P_b \leftarrow$ individual picked at random from P with replacement
4: **if** P_a Pareto Dominates P_b **then**
5:     **return** P_a
6: **else if** P_b Pareto Dominates P_a **then**
7:     **return** P_b
8: **else**
9:     **return** either P_a or P_b, chosen at random

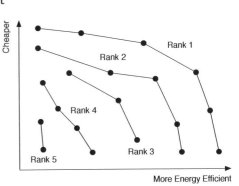

Figure 51 Pareto ranks.

Unfortunately, even if two individuals don't Pareto-dominate one another, and thus are equally attractive to the experimenter, one individual might still be preferred for optimization purposes. Specifically, if A has many individuals in the population who Pareto-dominate it, and B has none, then we're interested in selecting B because we'll probably select individuals better than A in the next generation anyway. Sure, B doesn't Pareto dominate A. But A is part of the rabble.

To get at this notion, we need a notion of how *close* an individual is to the Pareto front. There are various ways to do this, and we'll discuss additional one (**strength**) in the next section. But we start here with a new concept called a **Pareto Front Rank**. Individuals in the Pareto front are in Rank 1. If we *removed these individuals from the population*, then computed a new front, individuals in that front would be in Rank 2. If we removed *those* individuals, then computed a new front, we'd get Rank 3, and so on. It's like peeling an onion. Figure 51 shows the notion of ranks.

Let's start by defining how to compute a Pareto front. The trick is to go through the population and add an individual to the front if it isn't dominated by anyone presently in the front, and *remove* individuals from the front if they got dominated by this new individual. It's fairly straightforward:

Algorithm 100 *Computing a Pareto Non-Dominated Front*
1: $G \leftarrow \{G_1, ..., G_m\}$ Group of individuals to compute the front among   ▷ Often the population
2: $O \leftarrow \{O_1, ..., O_n\}$ objectives to assess with

3: $F \leftarrow \{\}$ ▷ The front
4: **for** each individual $G_i \in G$ **do**
5:     $F \leftarrow F \cup \{G_i\}$ ▷ Assume G_i's gonna be in the front
6:     **for** each individual $F_j \in F$ other than G_i **do**
7:         **if** F_j Pareto Dominates G_i given O **then**   ▷ Oh well, guess it's not gonna stay in the front
8:             $F \leftarrow F - \{G_i\}$
9:             **break** out of inner for-loop
10:         **else if** G_i Pareto Dominates F_j given O **then**   ▷ An existing front member knocked out!
11:             $F \leftarrow F - \{F_j\}$
12: **return** F

Computing the ranks is easy: figure out the first front, then remove the individuals, then figure out the front again, and so on. If we pre-process all the individuals with this procedure, we could then simply use the Pareto Front Rank of an individual as its fitness. Since lower Ranks are better, we could convert it into a fitness like this:

$$\text{Fitness}(i) = \frac{1}{1 + \text{ParetoFrontRank}(i)}$$

The algorithm to compute the ranks builds two results at once: first it *partitions* the population P into ranks, with each rank (a group of individuals) stored in the vector F. Second, it *assigns* a rank number to an individual (perhaps the individual gets it written internally somewhere). That way later on we can ask both: (1) which individuals are in rank i, and (2) what rank is individual j in? This procedure is called **Non-Dominated Sorting**, by N. Srinvas and Kalyanmoy Deb.[115]

Algorithm 101 *Front Rank Assignment by Non-Dominated Sorting*
1: $P \leftarrow$ population
2: $O \leftarrow \{O_1, ..., O_n\}$ objectives to assess with

3: $P' \leftarrow P$ ▷ We'll gradually remove individuals from P'
4: $R \leftarrow \langle \ \rangle$ ▷ Initially empty ordered vector of Pareto Front Ranks
5: $i \leftarrow 1$
6: **repeat**
7: $\quad R_i \leftarrow$ Pareto Non-Dominated Front of P' using O
8: $\quad$ **for** each individual $A \in R_i$ **do**
9: $\quad\quad$ ParetoFrontRank$(A) \leftarrow i$
10: $\quad\quad P' \leftarrow P' - \{A\}$ ▷ Remove the current front from P'
11: $\quad i \leftarrow i + 1$
12: **until** P' is empty
13: **return** R

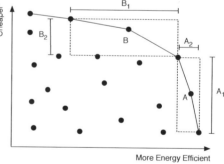

Sparsity We'd also like to push the individuals in the population towards being spread more evenly across the front. To do this we could assign a distance measure of some sort among individuals in the same Pareto Front Rank. Let's define the **sparsity** of an individual: an individual is in a more *sparse region* if the closest individuals on either side of it in its Pareto Front Rank aren't too close to it.

Figure 52 illustrates the notion we're more or less after. We'll define sparsity as **Manhattan distance**,[116] over every objective, between an individual's left and right neighbors

Figure 52 The sparsity of individual B is higher than individual A because $A_1 + A_2 < B_1 + B_2$.

---
[115]First published in N. Srinivas and Kalyanmoy Deb, 1994, Multiobjective optimization using nondominated sorting in genetic algorithms, *Evolutionary Computation*, 2, 221–248. This paper also introduced Algorithm 100.

[116]Manhattan lies on a grid, so you can't go directly from point A to point B unless you're capable of leaping tall buildings in a single bound. Instead you must walk horizontally so many blocks, then vertically so many blocks. That's the Manhattan distance from A to B.

along its Pareto Front Rank. Individuals at the far ends of the Pareto Front Rank will be assigned an infinite sparsity. To compute sparsity, you'll likely need to know the range of possible values that any given objective can take on (from min to max). If you don't know this, you may be forced to assume that the range equals 1 for all objectives.

Algorithm 102 *Multiobjective Sparsity Assignment*
1: $F \leftarrow \langle F_1, ..., F_m \rangle$ a Pareto Front Rank of Individuals
2: $O \leftarrow \{O_1, ..., O_n\}$ objectives to assess with
3: $\text{Range}(O_i)$ function providing the range (max $-$ min) of possible values for a given objective O_i

4: **for** each individual $F_j \in F$ **do**
5:     $\text{Sparsity}(F_j) \leftarrow 0$
6: **for** each objective $O_i \in O$ **do**
7:     $F' \leftarrow F$ sorted by ObjectiveValue given objective O_i
8:     $\text{Sparsity}(F'_1) \leftarrow \infty$
9:     $\text{Sparsity}(F'_{||F||}) \leftarrow \infty$ ▷ Each end is really *really* sparse!
10:    **for** j from 2 to $||F'|| - 1$ **do**
11:        $\text{Sparsity}(F'_j) \leftarrow \text{Sparsity}(F'_j) + \dfrac{\text{ObjectiveValue}(O_i, F'_{j+1}) - \text{ObjectiveValue}(O_i, F'_{j-1})}{\text{Range}(O_i)}$
12: **return** F with Sparsities assigned

To compute the sparsities of the whole population, use Algorithm 101 to break it into Pareto Front ranks, then for each Pareto Front rank, call Algorithm 102 to assign sparsities to the individuals in that rank.

We can now use sparsity to do a kind of crowding, but one which is in the *multiobjective space* rather than in a genotype or phenotype space. We define a tournament selection to select first based on Pareto Front Rank, but to break ties by using sparsity. The idea is to get individuals which are not only close to the true Pareto front, but also nicely spread out along it.

Algorithm 103 *Non-Dominated Sorting Lexicographic Tournament Selection With Sparsity*
1: $P \leftarrow$ population with Pareto Front Ranks assigned
2: $Best \leftarrow$ individual picked at random from P with replacement
3: $t \leftarrow$ tournament size, $t \geq 1$

4: **for** i from 2 to t **do**
5:     $Next \leftarrow$ individual picked at random from P with replacement
6:     **if** $\text{ParetoFrontRank}(Next) < \text{ParetoFrontRank}(Best)$ **then**   ▷ Lower ranks are better
7:         $Best \leftarrow Next$
8:     **else if** $\text{ParetoFrontRank}(Next) = \text{ParetoFrontRank}(Best)$ **then**
9:         **if** $\text{Sparsity}(Next) > \text{Sparsity}(Best)$ **then**
10:            $Best \leftarrow Next$ ▷ Higher sparsities are better
11: **return** $Best$

This alone does a good job. But the **Non-Dominated Sorting Genetic Algorithm II** (or **NSGA-II**, by Kalyanmoy Deb, Amrit Pratap, Sameer Agarwal, and T. Meyarivan),[117] goes a bit further: it also keeps around *all* the best known individuals so far, in a sort of $(\mu + \lambda)$ or elitist fashion.

Algorithm 104 *An Abstract Version of the Non-Dominated Sorting Genetic Algorithm II (NSGA-II)*

1: $m \leftarrow$ desired population size
2: $a \leftarrow$ desired archive size   ▷ Typically $a = m$

3: $P \leftarrow \{P_1, ..., P_m\}$ Build Initial Population
4: $A \leftarrow \{\}$ archive
5: **repeat**
6:      AssessFitness(P)   ▷ Compute the objective values for the Pareto front ranks
7:      $P \leftarrow P \cup A$ ▷ Obviously on the first iteration this has no effect
8:      *BestFront* $\leftarrow$ Pareto Front of P
9:      $R \leftarrow$ Compute Front Ranks of P
10:      $A \leftarrow \{\}$
11:      **for** each Front Rank $R_i \in R$ **do**
12:          Compute Sparsities of Individuals in R_i ▷ Just for R_i, no need for others
13:          **if** $||A|| + ||R_i|| \geq a$ **then**   ▷ This will be our last front rank to load into A
14:             $A \leftarrow A \cup$ the Sparsest $a - ||A||$ individuals in R_i, breaking ties arbitrarily
15:             **break** from the **for** loop
16:          **else**
17:             $A \leftarrow A \cup R_i$ ▷ Just dump it in
18:      $P \leftarrow$ Breed(A), using Algorithm 103 for selection (typically with tournament size of 2)
19: **until** *BestFront* is the ideal Pareto front or we have run out of time
20: **return** *BestFront*

The general idea is to hold in A an **archive** of the best n individuals discovered so far. We then breed a new population P from A, and everybody in A and P gets to compete for who gets to stay in the archive. Such algorithms are sometimes known as **archive algorithms**. Ordinarily an approach like this would be considered *highly* exploitative. But in multiobjective optimization things are a little different because we're not looking for just a *single point* in space. Instead we're looking for an entire *Pareto front* which is spread throughout the space, and that front alone imposes a bit of exploration on the problem.

Note that we only compute Sparsities for a select collection of Pareto Front Ranks. This is because they're the only ones that ever use them: the other ranks get thrown away. You can just compute Sparsities for all of Q if you want to, it's no big deal.

7.3 Pareto Strength

Pareto Front Ranks are not the only way we can use Pareto values to compute fitness. We could also identify the **strength** of an individual, defined as the *number* of individuals in the population that the individual Pareto dominates.

---

[117]Kalyanmoy Deb, Amrit Pratap, Sameer Agarwal, and T. Meyarivan, 2000, A fast elitist non-dominated sorting genetic algorithm for multi-objective optimization: NSGA-II, in Marc Schoenauer, *et al.*, editors, *Parallel Problem Solving from Nature (PPSN VI)*, pages 849–858, Springer. This paper also introduced Algorithm 102.

We could use an individual's strength as his fitness. There's a problem with this, however. Strength doesn't necessarily correspond with how close an individual is to the Pareto front. Indeed, individuals near the corners of the front are likely to not be very strong compared to individuals fairly distant from the front, as shown in Figure 53. Alternatively, we may define the **weakness** of an individual to be *the number of individuals which dominate the individual*. Obviously individuals on the Pareto front have a 0 weakness, and individuals far from the front are likely to have a high weakness. A slightly more refined version of weakness is the **wimpiness**[118] of an individual: the sum total strength of *everyone who dominates the individual*, for an individual i and a group G, that is,

$$\text{Wimpiness}(i) = \sum_{g \in G \text{ that Pareto Dominate } i} \text{Strength}(g)$$

Ideally we'd like the wimpiness of an individual to be as *low* as possible. A non-dominated individual has a 0 wimpiness. We could use some kind of *non*-wimpiness as a fitness too. To do this, we could convert wimpiness such that wimpier individuals have lower values. Perhaps:

$$\text{Fitness}(i) = \frac{1}{1 + \text{Wimpiness}(i)}$$

Eckart Zitzler, Marco Laumanns, and Lothar Thiele built an archive-based algorithm around the notion of strength (or more correctly, wimpiness), called the **Strength Pareto Evolutionary Algorithm** (or **SPEA**). The current version, **SPEA2**, competes directly with NSGA-II and various other multiobjective stochastic optimization algorithms.[119] Like NSGA-II, SPEA2 maintains an archive of the best known Pareto front members plus some others. SPEA2 also similarly employs both a Pareto measure and a crowding measure in its fitness procedure. However, SPEA2's Pareto measure is Wimpiness, and its crowding measure is based on distance to other individuals in the multiobjective space, rather than distance along ranks.

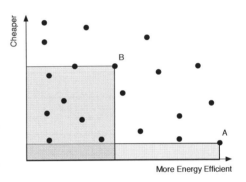

Figure 53 Individual A is closer to the Pareto front, but individual B is Stronger.

SPEA2's similarity measure computes a distance to other individuals in the population, and specifically, to the kth closest individual in the population. There are many fancy ways of computing this in a reasonably efficient manner. Here I'm just going to suggest a grotesquely inefficient, but simple, approach.[120] Basically we compute the distance from everyone to everyone. Then, for each individual in the population, we sort the population by distance to that individual, and take the kth closest individual. This is $O(n^2 \lg n)$, where n is the population size. That's not great.

---

[118]Of *course* I made up these names (except for strength).

[119]They're sort of intertwined. SPEA was introduced in Eckart Zitzler and Lothar Thiele, 1999, Multiobjective evolutionary algorithms: A comparitive case study and the strength pareto approach, *IEEE Transactions on Evolutionary Computation*, 3(4), 257–271. NSGA-II then came out in 2000, and SPEA2 then came out as Eckart Zitzler, Marco Laumanns, and Lothar Thiele, 2002, SPEA2: Improving the strength pareto evolutionary algorithm for multiobjective optimization, in K. Giannakoglou, *et al.*, editors, *Evolutionary Methods for Design, Optimization, and Control*, pages 19–26.

[120]Hey, fitness assessment time is the dominant factor timewise nowadays anyway!

Algorithm 105 *Compute the Distance of the Kth Closest Individual*
1: $P \leftarrow \{P_1, ..., P_m\}$ population
2: $O \leftarrow \{O_1, ..., O_n\}$ objectives to assess with
3: $P_l \leftarrow$ individual to compute kth closest individual to
4: $k \leftarrow$ desired individual index (the kth individual from l)

5: **global** $D \leftarrow m$ vectors, each of size m ▷ D_i holds a vector of distances of various individuals i
6: **global** $S \leftarrow \{S_1, ..., S_m\}$ ▷ S_i will be true if D_i has already been sorted
7: **perform once only**
8:   **for** each individual $P_i \in P$ **do**
9:     $V \leftarrow \{\}$ ▷ Our distances
10:    **for** each individual $P_j \in P$ **do**
11:      $V \leftarrow V \cup \left\{ \sqrt{\sum_{m=1}^{n}(\text{ObjectiveValue}(O_m, P_i) - \text{ObjectiveValue}(O_m, P_j))^2} \right\}$
12:    $D_i \leftarrow V$
13:    $S_i \leftarrow$ false
14: **perform each time**
15:   **if** S_l is false **then**   ▷ Need to sort
16:     Sort D_l, smallest first
17:     $S_l \leftarrow$ true
18:   $W \leftarrow D_l$
19:   **return** W_{k+1} ▷ It's W_{k+1} because W_1 is always 0: the distance to the same individual

Given the Wimpiness of an individual and the kth closest individual to it, we can finally define a fitness. Define a pre-fitness value G_i as follows:

$$G_i \leftarrow \text{Wimpiness}(i) + \frac{1}{2+d_i}$$

d_i is the distance to the kth closest individual to i, where $k = \left\lceil \sqrt{||P||} \right\rceil$ typically.[121] The smaller the value of G_i the better. The idea is that a big distance d_i makes G_i smaller (because it's far away from other individuals — we want diversity!) and likewise a small Wimpiness makes G_i smaller.

SPEA2 in reality uses G_i as the fitness of individual i: but in keeping with our tradition (higher fitness is better), let's convert it into a final fitness like we've done before:

$$\text{Fitness}(i) = \frac{1}{1+G_i}$$

Each iteration, SPEA2 will build an archive consisting of the current Pareto front of the population. The archive is supposed to be of size n. If there aren't enough individuals in the front to fill all those n, SPEA2 will fill the rest with other fit individuals selected from the population. If there are instead *too many* individuals in the Pareto front to fit into n, SPEA2 needs to trim some individuals. It does this by iteratively deleting individuals who have the smallest kth closest distance (starting with $k = 1$, breaking ties with $k = 2$, and so on). The goal is to get in the archive those individuals in the Pareto front which are furthest away from one another and other individuals in the population. The algorithm for constructing the archive looks like this:

---
[121] Actually, Zitzler and Thiele don't say how you should round it: you could just as well do $k = \left\lfloor \sqrt{||P||} \right\rfloor$ I suppose.

Algorithm 106 *SPEA2 Archive Construction*
1: $P \leftarrow \{P_1, ..., P_m\}$ population
2: $O \leftarrow \{O_1, ..., O_n\}$ objectives to assess with
3: $a \leftarrow$ desired archive size

4: $A \leftarrow$ Pareto non-dominated front of P ▷ The archive
5: $Q \leftarrow P - A$ ▷ All individuals not in the front
6: **if** $||A|| < a$ **then** ▷ Too small! Pack with some more individuals
7:     Sort Q by fitness
8:     $A \leftarrow A \cup$ the $a - ||A||$ fittest individuals in Q, breaking ties arbitrarily
9: **while** $||A|| > a$ **do** ▷ Too big! Remove some "k-closest" individuals
10:     $Closest \leftarrow A_1$
11:     $c \leftarrow$ index of A_1 in P
12:     **for** each individual $A_i \in A$ except A_1 **do**
13:         $l \leftarrow$ index of A_i in P
14:         **for** k from 1 to $m-1$ **do** ▷ Start with $k = 1$, break ties with larger values of k
15:             **if** DistanceOfKthNearest$(k, P_l) <$ DistanceOfKthNearest(k, P_c) **then**
16:                 $Closest \leftarrow A_i$
17:                 $c \leftarrow l$
18:                 **break** from inner **for**
19:             **else if** DistanceOfKthNearest$(k, P_l) >$ DistanceOfKthNearest(k, P_c) **then**
20:                 **break** from inner **for**
21:     $A \leftarrow A - \{Closest\}$
22: **return** A

Now we're ready to describe the SPEA2 top-level algorithm. It's very similar to NSGA-II (Algorithm 104): the primary difference is that the archive construction mechanism, which is more complex in SPEA2, was broken out into a separate algorithm, which simplifies the top-level:

Algorithm 107 *An Abstract Version of the Strength Pareto Evolutionary Algorithm 2 (SPEA2)*
1: $m \leftarrow$ desired population size
2: $a \leftarrow$ desired archive size ▷ Typically $a = m$

3: $P \leftarrow \{P_1, ..., P_m\}$ Build Initial Population
4: $A \leftarrow \{\}$ archive
5: **repeat**
6:     AssessFitness(P)
7:     $P \leftarrow P \cup A$ ▷ Obviously on the first iteration this has no effect
8:     $BestFront \leftarrow$ Pareto Front of P
9:     $A \leftarrow$ Construct SPEA2 Archive of size a from P
10:     $P \leftarrow$ Breed(A), using tournament selection of size 2 ▷ Fill up to the old size of P
11: **until** $BestFront$ is the ideal Pareto front or we have run out of time
12: **return** $BestFront$

In short: given a population P and an (initially empty) archive A, we build a new archive of the Pareto Front from $P \cup A$, trimmed if necessary of "close" individuals, plus some other fit individuals from P to fill in any gaps. Then we create a new population P by breeding from A (which eventually comes close to random selection as the Pareto front improves). Note that unlike in NSGA-II, in SPEA2 you can specify the archive size, though usually it's set to the same value as NSGA-II anyway ($a = m$).

SPEA2 and NSGA-II both are basically versions of $(\mu + \lambda)$ in multiobjective space, coupled with a diversity mechanism and a procedure for selecting individuals that are closer to the Pareto front. Both SPEA2 and NSGA-II are fairly impressive algorithms,[122] though NSGA-II is a bit simpler and has lower computational complexity in unsophisticated versions.

---

[122]Believe me, I know. Zbigniew Skolicki and I once constructed a massively parallel island model for doing multiobjective optimization. If there were n objectives, the islands were organized in a grid with n corners, one per objective. For example with 2 objectives, the grid was a line. If there were 3 objectives, the grid was a triangle mesh. If there were 4 objectives, the grid was a mesh filling the volume of a tetrahedron (three-sided pyramid). Each island assessed fitness as a weighted sum of the objectives. The closer an island was to a corner, the more it weighted that corner's objective. Thus islands in the corners or ends were 100% a certain objective, while (for example) islands near the center weighted each objective evenly. Basically each island was searching for its own part of the Pareto front, resulting in (hopefully) a nicely distributed set of points along the front. We got okay results. But SPEA2, on a single machine, beat our pants off.

8 Combinatorial Optimization

So far the kinds of problems we've tackled are very general: any arbitrary search space. We've seen spaces in the forms of permutations of variables (fixed-length vectors); spaces that have reasonable distance metrics defined for them; and even spaces of trees or sets of rules.

One particular kind of space deserves special consideration. A **combinatorial optimization problem**[123] is one in which the solution consists of a combination of unique **components** selected from a typically finite, and often small, set. The objective is to find the optimal combination of components.

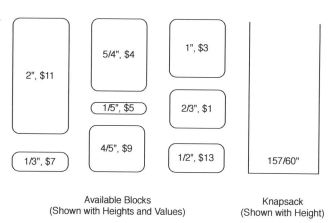

Figure 54 A knapsack problem. Fill the knapsack with as much value ($$$) without exceeding the knapsack's height.

A classic combinatorial optimization problem is a simple form of the **knapsack problem**: we're given *n blocks* of different heights and worth different amounts of money (unrelated to the heights) and a *knapsack*[124] of a certain larger height, as shown in Figure 54. The objective is to fill the knapsack with blocks worth the most $$$ (or €€€ or ¥¥¥) without overfilling the knapsack.[125] Blocks are the components. Figure 55 shows various combinations of blocks in the knapsack. As you can see, just because the knapsack is maximally filled doesn't mean it's optimal: what counts is how much value can be packed into the knapsack without going over. Overfull solutions are **infeasible** (or *illegal* or *invalid*).

This isn't a trivial or obscure problem. It's got a lot of literature behind it. And lots of real-world problems can be cast into this framework: knapsack problems show up in the processor queues of operating systems; in allocations of delivery trucks along routes; and in determining how to get exactly $15.05 worth of appetizers in a restaurant.[126]

Another example is the classic **traveling salesman problem** (or **TSP**), which has a set of *cities* with some number of *routes* (plane flights, say) between various pairs cities. Each route has a *cost*. The salesman must construct a *tour* starting at city A, visiting all the cities at least once, and finally

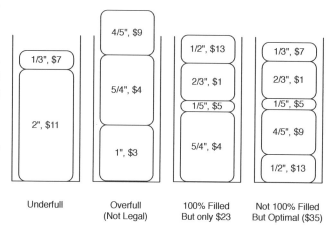

Figure 55 Filling the knapsack.

---

[123]Not to be confused with *combinatorics*, an overall field of problems which could reasonably include, as a small subset, practically everything discussed so far.

[124]Related are various **bin packing** problems, where the objective is to figure out how to arrange blocks so that they will fit correctly in a multi-dimensional bin.

[125]There are various knapsack problems. For example, another version allows you to have as many copies of a given block size as you need.

[126]http://xkcd.com/287/

returning to A. Crucially, this tour must have the lowest cost possible. Put another way, the cities are nodes and the routes are edges in a graph, labelled by cost, and the object is to find a minimum-cost cycle which visits every node at least once. Here the components aren't blocks but are rather the edges in the graph. And the arrangement of these edges matters: there are lots of sets of edges which are nonsense because they don't form a cycle.

Costs and Values   While the TSP has **cost** (the edge weights) which must be minimized, Knapsack instead has **value** ($$$) which must be maximized. These are really just the same thing: simply negate or invert the costs to create values. Most combinatorial optimization algorithms traditionally assume costs, but we'll include both cases. At any rate, one of many ways you might convert the cost of a component C_i into a value (or vice versa) would be something along the lines of:

$$\text{Value}(C_i) = \frac{1}{\text{Cost}(C_i)}$$

That's the relationship we'll assume in this Section. This of course assumes that your costs (and values) are > 0, which is the usual case. If your costs or values are both positive and negative, some of the upcoming methods do a kind value-proportional selection, so you'll need to add some amount to make them all positive. Finally, there exist problems in which components all have exactly the same value or cost. Or perhaps you might be able to provide your algorithm with a **heuristic**[127] that you as a user have designed to favor certain components over others. In this case you could use $\text{Value}(C_i) = \text{Heuristic}(C_i)$.

Knapsack does have one thing the TSP doesn't have: it has additional **weights**[128] (the block heights) and a maximum "weight" which *must not* be exceeded. The TSP has a different notion of infeasible solutions than simply ones which exceed a certain bound.

8.1 General-Purpose Optimization and Hard Constraints

Combinatorial optimization problems can be solved by most general-purpose metaheuristics such as those we've seen so far, and in fact certain techniques (Iterated Local Search, Tabu Search, etc.) are commonly promoted as combinatorics problem methods. But some care must be taken because most metaheuristics are really designed to search much more general, wide-open spaces than the constrained ones found in most combinatorial optimization problems. We can adapt them but need to take into consideration these restrictions special to these kinds of problems.[129]

As an example, consider the use of a boolean vector in combination with a metaheuristic such as simulated annealing or the genetic algorithm. Each slot in the vector represents a component, and if the slot is true, then the component is used in the candidate solution. For example, in Figure 54 we have blocks of height 2, $\frac{1}{3}$, $\frac{5}{4}$, $\frac{1}{5}$, $\frac{4}{5}$, 1, $\frac{2}{3}$, and $\frac{1}{2}$. A candidate solution to the problem in this Figure would be a vector of eight slots. The optimal answer shown in Figure 55 would be ⟨false, true, false, true, true, false, true, true⟩, representing the blocks $\frac{1}{3}$, $\frac{1}{5}$, $\frac{4}{5}$, $\frac{2}{3}$, and $\frac{1}{2}$.

The problem with this approach is that it's easy to create solutions which are infeasible. In the knapsack problem we have declared that solutions which are larger than the knapsack are

---

[127] A heuristic is a rule of thumb provided by you to the algorithm. It can often be wrong, but is right often enough that it's useful as a guide.

[128] Yeah, confusing. TSP edge weights vs. combinatorial component weights. That's just the terminology, sorry.

[129] A good overview article on the topic, by two greats in the field, is Zbigniew Michalewicz and Marc Schoenauer, 1996, Evolutionary algorithms for constrained parameter optimization problems, *Evolutionary Computation*, 4(1), 1–32.

simply illegal. In Knapsack, it's not a disaster to have candidate solutions like that, as long as the final solution is feasible — we could just declare the quality of such infeasible solutions to be their distance from the optimum (in this case perhaps how overfull the knapsack is). We might punish them further for being infeasible. But in a problem like the Traveling Salesman Problem, our boolean vector might consist of one slot per edge in the TSP graph. It's easy to create infeasible solutions for the TSP which are simply nonsense: how do we assess the "quality" of a candidate solution whose TSP solution isn't even a tour?

The issue here is that these kind of problems, as configured, have **hard constraints**: there are large regions in the search space which are simply invalid. Ultimately we want a solution which is feasible; and during the search process it'd be nice to have feasible candidate solutions so we can actually think of a way to assign them quality assessments! There are two parts to this: initialization (construction) of a candidate solution from scratch, and Tweaking a candidate solution into a new one.

Construction Iterative construction of components within hard constraints is sometimes straightforward and sometimes not. Often it's done like this:

1. Choose a component. For example, in the TSP, pick an edge between two cities A and B. In Knapsack, it's an initial block. Let our current (partial) solution start with just that component.

2. Identify the subset of components that can be concatenated to components in our partial solution. In the TSP, this might be the set of all edges going out of A or B. In Knapsack, this is all blocks that can still be added into the knapsack without going over.

3. Tend to discard the less desirable components. In the TSP, we might emphasize edges that are going to cities we've not visited yet if possible.

4. Add to the partial solution a component chosen from among those components not yet discarded.

5. Quit when there are no components left to add. Else go to step 2.

This is an intentionally vague description because iterative construction is almost always highly problem-specific and often requires a lot of thought.

Tweaking The Tweak operator can be even harder to do right, because in the solution space feasible solutions may be surrounded on all sides by infeasible ones. Four common approaches:

- Invent a **closed** Tweak operator which automatically creates feasible children. This can be a challenge to do, particularly if you're including crossover. And if you create a closed operator, can it generate all possible feasible children? Is there a bias? Do you know what it is?

- Repeatedly try various Tweaks until you create a child which is feasible. This is relatively easy to do, but it may be computationally expensive.

- Allow infeasible solutions but construct a quality assessment function for them based on their distance to the nearest feasible solution or to the optimum. This is easier to do for some problems than others. For example, in the Knapsack problem it's easy: the quality of an overfull solution could be simply based on how overfull it is (just like underfull solutions).

- Assign infeasible solutions a poor quality. This essentially eliminates them from the population; but of course it makes your effective population size that much smaller. It has another problem too: moving *just* over the edge between the feasible and infeasible regions in the space results in a huge decrease in quality: it's a Hamming Cliff (see Representation, Section 4). In Knapsack, for example, the best solutions are very close to infeasible ones because they're close to filled. So one little mutation near the best solutions and whammo, you're infeasible and have big quality punishment. This makes optimizing near the best solutions a bit like walking on a tightrope.

None of these is particularly inviting. While it's often easy to create a valid construction operator, making a good Tweak operator that's closed can be pretty hard. And the other methods are expensive or allow infeasible solutions in your population.

Component-Oriented Methods   The rest of this Section concerns itself with methods specially designed for certain kinds of spaces often found in combinatorial optimization, by taking advantage of the fact that the that solutions in these spaces consist of *combinations of components* drawn from a typically *fixed set*. It's the presence of this fixed set that we can take advantage of in a greedy, local fashion by maintaining historical "quality" values, so to speak, of individual components rather than (or in addition to) complete solutions. There are two reasons you might want to do this:

- While constructing, to tend to select from components which have proven to be better choices.

- While Tweaking, to modify those components which appear to be getting us in a local optimum.

We'll begin with a straightforward metaheuristic called **Greedy Randomized Adaptive Search Procedures** (or **GRASP**) which embodies the basic notion of constructing combinatorial solutions out of components, then Tweaking them. From there we will move to a related technique, **Ant Colony Optimization**, which assigns "historical quality" values to these components to more aggressively construct solutions from the historically "better" components. Finally, we'll examine a variation of Tabu Search called **Guided Local Search** which focuses instead on the Tweak side of things: it's designed to temporarily "punish" those components which have gotten the algorithm into a rut.

Some of these methods take advantage of the "historical quality" values of individual components, but use them in quite different ways. Ant Colony Optimization tries to favor the best-performing components; but Guided Local Search gathers this information to determine which low-performing components appear to show up often in local optima.

The meaning of Quality or Fitness   Because combinatorial problems can be cast as either cost or as value, the meaning of *quality* or *fitness* of a candidate solution is shaky. If your problem is in terms of *value* (such as Knapsack), it's easy to define quality or fitness simply as the sum total value, that is, $\sum_i \text{Value}(C_i)$, of all the components C_i which appear in the candidate solution. If your problem is in terms of *cost* (such as the TSP), it's not so easy: you want the presence of many low-cost components to collectively result in a high-quality solution. A common approach is to define quality or fitness as $1/(\sum_i \text{Cost}(C_i))$, for each component C_i that appears in the solution.

8.2 Greedy Randomized Adaptive Search Procedures

At any rate, let's start easy with a single-state metaheuristic which is built on the notions of constructing and Tweaking feasible solutions, but which doesn't use any notion of component-level "historical quality": **Greedy Randomized Adaptive Search Procedures** or **GRASP**, by Thomas Feo and Mauricio Resende.[130] The overall algorithm is really simple: we create a feasible solution by constructing from among highest value (lowest cost) components (basically using the approach outlined earlier) and then do some hill-climbing on the solution.

Algorithm 108 *Greedy Randomized Adaptive Search Procedures (GRASP)*
1: $C \leftarrow \{C_1, ..., C_n\}$ components
2: $p \leftarrow$ percentage of components to include each iteration
3: $m \leftarrow$ length of time to do hill-climbing

4: $Best \leftarrow \square$
5: **repeat**
6:     $S \leftarrow \{\}$ ▷ Our candidate solution
7:     **repeat**
8:         $C' \leftarrow$ components in $C - S$ which could be added to S without being infeasible
9:         **if** C' is empty **then**
10:             $S \leftarrow \{\}$ ▷ Try again
11:         **else**
12:             $C'' \leftarrow$ the $p\%$ highest value (or lowest cost) components in C'
13:             $S \leftarrow S \cup \{$component chosen uniformly at random from $C''\}$
14:     **until** S is a complete solution
15:     **for** m times **do**
16:         $R \leftarrow \text{Tweak}(\text{Copy}(S))$ ▷ Tweak must be closed, that is, it must create feasible solutions
17:         **if** Quality(R) > Quality(S) **then**
18:             $S \leftarrow R$
19:     **if** $Best = \square$ or Quality(S) > Quality($Best$) **then**
20:         $Best \leftarrow S$
21: **until** $Best$ is the ideal solution or we have run out of time
22: **return** $Best$

Instead of picking the $p\%$ best available components, some versions of GRASP pick components from among the components whose value is no less than (or cost is no higher than) some amount. GRASP is more or less using a truncation selection among components to do its initial construction of candidate solutions. You could do something else like a tournament selection among the components, or a fitness-proportionate selection procedure (see Section 3 for these methods).

GRASP illustrates one way how to construct candidate solutions by iteratively picking components. But it's still got the same conundrum that faces evolutionary computation when it comes to the Tweak step: you have to come up with some way of guaranteeing closure.

---

[130]The first GRASP paper was Thomas A. Feo and Mauricio G. C. Resende, 1989, A probabilistic heuristic for a computationally difficult set covering problem, *Operations Research Letters*, 8, 67–71. Many of Resende's current publications on GRASP may be found at http://www.research.att.com/~mgcr/doc/

8.3 Ant Colony Optimization

Marco Dorigo's Ant Colony Optimization (or ACO)[131] is an approach to combinatorial optimization which gets out of the issue of Tweaking by making it optional. Rather, it simply assembles candidate solutions by selecting components which compete with one another for attention.

ACO is population-oriented. But there are two different kinds of "populations" in ACO. First, there is the set of *components* that make up a candidate solutions to the problem. In the Knapsack problem, this set would consist of all the blocks. In the TSP, it would consist of all the edges. The set of components never changes: but we will adjust the "fitness" (called the **pheromone**) of the various components in the population as time goes on.

Each generation we build one or more candidate solutions, called **ant trails** in ACO parlance, by selecting components one by one based, in part, on their pheromones. This constitutes the second "population" in ACO: the collection of trails. Then we assess the fitness of each trail. For each trail, each of the components in that trail is then updated based on that fitness: a bit of the trail's fitness is rolled into each component's pheromone. Does this sound like some kind of one-population cooperative coevolution?

The basic abstract ACO algorithm:

Algorithm 109 *An Abstract Ant Colony Optimization Algorithm (ACO)*
1: $C \leftarrow \{C_1, ..., C_n\}$ components
2: *popsize* ← number of trails to build at once ▷ "ant trails" is ACOspeak for "candidate solutions"
3: $\vec{p} \leftarrow \langle p_1, ..., p_n \rangle$ pheromones of the components, initially zero
4: *Best* ← □
5: **repeat**
6:      $P \leftarrow$ *popsize* trails built by iteratively selecting components based on pheromones and costs or values
7:      **for** $P_i \in P$ **do**
8:          $P_i \leftarrow$ Optionally Hill-Climb P_i
9:          **if** *Best* = □ or Fitness(P_i) > Fitness(*Best*) **then**
10:              *Best* ← P_i
11:      Update $\vec{p}$ for components based on the fitness results for each $P_i \in P$ in which they participated
12: **until** *Best* is the ideal solution or we have run out of time
13: **return** *Best*

I set this up to highlight its similarities to GRASP: both algorithms iteratively build candidate solutions, then hill-climb them. There are obvious differences though. First, ACO builds some *popsize* candidate solutions all at once. Second, ACO's hill-climbing is *optional*, and indeed it's often not done at all. If you're finding it difficult to construct a closed Tweak operator for your particular representation, you can entirely skip the hill-climbing step if need be.

Third, and most importantly, components are selected not just based on component value or cost, but also on *pheromones*. A pheromone is essentially the "historical quality" of a component:

---

[131] ACO's been around since around 1992, when it Dorigo proposed it in his dissertation: Marco Dorigo, 1992, *Optimization, Learning and Natural Algorithms*, Ph.D. thesis, Politecnico di Milano, Milan, Italy. The algorithms here are loosely adapted from Dorigo and Thomas Stützle's excellent recent book: Marco Dorigo and Thomas Stützle, 2004, *Ant Colony Optimization*, MIT Press.

often approximately the sum total (or mean, etc.) fitness of all the trails that the component has been a part of. Pheromones tell us how good a component would be to select regardless of its (possibly low) value or (high) cost. After assessing the fitness of trails, we update the pheromones in some way to reflect new fitness values we've discovered so those components are more or less likely to be selected in the future.

So where are the ants? Well, here's the thing. ACO was inspired by earlier research work in pheromone-based ant foraging and trail formation algorithms: but the relationship between ACO and actual ants is... pretty thin. ACO practitioners like to weave the following tale: to solve the Traveling Salesman Problem, we place an Ant in Seattle and tell it to go wander about the graph, from city to city, eventually forming a cycle. The ant does so by picking edges (trips to other cities from the ant's current city) that presently have high pheromones and relatively good (low) edge costs. After the ant has finished, it lays a fixed amount of pheromone on the trail. If the trail is shorter (lower costs), then of course that pheromone will be distributed more densely among its edges, making them more desirable for future ants.

That's the story anyway. The truth is, there are no ants. There are just components with historical qualities ("pheromones"), and candidate solutions formed from those components (the "trails"), with fitness assessed to those candidate solutions and then divvied up among the components forming them.

8.3.1 The Ant System

The first version of ACO was the **Ant System** or **AS**. It's not used as often nowadays but is a good starting point to illustrate these notions. In the Ant System, we select components based on a fitness-proportionate selection procedure of sorts, employing both costs or values and pheromones (we'll get to that). We then always *add* fitnesses into the component pheromones. Since this could cause the pheromones to go sky-high, we also always *reduce* (or **evaporate**) all pheromones a bit each time.

The Ant System has five basic steps:

1. Construct some trails (candidate solutions) by selecting components.

2. (Optionally) Hill-Climb the trails to improve them.

3. Assess the fitness of the final trails.

4. "Evaporate" all the pheromones a bit.

5. Update the pheromones involved in trails based on the fitness of those solutions.

In the original AS algorithm, there's no hill-climbing: I've added it here. Later versions of ACO include it. Here's a version of the algorithm (note certain similarities with GRASP):

Algorithm 110 *The Ant System (AS)*

1: $C \leftarrow \{C_1, ..., C_n\}$ components
2: $e \leftarrow$ evaporation constant, $0 < e \leq 1$
3: *popsize* $\leftarrow$ number of trails to construct at once
4: $\gamma \leftarrow$ initial value for pheromones
5: $t \leftarrow$ iterations to Hill-Climb

6: $\vec{p} \leftarrow \langle p_1, ..., p_n \rangle$ pheromones of the components, all set to γ
7: $Best \leftarrow \square$
8: **repeat**
9:     $P \leftarrow \{\}$ ▷ Our trails (candidate solutions)
10:    **for** *popsize* times **do**   ▷ Build some trails
11:        $S \leftarrow \{\}$
12:        **repeat**
13:           $C' \leftarrow$ components in $C - S$ which could be added to S without being infeasible
14:           **if** C' is empty **then**
15:              $S \leftarrow \{\}$ ▷ Try again
16:           **else**
17:              $S \leftarrow S \cup \{$component selected from C' based on pheromones and values or costs$\}$
18:        **until** S is a complete trail
19:        $S \leftarrow$ Hill-Climb(S) for t iterations   ▷ Optional. By default, not done.
20:        AssessFitness(S)
21:        **if** $Best = \square$ or Fitness(S) > Fitness($Best$) **then**
22:           $Best \leftarrow S$
23:        $P \leftarrow P \cup \{S\}$
24:    **for** each $p_i \in \vec{p}$ **do**   ▷ Decrease all pheromones a bit ("evaporation")
25:        $p_i \leftarrow (1 - e) p_i$
26:    **for** each $P_j \in P$ **do**   ▷ Update pheromones in components used in trails
27:        **for** each component C_i **do**
28:           **if** C_i was used in P_j **then**
29:              $p_i \leftarrow p_i +$ Fitness(P_j)
30: **until** $Best$ is the ideal solution or we have run out of time
31: **return** $Best$

Component Values or Costs, and Selecting Components   We construct trails by repeatedly selecting from those components which, if added to the trail, wouldn't make it infeasible. Knapcksack is easy: keep on selecting blocks until it's impossible to select one without going over. But the TSP is more complicated. For example, in the TSP we could just keep selecting edges until we have a complete tour. But we might wind up with edges we didn't need, or a bafflingly complex tour. Another approach might be to start with a city, then select from among those edges going out of the city to some city we've not seen yet (unless we have no choice), then select from among edges going out of *that* city, and so on. However it may be the case that the optimal tour requires that we go through certain cities repeatedly. Or what if the only possible tours require that you go from

Salt Lake City to Denver, yet that's got a high cost (low value) so we keep avoiding it and picking other cities, only to be forced to backtrack? We could have some pretty ugly tours. Anyway: the point is, trail construction can require some forethought.

AS selects using what I'll call a component's **desirability**: combining values and pheromones:

$$\text{Desirability}(C_i) = p_i^\delta \times (\text{Value}(C_i))^\epsilon$$

...or if your problem is using costs...

$$\text{Desirability}(C_i) = p_i^\delta \times \left(\frac{1}{\text{Cost}(C_i)}\right)^\epsilon$$

δ and ϵ are tuning parameters.[132] Note that as the pheromone goes up the quality goes up. Likewise, if a component has a higher value (or lower cost), then the quality goes up. Now AS simply does a "desirability-proportionate" selection among the components we're considering, similar to Algorithm 30. If you like you could perform some other selection procedure among your components, like tournament selection or GRASP-style truncation to $p\%$ based on desirability.

Initializing the Pheromones You could set them all to $\gamma = 1$. For the TSP, the ACO folks often set them to $\gamma = \textit{popsize} \times (1/\text{Cost}(D))$, where D is some costly, absurd tour like the Nearest Neighbor Tour (construct a TSP tour greedily by always picking the lowest cost edge).

Evaporating Pheromones The Ant System evaporates pheromones because otherwise the pheromones keep on piling up. But there's perhaps a better way to do it: adjust the pheromones up or down based on how well they've performed on average. Instead of evaporating and updating as was shown in the Ant System, we could just take each pheromone p_i and adjust it as follows:

Algorithm 111 *Pheromone Updating with a Learning Rate*
1: $C \leftarrow \{C_1, ..., C_n\}$ components
2: $\vec{p} \leftarrow \langle p_1, ..., p_n \rangle$ pheromones of the components
3: $P \leftarrow \{P_1, ..., P_m\}$ population of trails
4: $\alpha \leftarrow$ learning rate

5: $\vec{r} \leftarrow \langle r_1, ..., r_n \rangle$ total desirability of each component, initially 0
6: $\vec{c} \leftarrow \langle c_1, ..., c_n \rangle$ component usage counts, initially 0
7: **for** each $P_j \in P$ **do** ▷ Compute the average fitness of trails which employed each component
8:     **for** each component C_i **do**
9:         **if** C_i was used in P_j **then**
10:             $r_i \leftarrow r_i +$ Desirability(P_j)
11:             $c_i \leftarrow c_i + 1$
12: **for** each $p_i \in \vec{p}$ **do**
13:     **if** $c_i > 0$ **then**
14:         $p_i \leftarrow (1-\alpha)p_i + \alpha \frac{r_i}{c_i}$ ▷ $\frac{r_i}{c_i}$ is the average fitness computed earlier
15: **return** $\vec{p}$

---

[132]This isn't set in stone. For example, we could do Desirability(C_i) = $p_i^\delta + (\text{Value}(C_i))^\epsilon$. Or we could do Desirability(C_i) = $\delta p_i + (1-\delta)\text{Value}(C_i)$.

$0 \leq \alpha \leq 1$ is the **learning rate**. For each component, we're computing the average fitness of every trail which used that component. Then we're throwing out a small amount of what we know so far ($1 - \alpha$'s worth) and rolling in a little bit of what we've just learned this iteration about how good a component is (α's worth). If α is large, we quickly adopt new information at the expense of our historical knowledge. It's probably best if α is small.[133]

Optional Hill-Climbing: More Exploitation AS doesn't have hill-climbing by default. But we could hill-climb the ant trail S it right after the AssessFitness step, just like we do in GRASP. And just like in GRASP we're going to have the same issue: guaranteeing that each time we Tweak an ant trail, the child is still a valid ant trail. For some problems this is easy, for others, not so easy. Anyway, hill-climbing adds more exploitation to the problem, directly moving towards the locally best solutions we can find. Often this is a good approach for problems like TSP, which tend to benefit from a high dose of exploitation.

8.3.2 The Ant Colony System: A More Exploitative Algorithm

There have been a number of improvements on AS since it was first proposed (some of which were mentioned earlier). Here I'll mention one particularly well-known one: the **Ant Colony System (ACS)**.[134] ACS works like the Ant System but with the following changes:

1. The use of an **elitist** approach to updating pheromones: only increase pheromones for components used in the best trail discovered so far. In a sense this starts to approach $(1 + \lambda)$.

2. The use of a learning rate in pheromone updates.

3. A slightly different approach for evaporating pheromones.

4. A strong tendency to select components that were used in the best trail discovered so far.

Elitism ACS only improves the pheromones of components that were used in the best-so-far trail (the trail we store in *Best*), using the learning rate method stolen from Algorithm 111. That is, if a component is part of the best-so-far trail, we increase its pheromones as $p_i \leftarrow (1 - \alpha)p_i + \alpha \,\text{Fitness}(Best)$.

This is very strongly exploitative, so all pheromones are also *decreased* whenever they're used in a solution, notionally to make them less desirable for making future solutions in order to push the system to explore a bit more in solution space. More specifically, whenever a component C_i is used in a solution, we adjust its pheromone $p_i \leftarrow (1 - \beta)p_i + \beta\gamma$, where β is a sort of evaporation or "unlearning rate", and γ is the value we initialized the pheromones to originally. Left alone, this would eventually reset the pheromones to all be γ.

Elitist Component Selection Component selection is also pretty exploitative. We flip a coin of probability q. If it comes up heads, we select the component which has the highest Desirability. Otherwise we select in the same way as AS selected: though ACS simplifies the selection mechanism by getting rid of δ (setting it to 1).

---

[133] We'll see the $1 - \alpha$ vs. α learning rate metaphor again in discussion of Learning Classifier Systems. It's a common notion in reinforcement learning too.

[134] Again by Marco Dorigo and Luca Gambardella — no, there are plenty of people doing ACO besides Marco Dorigo!

Now we're ready to do the Ant Colony System. It's not all that different from AS in structure:

Algorithm 112 *The Ant Colony System (ACS)*
1: $C \leftarrow \{C_1, ..., C_n\}$ Components
2: *popsize* ← number of trails to construct at once
3: $\alpha \leftarrow$ elitist learning rate
4: $\beta \leftarrow$ evaporation rate
5: $\gamma \leftarrow$ initial value for pheromones
6: $\delta \leftarrow$ tuning parameter for heuristics in component selection   ▷ Usually $\delta = 1$
7: $\epsilon \leftarrow$ tuning parameter for pheromones in component selection
8: $t \leftarrow$ iterations to Hill-Climb
9: $q \leftarrow$ probability of selecting components in an elitist way

10: $\vec{p} \leftarrow \langle p_1, ..., p_n \rangle$ pheromones of the components, all set to γ
11: *Best* ← □
12: **repeat**
13:     $P \leftarrow \{\}$ ▷ Our candidate solutions
14:     **for** *popsize* times **do**   ▷ Build some trails
15:         $S \leftarrow \{\}$
16:         **repeat**
17:             $C' \leftarrow$ components in $C - S$ which could be added to S without being infeasible
18:             **if** C' is empty **then**
19:                 $S \leftarrow \{\}$ ▷ Try again
20:             **else**
21:                 $S \leftarrow S \cup \{$ component selected from C' using Elitist Component Selection $\}$
22:         **until** S is a complete trail
23:         $S \leftarrow$ Hill-Climb(S) for t iterations   ▷ Optional. By default, not done.
24:         AssessFitness(S)
25:         **if** *Best* = □ or Fitness(S) > Fitness(*Best*) **then**
26:             *Best* ← S
27:     **for** each $p_i \in \vec{p}$ **do**   ▷ Decrease all pheromones a bit ("evaporation")
28:         $p_i \leftarrow (1 - \beta)p_i + \beta\gamma$
29:     **for** each component S_i **do**   ▷ Update pheromones only of components in *Best*
30:         **if** S_i was used in *Best* **then**
31:             $p_i \leftarrow (1 - \alpha)p_i + \alpha$ Fitness(*Best*)
32: **until** *Best* is the ideal solution or we have run out of time
33: **return** *Best*

As before, we might be wise to do some hill-climbing right after the AssessFitness step.

At this point you may have picked up on an odd feature about ACO. The selection of components in candidate solutions is greedily based on how well a component has appeared in high-quality solutions (or perhaps even the *best* solution so far). It doesn't consider the possibility that a component needs to always appear with some other component in order to be good, and without the second component it's terrible. That is, ACO *completely disregards linkage among components*.

That's a pretty bold assumption. This could, in theory, lead to the same problems that cooperative coevolution has: jacks-of-all-trades. ACS tries to get around this by pushing hard for the best-so-far result, just as cooperative coevolution's best-of-n approaches and archive methods try to view components in the light of their best situation. I think ACO has a lot in common with coevolution, although it's not been well studied. In some sense we may view ACO as a **one population pseudo-cooperative coevolution** algorithm.

It's possible to surmount this by trying a population not of components but of (say) all possible *pairs* of components. We could select pairs that have been performing well. This would move up the chain a little bit as far as linkage is concerned, though it'd make a much bigger population. Pheromones for pairs or triples, etc., of components are known as **higher-order pheromones**.

ACO also has a lot in common with Univariate Estimation of Distribution Algorithms (discussed in Section 9.2)[135] Here's how to look at it: the components' fitnesses may be viewed as **probabilities** and the whole population is thus one **probability distribution** on a per-component basis. Contrast this to the evolutionary model, where the population may also be viewed as a sample distribution over the *joint* space of all possible candidate solutions, that is, all possible *combinations* of components. It should be obvious that ACO is searching a radically simpler (perhaps simplistic) space compared to the evolutionary model. For general problems that may be an issue. But for many combinatorial problems, it's proven to be a good tradeoff.

8.4 Guided Local Search

There's another way we can take advantage of the special component-based space found in combinatorial optimization problems: by marking certain components which tend to cause local optima and trying to avoid them.

Recall that **Feature-based Tabu Search** (Algorithm 15, in Section 2.5) operated by identifying "features" in solutions found in good solutions, and then made those features "taboo", temporarily banned from being returned to by later Tweaks. The idea was to prevent the algorithm from revisiting, over and over again, those local optima in which those features tended to be commonplace.

If you can construct a good, closed Tweak operator, it turns out that Feature-based Tabu Search can be nicely adapted to the combinatorial optimization problem. Simply define "features" to be the components of the problem. For example, Feature-based Tabu Search might hill-climb through the space of Traveling Salesman Problem solutions, temporarily making certain high-performing edges taboo to force it out of local optima in the TSP.

A variant of Feature-based Tabu Search called **Guided Local Search (GLS)** seems to be particularly apropos for combinatorial optimization: it assigns "historical quality" measures to components, like Ant Colony Optimization does. But interestingly, it uses this quality information not to home in on the best components to use, but rather to make troublesome components taboo and force more exploration.

GLS is by Chris Voudouris and Edward Tsang.[136] The algorithm is basically a variation of Hill-Climbing that tries to identify components which appear too often in local optima, and penalizes later solutions which use those components so as to force exploration elsewhere.

---

[135]This has been noted before, and not just by me: see p. 57 of Marco Dorigo and Thomas Stützle, 2004, *Ant Colony Optimization*, MIT Press. So we've got similarities to coevolution *and* to EDAs... hmmm....

[136]Among the earlier appearances of the algorithm is Chris Voudouris and Edward Tsang, 1995, Guided local search, Technical Report CSM-247, Department of Computer Science, University of Essex. This technical report was later updated as Chris Voudouris and Edward Tsang, 1999, Guided local search, *European Journal of Operational Research*, 113(2), 469–499.

To do this, Guided Local Search maintains a vector of pheromones,[137] one per component, which reflect how often each component has appeared in high-quality solutions. Instead of hill-climbing by Quality, GLS hill-climbs by an AdjustedQuality function which takes both Quality and the presence of these pheromones into account.[138] Given a candidate solution S, a set of components C for the problem, and a vector $\vec{p}$ of current pheromones, one per component, the adjusted quality of S is defined as:

$$\text{AdjustedQuality}(S, C, \vec{p}) = \text{Quality}(S) - \beta \sum_i \begin{cases} p_i & \text{if component } C_i \text{ is found in } S \\ 0 & \text{otherwise} \end{cases}$$

Thus the hill-climber is looking for solutions both of high quality but also ones which are relatively *novel*: they use components which haven't been used much in high-quality solutions before. High pheromones are *bad* in this context. The parameter β determines the degree to which novelty figures in the final quality computation, and it will need to be tuned carefully.

After doing some hill-climbing in this adjusted quality space, the algorithm then takes its current candidate solution S, which is presumably at or near a local optimum, and increases the pheromones on certain components which can be found in this solution. To be likely to have its pheromones increased, a component must have three qualities. First, it must appear in the current solution — that is, it's partly responsible for the local optimum and should be avoided. Second, it will tend to have lower value or higher cost: we wish to move away from the least important components in the solution first. Third, it will tend to have lower pheromones. This is because GLS doesn't just want to penalize the same components forever: it'd like to turn its attention to other components for some exploration. Thus when a component's pheromone has increased sufficiently, it's not chosen for further increases. Spread the love!

To determine the components whose pheromones should be increased, GLS first computes the *penalizability* of each component C_i with current pheromone p_i as follows:[139]

$$\text{Penalizability}(C_i, p_i) = \frac{1}{(1 + p_i) \times \text{Value}(C_i)}$$

...or if your problem is using costs...

$$\text{Penalizability}(C_i, p_i) = \frac{\text{Cost}(C_i)}{(1 + p_i)}$$

Guided Local Search then picks the *most* penalizable component *presently found in the current solution S* and increments its pheromone p_i by 1. If there's more than one such component (they're tied), their pheromones are all increased.

Compare the Penalizability function with the Desirability function in Section 8.3.1: note that components with high Desirability generally have low Penalizability and vice versa. While ACO seeks to *build* new candidate solutions from historically desirable components, GLS punishes components which have often appeared in local optima, though the ones it punishes the most are the least desirable such components.

---

[137]I'm borrowing ACO terminology here: GLS calls them **penalties**.

[138]In the name of consistency I'm beginning to deviate from the standard GLS formulation: the algorithm traditionally is applied to minimization rather than maximization problems.

[139]GLS traditionally uses the term *utility* rather than my made-up word *penalizability*. Utility is a highly loaded term that usually means something quite different — see Section 10 for example — so I'm avoiding it.

Now that we have a way to adjust the quality of solutions based on pheromones, and a way to increase pheromones for components commonly found in local optima, the full algorithm is quite straightforward: it's just hill-climbing with an additional, occasional, adjustment of the current pheromones of the components. There's no evaporation (which is quite surprising!).

Guided Local Search doesn't specify how we determine that we're stuck in a local optimum and must adjust pheromones to get ourselves out. Usually there's no test for local optimality. Thus below the approach I've taken is borrowed from Algorithm 10 (Hill-Climbing with Random Restarts, Section 2.2), where we hill-climb until a random timer goes off, then update pheromones under the presumption that we've hill-climbed long enough to roughly get ourselves trapped in a local optimum.

Algorithm 113 *Guided Local Search (GLS) with Random Updates*

1: $C \leftarrow \{C_1, ..., C_i\}$ set of possible components a candidate solution could have
2: $T \leftarrow$ distribution of possible time intervals

3: $\vec{p} \leftarrow \langle p_1, ..., p_i \rangle$ pheromones of the components, initially zero
4: $S \leftarrow$ some initial candidate solution
5: $Best \leftarrow S$
6: **repeat**
7:     $time \leftarrow$ random time in the near future, chosen from T
8:     **repeat**   ▷ First do some hill-climbing in the pheromone-adjusted quality space
9:         $R \leftarrow \text{Tweak}(\text{Copy}(S))$
10:         **if** Quality(R) > Quality($Best$) **then**
11:             $Best \leftarrow R$
12:         **if** AdjustedQuality($R, C, \vec{p}$) > AdjustedQuality($S, C, \vec{p}$) **then**
13:             $S \leftarrow R$
14:     **until** $Best$ is the ideal solution, *time* is up, or we have run out of time
15:     $C' \leftarrow \{\}$
16:     **for** each component $C_i \in C$ appearing in S **do**   ▷ Find the most penalizable components
17:         **if** for all $C_j \in C$ appearing in S, Penalizability(C_i, p_i) $\geq$ Penalizability(C_j, p_j) **then**
18:             $C' \leftarrow C' \cup \{C_i\}$
19:     **for** each component $C_i \in C$ appearing in S **do** ▷ Penalize them by increasing their pheromones
20:         **if** $C_i \in C'$ **then**
21:             $p_i \leftarrow p_i + 1$
22: **until** $Best$ is the ideal solution or we have run out of time
23: **return** $Best$

The general idea behind Guided Local Search doesn't have to be restricted to hill-climbing: it could be used for population-based methods as well (and indeed is, where one version is known as the **Guided Genetic Algorithm**).

9 Optimization by Model Fitting

Most of the methods we've examined so far sample the space of candidate solutions and select the high-quality ones. Based on the samples, new samples are generated through Tweaking. Eventually the samples (if we're lucky) start migrating towards the fitter areas in the space.

But there's an alternative to using selection and Tweak. Instead, from our samples we might build a **model** (or update an existing one) which gives us an idea of where the good areas of the space are. From that model we could then generate a new set of samples.

Models can take many forms. They could be **neural networks** or **decision trees** describing how good certain regions of the space are. They could be sets of rules delineating regions in the space. They could be **distributions** over the space suggesting where most of the population should go. The process of fitting a model (sometimes known as a **hypothesis**) to a sample of data is commonly known as **induction**, and is one of the primary tasks of **machine learning**.

This model building and sample generation is really just an elaborate way of doing selection and Tweaking, only we're not generating children *directly* from other individuals, but instead created uniformly from the *region* in which the fitter individuals generally reside.

Much of the model-fitting literature in the metaheuristics community has focused on models in the form of distributions, especially simplified distributions known as **marginal distributions**. This literature is collectively known as **Estimation of Distribution Algorithms (EDAs)**. But there are other approaches, largely cribbed from the machine learning community. We'll begin with one such alternative, then get to EDAs afterwards.

9.1 Model Fitting by Classification

A straightforward way to fit a model to a population is to simply divide the population into the fit individuals and the unfit individuals, then tell a learning method to use this information to identify the "fitter" regions of the space as opposed to the "unfit" regions. This is basically a binary **classification** problem.[140]

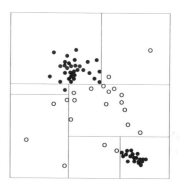

Figure 56 Model fitting by classification via a decision tree. Black circles are "fit" and white circles are "unfit" individuals in the population. The learned model delimits fit and unfit regions of the genotype space.

One of the better-known variations on model-fitting by classification is the **Learnable Evolution Model (LEM)**, by Ryszard Michalski.[141] The overall technique is very simple: first, do some evolution. Then when your population has run out of steam, break it into two groups: the "fit" and "unfit" individuals (and possibly a third group of "middling" individuals). Use a classification algorithm to identify the regions of the space containing the fit individuals but *not* containing the unfit individuals. Replace the "unfit" individuals with individuals sampled at random from those identified regions. Then go back to do some more evolution.

There are plenty of binary classification algorithms available in the machine learning world: for example, **decision trees**, **Support Vector Machines (SVMs)**, **k-Nearest-Neighbor (kNN)**, even

---

[140]Classification is the task of identifying the regions of space which belong to various *classes* (or *categories*). Here, we happen to be dividing the genotype space into two classes: the *fit individuals* class and the *unfit individuals* class. Hence the term *binary classification*.

[141]Ryszard Michalski, 2000, Learnable evolution model: Evolutionary processes guided by machine learning, *Machine Learning*, 38(1–2), 9–40.

Michalski's own **AQ**[142] algorithm. LEM doesn't care all that much. Figure 56 shows the results of applying a decision tree to divide up the "fit" from "unfit" regions. Note some portions of the space could have been fit better: part of this is due to the particular **learning bias** of the decision tree algorithm, which emphasizes rectangles. Every learning method has a bias: pick your poison. The algorithm:

Algorithm 114 *An Abstract Version of the Learnable Evolution Model (LEM)*
1: $b \leftarrow$ number of "best individuals"
2: $w \leftarrow$ number of "worst individuals" ▷ $b + w \leq ||P||$. If you wish, you can make $b + w = ||P||$.

3: $P \leftarrow$ Build Initial Population
4: $Best \leftarrow \square$
5: **repeat**
6:     **repeat** ▷ Do some evolution
7:         AssessFitness(P)
8:         **for** each individual $P_i \in P$ **do**
9:             **if** $Best = \square$ or Fitness(P_i) > Fitness($Best$) **then**
10:                 $Best \leftarrow P_i$
11:         $P \leftarrow$ Join(P, Breed(P))
12:     **until** neither P nor $Best$ seem to be improving by much any more
13:     $P^+ \subset P \leftarrow$ fittest b individuals in P ▷ Fit a model
14:     $P^- \subset P \leftarrow$ least fit w individuals in P
15:     $M \leftarrow$ learned model which describes the region of space containing members of P^+ but not P^-
16:     $Q \leftarrow w$ children generated randomly from the region described in M ▷ Generate children
17:     $P \leftarrow$ Join(P, Q) ▷ Often $P \leftarrow (P - P^-) \cup Q$
18: **until** $Best$ is the ideal solution or we have run out of time
19: **return** $Best$

Some notes. First, the Join operation in Line 17 is often done by simply replacing the w worst individuals in P, that is, P^-, with the Q new children. In other words, $P \leftarrow (P - P^-) \cup Q$. But you could do Join in other ways as well. Second, M could also be based not on P but on *all* previously tested individuals: why waste information?

Third, it's plausible, and in fact common, to do *no* evolution at all, and do only model building: that is, eliminate Lines 6, 11, and 12. This model-building-only approach will be used in later algorithms in this Section. Or, since it's sometimes hard to determine if things are "improving", you could jut run the evolution step for some n times and then head into model-building, or apply a timer a-la Hill-Climbing with Random Restarts (Algorithm 10).

Generating Children from the Model The models produced by classification algorithms fall into two common categories: **generative models** and **discriminative models**. Generative models can easily generate random children for you. Discriminative models cannot. But many common classification algorithms (including all mentioned so far) produce discriminative models! What to do? We could apply **rejection sampling** to our discriminative models: repeatedly generate random individuals until one falls in the "high fitness" region according to our model.

---
[142]Originally called A^q, later restyled as AQ. I don't know why.

Algorithm 115 *Simple Rejection Sampling*
1: $n \leftarrow$ desired number of samples
2: $M \leftarrow$ learned model

3: $P \leftarrow \{\}$
4: **for** n times **do**
5:     **repeat**
6:         $S \leftarrow$ individual generated uniformly at random
7:     **until** S is in a "fit" region as defined by M
8:     $P \leftarrow P \cup \{S\}$
9: **return** P

As the run progresses and the population homes in on the optima in the space, the regions of "fit" individuals become very small, and rejection sampling starts getting expensive. Alternatively, you could try to gather the list of regions that are considered valid, and sample from them according to their size. Imagine that you've gone through the model (a decision tree say) and have gathered a list of "fit" regions. For each region you have computed a volume. You could perform a kind of **region-based sampling** where you first pick a region proportional to their volumes (using Fitness Proportionate Selection, but with volumes rather than fitnesses), and then select a point uniformly at random within the chosen region. This would also create an entirely uniform selection.

Algorithm 116 *Region-based Sampling*
1: $n \leftarrow$ desired number of samples
2: $M \leftarrow$ learned model

3: $P \leftarrow \{\}$
4: $R \leftarrow \{R_1, ..., R_m\}$ "fit" regions from M, each with computed volumes
5: **for** n times **do**
6:     $R_i \leftarrow$ selected from R using Volume-Proportionate Selection ▷ (Like algorithm 30, so to speak)
7:     $P \leftarrow P \cup \{$ individual generated uniformly from within the bounds of $R_i\}$
8: **return** P

It turns out that many discriminative models don't just create boundaries delimiting regions, but really define fuzzy functions specifying the probability that a given point belongs to one class or another. Deep in the "low fitness" regions, the probability of a point being "high fitness" is very small; while deep in the "high fitness" regions it's quite big. On the borders, it's half/half. Furthermore, there exist approximate probability estimation functions even for those algorithms which are notionally boundary-oriented, such as k-Nearest-Neighbor, SVMs, and decision trees. For example, in a decision tree, the probability of a region belonging to the "high fitness" class could be assumed to be proportional to the number of "high fitness" individuals from the population from which we built the model which were located in that region.

Assuming we have this probability, we could apply a **weighted rejection sampling**, where we keep kids only with a probability matching the model:

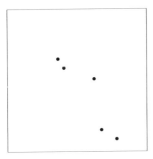   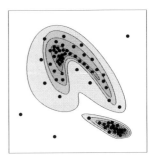

(a) A population of 5 individuals

(b) A population of 20 individuals

(c) A population of 75 indivdiuals

(d) A distribution of an infinite number of individuals, with Subfigure (c) overlaid for reference.

Figure 57 The distribution of a population candidate solutions, using samples of 5, 20, and 75, plus an infinite population distribution.

Algorithm 117 *Weighted Rejection Sampling*
1: $n \leftarrow$ desired number of samples
2: $M \leftarrow$ learned model

3: $P \leftarrow \{\}$
4: **for** n times **do**
5:    **repeat**
6:       $S \leftarrow$ individual generated uniformly at random
7:       $p \leftarrow$ probability that S is "fit", according to M
8:    **until** $p \geq$ random number chosen uniformly from 0.0 to 1.0 inclusive
9:    $P \leftarrow P \cup \{S\}$
10: **return** P

Algorithm 115 (simple rejection sampling) is just a degenerate version of weighted sampling, where the probability is 1.0 if you're in the "fit" region and 0.0 of you're in the "unfit" region.

9.2 Model Fitting with a Distribution

An alternative form of model is a **distribution of an infinite-sized population** using some mathematical function. This is the basic idea behind **Estimation of Distribution Algorithms (EDAs)**. To conceptualize this, let's begin with an approach to a distribution which in fact no EDAs (to my knowledge) use, but which is helpful for illustration. Figure 57(a) shows a population of 5 individuals sampling the space roughly in proportion to the fitness of those regions. Figure 57(b) has increased this to 20 individuals, and Figure 57(c) to 75 individuals. Now imagine that we keep increasing the population clear to ∞ individuals. At this point our infinite population has become a **distribution** of the sort shown in Figure 57(d), with different densities in the space. Thus in some sense we may view Figures 57(a), (b), and (c) as **sample distributions** of the true underlying infinite distribution shown in Figure 57(d).

That's basically what a population actually is: in an ideal world we'd have an infinite number of individuals to work with. But we can't, because, well, our computers can't hold that many. So we work with a sample distribution instead.

The idea behind an Estimation of Distribution Algorithm is to represent that infinite population in some way other than with a large number of samples. From this distribution we will typically sample a set of individuals, assess them, then adjust the distribution to reflect the new fitness results we've discovered. This adjustment imagines that the entire distribution is undergoing selection[143] such that fitter regions of the space increase in their proportion of the distribution, and the less fit regions decrease in proportion. Thus the next time we sample from the distribution, we'll be sampling more individuals from the fitter areas of the space (hopefully).

Algorithm 118 *An Abstract Estimation of Distribution Algorithm (EDA)*
1: $D \leftarrow$ Build Initial Infinite Population Distribution
2: $Best \leftarrow \square$
3: **repeat**
4:     $P \leftarrow$ a sample of individuals generated from D
5:     AssessFitness(P)
6:     **for** each individual $P_i \in P$ **do**
7:         **if** $Best = \square$ or Fitness(P_i) > Fitness($Best$) **then**
8:             $Best \leftarrow P_i$
9:     $D \leftarrow$ UpdateDistribution(D, P)   ▷ Using P's fitness results, D undergoes "selection"
10: **until** *Best* is the ideal solution or we have run out of time
11: **return** *Best*

At this point you may have noticed that estimation of distribution algorithms are really just a fancy way of fitting **generative models** to your data. Such models are often essentially telling you the probability that a given point in space is going to be "highly fit". Because they're generative, we don't need to do rejection sampling etc.: we can just produce random values under the models. In theory.

Representing Distributions So far we've assumed our space is real-valued and multidimensional. Let's go with that for a while. How could you represent a distribution over such a monster? One way is to represent the distribution as an *n*-dimensional histogram. That is, we discretize the space into a grid, and for each grid point we indicate the proportion of the population which resides at that grid point. This approach is shown in Figure 58. The difficulty with this method is twofold. First, we may need a fairly high-resolution grid to accurately represent the distribution (though we could do better by allowing the grid squares to vary in size, as in a **kd-tree** or **quadtree**). Second, if we have a high dimensional space, we're going to need a *lot* of grid points. Specifically, if we have *n* genes in our genome, and each has been discretized into *a* pieces, we'll need a^n numbers. Eesh.

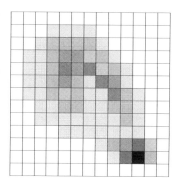

Figure 58 Approximating the distribution in Figure 57(d) with a histogram.

---
[143] As it's an *infinite* population, Tweaking is not actually necessary. Just selection.

Another way to represent our infinite population is with some kind of parametric distribution. For example, we could use some m number of gaussian curves to approximate the real distribution as shown in Figure 59 (with $m = 3$). This has the advantage of not requiring a massive number of grid squares. But it too has some problems. First off, how many gaussian curves do we need to accurately describe this population? Second, gaussian curves may not give you the cost savings you were expecting. A one-dimensional gaussian, like everyone's seen in grade school, just needs a mean μ and variance σ^2 to define it. But in an n-dimensional space, a multinomial gaussian which can be stretched and tilted in any dimension requires a **mean vector** $\vec{\mu}$ of size n and a **covariance matrix**[144] Σ which is n^2 in size. So if you have 1000 genes, you need a covariance matrix of size 1,000,000 for a single gaussian.

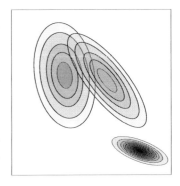

Figure 59 Approximating the distribution in Figure 57(d) with three multivariate Gaussian curves.

Still though, n^2 is lots better than a^n. But it's not nearly good enough. Thus most estimation of distribution algorithms cheat and use a different representation which is radically simpler but at a huge cost: a set of **marginal distributions**.

A marginal distribution is a projection of the full distribution onto (usually) a single dimension. For example, Figure 60 shows the projection of the full joint distribution in two different directions, one for x and one for y. If we just use the marginal distributions in each dimension, then instead of a joint distribution of n dimensions, we just have n 1-dimensional distributions. Thus a marginal distribution contains proportions of an infinite population which contain the various possible values for a *single gene*. There is one marginal distribution per gene.

We've not come up with a new representation: just a way to reduce the dimensionality of the space. So we'll still need to have some way of representing each of the marginal distributions. As usual, we could use (for example) a parametric representation like one or more 1-dimensional gaussians; or we could use a 1-dimensional array as a histogram, as shown in Figure 61.

From Figure 60 it appears that we could probably get away with representing each marginal distribution with, it appears, roughly two 1-dimensional gaussians. Each such gaussian requires a mean and a variance: that's just *8 numbers* (a mean and variance for each gaussian, two gaussians per marginal distribution, two marginal distributions). In general, if we needed b gaussians per dimension, we'd need $2bn$ numbers. A tiny amount compared to n^2. Or if we chose to use a histogram, discretizing our one-dimensional distributions each into b buckets, that's still bn numbers, instead of the a^n we needed for the joint histogram. Great! (Actually, there's an ugly problem, but we'll get to that in a bit.)

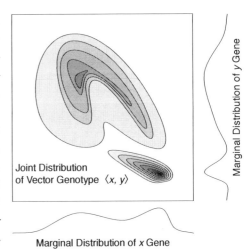

Figure 60 Marginalized versions of the distribution in Figure 57(d). Since each distribution has two peaks, each could probably be reasonably approximated with two gaussians per distribution (four in total).

---

[144]Yes. Σ is classically used to represent covariance matrices. Not to be confused with the summation symbol $\sum$. Ugh. Try summing covariance matrices some time: $\sum_i \sum_j \Sigma_{ij}$. Wonderful.

Now that we've burned out on real-valued spaces, consider (finite[145]) discrete spaces. Representing a joint discrete space is exactly like the grid in Figure 58, except (of course) don't need to discretize: we're already discrete. However we still have a potentially huge number of points, making attractive the marginal distributions again. Each marginal distribution is, as usual, a description of the fractions of the population which have a particular value for their gene. Each gene thus has a marginal distribution consisting of just an array of fractions, one for every possible gene value. Similar to the marginalized histogram example.

In fact, if you have w possible gene values, you don't *really* need an array of size w. You just need the first $w - 1$ elements. The array must sum to 1 (it's a distribution), so it's clear what the last element value is.

We can get even simpler still: what if our space is simply multidimensional boolean? That is, each point in space is just a vector of booleans? You couldn't get simpler: the marginal distribution for each gene is represented by just a single number: the fraction of the population which has a 1 in that gene position (as opposed to a 0). Thus you can think of all marginal distributions for an n dimensional boolean problem as a single real-valued vector of length n, with each value between 0.0 and 1.0.

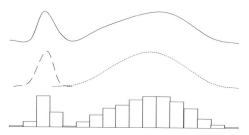

Figure 61 Gaussian and histogram representations of a 1-dimensional marginal distribution.

9.2.1 Univariate Estimation of Distribution Algorithms

Now that we have a way of reducing the space complexity through marginalization, and can represent marginal distributions in various ways, we can look at some actual EDAs. The first EDAs were **univariate** EDAs: they used the marginalizing trick described earlier. Most of them also operated over **discrete** or even **boolean** spaces.

Among the earliest such EDAs was **Population-Based Incremental Learning (PBIL)**, by Shumeet Baluja.[146] PBIL assumes a finite discrete space. This algorithm begins with n marginal distributions, one per gene. Each distribution is initially uniform, but that'll change soon. The algorithm then repeatedly samples individuals by picking one gene from each distribution. It then assesses the fitness of the individuals, and applies truncation selection to throw out the worst ones. It then updates each marginal distribution by throwing out a little of its old probabilities and rolling in a little of the proportions of values for that gene which exist among the remaining (fitter) individuals. We then throw away the individuals and go back to making new ones from the revised distribution.

---

[145]Countably infinite spaces, like the space of all integers or the space of trees or graphs, present a much yuckier problem and typically aren't handled by EDAs.

[146]The first PBIL document was Shumeet Baluja, 1994, Population-based incremental learning: A method for integrating genetic search based function optimization and competitive learning, Technical Report CMU-CS-94-163, Carnegie Mellon University. The first formal publication, with Rich Caruana, was Shumeet Baluja and Rich Caruana, 1995, Removing the genetics from the standard genetic algorithm, in Armand Prieditis and Stuart Russell, editors, *Proceedings of the Twelfth International Conference on Machine Learning (ICML)*, pages 38–46, Morgan Kaufmann.

Algorithm 119 *Population-Based Incremental Learning (PBIL)*
1: *popsize* ← number of individuals to generate each time
2: *b* ← how many individuals to select out of the generated group
3: α ← learning rate: how rapidly to update the distribution based on new sample information

4: $D \leftarrow \{D_1, ..., D_n\}$ marginal distributions, one per gene   ▷ Each uniformly distributed
5: *Best* ← □
6: **repeat**
7:     $P \leftarrow \{\}$ ▷ Sample from D
8:     **for** *i* from 1 to *popsize* **do**
9:        S ← individual built by choosing the value for each gene *j* at random under distribution D_j
10:        AssessFitness(S)
11:        **if** *Best* = □ or Fitness(S) > Fitness(*Best*) **then**
12:           *Best* ← S
13:        $P \leftarrow P \cup \{S\}$
14:     P ← the fittest *b* individuals in P ▷ Truncation selection
15:     **for** each gene *j* **do**   ▷ Update D
16:        N ← distribution over the possible values for gene *j* found among the individuals in P
17:        $D_j \leftarrow (1-\alpha)D_j + \alpha N_j$
18: **until** *Best* is the ideal solution or we have run out of time
19: **return** *Best*

That last equation ($D_j \leftarrow (1-\alpha)D_j + \alpha N_j$) deserves some explanation. Keep in mind that because PBIL operates over discrete spaces, each distribution D_j is just a vector of fractions, one for each value that gene *j* can be. We multiply each of these fractions by $1 - \alpha$, and add in α's worth of fractions from N_j. N_j is the vector, one per value that gene *j* can be, of the fraction of members of P that have that particular value for gene *j*. So α helps us to *gradually* change the distribution.

In short: we sampled from D, threw out the least fit samples, and rolled their resulting distributions back into D. As a result D has shifted to be closer to the fitter parts of the space.

A variation on PBIL is the **Univariate Marginal Distribution Algorithm (UMDA)**, by Heinz Mühlenbein.[147] UMDA differs from PBIL only in two small respects. First, UMDA doesn't specify truncation selection as the way to reduce P: any selection procedure is allowed. Second, UMDA entirely replaces the distribution D each time around. That is, $\alpha = 1$. Because there's no gradualness, if our latest sample doesn't contain a given value for a certain gene, that value is lost forever, just like using crossover without mutation in the genetic algorithm. As a result, to maintain diversity we will require a large sample each time if the number of discrete values each gene can take on is large. Perhaps for this reason, UMDA is most often applied to boolean spaces.

Next, we consider the **Compact Genetic Algorithm (cGA)** by Georges Harik, Fernando Lobo, and David Goldberg, which operates solely over boolean spaces.[148] cGA is different from PBIL in important ways. Once again, we have a distribution and use it to generate some collection of individuals, but rather than do selection on those individuals, we instead compare every pair of

---

[147] Heinz Mühlenbein, 1997, The equation for response to selection and its use for prediction, *Evolutionary Computation*, 5(3), 303–346.

[148] It's never been clear to me why it's cGA and not CGA. Georges Harik, Fernando Lobo, and David Goldberg, 1999, The compact genetic algorithm, *IEEE Transactions on Evolutionary Computation*, 3(4), 287–297.

individuals P_i and P_k in our sample. Assume P_i is fitter. For each gene j, if P_i and P_k differ in value at gene j, we shift D_j so that it will generate P_i's gene value more often in the future. Since cGA works only with booleans, gene values can only be 1 or 0, and each distribution D_j is represented by just a real-valued number (how often we pick a 1 versus a 0). If P_i was 1 and P_k was 0, we increase D_j by a small amount. Thus not only do the "fit" individuals have a say in how the distribution changes, but the "unfit" individuals do as well: they're telling the distribution: "don't be like me!"

The cGA doesn't model an infinite population, but rather a very large but *finite* population. Thus the cGA has "steps" for incrementing or decrementing distributions, each step $\frac{1}{discretization}$ in size. Moving one step up in a discretization represents one more member of that large population taking on that particular gene value. Though I'm not sure why you couldn't just say

$$D_j \leftarrow (1 - \alpha)D_j + \alpha(\text{value of gene } j \text{ in } P_i - \text{value of gene } j \text{ in } P_k)$$

(or in the notation of the algorithm below, use U and V instead of P_i and P_k).

Algorithm 120 *The Compact Genetic Algorithm (cGA)*

1: *popsize* ← number of individuals to generate each time
2: *discretization* ← number of discrete values our distributions can take on   ▷ Should be odd, ≥ 3

3: $D \leftarrow \{D_1, ..., D_n\}$ marginal boolean distributions, one per gene   ▷ Each uniform: set to 0.5
4: *gameover* ← false
5: *Best* ← □
6: **repeat**
7:     **if** for all genes j, $D_j = 1$ or $D_j = 0$ **then**   ▷ D has converged, so let's quit after this loop
8:         *gameover* ← true
9:     $P \leftarrow \{\}$ ▷ Sample from D
10:    **for** i from 1 to *popsize* **do**
11:        $S \leftarrow$ individual built by choosing the value for each gene j at random under distribution D_j
12:        AssessFitness(S)
13:        **if** *Best* = □ or Fitness(S) > Fitness(*Best*) **then**
14:            *Best* ← S
15:        $P \leftarrow P \cup \{S\}$
16:    **for** i from 1 to $||P||$ **do**   ▷ For all pairs P_i and P_k, $i \neq k$...
17:        **for** k from $i + 1$ to $||P||$ **do**
18:            $U \leftarrow P_i$
19:            $V \leftarrow P_k$
20:            **if** Fitness(V) > Fitness(U) **then**   ▷ Make sure U is the fitter individual of the two
21:                Swap U and V
22:            **for** each gene j **do**   ▷ Update each D_j only if U and V are different
23:                **if** the value of gene j in U > the value of gene j and $D_j < 1$ **then**   ▷ 1 vs. 0
24:                    $D_j \leftarrow D_j + \frac{1}{discretization}$ ▷ Push closer to a 1
25:                **else if** the value of gene j in U < the value of gene j and $D_j > 0$ **then**   ▷ 0 vs. 1
26:                    $D_j \leftarrow D_j - \frac{1}{discretization}$ ▷ Push closer to a 0
27: **until** *Best* is the ideal solution, or *gameover*=true, or we have run out of time
28: **return** *Best*

I augmented this with our standard "Best" mechanism: though in fact the cGA doesn't normally include that gizmo. Instead the cGA normally runs until its distributions are all 1's or 0's, which indicates that the entire "population" has converged to a given point in the space. Then it just returns that point (this is easily done by just sampling from the D_j distributions one last time). To augment with the "Best" mechanism, I'm just running the loop one final time (using the *gameover* counter) to give this final sampling a chance to compete for the "Best" slot.

The version of cGA shown here is the more general "round robin tournament" version, in which every individual is compared against every other individual. A more common version of cGA just generates two individuals at a time and compares them. This can be implemented simply by setting the size of P to 2 in the round-robin tournament version.

In the round robin tournament version, we have to ensure that $0 \leq D_j \leq 1$; but in the $||P|| = 2$ version, it so happens that happens automagically. When D_j reaches (say) 0, then 100% of the individuals sampled from it will have 0 in that gene slot. That includes U and V. U and V will now always have the same value in that slot and the if-statements (lines 23 and 25) will be turned off.

Real-Valued Representations So far we've seen algorithms for boolean and discrete marginal distributions. How about real-valued ones?

Once we've marginalized a real-valued distribution, we're left with m separate 1-dimensional real-valued distributions. As discussed earlier, we could just discretize those distributions, so each gene would have some n (discrete) gene values. At this point we could just use PBIL: generate an individual by, for each gene, first picking one of those discrete gene values, then picking a random real-valued number within that discretized region. Likewise, to determine if a (discretized) gene value is found in a given individual, you just discretize the current value and see if it matches.

There are other approaches too. For example, you could represent each marginal distribution with a single gaussian. This would require two numbers, the mean μ and variance σ^2, per distribution. To create an individual, for each gene you just pick a random number under the gaussian distribution defined by μ and σ^2, that is, the Normal distribution $N(\mu, \sigma^2)$ (see Algorithm 12).

In PBIL, to adjust the distribution to new values of μ and σ^2 based on the fitness results, we first need to determine the mean μ_{N_j} and variance $\sigma^2_{N_j}$ of the distribution N_j described by the fit individuals stored in P. The mean is obvious:

$$\mu_{N_j} = \frac{1}{||P||} \sum_{P_i \in P} \text{value of gene } j \text{ of } P_i$$

We could use the **unbiased estimator**[149] for our variance:

$$\sigma^2_{N_j} = \frac{1}{||P|| - 1} \sum_{P_i \in P} (\text{value of gene } j \text{ of } P_i - \mu_{N_j})^2$$

Now we just update the distribution D_j. Instead of using this line:

$$D_j \leftarrow (1 - \alpha) D_j + \alpha N_j$$

We could do:

$$\mu_{D_j} \leftarrow (1 - \alpha) \mu_{D_j} + \alpha \mu_{N_j}$$
$$\sigma^2_{D_j} \leftarrow (1 - \beta) \sigma^2_{D_j} + \beta \sigma^2_{N_j}$$

---

[149] I *think* this is what we want. If it isn't, then it's $\frac{1}{||P||}$ rather than $\frac{1}{||P||-1}$.

The idea is to make the distribution in D_j more similar to the sample distribution we gathered in N_j. To be maximally general, σ^2 has its own learning rate β, but if you like you could set $\beta = \alpha$.

Of course, in Figure 60 the distributions weren't described easily with a single gaussian, but rather would be okay with *two* gaussians each. Updating a multimodal distribution like that is perfectly doable but trickier, involving a variant of gradient descent called the **Expectation Maximization** or **EM** algorithm. That's a whole topic in and of itself, so I'll just leave it there. But in truth, I'd use several gaussians per marginal distribution in most cases.

9.2.2 Multivariate Estimation of Distribution Algorithms

There is a **very big problem** with using marginal distributions, and it turns out it is the *exact same problem* that is faced by Cooperative Coevolution: it assumes that there is no linkage at all between genes. Each gene can be relegated to its own separate distribution without considering the joint distribution between the genes. We're throwing information away. As a result, marginal distributions suffer from essentially the same maladies that Cooperative Coevolution does.[150] As a result, univariate EDAs may easily get sucked into local optima for many nontrivial problems.

Recognizing this problem, recent EDA research has focused on coming up with more sophisticated EDAs which don't just use simple marginal distributions. But we can't just go to the full joint distribution: it's too huge. Instead they've moved a *little* towards the joint by using **bivariate** distributions: one distribution for every *pair* of genes in the individual. If you have n genes, this results in $n^2 - n$ distributions, and that's prohibitively expensive. And if we go to triples or quadruples of genes per distribution, it gets uglier still.

Various algorithms have been proposed to deal with this. The prevailing approach seems to be to find the pairs (or triples, or quadruples, etc.) of genes which appear to have the strongest linkage, rather than computing *all* the combinations. We can then represent the joint distribution of the space as a collection of univariate distributions and the most strongly-linked bivariate (or multivariate) distributions. This sparse approximate representation of the space is known as a **Bayes Network**. Now instead of building the distribution D from our samples, we build a Bayes Network N which *approximates* the true distribution D as well as possible. N is likewise used to generate our new collection of samples.

Here I'm going to disappoint you: I'm not going explain how to build a Bayes Network from a collection of data (in our case, a small population), nor explain how to generate a new data point (individual) from the same. There is an *entire research field* devoted to these topics. It's complex! And depending on the kind of data (real-valued, etc.), and the models used to represent them (gaussians, histograms, whatnot), it can get *much* more complex still. Instead, it might be wise to rely on an existing Bayes Network or Graphical Model package to do the hard work for you.

With such a package in hand, the procedure is pretty easy. We begin with a random sample (population) and cut it down to just the fitter samples. We then build a network from those samples

---

[150]The model behind Cooperative Coevolution is basically identical to univariate estimation of distribution algorithms in its use of marginalization. The only difference is that Cooperative Coevolution uses samples (individuals in populations) for its "marginal distributions", while univariate EDAs use something else — gaussians, histograms, what have you. Compare Figures 45 and 46 in the Coevolution Section with Figure 60 showing marginalized distributions: they're *very* similar. Christopher Vo, Liviu Panait, and I had a paper on all this: Christopher Vo, Liviu Panait, and Sean Luke, 2009, Cooperative coevolution and univariate estimation of distribution algorithms, in *FOGA '09: Proceedings of the Tenth ACM SIGEVO Workshop on the Foundations of Genetic Algorithms*, pages 141–150, ACM. It's not a giant result but it was fun to write.

which approximates their distribution in the space. From this distribution we generate a bunch of new data points (the "children"). Then the children get joined into the population. This is the essence of the **Bayesian Optimization Algorithm (BOA)** by Martin Pelikan, David Goldberg, and Eric Cantú-Paz. A more recent version, called the **Hierarchical Bayesian Optimization Algorithm (hBOA)**,[151] is presently the current cutting edge, but BOA suffices for our purposes here:

Algorithm 121 *An Abstract Version of the Bayesian Optimization Algorithm (BOA)*

1: $p \leftarrow$ desired initial population size
2: $\mu \leftarrow$ desired parent subset size
3: $\lambda \leftarrow$ desired child subset size

4: $Best \leftarrow \square$
5: $P \leftarrow \{P_1, ..., P_p\}$ Build Initial Random Population
6: AssessFitness(P)
7: **for** each individual $P_i \in P$ **do**
8:     **if** $Best = \square$ or Fitness(P_i) > Fitness($Best$) **then**
9:         $Best \leftarrow P_i$
10: **repeat**
11:     $Q \subseteq P \leftarrow$ Select μ fit individuals from P ▷ Truncation selection is fine
12:     $N \leftarrow$ construct a Bayesian Network distribution from Q
13:     $R \leftarrow \{\}$
14:     **for** λ times **do**
15:         $R \leftarrow R \cup \{$ individual generated at random under $N\}$
16:     AssessFitness(R)
17:     **for** each individual $R_j \in R$ **do**
18:         **if** Fitness(R_j) > Fitness($Best$) **then**
19:             $Best \leftarrow R_j$
20:     $P \leftarrow$ Join(P, R)   ▷ You could do $P \leftarrow Q \cup R$, for example
21: **until** $Best$ is the ideal solution or we have run out of time
22: **return** $Best$

So what's really going on with algorithms like these? They're actually little more than extravagant methods for doing population resampling. But they're different in an important way: the Bayes Network is essentially finding not just highly fit individuals to resample into a new population, it's trying to identify *why* they're highly fit. What features do they appear to have in common? Which elements in the individuals appear to matter and which ones don't?

This is a big deal: it can home in on the best parts of the space fairly rapidly. But it comes at a considerable cost: Algorithms along these lines can get *very* complex due to manipulation of the Bayes Network, particularly if the space isn't something simple like a boolean space.

---

[151] I have no idea why it's not HBOA. The BOA algorithm was introduced in Martin Pelikan, David E. Goldberg, and Erick Cantú-Paz, 1999, BOA: The bayesian optimization algorithm, in Wolfgang Banzhaf, *et al.*, editors, *Proceedings of the Genetic and Evolutionary Computation Conference GECCO-1999*, pages 525–532, Morgan Kaufmann. Two years later, hBOA was published in Martin Pelikan and David E. Goldberg, 2001, Escaping hierarchical traps with competent genetic algorithms, in *Proceedings of the Genetic and Evolutionary Computation Conference (GECCO-2001)*, pages 511–518, Morgan Kaufmann. Warning: hBOA is patented.

10 Policy Optimization

Section 4.5.1 introduced the notion of an **agent** which follows a simple program called a **policy**. Much of this section concerns methods for an agent to learn or optimize its policy.[152] To do so, the agent will wander about doing what an agent does, and occasionally receive a **reward** (or **reinforcement**) to encourage or discourage the agent from doing various things. This reward ultimately trickles back through earlier actions the agent did, eventually teaching the agent which actions help to lead to good rewards and away from bad ones.

In the machine learning community, non-metaheuristic methods for learning policies are well established in a subfield called **reinforcement learning**. But those methods learn custom rules for every single state of the world. In contrast, there are evolutionary techniques, known as **Michigan-Approach Learning Classifier Systems (LCS)** or **Pitt-Approach Rule Systems**, which find much smaller, sparse descriptions of the entire state space. We'll begin by examining reinforcement learning because it is so closely associated with the evolutionary methods both historically and theoretically. Specifically, we'll spend quite a few pages on a **non-metaheuristic** reinforcement learning method called *Q-Learning*. Then we'll move to the evolutionary techniques.

I won't kid you. This topic can be very challenging to understand. You've been warned.[153]

10.1 Reinforcement Learning: Dense Policy Optimization

We begin with a non-metaheuristic set of techniques for learning dense policies, collectively known as **reinforcement learning**, partly to put the metaheuristic methods (in Section 10.2) in context, and partly because it teaches some concepts we'll need as we go on.

Reinforcement learning is a strange term. Generally speaking, it refers to any method that learns or adapts based on receiving quality assessments (the rewards or punishments — the *reinforcement*). Thus every single topic discussed up to this point could be considered reinforcement learning. Unfortunately this very general term has been co-opted by a narrow sub-community interested in learning policies consisting of sets of *if→then* rules. Recall that in Section 4.5 such rules were called **state-action rules**, and collectively described what to do in all situations the agent might find itself in. The reinforcement learner figures out what the optimal state-action ruleset is for a given environment, based solely on reinforcement received when trying out various rulesets in the environment.

What kinds of environments are we talking about? Here's an example: a cockroach robot's world is divided into grid squares defined by GPS coordinates. When the robot tries to move from grid square to grid square (say, going north, south, east, or west), sometimes it succeeds, but with a certain probability it winds up in a different neighboring square by accident. Some grid squares block the robot's path in certain directions (perhaps there's a wall). In some grid locations there are yummy things to eat. In other places the robot gets an electric shock. The robot does not know which squares provide the food or the shocks. It's just trying to figure out, for each square in its world,

---

[152]Unlike most other topics discussed so far, this is obviously a specific application to which metaheuristics may be applied, rather than a general area. But it's included here because this particular application has spawned unusual and important metaheuristics special to it; and it's a topic of some pretty broad impact. So we're going with it.

[153]If you want to go deeper into *Q-Learning* and related methods, a classic text on reinforcement learning is Richard Sutton and Andrew Barto, 1998, *Reinforcement Learning: an Introduction*, MIT Press. This excellent book is available online at http://www.cs.ualberta.ca/~sutton/book/the-book.html for free.

what direction should he go so as to maximize the yummy food and minimize the shocks over the robot's lifetime.

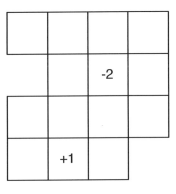

At right is a possible robot cockroach world, where if the cockroach stumbles into one area it gets a yummy treat (+1), and if it stumbles into another area it gets an electric shock (−2).

In this example, the cockroach robot is our **agent**. The grid squares are the **external states** (or just **states**) the agent may find itself in. The directions the cockroach tries to move are the **actions** available to the agent; different states may have different actions (in this case, because of the presence of walls). The yummy things to eat are **positive reinforcement** or **positive reward**, and the electric shocks are likewise **negative reinforcement**, or **punishment**, or **negative reward** (so to speak). The agent's attempt to maximize positive reinforcement over its lifetime is also known as trying to maximize the agent's **utility**[154] (or **value**). The probability of winding up in a new state based on the current state and chosen action is known as the **transition model**. Our agent usually doesn't know the transition model, but one exists.

Figure 62 Robot cockroach world with rewards (all unlabeled states have zero reward).

The reason each *if→then* rule is called a *state-action rule* in this context is because the *if* side indicates a possible external state, and the *then* side indicates what action to take when in that state. The agent is trying to construct a set of such rules, one for each possible external state, which collectively describe all the actions to take in the world. This collection of rules is known as a **policy**, and it is traditionally[155] denoted as a function $\pi(s)$ which returns the action a to take when in a given state s. Figure 63 shows a likely optimal policy for the cockroach world.

Let's do another example. We want to learn how to play Tic-Tac-Toe (as X) against a random opponent based entirely on wins and losses. Each possible board situation where X is about to play may be considered a *state*. For each such state, there are some number of moves X could make; these are available *actions* for the state. Then our opponent plays a random move against us and we wind up in a new state: the probability that playing a given action in a given state will wind up in a given new state is the *transition model*. Doing actions in certain states wind up punishing us or rewarding us because they cause us to immediately win or lose. Those are our *reinforcements*.

For example, if X plays at the location + in the state
X	X	+
O	−	X
O	△	O

then X receives a positive reinforcement because X wins the game. If X plays at the location −, X probably loses immediately and receives negative reinforcement provided the opponent isn't stupid[156] (keep in mind, the next state is *after* the opponent makes *his* move too). And if X plays at △ then X doesn't get any reinforcement immediately as the game must still continue (for a bit). Not getting reinforcement is also a kind of reinforcement: it's just a reinforcement of zero. Ultimately we're trying to learn a policy which tells us what to do in each board configuration.

Figure 63 An optimal policy for the cockroach robot world.

---

[154]Not to be confused with *utility* in Section 8.4.

[155]Yes, using π as a function name is stupid.

[156]Of course, to get in this situation in the first place, our random opponent wasn't the sharpest knife in the drawer.

Here's a third example, stolen from Minoru Asada's[157] work in robot soccer. A robot is trying to learn to push a ball into a goal. The robot has a camera and has boiled down what it sees into the following simple information: the ball is either *not visible* or it is in the *left*, *right*, or *center* of the field of view. If the ball is visible, it's also either *small* (far away), *medium*, or *large* (near). Likewise the goal is either not visible, on the left, right, or center, and if visible it's either small, medium, or large. All told there are ten ball situations (not visible, left small, left medium, left large, center small, center medium, center large, right small, right medium, right large) and likewise ten goal situations. A state is a pair of goal and ball situations: so there are 100 states. The robot can move forward, curve left, curve right, move backward, back up to the left, and back up to the right. So there are 6 actions for each state. The robot receives a positive reward for getting the ball in the goal and zero for everything else.

It's not just robots and games: reinforcement learning is in wide use in everything from factory-floor decision making to gambling to car engines deciding when and how to change fuel injection to maximize efficiency to simulations of competing countries or businesses. It's used a lot.

All these examples share certain common traits. First, we have a **fixed number of states**. Second, each state has a **fixed number of actions**, though the number and makeup of actions may differ from state to state. Third, we're assuming that performing an action in a given state **transfers** to other states with a **fixed probability**. That's nonsense but it's necessary nonsense to make the problem tractable. Fourth, we're also assuming that we receive rewards for doing certain actions in certain states, and that these rewards are either **deterministic** or also occur with a **fixed probability** on a per state/action basis. That's also a somewhat ridiculous assumption but keeps things tractable. And now the final nonsense assumption: the transition probabilities are based *entirely* on our current state and action — earlier actions or states do not influence the probabilities except through the fact that they helped us to land in our current state and action. That is, to figure out what the best possible action is for a given state, we **don't need to have any memory** of what we did a while back. We just need a simple *if→then* describing what to do given the situation we are in *now*. This last assumption is commonly known as an assumption of a **Markovian**[158] **environment**. Very few real situations are Markovian: but this assumption truly makes the problem tractable, so we try to make it whenever possible if it's not totally crazy.

10.1.1 *Q-Learning*

Q-Learning is a popular reinforcement learning algorithm which is useful to understand before we get to the evolutionary models. In *Q*-Learning, the agent maintains a current policy $\pi(s)$ (the best policy it's figured out so far) and wanders about its environment following that policy. As it learns that some actions aren't very good, the agent updates and changes its policy. The goal is ultimately to figure out the optimal (smartest possible) policy, that is, the policy which brings in the highest expected rewards over the agent's lifetime. The optimal policy is denoted with $\pi^*(s)$.

The agent doesn't actually store the policy: in fact the agent stores something more general than that: a *Q*-table. A *Q*-table is a function $Q(s, a)$ over every possible state s and action a that could be performed in that state. The *Q*-table tells us how good it would be to be presently in s, and

---

[157] Among lots of other things, Minoru Asada is the co-founder of the RoboCup robot soccer competition.

[158] Andrey Andreyevich Markov was a Russian mathematician from 1856–1922, and was largely responsible for *Markov chains*, which are lists of states $s_1, s_2, ...$ the agent finds itself in as it performs various actions in a Markovian environment. This field, a major area in probability theory, is a large part of what are known as **stochastic processes**, not to be confused with stochastic optimization.

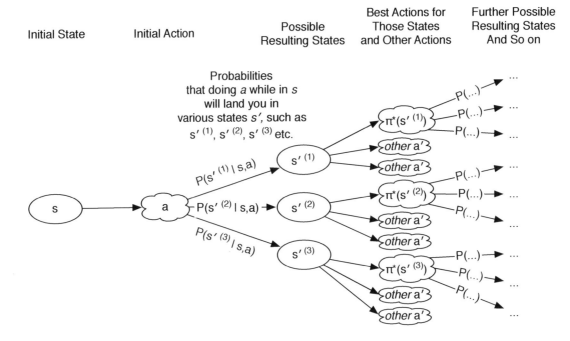

Figure 64 The Q-Learning state-action model. We are presently in some state s and decide to perform an action a. With a certain probability $P(s'|s,a)$, doing that action a while in s leads to a state s' (here there are three possible s' we could land in, $s'^{(1)}, s'^{(2)}$, and $s'^{(3)}$). We presume that from then on out we make the *smartest possible action* $\pi^*(s')$ for each state s', leading to still further states and and smartest possible actions for *them*, and so on. Note that in this model the first action we do (a) may not be the smartest action for s.

then perform action a, and *then follow the optimal policy from then on*. Thus the Q-value tells us the **utility** of doing action a when in s if we were a perfect agent (other than our initial choice of a). The agent starts with crummy Q-tables with lots of incorrect information, and then tries to update them until they approach the *optimal Q-table*, denoted $Q^*(s,a)$, where all the information is completely accurate. For a given state s, we would expect the best action a for that state (that is, $\pi^*(s)$) to have a higher Q^* value than the other actions. Thus we can define $\pi^*(s) = \text{argmax}_a Q^*(s,a)$, meaning, "the action a which makes $Q^*(s,a)$ the highest").

The world is a Markovian world: when an agent performs an action a in a given state s, the agent will then transition to another state s' with a certain transition probability $P(s'|s,a)$. The agent also receives a reward $R(s,a)$ as a result. Figure 64 shows the Q-learning state-action model: an agent performs some action a, leading to one of several possible states s', and we'll assume (perhaps wrongly) that the agent will choose perfect actions from π^* thereafter.

In a perfect world, where we actually *knew* $P(s'|s,a)$, there's a magic equation which we can use to compute $Q^*(s,a)$:

$$Q^*(s,a) = R(s,a) + \gamma \sum_{s'} P(s'|s,a) \max_{a'} Q^*(s',a') \qquad (1)$$

This equation says: the Q^* value of doing action a while in state s is equal to the expected sum of all future rewards received thereafter. This is equal to the first reward received, followed by the

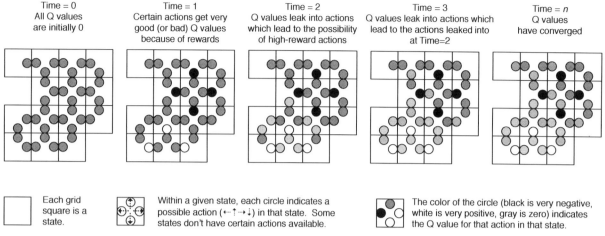

Figure 65 Illustration of Q-Learning with a model in the cockroach robot world. By time=n, the best (lightest color) action in each state corresponds to the optimal policy action in Figure 63.

sum, over all possible new states s' we might land in, of the likelihood that we land there, times the Q^* value of the smartest action a' we could perform at that point. It's a recursive definition.[159]

This is hard to get your head around, so think of it this way. At different times t the agent finds itself in various states s_t and performs various actions a_t. For doing this, the agent receives various rewards along the way (which might be 0). Thus the agent's total rewards are:

$$R(s_0, a_0) + R(s_1, a_1) + R(s_2, a_2) + R(s_3, a_3) + ...$$

Let's assume these are all optimal actions, and to keep things simple, there's no probability: when you do an action in a given state, you *will* wind up in a specific new state. Then the $Q^*(s_2, a_2)$ value at time 2 is equal to the sum total rewards from then on, that is, $R(s_2, a_2) + R(s_3, a_3) + ...$ Similarly the $Q^*(s_1, a_1)$ value at time 1 is equal to $R(s_1, a_1) + R(s_2, a_2) + R(s_3, a_3) + ...$ Thus $Q^*(s_1, a_1) = R(s_1, a_1) + Q^*(s_2, a_2)$. Similarly, $Q^*(s_0, a_0) = R(s_0, a_0) + Q^*(s_1, a_1)$. See the similarity with Equation 1? That equation had the additional term $\sum_{s'} P(s'|s,a) \max_{a'} Q^*(s', a')$, rather than just $Q^*(s', a')$. This is because of the transition probability P. The term tells us the weighted average Q^* received in the future.

So what's the γ? This is a cut-down constant between 0 and 1. It makes future rewards worth less than earlier rewards, and without it, the Q^* values could be infinite (which isn't good).

If we had the $P(s'|s,a)$ distribution and $R(s,a)$ function at our disposal, we could use this magic equation to figure out Q^*. It works like this:

---

[159]The Q^* equation is derived from a famous simpler equation by Richard Bellman called the **Bellman Equation**. That equation doesn't have actions explicitly listed, but rather assumes that the agent is performing some (possibly suboptimal) hard-coded policy π. The Bellman equation looks like this:

$$U(s) = R(s) + \gamma \max_a \sum_{s'} P(s'|s,a) U(s')$$

The $U(s)$ bit is the equivalent of $Q^*(s, a)$, but it assumes that the a we do is always $\pi(s)$. By the way, it's U for *Utility*, just as it's R for *Reward* or *Reinforcement*. Sometimes instead of U you'll see V (for the synonymous *Value*). The probability function isn't usually denoted $P(s'|s,a)$ — I wrote it that way to be consistent with probability theory — but is rather usually written $T(s, a, s')$. That is, T for *Transition Probability*. Hmmm, I wonder we if could use Q for *Q-tility*...

Algorithm 122 *Q-Learning with a Model*
1: $R(S, A) \leftarrow$ reward function for doing a while in s, for all states $s \in S$ and actions $a \in A$
2: $P(S'|S, A) \leftarrow$ probability distribution that doing a while in s results in s', for all $s, s' \in S$ and $a \in A$
3: $\gamma \leftarrow$ cut-down constant ▷ $0 < \gamma < 1$. 0.5 is fine.

4: $Q^*(S, A) \leftarrow$ table of utility values for all $s \in S$ and $a \in A$, initially all zero
5: **repeat**
6:   $Q'(S, A) \leftarrow Q^*(S, A)$ ▷ Copy the whole table
7:   **for** each state s **do**
8:     **for** each action a performable in s **do**
9:       $Q^*(s, a) \leftarrow R(s, a) + \gamma \sum_{s'} P(s'|s, a) \max_{a'} Q'(s', a')$
10: **until** $Q^*(S, A)$ isn't changing much any more
11: **return** $Q^*(S, A)$

That is, we start with absurd notions of Q^*, assume they're correct, and slowly fold in rewards until our Q^* values don't change any more. This notion is called **bootstrapping**, and it may seem crazy but it's perfectly doable because of a peculiarity of Q-learning made possible by Markovian environments: the Q-learning world has **no local optima**. Just one big global optimum. Basically this is an obsfucated way of doing hill-climbing.

Q-Learning as Reinforcement Learning   The algorithm just discussed is an example of what is known in engineering and operations research circles as **dynamic programming**. This isn't to be confused with the use of the same term in computer science.[160] In computer science, dynamic programming is an approach to solve certain kinds of problems faster because they can be broken into subproblems which overlap. In engineering, dynamic programming usually refers to figuring out policies for agents in Markovian environments where the transition probability P and reward function R are known beforehand.

From an artificial intelligence perspective, if we have P and R, this isn't a very interesting algorithm. Instead, what we *really* want is an algorithm which discovers Q^* without the help of P or R, simply by wandering around in the environment and, essentially, experiencing P and R first-hand. Such algorithms are often called **model-free** algorithms, and reinforcement learning is distinguished from dynamic programming by its emphasis on model-free algorithms.

We can gather Q^* without P or R by discovering interesting facts from the environment as we wander about. R is easy: we just fold in the rewards as we receive them. P is more complex to explain. We need to replace the $\sum_{s'} P(s'|s, a)$ portion of Equation 1. This portion added in the various $Q^*(s', a')$ according to how often they occur. Instead, now we'll just add them in as we wind up in various s'. Wander around enough and the distribution of these s' approaches $P(s'|s, a)$.

So: we'll build up an *approximation* of Q^*, based on samples culled from the world, called Q. The table is initially all zeros. As we're wandering about, we perform various actions in states, transitioning us to new states and triggering rewards. Let's say we're in state s and have decided to perform action a. Performing this action transitioned us to state s' and incurred a reward r. We then update our Q table as:

---
[160] Actually there's a historical relationship between the two: but it's a long story. Suffice it to say, the engineering usage predates the computer science usage by quite a bit.

$$Q(s,a) \leftarrow (1-\alpha)Q(s,a) + \alpha(r + \gamma \max_{a'} Q(s',a')) \tag{2}$$

Notice that we're throwing away a bit of what we know so far, using the $1 - \alpha$ trick—we saw this before in Ant Colony Optimization (in Section 8.3) and in Estimation of Distribution Algorithms (in Section 9.2.1)—and roll in a bit of the new information we've learned. This new information is set up in what should by now be a familiar fashion: the reward r plus the biggest Q of the next state s'. Notice the relationship to Equation 1. The revised algorithm is then:

Algorithm 123 *Model-Free Q-Learning*
1: $\alpha \leftarrow$ learning rate $\qquad\qquad\qquad\qquad\qquad\qquad\qquad\qquad\qquad\qquad$ ▷ $0 < \alpha < 1$. Make it small.
2: $\gamma \leftarrow$ cut-down constant $\qquad\qquad\qquad\qquad\qquad\qquad\qquad\qquad\qquad$ ▷ $0 < \gamma < 1$. 0.5 is fine.

3: $Q(S, A) \leftarrow$ table of utility values for all $s \in S$ and $a \in A$, initially all zero
4: **repeat**
5: $\qquad$ Start the agent at an initial state $s \leftarrow s_0$ $\qquad\qquad$ ▷ It's best if s_0 isn't the same each time.
6: $\qquad$ **repeat**
7: $\qquad\qquad$ Watch the agent make action a, transition to new state s', and receive reward r
8: $\qquad\qquad$ $Q(s,a) \leftarrow (1-\alpha)Q(s,a) + \alpha(r + \gamma \max_{a'} Q(s',a'))$
9: $\qquad\qquad$ $s \leftarrow s'$
10: $\qquad$ **until** the agent's life is over
11: **until** $Q(S, A)$ isn't changing much any more, or we have run out of time
12: **return** $Q(S, A)$ $\qquad\qquad\qquad\qquad\qquad\qquad\qquad\qquad\qquad$ ▷ As our approximation of $Q^*(S, A)$

How does the agent decide what action to make? The algorithm will converge, slowly, to the optimum if the action is picked entirely at random. Alternatively, you could pick the best action possible for the state s, that is, use $\pi^*(s)$, otherwise known as argmax$_a Q^*(s, a)$. Oh that's right, we don't have Q^*. Well, we could fake it by picking the best action we've discovered so far with our (crummy) Q-table, that is, argmax$_a Q(s, a)$.

That seems like a nice answer. But it's got a problem. Let's go back to our cockroach example. The cockroach is wandering about and discovers a small candy. Yum! As the cockroach wanders about in the local area, nothing's as good as that candy; and eventually for every state in the local area the cockroach's Q table tells it to go back to the candy. That'd be great if the candy was the only game in town: but if the cockroach just wandered a *bit further*, it'd discover a giant pile of sugar! Unfortunately it'll never find that, as it's now happy with its candy. Recognize this problem? It's **Exploration versus Exploitation** all over again. If we use the best action a that we've discovered so far, Q-learning is 100% exploitative. The problem is that the model-free version of the algorithm, unlike the dynamic programming version, **has local optima**. We're getting trapped in a local optimum. And the solution is straight out of stochastic optimization: force more exploration. We can do this by adding *some* randomness to our choices of action. Sometimes we do the best action we know about so far. Sometimes we just go crazy. This approach is called ϵ-**greedy action selection**, and is guaranteed to escape local optima, though if the randomness is low, we may be waiting a *long* time. Or we might do a Simulated Annealing kind of approach and initially just do crazy things all the time, then little by little only do the best thing we know about.

Last, it's fine to have α be a constant throughout the run. Though you may get better results if you reduce α for those $Q(s, a)$ entries which have been updated many times.

Generalization Believe it or not, there was a reason we covered all this. Reinforcement Learning would be the end of the story except for a problem with the technique: **it doesn't generalize**. Ordinarily a learner should be able to make general statements about the entire environment based on just a few samples of the environment. That's the whole point of a learning algorithm. If you have to examine every point in the space, what's the point of using a learning algorithm? You've already got knowledge of the entire universe.

Reinforcement Learning learns a separate action for every point in the entire space (every single state). Actually it's worse than that: Q-learning develops a notion of utility for *every possible combination of state and action*. Keep in mind that in the Soccer Robot example, there were 100 states and 6 actions. That's a database of 600 elements! And that's a *small environment*. Reinforcement Learning doesn't scale very well.

Many approaches to getting around this problem are basically versions of discretizing the space to reduce its size and complexity. Alternatively you could embed a *second* learning algorithm — typically a neural network — into the reinforcement learning framework to try to learn a simple set of state action rules which describe the entire environment.

Another approach is to use a metaheuristic to learn a simple set of rules to describe the environment in a general fashion. Such systems typically use an evolutionary algorithm to cut up the space of states into regions all of which are known to require the same action. Then each rule is simply of the form *region description→action*. Instead of having one rule per state, we have one rule per region, and we can have as few regions as it takes to describe the entire space properly. We'll cover those next. But first...

A Final Derivation You can skip this if you like. The goal is to show where the magic equation

$$Q^*(s,a) = R(s,a) + \gamma \sum_{s'} P(s'|s,a) \max_{a'} Q^*(s',a')$$

came from. We're going to go through the derivation of Q^* in a very pedantic fashion. First, we define Q^* as telling us, for any given state s and action a, how good it would be to *start* in state s, then perform action a, and then perform the smartest possible actions thereafter (that is, thereafter, we use $\pi^*(s)$ for all of our a). We can define Q^* as the *expected value*, over all possible future strings of states and actions, of the sum total reward we'd get for starting in s and doing a, and then being smart from then on. Here's how to write that:

$$Q^*(s,a) = E[\sum_{t=0}^{\infty} R(s_t, a_t) | s_0 = s, a_0 = a, a_{t \geq 1} = \pi^*(s_t)]$$

There's a problem. Imagine that there are two actions A and B, and if you always do action A, regardless of your state, you get a reward of 1. But if you always do action B, you always get a reward of 2. If our agent's lifetime is infinite, both of these sum to infinity. But clearly B is preferred. We can solve this by cutting down future rewards so they don't count as much. We do this by adding a multiplier $0 < \gamma < 1$, raised to the power of t so it makes future rewards worth less. This causes the sums to always be finite, and B's sum to be higher than A's sum.

$$Q^*(s,a) = E[\sum_{t=0}^{\infty} \gamma^t R(s_t, a_t) | s_0 = s, a_0 = a, a_{t \geq 1} = \pi^*(s_t)] \tag{3}$$

Now let's pull our first actions s and a out of the sum. In the sum they're known as s_0 and a_0. They'll come out with their associated γ, which happens to be γ^0.

$$Q^*(s,a) = E[\gamma^0 R(s_0, a_0) + \sum_{t=1}^{\infty} \gamma^t R(s_t, a_t) | s_0 = s, a_0 = a, a_{t \geq 1} = \pi^*(s_t)]$$

From now on out, the goal is going to be to massage the stuff inside the expectation so that it *looks like the expectation in Equation 3 again*. Let's get going on that. Obviously $\gamma^0 = 1$ so we can get rid of it. Now there's nothing in the expectation that $R(s_0, a_0)$ relies on so it can be pulled straight out, at which time we can rename s_0 and a_0 back to s and a.

$$Q^*(s,a) = R(s,a) + E[\sum_{t=1}^{\infty} \gamma^t R(s_t, a_t) | s_0 = s, a_0 = a, a_{t \geq 1} = \pi^*(s_t)]$$

Next comes the most complex part of the derivation. We'd like to get rid of the s_0 and a_0 still inside the expectation. So we'll create a new state s' to be the next state s_1. But recall from Figure 64, there are actually many possible states $s'^{(1)}, s'^{(2)}, \ldots$ each with an associated probability $P(s'^{(1)}|s, a), P(s'^{(2)}|s, a), \ldots$ that the given s' state will be the one we wind up landing in after doing action a in state s. So if we pull s_0 out of the expectation, nothing in the expectation will reflect this fact, and we'll have to explicitly state that the old expectation has been broken into multiple expectations, one per s', and we're adding them up, multiplied by the probabilities that they'd occur. Here we go:

$$Q^*(s,a) = R(s,a) + \sum_{s'} P(s'|s,a) E[\sum_{t=1}^{\infty} \gamma^t R(s_t, a_t) | s_1 = s', a_{t \geq 1} = \pi^*(s_t)]$$

Now we can change the inner sum back to $t = 0$, because there's nothing inside the expectation that relies on timestep 0 anymore. So inside the expectation we'll just redefine $t = 1$ to be $t = 0$. This will cause everything to be multiplied by one fewer γ so we'll need to add a γ as well:

$$Q^*(s,a) = R(s,a) + \sum_{s'} P(s'|s,a) E[\gamma \sum_{t=0}^{\infty} \gamma^t R(s_t, a_t) | s_0 = s', a_{t \geq 0} = \pi^*(s_t)]$$

That γ isn't dependent on anything, so we can pull it clear out of the expectation and the sum:

$$Q^*(s,a) = R(s,a) + \gamma \sum_{s'} P(s'|s,a) E[\sum_{t=0}^{\infty} \gamma^t R(s_t, a_t) | s_0 = s', a_{t \geq 0} = \pi^*(s_t)]$$

Notice that inside the expectation we now have a new s_0 but no a_0. We remedy that by breaking our $a_{t \geq 0}$ up again. Instead of defining a_0 to be $\pi^*(s_0)$, we're going to invent a new symbol a' to represent the action we perform when we're in s', that is, $a' = a_0$. This allows us to move the a' definition outside of the expectation. But once again to do this we have to keep around the notion that a' is the smartest possible action to perform when in a given s'. We do this by introducing the operator *max* to select the a' that yields the highest possible expectation (that is, it's the smartest pick, and so is clearly $\pi^*(s_0)$):

$$Q^*(s,a) = R(s,a) + \gamma \sum_{s'} P(s'|s,a) \max_{a'} E[\sum_{t=0}^{\infty} \gamma^t R(s_t, a_t) | s_0 = s', a_0 = a', a_{t \geq 1} = \pi^*(s_t)]$$

And now the payoff for all this manipulation. Notice that the expectation (everything after the *max*) now looks *very similar* to Equation 3. The only difference is that we're using s' instead of s and a' instead of a. This allows us to just say:

$$Q^*(s,a) = R(s,a) + \gamma \sum_{s'} P(s'|s,a) \max_{a'} Q^*(s',a')$$

Ta-da! A recursive definition pops out by magic!

10.2 Sparse Stochastic Policy Optimization

As mentioned before, the primary issue with reinforcement learning is that it constructs a unique rule for every possible state. *Q*-learning is even worse, as it builds a table for every state/action combination. If there are lots of states (and lots of actions), then there are going to be a lot of slots in that table. There are a variety of ways to counter this, including simplifying the state space or trying to use a learning method like a neural network to learn which states all have the same action. Popular current methods include Ronald Williams's REINFORCE[161] algorithms and Andrew Ng and Michael Jordan's PEGASUS,[162] techniques collectively known as **policy search**.

We could also use metaheuristics to learn a sparse representation of this rule space. The idea is to learn a set of rules, each of which attach an action not to a single state but to a *collection* of states with some feature in common. Rather than have one rule per state, we search for a small set of rules which collectively explain the space in some general fashion.

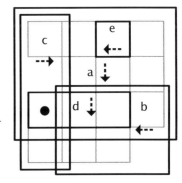

Imagine that states describe a point in *N*-dimensional space. For example, in our soccer robot example, we might have four dimensions: ball size, ball position (including "not there"), goal size, and goal position (including "not there"). In the cockroach example, we might have two dimensions: the *x* and *y* values of the grid location of the cockroach. In the Tic-Tac-Toe example we might have nine dimensions: each of the board positions. Given an *N*-dimensional space, one kind of rule might describe a **box** or **rectangular region** in that space rather than a precise location. For example, here's a possible rule for the cockroach robot:

Figure 66 A sparse version of the optimal policy for the cockroach robot world, with five rules (*a...e*). Compare to Figure 63. The state marked • is covered by three different rules (*a, c,* and *d*), with *d* being the most specific.

$$x \geq 4 \text{ and } x \leq 5 \text{ and } y \geq 1 \text{ and } y \leq 9 \rightarrow \text{go up}$$

Such a rule is called a **classification rule**, as it has classified (or labelled) the rectangular region from $\langle 4, 1 \rangle$ and $\langle 5, 9 \rangle$ with the action "go up". The rule is said to **cover** this rectangular region. The objective is to find a set of rules which cover the entire state space and properly classify the states in their covered regions with the actions from the optimal policy. For example, in Figure 66 we have a small set of rules which collectively define exactly the same policy as shown in Figure 63.

If rules overlap (if the problem is **over-specified**), we may need an **arbitration scheme**. Were I to hand-code such a ruleset, the arbitration scheme I'd pick would be based on **specificity**: rules

---

[161] Ronald J. Williams, 1992, Simple statistical gradient-following algorithms for connectionist reinforcement learning, in *Machine Learning*, pages 229–256.

[162] This is a nontrivial paper to read. Andrew Ng and Michael Jordan, 2000, PEGASUS: A policy search method for large MDPs and POMDPs, in *Proceedings of the Sixteenth Conference on Uncertainty in Artificial Intelligence*, pages 406–415.

covering smaller regions defeat rules covering larger regions. Figure 66 does exactly that. But the methods discussed later use different approaches to arbitration.

There are two basic ways we could use a metaheuristic to learn rulesets of these kinds:

- A candidate solution (or individual) is a complete set of rules. Evolving rulesets is known as **Pitt Approach** Rule Systems.

- An individual is a single rule: and the whole population is the complete set of rules. Evolving individual rules and having them participate collectively is known as the **Michigan Approach** to Learning Classifier Systems, or just simply **Learning Classifier Systems (LCS)**.[163]

10.2.1 Rule Representation

State-action rules in Q-learning took the following form:

If I am in the following state... → Then do this...

The first part is the **rule body**, which defines the kinds of world states which would trigger the rule. The second part is the **rule head**, which defines the action to take when the rule is triggered. We can generalize the rule body in two different ways to cover more than one state. First, rule bodies might require exact matches:

If I am in a state which exactly fits the following features... → Then do this...

Or we can have rules which describe imprecise matches:

If I am in a state which sort of looks like this, even with a few errors... → Then do this...

In the first case, we have the issue of **under-specification**: we need to make sure that for every possible state, there's *some* rule which covers that state. To guarantee this we might need to rely on some kind of **default rule** which is assumed to match when no others do. Alternatively, the algorithm might generate a rule on-the-fly, and insert it into the ruleset, to match a state if it suddenly shows up.

In the second case, we don't need to worry about under-specification, since every rule matches every state to *some* degree. But we will need to define a notion of *how well* a rule matches. This is known as a rule's **match score**. The rule which the best match score might be selected.

In either case, we'll still need to worry about over-specification, requiring an arbitration scheme. Instead of specificity, the later methods use some combination of:

- The utility of the rule — essentially its Q-value, determined by the agent as it has tried out the rule in various situations. Recall that utility is a measure of how often the rule led to high rewards. Higher utility rules might be preferred over lower-utility rules.

- The **variance** in the rule's utility: if the rule is consistent in yielding high rewards, it might be preferred over more tenuous rules which occasionally get lucky.

---

[163]Don't confuse these with classification algorithms from machine learning, such as those mentioned in Section 9.1. Those algorithms find classifications for whole regions of space based on provided samples in the space which have been pre-labelled for them (part of an area called **supervised learning**). Whereas the metaheursistics described here find classifications for regions based solely on reinforcement information gleaned while wandering about in the space.

- The **error** in the rule's utility: the difference between the rule's utility and the utilities of rules which it leads to.

- The **match score** of the rule: rules more apropos to the current situation would be preferred over ones whose bodies don't match the situation very well.

Much of rule representation concerns itself with the rule body, which can take on many forms, so it's worth considering them:

Real-Valued or Integer Metric Spaces This state space is particularly common in Pitt-approach rule systems, though it's being increasingly studied in Michigan-approach methods too. There are lots of ways you could describe the space, though boxes are the most common. Here are a few:

- **Boxes** We've seen these already.
    - *Example:* $x \geq 20$ and $x \leq 30$ and $y \geq 1$ and $y \leq 9 \to$ go up
    - *Match Score:* If the point's in the box, it's got a perfect match score (1.0 maybe?); else perhaps its match score is equal to the percentage of dimensions in whose ranges it lies. For example, $\langle 40, 5 \rangle$ is covered by y but not by x, which might result in a match score of 0.5. Another approach: the match score decreases with distance from the box boundary.

- **Toroidal Boxes** If your state space is bounded, a box could go off of one side and wrap around to the other. Imagine if the space was toroidal in the x direction and bounded from 0 to 360. The rule below would be true either when $60 \leq x \leq 360$ or $0 \leq x \leq 20$ (assuming y is in the right region). This isn't totally nuts: it's useful if x described an angle, for example.
    - *Example:* $x \geq 60$ and $x \leq 20$ and $y \geq 1$ and $y \leq 9 \to$ go up
    - *Match Score:* Same as regular boxes.

- **Hyperspheres or Hyperellipsoids** A rule might be defined as a point (the center of the sphere) and a radius. Or a rule might be defined as a point and associated data describing a rotated multidimensional ellipsoid (perhaps a covariance matrix like those used to describe multidimensional Gaussian curves). Here's an example of a simple hypersphere:
    - *Example:* If the state $\langle x, y, z \rangle$ lies within a sphere centered at $\langle 4, 7, 2 \rangle$ and of radius 9.3 $\to$ go up
    - *Match Score:* Same notion as regular boxes.

- **Exemplars** Specific points in the space which serve as examples for the regions around them. A ruleset of exemplars divides the environment up into a **Voronoi tessellation**: regions of space delimited by which exemplar each region is closest to.[164] Such rules rely entirely on match scores, so certain techniques (often Michigan approach methods) might not be able to use them. You may think of exemplars as infinitely small hyperspheres.
    - *Example:* If the state is nearest to $\langle 4, 7, 2 \rangle \to$ go up
    - *Match Score:* The further from the exemplar, the lower the match score.

---

[164] After Georgy Feodosevich Voronoi, 1868–1908, a Russian mathematician. Voronoi tesselations (sometimes called "Voronoi diagrams") are widely used in lots of areas of computational geometry, everything from graphics to wireless networks to robotics. The notion of dividing space up by exemplars also forms the basis of the **k-Nearest-Neighbor (kNN)** machine learning algorithm.

- **Hyperplanes**[165] The rule cuts a plane through the space, dividing an area on which we have an opinion from an area in which the rule has no opinion. Hyperplanes may likewise be problematic for some Michigan approach methods.

    Example: If $2.3x + 9.2y - 7.3z > 4.2 \to$ go up
    Match Score: If the point is on the matching side of the hyperplane, it matches perfectly (or its match score improves if further away from the plane). If the point is on the non-matching side of the hyperplane, its match score is worse, but improves as it approaches the hyperplane.

Non-Metric Integer Spaces As we've seen earlier in the Section 4 (Representation), integer spaces might describe **metric spaces** or simply define **unordered sets of objects** (0 = "red", 1 = "blue", etc.). Integer-space rule bodies are no different. An unordered integer rule might look like this:

$$x = \text{"red"} \text{ and } y = \text{"soft"} \text{ and } z = \text{"hollow"} \to \text{go up}$$

Here the rule, like exemplars, describes an exact point in the (unordered) space. A match score might be defined in terms of the number of variables which exactly match the given state.

Unordered set rules might also have disjunctions:

$$x = \text{"red"} \text{ and } y = \text{"soft"} \text{ and } z = (\text{"hollow"} \text{ or } \text{"solid"}) \to \text{go up}$$

A disjunction would be considered a single condition, and it'd be true if any of its parts were true.

Boolean Spaces Though they have lately been generalized to other kinds of rules, Michigan Approach classifier systems have traditionally focused on a single kind of rule: one involving boolean conditions.

Because they're so simple, boolean rules tend to take on a certain standard pattern: combinations of "yes", "no", and "doesn't matter". Let's say each state in your state space is described by three boolean values, x, y, and z. Thus your space has eight states. A boolean rule over three dimensions, might look like this:

$$x = 1 \text{ and } y = 0 \text{ (and } z \text{ doesn't matter)} \to \text{go up}$$

In the parlance of Michigan Approach classifier systems, such a rule is usually written like this:

$$10\# \to \text{go up}$$

Note that the # sign means "this one doesn't matter". The more "doesn't matter" dimensions in the rule, the less specific. Match scores might again be defined in terms of the number of values (that "matter") which exactly match the state.

Could rule bodies be trees or graphs? More complex functions? Who knows?

---

[165]There's a clever way of converting hyperplanes into more complex subregions of space, called **kernelization**, a technique made popular by **Support Vector Machines (SVMs)** in machine learning. I've not had much luck with kernelization in the context of rule systems though.

10.3 Pitt Approach Rule Systems

The **Pitt Approach**[166] applies an evolutionary algorithm to find a set of rules which best describes the optimal policy. A candidate solution is simply a set of such rules. Section 4.5 introduced the notions of rulesets popularly used in Pitt Approach rule systems and suggested approaches to initializing, recombining, and mutating them. Here we will discuss a particularly well-known Pitt Approach algorithm, SAMUEL.[167]

SAMUEL was developed by John Grefenstette, Connie Ramsey, and Alan Schultz at the Naval Research Laboratory.[168] The idea is to employ a Pitt Approach to optimizing rulesets as entire candidate solutions in stochastic optimization, and to also use reinforcement learning ideas to improve the rules within a candidate solution. SAMUEL traditionally uses a genetic algorithm, but most any optimization method is plausible. All the actual magic is in the fitness assessment function — where rule utilities are computed in addition to the fitness of the whole ruleset — and in the breeding operators. SAMUEL iterates through four basic steps:

1. Each individual is tested n times and the results are used to update the utilities of its rules.

2. Using the updated utility information, each individual's rules are improved in a special rule mutation procedure.

3. Each individual is tested *again* some m additional times and the results are used to update the fitness of the individual (ruleset) as a whole.

4. After all individuals have undergone the first three steps, we perform traditional evolutionary algorithm style breeding and selection on the individuals based on fitness.

Fitness and Utility Assessment The two assessment steps (1 and 3 above) are nearly identical except for the statistics they update: so we'll treat them together here, and in fact Algorithm 124 is used to describe both steps.

Both assessment procedures involve placing the agent in the world and having it follow the policy as dictated by the ruleset being tested. As the agent is wandering about, we'll need to decide which action the agent will choose at any given step. This is first done by computing a **match set** consisting of rules which best match the current state, that is, those with the highest match score. Next, only the highest-scoring rules for each action are retained. SAMUEL then chooses a rule to perform from the match set using some kind of score-based selection procedure. For example, we might simply choose the rule with the highest score; or select with a probability proportional to the rule's score (as in fitness-proportionate selection, Algorithm 30). This two-level mechanism

---

[166] Ken De Jong and students developed the Pitt Approach at the University of Pittsburgh. Hence the name.

[167] SAMUEL is an acronym for Strategy Acquisition Method Using Empirical Learning. Yes, it's pushing it. In reality, Grefenstette, Ramsey, and Shultz were looking for a way to name the algorithm after Arthur Samuel, a famous machine learning pioneer who (coincidentally I believe) died the same year as the seminal SAMUEL paper. While at IBM in the 1950s, Arthur Samuel developed a program which learned on its own how to play checkers, and this program is considered a major landmark in artificial intelligence history. Hmm, I seem to have a lot of footnotes about checkers....

SAMUEL was first defined in John Grefenstette, Connie Ramsey, and Alan Schultz, 1990, Learning sequential decision rules using simulation models and competition, *Machine Learning*, 5(4), 355–381. Though you can get a roughly current version of the manual online via CiteSeer^x, presently at http://citeseerx.ist.psu.edu/viewdoc/summary?doi=10.1.1.48.9876

[168] NRL was instrumental in the development of GPS and much of modern radar.

(truncation followed by score-based selection) is intended to prevent large numbers of identical crummy rules from being selected over a few high-quality ones.

The first fitness assessment procedure updates utility information about the rules. Recall that Q-learning assumes that rewards occur throughout the agent's life. In contrast, SAMUEL assumes that rewards tend to happen at the end of an agent's life. This leads to different strategies for distributing rewards. In Q-learning, when a reward is received, it is stored in the Q-value for that state-action combination; and later on when another state-action combination leads to this state, the Q-value is then partially distributed to the earlier combination. We'll see this assumption again in Michigan Approach methods, in Section 10.4. But SAMUEL instead directly and immediately distributes rewards to all state-action rules which led to the reward. Such rules are called **active**. More specifically: if a rule contained an action which was used at some time in the past, prior to a reward r appearing, then when r is finally received, the utility of the rule is updated as:

$$\text{Utility}(R_i) \leftarrow (1 - \alpha)\,\text{Utility}(R_i) + \alpha r$$

SAMUEL also maintains an approximation of the **variance** of the utilities of each rule because we want to have rules which both lead to high rewards *and are consistent in leading to them*. Each time the utility is updated, variance in utility is also updated as:

$$\text{UtilityVariance}(R_i) \leftarrow (1 - \alpha)\,\text{UtilityVariance}(R_i) + \alpha(\text{Utility}(R_i) - r)^2$$

Finally, SAMUEL uses this information to build up a "quality" of sorts of each rule, called the rule's **strength**,[169] which is a combination its utility and utility variance. Strength affects how likely the rule is to be mutated later on.

$$\text{Strength}(R_i) \leftarrow \text{Utility}(R_i) + \gamma\,\text{UtilityVariance}(R_i)$$

We commonly set γ to a low value less than 1, as utility is more important than variance.

Distributing reward evenly among all rules is an odd choice. I would have personally distributed so that later rules received more reward than earlier rules. Interestingly, SAMUEL maintains information about how long ago a rule was active, though it uses it only to determine which rules to delete. This value is called the **activity level** of a rule. Rules start with an activity level of $\frac{1}{2}$, and are updated each time the agent performs an action. Rules which had that particular action in their heads are increased like this:

$$\text{Activity}(R_i) \leftarrow (1 - \beta)\,\text{Activity}(R_i) + \beta$$

Given an $0 \leq \beta \leq 1$, this has the effect of shifting a rule's activity towards 1 when the rule's action is chosen. Rules without that action in their heads have their activity levels decreased:

$$\text{Activity}(R_i) \leftarrow \delta\,\text{Activity}(R_i)$$

for $0 \leq \delta \leq 1$. This has the effect of slowly decreasing the rule's activity level towards zero.

The second assessment procedure in SAMUEL is used to compute the fitness of the entire individual (the ruleset). This is simply defined as the sum of rewards received by the individual during testing. The following algorithm describes both fitness procedures: the particular procedure being done (utility or fitness) is determined by the *dofitness* variable.

---

[169]Not to be confused with Pareto "strength" (Section 7.3).

Algorithm 124 SAMUEL *Fitness Assessment*
1: $S \leftarrow$ individual being assessed
2: $\alpha \leftarrow$ learning and decay rate
3: $\beta \leftarrow$ activity level increase rate
4: $\gamma \leftarrow$ how much variance to include
5: $\delta \leftarrow$ activity level decay rate
6: *dofitness* $\leftarrow$ are we assessing to compute fitness (as opposed to rule strength)?
7: $n \leftarrow$ number of times to test the agent

8: $f \leftarrow 0$
9: $R \leftarrow \{R_1, ..., R_l\}$ rules in the ruleset of the individual S
10: **for** n times **do**
11:     $s \leftarrow$ an initial state of agent
12:     $Z \leftarrow \{\}$ ▷ Active Rule Set
13:     **for** each rule $R_i \in R$ **do**   ▷ All rules which were in an action set this time around
14:         Activity$(R_i) \leftarrow 0.5$
15:     **repeat**
16:         **for** each rule $R_i \in R$ **do**   ▷ No matter how badly they match the state
17:             ComputeMatchScore(R_i, s)
18:         $N \leftarrow$ all actions which appear in the head of any rule in R
19:         $M \leftarrow \{\}$ ▷ Match Set
20:         **for** each action $N_j \in N$ **do**   ▷ Find the highest-scoring rule for each action
21:             $R' \subseteq R \leftarrow$ all rules in R whose heads are action N_j
22:             $M \leftarrow M \cup \{$ the rule $R'_i \in R'$ whose match score is highest $\}$
23:         $R_a \leftarrow$ SelectWithReplacement(M) ▷ Select among the highest-scoring rules
24:         $A \subseteq R \leftarrow$ all rules whose heads (actions) are the same as the head of R_a ▷ Action Set
25:         **for** each rule $A_i \in A$ **do**   ▷ Increase activity
26:             Activity$(A_i) \leftarrow (1 - \beta)$ Activity$(A_i) + \beta$
27:             **if** $A_i \notin Z$ **then**
28:                 $Z \leftarrow Z \cup \{A_i\}$
29:         **for** each rule $R_i \in R - A$ **do**   ▷ Decrease activity
30:             Activity$(R_i) \leftarrow \delta$ Activity(R_i)
31:         Perform action R_a, transitioning to a new state s ▷ Notice no reward
32:     **until** the agent's life is over
33:     $r \leftarrow$ cumulative reward (assessment) of the agent   ▷ Ah, here's the reward. Only at the end.
34:     **if** *dofitness* is false **then**   ▷ We're doing runs to update the strengths of the rules
35:         **for** each rule $Z_i \in Z$ **do**
36:             Utility$(Z_i) \leftarrow (1 - \alpha)$ Utility$(Z_i) + \alpha r$
37:             UtilityVariance$(Z_i) \leftarrow (1 - \alpha)$ UtilityVariance$(Z_i) + \alpha($Utility$(Z_i) - r)^2$
38:             Strength$(Z_i) \leftarrow$ Utility$(Z_i) - \gamma$ UtilityVariance(Z_i)
39:     **else**   ▷ We're doing runs to update fitness
40:         $f \leftarrow f + r$
41: **if** *dofitness* is true **then**
42:     fitness of $S \leftarrow f$

Mutation   SAMUEL has two mutation steps, each following one of the assessment steps. After the first assessment procedure (which determines rule strength), the *rules* in the individual are modified. Hopefully this improves the individual for the second fitness assessment (whose purpose is to compute the actual fitness of the individual). After the second fitness procedure, we do regular breeding of the population with more bulk-style, traditional operations.

Let's start with the first mutation step: improving the rules. SAMUEL performs any of the following mutations on the individual to try to improve it for the second stage:

- **Rule Deletion**   If a rule is sufficiently old (brand new rules are never deleted), has a sufficiently low activity value (it's not fired recently), or its strength is sufficiently low, or if the rule is subsumed by another rule with greater strength, then the rule is a candidate for deletion. We may also delete a few rules randomly. It's up to you to decide these thresholds and how many deletions occur. We say that a rule A is *subsumed* by another rule B if every state that A covers is also covered by B, and B covers some additional states as well, *and* the two rules have the same actions in their heads.

- **Rule Specialization**   If a rule is not very strong and covers a large number of states, it is a candidate for *specialization* since it may be crummy *because* of the large region it's covering. We add to the ruleset a new rule subsumed by the old rule (and thus more specific) and which has the same action in its head. The original rule is retained. For example, the rule

$$x \geq 4 \text{ and } x \leq 5 \text{ and } y \geq 1 \text{ and } y \leq 9 \rightarrow \text{go up}$$

  Might be specialized to

$$x = 5 \text{ and } y \geq 6 \text{ and } y \leq 9 \rightarrow \text{go up}$$

- **Rule Generalization**   This is the opposite of rule specialization. If a rule is very strong and covers a *small* number of states, it is a candidate for *generalization* because it might do well with more states. We add to the ruleset a new rule which subsumes the old rule (and thus is more general) and has the same action in its head. The original rule is retained.

- **Rule Covering**   Covering is similar to generalization, but is based on information we gleaned from the assessment process. Let's say that during assessment we discovered that a certain rule had often fired but was fairly consistent in not *completely* matching the state. For example, returning to our rule

$$x \geq 4 \text{ and } x \leq 5 \text{ and } y \geq 1 \text{ and } y \leq 9 \rightarrow \text{go up}$$

  Imagine that this rule had been selected a number of times when $y = 4, x = 6$. Obviously $x = 6$ is out of bounds for the rule, but the $y = 4$ match was good enough, and the rule was strong enough, for it to win even with only a partial match. Rule covering would select this rule and create a new one more likely to match, for example:

$$x \geq 4 \text{ and } x \leq 6 \text{ and } y \geq 1 \text{ and } y \leq 9 \rightarrow \text{go up}$$

  The original rule is retained.

- **Rule Merging**   If two rules are sufficiently strong, share the same action in their heads, and overlap sufficiently in the number of states they cover, they're candidates for merging into a single rule which is the union of them. The original rules are retained.

Notice that all these mutation mechanisms are **directed**, that is, they're explicitly exploitative, aimed at pushing the rules so that they perform better next time. For this reason, John Grefenstette refers to this mutation step as **Lamarckian** (see Section 3.3.4) — it improves the individuals during the course of assessment.

The remaining mutation operators occur during breeding just like any other evolutionary algorithm, and have more of an explorative nature to them:

- **Plain Old Mutation**   Make random mutations to some rules. The original rules are not retained. This is the more explorative mutation.
- **Creep Mutation**[170]   Make a very small, local random change to a few rules. The objective here is to push a little bit for hill-climbing.

Recombination   Section 4.5.5 mentioned various approaches to crossing over rulesets. SAMUEL offers other possibilities:

- A version of **Uniform Crossover**   Some n times, the two individuals trade a rule at random.
- **Clustered Crossover**   From the fitness assessment procedure we gather some statistics: specifically, we want to know which sequences of rules led to a reward. From this we identify pairs of rules which often led to a reward when they *both* appeared in a sequence. We then do a uniform crossover, but at the end try to ensure that these pairs don't get split up: if one rule winds up in individual A and the other in individual B, we move one of the two rules to the other individual (swapping over some other rule instead). The idea is to recognize that there is *very strong linkage* among rules in rulesets, and we want to cross over whole *teams* of rules which have performed well as a group.

Notice that both of these recombination operators don't change the size of either ruleset. Nor do the mutation operators during breeding. SAMUEL appears to restrict ruleset size changes to the exploitative "Lamarckian" mutation operators which occur after the first assessment procedure.

Selection   You can use any old fitness-based selection procedure. Though SAMUEL traditionally uses an odd combination of truncation selection and Stochastic Universal Sampling. Specifically, we compute the mean fitness over the whole population, as well as the variance in the fitness. We then update a **baseline fitness** as follows:

$$\text{baseline} \leftarrow (1-v)\,\text{baseline} + v(\text{mean fitness} - \psi\,\text{variance in fitness})$$

... where $0 \leq v \leq 1$, and ψ is a parameter indicating how important variance is. Once we have our baseline fitness, the only individuals which are even *considered* for selection are those whose fitness is higher than the baseline. We then use a standard selection procedure (SAMUEL used Stochastic Universal Sampling) to select among those individuals.

In truth, I wonder if just doing plain-old truncation selection would do just as well.

---
[170]My vote for creepiest mutation name.

Initialization   There are lots of ways to initialize the ruleset. In SAMUEL three are common:

- Create a set of random rules.

- Seed the rules in each individual with rules you believe to be helpful to the agent.

- Perform **adaptive initialization**. Each individual starts with a set of rules that are totally general, one for each possible action:

$$\text{In all cases} \to \text{go up} \qquad \text{In all cases} \to \text{go down} \qquad ...etc...$$

Run this for a while to get an idea of the strength of each rule. As you're doing this, apply a fair number of **Rule Specialization** operators, as described earlier, to make these general rules more specific. The idea is to gracefully let SAMUEL find good initial operators based on a bit of initial experience in a sandbox.

Self-Adaptive Operators   SAMUEL has an optional gimmick for adjusting the probability that various mutation operators will occur (particularly the "Lamarckian" ones). Each individual contains its own operator probabilities. Let's say that $P(O_i, I_j)$ is the probability that operator O_i is performed on individual I_j. This probability is stored in individual I_j itself, and children receive the same set of probabilities that their parents had. Each timestep all the operator probabilities in all individuals are decreased like this:

$$P(O_i, I_j) \leftarrow (1 - \tau) P(O_i, I_j)$$

... where $0 \leq \tau \leq 1$. This eventually pushes the probabilities towards 0. But when an individual is mutated or crossed over using an operator, the probability of that operator is increased for the resulting individual(s), perhaps something like:

$$P(O_i, I_j) \leftarrow (1 - \tau) P(O_i, I_j) + \tau$$

This pushes this probability, eventually, towards 1.

This is an example of **self-adaptive operators**, where the individuals contain their own mutation and crossover probabilities. Self-adaptive operators have been around for a long time, since early work in Evolution Strategies. But in my personal experience they're finicky.[171] I wouldn't bother.

10.4 Michigan Approach Learning Classifier Systems

After John Holland[172] developed the Genetic Algorithm around 1973, he turned his attention to a related topic: how to use an evolutionary process to discover a set of rules which describe, for each situation an agent finds himself in, what to do in that situation. I think Holland pitched it more generally than this—as a general machine learning classifier rather than one used for agent actions—and this is where the name **Learning Classifier Systems (LCS)** came from. Rather

---

[171] My proposed dissertation work was originally going to be using self-adaptive operators. Let's just say I wound up doing something else.

[172] John Holland is at the University of Michigan. Hence the name. Holland's earliest work on the topic is John Holland, 1975, *Adaptation in Natural and Artificial Systems*, University of Michigan Press. But the notion of learning classifier systems weren't formalized until a later paper, John Holland, 1980, Adaptive algorithms for discovering and using general patterns in growing knowledge bases, *International Journal of Policy Analysis and Information Systems*, 4(3), 245–268.

than having individuals being whole solutions (rulesets), Holland envisioned a *population* of individual rules which would fight for survival based on how effective they were in helping the classifier as a whole. Thus, like Ant Colony Optimization, Learning Classifier Systems have a very one-population coevolutionary feel to them.

Holland's original formulation was somewhat baroque. Since then, Stewart Wilson has created a streamlined version called the **Zeroth Level Classifier System (ZCS)**.[173] ZCS is a steady-state evolutionary computation technique. The evolutionary computation loop iterates only occasionally. Instead, most of the time is spent updating the fitness values of the entire generation based on their collective participation, as rules, in a reinforcement learning setting. Then after a while a few new rules are bred from the population and reinserted into it, displacing some existing low-fitness rules.

ZCS maintains a population of sparse *if→then* rules. Each rule is associated with a current *fitness* which reflects the utility of the rule. To test the rules, the agent is placed in a starting state, and then begins performing actions chosen from the population. This is done by first selecting all the rules which cover the current state of the agent. This set of rules forms the **match set** M. If there is more than one such rule, ZCS's arbitration scheme selects from among the match set using a fitness-based selection method (traditionally fitness-proportionate selection).

One way in which ZCS differs from SAMUEL is that it expects a *complete* match rather than allowing partial matches. Match scores are never used. If the match set is in fact empty—not a single rule covers the current state—ZCS creates a random rule which covers the state (and possibly others), and which has a random action. The fitness of the rule is set to the average fitness of the population at present. ZCS then marks an existing rule for death in the population and replaces it with this new rule. Rules are usually marked for death via a fitness-based selection method, tending to select less-fit rules more often.

Once ZCS has a winning rule, it extracts the action from the head of the rule, then creates a subset of the match set called the **action set** A, consisting of all the rules whose head was also that action. The action is performed, and the agent receives a reward r and transitions to a new state s', at which point ZCS constructs the next match set M' and action set A'. Each rule $A_i \in A$ then has its fitness updated as:

$$\text{Fitness}(A_i) \leftarrow (1-\alpha)\,\text{Fitness}(A_i) + \alpha \frac{1}{||A||}(r + \gamma \sum_{A'_j \in A'} \text{Fitness}(A'_j)) \qquad (4)$$

Look familiar? Hint: let's define a function G, consisting of the combined fitness (utility) of all the rules in the present action set A. That is, $G(A) = \sum_i \text{Fitness}(A_i)$. Equation 4 above would result in the equivalent equation for G:

$$G(A) \leftarrow (1-\alpha)\,G(A) + \alpha \frac{1}{||A||}(r + \gamma\,G(A'))$$

Compare this to Equation 2. Unlike SAMUEL, ZCS updates utility (ZCS's rule fitness) in basically a Q-learning fashion. ZCS also punishes rules for not getting picked (that is, the rules in $M - A$). Let $B = M - A$. Then the fitness of each rule $B_i \in B$ is decreased as:

$$\text{Fitness}(B_i) \leftarrow \beta\,\text{Fitness}(B_i)$$

This has basically the same effect as evaporation did in Ant Colony Optimization (see Section 8.3.1). β can be a value between 0 and 1, and shouldn't be very large. All told, the algorithm for updating fitnesses in the match set is:

---

[173]Introduced in Stewart Wilson, 1994, ZCS: A zeroth level classifier system, *Evolutionary Computation*, 2(1), 1–18.

Algorithm 125 *Zeroth Classifier System Fitness Updating*

1: $M \leftarrow$ previous match set
2: $M' \leftarrow$ next match set ▷ Unused. We keep it here to be consistent with Algorithm 131.
3: $A \leftarrow$ previous action set
4: $A' \leftarrow$ next action set
5: $r \leftarrow$ reward received by previous action
6: $\alpha \leftarrow$ learning rate ▷ $0 < \alpha < 1$. Make it small.
7: $\beta \leftarrow$ evaporation constant ▷ $0 < \beta < 1$. Make it large.
8: $\gamma \leftarrow$ cut-down constant ▷ $0 < \gamma < 1$. 0.5 is fine.

9: **for** each $A_i \in A$ **do**
10: $\quad$ Fitness$(A_i) \leftarrow (1-\alpha)$ Fitness$(A_i) + \alpha \frac{1}{||A||}(r + \gamma \sum_{A'_j \in A'}$ Fitness$(A'_j))$
11: $B \leftarrow M - A$
12: **for** each $B_i \in B$ **do**
13: $\quad$ Fitness$(B_i) \leftarrow \beta$ Fitness(B_i)

Because ZCS uses fitness as utility, when ZCS produces children as a result of steady-state breeding, it needs to assign them an initial fitness: otherwise they would never even be considered for match sets. To this end, half the fitness of each parent is removed from the parent and added into each child (because we want to approximately maintain the sum total fitness in our population):

Algorithm 126 *Zeroth Classifier System Fitness Redistribution*

1: $P_a, P_b \leftarrow$ parents
2: $C_a, C_b \leftarrow$ children
3: *crossedover* $\leftarrow$ are the children the result of crossover?

4: **if** *crossedover* = true **then**
5: $\quad$ Fitness(C_a), Fitness$(C_b) \leftarrow \frac{1}{4}$ (Fitness(P_a) + Fitness(P_b))
6: **else**
7: $\quad$ Fitness$(C_a) \leftarrow \frac{1}{2}$ Fitness(P_a)
8: $\quad$ Fitness$(C_b) \leftarrow \frac{1}{2}$ Fitness(P_b)
9: Fitness$(P_a) \leftarrow \frac{1}{2}$ Fitness(P_a)
10: Fitness$(P_b) \leftarrow \frac{1}{2}$ Fitness(P_b)

Now we can examine the top level ZCS loop. The loop has two parts:

1. We update the utilities (fitnesses) of the rules by testing them with the agent: we repeatedly create a match set, pick an action from the match set, determine the action set, perform the action and receive reward, and update the fitness values of the rules in the match set. Fitness values are updated with Algorithm 125.

2. After doing this some n times, we then perform a bit of steady-state breeding, producing a few new rules and inserting them into the population. The fitness of the new children is initialized using Algorithm 126.

Algorithm 127 *The Zeroth Level Classifier System (ZCS)*
1: $popsize \leftarrow$ desired population size
2: $n \leftarrow$ agent runs per evolutionary loop ▷ Make it large.
3: $c \leftarrow$ probability of crossover occurring ▷ Make it small.

4: $P \leftarrow$ Generate Initial Population, given *popsize* ▷ See Text
5: **repeat** ▷ First we do the reinforcement stage to build up fitness values
6:     **for** n times **do**
7:         $s \leftarrow$ an initial state of agent
8:         $r \leftarrow 0$
9:         $M \leftarrow \{\}$
10:        $A \leftarrow \{\}$
11:        **repeat**
12:            $M' \subseteq P \leftarrow$ match set for state s ▷ That is, all $P_i \in P$ which cover s
13:            **if** M' is empty **then** ▷ Oops, nothing's covering s, make something
14:                $M' \leftarrow \{$ Create New Individual Covering s $\}$ ▷ See Text
15:                **if** $||P|| = popsize$ **then** ▷ We're full, delete someone
16:                    $P \leftarrow P - \{\text{SelectForDeath}(P)\}$
17:                $P \leftarrow P \cup M'$
18:            $a \leftarrow$ best action from M' ▷ The action of the winner of SelectWithReplacement(M')
19:            $A' \subseteq M' \leftarrow$ action set for action a ▷ That is, all $M'_j \in M$ whose action is a
20:            UpdateFitnesses with M, M', A, A' and r
21:            Have agent perform action a, resulting in new reward r and transitioning to new state s
22:            $M \leftarrow M'$
23:            $A \leftarrow A'$
24:        **until** the agent's life is over
25:        UpdateFitnesses with $M, M', A, \{\}$ and r ▷ Final iteration. Note $M = M'$, and $A' = \{\}$
26:     Parent $P_a \leftarrow$ SelectWithReplacement(P) ▷ And now we begin the breeding stage
27:     Parent $P_b \leftarrow$ SelectWithReplacement(P)
28:     Child $C_a \leftarrow$ Copy(P_a)
29:     Child $C_b \leftarrow$ Copy(P_b)
30:     **if** $c \geq$ random number chosen uniformly from 0.0 to 1.0 **then**
31:         $C_a, C_b \leftarrow$ Crossover(C_a, C_b)
32:         RedistributeFitnesses(P_a, P_b, C_a, C_b, true)
33:     **else**
34:         RedistributeFitnesses(P_a, P_b, C_a, C_b, false)
35:     $C_a \leftarrow$ Mutate(C_a)
36:     $C_b \leftarrow$ Mutate(C_b)
37:     **if** $||P|| = popsize$ **then** ▷ Make room for at least 2 new kids
38:         $P \leftarrow P - \{\text{SelectForDeath}(P)\}$
39:     **if** $||P|| + 1 = popsize$ **then**
40:         $P \leftarrow P - \{\text{SelectForDeath}(P)\}$
41:     $P \leftarrow P \cup \{C_a, C_b\}$
42: **until** we have run out of time
43: **return** P

The parameter n specifies the number of fitness updates performed before another iteration of steady-state evolution. If n is too small, the algorithm starts doing evolution on sketchy information, and becomes unstable. If n is too large, the algorithm wastes time getting very high-quality fitness information when it could be spending it searching further. Usually, n needs to be large.

There are various ways to generate the initial population. One obvious way is to fill P with *popsize* random individuals, each assigned a small initial fitness (like 1). Another common approach is to keep P initially empty. P will then fill with individuals generated on-the-fly as necessary.

Given a state s, ZCS creates an individual on-the-fly at random with the constraint that its condition must cover s. The fitness of this individual is typically set to the population mean; or if there is no population yet, then it is set to an arbitrary initial fitness (again something small, like 1).

In ZCS, crossover is optional. This is of course the case in many algorithms, but in ZCS it's particularly important because crossover is often highly destructive. The parameter p reflects how often crossover is done in creating children (usually not often). If crossover occurs, the redistributor is informed so as to average out the fitness values between them.

The ZCS algorithm is the first metaheuristic covered so far which doesn't return a "best result": rather the *entire population* is the result. The population itself is the solution to the problem.

The XCS Algorithm Building on ZCS, Stewart Wilson developed a next-generation version which he called **XCS**.[174] XCS has since gone through a number of iterations, including additions from Pier Luca Lanzi and Martin Butz. Basically XCS differs from ZCS in four primary places:

- How the action is selected
- How UpdateFitnesses is performed
- How SelectWithReplacement is done in the evolutionary portion of the algorithm
- How RedistributeFitnesses is performed

The *big change* is that XCS has *four* measures of quality, rather than just fitness:

- XCS has an explicit measure of rule *utility*[175] separate from fitness. It is essentially a rough notion of Q-value, and, when weighted by fitness, is used to select actions.

- XCS maintains a rule *utility error* measure, a historical estimate of the difference between the current utility of the rule and the current utility of the rules in the *next* time step. This is used in calculating the fitness, not in selecting actions. We'll use the $1 - \alpha$ trick to fold in newer results, so recent utility errors count more than older ones.

- From the rule's utility error, XCS derives an *accuracy* measure: lower error, higher accuracy. Below a certain amount of error, the accuracy is thresholded to 1 (perfect).

- XCS's rule *fitness* isn't utility, but an estimate of the historical accuracy of the rule. Beyond its role in evolution, fitness is used in weighting the utility when determining action selection.

---

[174]XCS doesn't appear to stand for anything! The earliest version of the algorithm appeared in Stewart Wilson, 1995, Classifier fitness based on accuracy, *Evolutionary Computation*, 3(2), 149–175.

XCS is complex. For a more accurate description of the algorithm, see Martin Butz and Stewart Wilson, 2001, An algorithmic description of XCS, in *Advances in Learning Classifier Systems*, volume 1996/2001, pages 267–274, Springer. Much of the code in these lecture notes was derived from this paper. Note that my version has some simplifying syntactic changes (no "prediction array" for example) but it should operate the same (knock on wood).

[175]What I am calling *utility* and *utility error* of a rule, XCS calls the **prediction** and **prediction error**.

Picking an Action XCS picks an action from the match set M by first determining the "best" action in M. To do this it gathers all the rules in M which propose the same action. XCS then adds up their utilities, probabilistically weighted by their fitnesses (fitter rules get to contribute more to the utility of the action).

Algorithm 128 *XCS Fitness-Weighted Utility of an Action*
1: $M \leftarrow$ match set
2: $N_i \leftarrow$ action

3: $R \subseteq M \leftarrow$ all rules in M whose heads are N_i
4: **if** $\sum_{r \in R} \text{Fitness}(r) \neq 0$ **then**
5:     **return** $\dfrac{\sum_{r \in R} (\text{Utility}(r) \times \text{Fitness}(r))}{\sum_{r \in R} \text{Fitness}(r)}$
6: **else**
7:     **return** 0

Now we can determine which of the actions is the "best one":

Algorithm 129 *XCS Best Action Determination*
1: $M \leftarrow$ match set
2: $N \leftarrow$ all actions which appear in the head of any rule in M

3: $Best \leftarrow \square$
4: $bestc \leftarrow 0$
5: **for** each action $N_i \in N$ **do**
6:     $c \leftarrow$ XCS Fitness-Weighted Utility of action N_i
7:     **if** $Best = \square$ or $c > bestc$ **then**
8:         $Best \leftarrow N_i$
9:         $bestc \leftarrow c$
10: **return** $Best$

Now we either pick a random action (with ϵ probability), or we choose our "best" action. This approach should look familiar: it's once again ϵ-greedy action selection, just like in Q-learning.[176]

Algorithm 130 *XCS Action Selection*
1: $M \leftarrow$ match set
2: $\epsilon \leftarrow$ exploration probability $\triangleright\ 0 \leq \epsilon \leq 1$

3: $N \leftarrow$ all actions which appear in the head of any rule in M
4: **if** $\epsilon \geq$ random number chosen uniformly from 0.0 to 1.0 inclusive **then**
5:     **return** a member of N chosen uniformly at random
6: **else**
7:     **return** the action provided by XCS Best Action Determination given M and N

---

[176]This was first proposed for XCS in Pier Luca Lanzi, 1999, An analysis of generalization in the XCS classifier system, *Evolutionary Computation*, 7(2), 125–149.

Updating Fitness During testing we no longer have just a fitness to update: we'll need to update all three elements: the utility, the utility error, and the fitness. The utility is updated Q-style:

$$\text{Utility}(A_i) \leftarrow (1 - \alpha) \times \text{Utility}(A_i) + \alpha(r + \gamma b)$$

What is b? It's the XCS Fitness-Weighted Utility (Algorithm 128) of the best action (Algorithm 129) the *next time around* — so you'll need to delay fitness updating of this iteration until you have gone one more iteration. Again, compare this to Equation 2.

The utility error is updated similarly, by rolling in the new error computed by subtracting the utility from the likely best utility of the *next* action set:

$$\text{UtilityError}(A_i) \leftarrow (1 - \alpha) \times \text{UtilityError}(A_i) + \alpha \, ||b - \text{Utility}(A_i)||$$

To compute the fitness, we first convert the error into an "accuracy" a_i. If the error is less than or equal to than some small value e, the accuracy a_i is considered to be perfect, that is, 1. Otherwise, the accuracy a_i is set to $\delta \left(\frac{e}{\text{UtilityError}(A_i)} \right)^\beta$. Finally the accuracy is rolled into the fitness:

$$\text{Fitness}(A_i) \leftarrow (1 - \alpha) \times \text{Fitness}(A_i) + \alpha \frac{a_i}{\sum_{A_j \in A} a_j}$$

Utility, Utility Error, and Fitness are initially set to something small, like 1. There's no evaporation. Here's the algorithm in full:

Algorithm 131 *XCS Fitness Updating*
1: $M \leftarrow$ previous match set ▷ Note: for the final iteration of the ZCS/XCS top loop, $M = M'$
2: $M' \leftarrow$ next match set
3: $A \leftarrow$ previous action set
4: $A' \leftarrow$ next action set ▷ Unused. We keep it here to be consistent with Algorithm 125.
5: $r \leftarrow$ reward received by previous action
6: $e \leftarrow$ the highest error in utility that should still warrant full fitness
7: $\alpha \leftarrow$ learning rate ▷ $0 < \alpha < 1$. Make it small.
8: $\beta \leftarrow$ fitness adjustment parameter ▷ $\beta > 1$
9: $\gamma \leftarrow$ cut-down constant ▷ $0 < \gamma < 1$. 0.5 is fine.
10: $\delta \leftarrow$ fitness adjustment parameter ▷ Presumably $0 \leq \delta \leq 1$. I'm guessing 1 is fine.

11: $n \leftarrow$ the action returned by XCS Best Action Selection on M'
12: $b \leftarrow$ the XCS Fitness-Weighted Utility of action n
13: $\vec{a} \leftarrow \langle a_1, ..., a_{||A||} \rangle$ vector of accuracies, one per rule in A
14: **for** each rule $A_i \in A$ **do**
15: $\quad$ Utility$(A_i) \leftarrow (1 - \alpha) \times$ Utility$(A_i) + \alpha(r + \gamma b)$
16: $\quad$ UtilityError$(A_i) \leftarrow (1 - \alpha) \times$ UtilityError$(A_i) + \alpha \, ||b - \text{Utility}(A_i)||$
17: $\quad$ **if** UtilityError$(A_i) > e$ **then** ▷ Convert error into "accuracy" (big error, low accuracy)
18: $\qquad a_i \leftarrow \delta \left(\frac{e}{\text{UtilityError}(A_i)} \right)^\beta$
19: $\quad$ **else**
20: $\qquad a_i \leftarrow 1$ ▷ Why it's not $a_i \leftarrow \delta$ I have no idea
21: **for** each rule $A_i \in A$ **do**
22: $\quad$ Fitness$(A_i) \leftarrow (1 - \alpha)$ Fitness$(A_i) + \alpha \frac{a_i}{\sum_{A_j \in A} a_j}$ ▷ Normalize the accuracies

Redistributing Fitness In addition to fitness, XCS now also needs to redistribute utility and utility error. And unlike ZCS, rather than redistribute fitness from the parents, XCS just cuts down the fitness of the child. Specifically:

Algorithm 132 *XCS Fitness Redistribution*
1: $P_a, P_b \leftarrow$ parents
2: $C_a, C_b \leftarrow$ children
3: $\nu \leftarrow$ fitness cut-down ▷ Use 0.1
4: *crossedover* $\leftarrow$ are the children the result of crossover?

5: **if** *crossedover* = true **then**
6: $\quad$ Fitness(C_a), Fitness(C_b) $\leftarrow \nu \frac{1}{4}$ (Fitness(P_a) + Fitness(P_b))
7: $\quad$ Utility(C_a), Utility(C_b) $\leftarrow \frac{1}{4}$ (Utility(P_a) + Utility(P_b))
8: $\quad$ UtilityError(C_a), UtilityError(C_b) $\leftarrow \frac{1}{4}$ (UtilityError(P_a) + UtilityError(P_b))
9: **else**
10: $\quad$ Fitness(C_a) $\leftarrow \nu \frac{1}{2}$ Fitness(P_a)
11: $\quad$ Fitness(C_b) $\leftarrow \nu \frac{1}{2}$ Fitness(P_b)
12: $\quad$ Utility(C_a) $\leftarrow \frac{1}{2}$ Utility(P_a)
13: $\quad$ Utility(C_b) $\leftarrow \frac{1}{2}$ Utility(P_b)
14: $\quad$ UtilityError(C_a) $\leftarrow \frac{1}{2}$ UtilityError(P_a)
15: $\quad$ UtilityError(C_b) $\leftarrow \frac{1}{2}$ UtilityError(P_b)

Performing SelectWithReplacement SelectWithReplacement is not performed over the whole population as it was in ZCS. Rather, it's just performed over the action set. That is, lines 28 and 29 of Algorithm 127 should look like this:

$\quad$ Parent $P_a \leftarrow$ SelectWithReplacement(A)
$\quad$ Parent $P_b \leftarrow$ SelectWithReplacement(A)

Other Gizmos To this basic algorithm, XCS normally adds some other gizmos. First, there's the notion of **microclassifiers**. XCS considers each individual not just as one rule, but actually as a whole lot of rules that are exactly the same. This is done by including with each individual a **count** variable which indicates how many "copies" of the rule are considered to be in the individual. When we do fitness updating (Algorithm 131), the very last line includes this count variable so that each of those "embedded" rules get a voice:

$$\text{Fitness}(A_i) \leftarrow (1-\alpha)\text{Fitness}(A_i) + \alpha \frac{a_i \times \text{Count}(A_i)}{\sum_{A_j \in A} a_j \times \text{Count}(A_j)}$$

Counts also figure when we're creating new rules or selecting rules for deletion. If we create a new rule, we check first to see if it's identical to an existing rule. If so, the existing rule has its count increased, and the new rule isn't actually added to the population. When we delete a rule, and its count is higher than 1, we just decrease the count and retain the rule; only when its count is 1 do we delete it. Note that this could result in the population size changing a bit. This gizmo is largely a mechanism to cut down on the total number of classifiers, but it doesn't really affect the results.

Because initial fitness and utility is arbitrarily set, XCS also grants new rules a bit of leeway, to give them a chance to get their utilities and utility errors ramped up. This is done by maintaining an **experience** counter for each rule which is incremented each time that rule appears in an action set. The learning rate is decreased little by little until the experience exceeds $1/\alpha$, at which point the learning rate is α thereafter.

Putting this all together, we can extend the XCS Fitness Updating algorithm (Algorithm 131) to include these additional gizmos:

Algorithm 133 *XCS Fitness Updating (Extended)*

1: $M \leftarrow$ previous match set ▷ Note: for the final iteration of the ZCS/XCS top loop, $M = M'$
2: $M' \leftarrow$ next match set
3: $A \leftarrow$ previous action set
4: $A' \leftarrow$ next action set ▷ Unused. We keep it here to be consistent with Algorithm 125.
5: $r \leftarrow$ reward received by previous action
6: $e \leftarrow$ the highest error in utility that should still warrant full fitness
7: $\alpha \leftarrow$ learning rate ▷ $0 < \alpha < 1$. Make it small.
8: $\beta \leftarrow$ fitness adjustment parameter ▷ $\beta > 1$
9: $\gamma \leftarrow$ cut-down constant ▷ $0 < \gamma < 1$. 0.5 is fine.
10: $\delta \leftarrow$ fitness adjustment parameter ▷ Presumably $0 \leq \delta \leq 1$. I'm guessing 1 is fine.

11: $n \leftarrow$ the action returned by XCS Best Action Selection on M'
12: $b \leftarrow$ the XCS Fitness-Weighted Utility of action n
13: $\vec{a} \leftarrow \langle a_1, ..., a_{||A||} \rangle$ vector of accuracies, one per rule in A
14: **for** each rule $A_i \in A$ **do**
15:    Experience(A_i) $\leftarrow$ Experience(A_i) $+1$
16:    $\alpha' \leftarrow \max(\frac{1}{\text{Experience}(A_i)}, \alpha)$
17:    Utility(A_i) $\leftarrow (1-\alpha') \times$ Utility(A_i) $+\alpha'(r+\gamma b)$
18:    UtilityError(A_i) $\leftarrow (1-\alpha') \times$ UtilityError(A_i) $+\alpha' ||b - $Utility$(A_i)||$
19:    **if** UtilityError(A_i) $> e$ **then** ▷ Convert error into "accuracy" (big error, low accuracy)
20:       $a_i \leftarrow \delta \left(\frac{e}{\text{UtilityError}(A_i)} \right)^\beta$
21:    **else**
22:       $a_i \leftarrow 1$ ▷ Why it's not $a_i \leftarrow \delta$ I have no idea
23: **for** each rule $A_i \in A$ **do**
24:    Fitness(A_i) $\leftarrow (1-\alpha)$ Fitness(A_i) $+\alpha \dfrac{a_i \times \text{Count}(A_i)}{\sum_{A_j \in A} a_j \times \text{Count}(A_j)}$

The big changes are on lines 15, 16, and 24.

Finally, XCS has optional **subsumption** procedures: it checks for a *subsumed* rule whose covered states are entirely covered by some other rule which is both reasonably fit and sufficiently old. The goal is, once again, to force diversity and eliminate redundancy. Subsumption could show up in two places. First, when a brand-new rule is created, XCS may refuse to include it in the population if it's subsumed by some other rule; instead, the subsuming rule has its count increased by one. Second, after building an action set A, XCS could check A to see if any rules subsume any others. If so, the subsumed rules are removed from the population.

10.5 Regression with the Michigan Approach

And now for a twist. Ordinarily algorithms like SAMUEL, ZCS, and XCS (and Q-learning) are used to find a policy $\pi(s) \to a$ which produces the right action (a) for a given state s for an agent under various Markovian assumptions. But there's another, distantly related use for XCS: regression. That is, fitting a real-valued function $y(s)$ to various states s.

The most common algorithm in this vein is **XCSF**, which hijacks XCS to do real-valued regression: the "states", so to speak, are sample points drawn from a multidimensional real-valued space, and the "actions" are real-valued numbers.[177] $y(s)$ is the function which maps the "states" to "actions". I put everything in "quotes" because although XCSF uses XCS to do its dirty work, it's not really learning a state-action policy at all. XCSF is not interested in agents and Markovian state-to-state transitions. Instead, it's just trying to learn $y(s)$.[178]

As a result, XCSF makes some big simplifications. XCSF doesn't have a *utility* per se: instead, each rule M_i in the match set M for a given $s \in S$ simply makes a **prediction**,[179] or guess, of $y(s)$ which we will call $p(M_i, s)$ (this is essentially the rule's "action"). XCSF's estimate of $y(s)$ is the fitness-weighted average prediction among all the rules in the match set. Rules are gradually modified so that that their predictions will more closely match $y(s)$ in the future, and so XCSF's estimate will as well.

In XCSF each state $s \in S$ (and for consistency with XCS I'll keep referring to it as s) is represented internally by a real-valued multidimensional point: let's call it $\vec{x}$. The condition part of a rule will be a region in this space; and the "action" will be some function over this region which explains how the rule predicts the value of those s which fall in this region. One classical way to define a rule in XCSF is as a real-valued box region with a gradient running through it from one corner to the other. The gradient is the "action". We define the rule in the form:

$$\{\vec{l} = \langle l_1, ... l_n \rangle, \quad \vec{u} = \langle u_1, ..., u_n \rangle, \quad \vec{w} = \langle w_0, w_1, ..., w_n \rangle \}$$

Notice that $\vec{w}$ has an extra value w_0 but $\vec{l}$ and $\vec{u}$ do not. This rule defines a box with a lower corner at $\vec{l}$ and an upper corner at $\vec{u}$. The rule predicts that $y(\vec{l}) = w_0$, and that $y(\vec{u}) = w_0 + \sum_{i=1}^{n} w_i(u_i - l_i)$. In general a point $\vec{x}$ within this box is predicted to have a $y(\vec{x})$ value of:[180]

$$y(\vec{x}) = w_0 + \sum_{i=1}^{n} w_i(x_i - l_i)$$

To be consistent with previous XCS notation we'll define the prediction abstractly as $p(M_j, s)$, where M_j is the rule in question, and s is an input point. In this case, M_j is $\{\vec{l}, \vec{u}, \vec{w}\}$ and s is $\vec{x}$.

Given this representation, XCSF estimates $y(s)$ using a **piecewise linear function**: it approximates $y(s)$ using a bunch of overlapping linear regions, one per rule. Multiple rules may cover a given point s (these are the match set for s), and in this case the prediction of $y(s)$ is be the fitness-weighted average of the $p(...)$ values for each of the these rules. Which leads us to...

---

[177] This also makes the "C" in XCSF a misnomer, though inexplicably the XCSF folks still refer to all this as "classification"! A good introduction to XCSF may be found in Stewart W. Wilson, 2002, Classifiers that approximate functions, *Natural Computing*, 1(2–3), 211–234. Like XCS, XCSF doesn't seem to stand for anything.

[178] This isn't to say you *couldn't* retain these features. See for example Pier Luca Lanzi, Daniele Loiacono, Stewart W. Wilson, and David E. Goldberg, 2005, XCS with computed prediction in continuous multistep environments, in *Congress on Evolutionary Computation*, pages 2032–2039.

[179] Recall from footnote 175 that XCS used the term *prediction* in a similar way: but recall that I opted for utility to be consistent with reinforcement learning. But here, stripped of agents and states, the term "prediction" is a good choice.

[180] In early papers, $y(\vec{x}) = w_0 + \sum_{i=1}^{n} w_i x_i$ (no l_i). This works but boxes far from the origin will be very sensitive to $\vec{w}$.

Algorithm 134 *XCSF Fitness-Weighted Collective Prediction*
1: $M \leftarrow$ match set

2: **if** $\sum_{M_i \in M} \text{Fitness}(r) \neq 0$ **then**
3:     **return** $\dfrac{\sum_{M_i \in M} \left(\text{p}(M_i, s) \times \text{Fitness}(M_i) \right)}{\sum_{M_i \in M} \text{Fitness}(M_i)}$
4: **else**
5:     **return** 0

Compare to Algorithm 128 (XCS Fitness-Weighted Utility of an Action). Once our population has converged to a good set of rules, now we have a way of interpreting them as a function which predicts $y(s)$ for any point s. Of course there are other ways of representing rules besides as boxes with linear gradients. For example, you could represent them as **hyperellipsoids** with radial gradients inside them. Or you could use neural networks, or a tile coding of some sort.

Eventually you'll want to use your learned XCSF model in the real world. But the model will probably be underspecified, and have regions that it doesn't cover: what if the match set M is empty? Returning 0 in this case isn't very satisfying. Instead, XCSF folks suggest that you pick a value $\theta > 0$. If during usage, $||M|| < \theta$, then M gets bulked up with the $||M|| - \theta$ rules *closest*, in some measure, to the testing point s, but not already in M. This can go for XCS and ZCS too.

The intuition behind XCSF is to adapt its rules so as to concentrate more rules on the "complex" parts of the space. It does this through evolution: but during Fitness Updating it also applies a special gradient descent operation which directly modifies a rule's condition so that it is more likely to produce the right prediction next time. This works as follows. When a rule doesn't predict the correct value during XCSF's, the rule is revised a bit so that next time it's more likely to be closer to the correct value. Recall that our s is represented by the point $\vec{x}$. Our rule is $\vec{l}, \vec{u}, \vec{w}$. Let $r = y(\vec{x})$. Recall that the rule's prediction of r is $w_0 + \sum_{i=1}^{n} w_i(x_i - l_i)$. So the difference b between the correct value r and the predicted value is simply $b = r - w_0 - \sum_{i=1}^{n} w_i(x_i - l_i)$.

Now we need an equation for updating $\vec{w}$ so that b is lessened next time. Let's use the **delta rule**[181] from neural networks:

$$\vec{w} \leftarrow \vec{w} + \langle \alpha b, \alpha b(x_1 - l_1), ..., \alpha b(x_n - l_n) \rangle$$

Now to the fitness. Recall that XCS didn't base fitness on utility, but rather "utility error", a historical average estimate of how the utility differed from the utility at the next state. But we don't have a "next state" any more, nor any notion of "utility" any more: we're not doing state-to-state

---

[181] Where did this magic rule come from? It's simple. We want to minimize the error: to do this we need some error function $\mathcal{E}$ which is zero when $b = 0$ and is more and more positive as b gets further from 0. Because it makes the math work out nicely, let's use $\mathcal{E} = \frac{1}{2}b^2 = \frac{1}{2}(r - w_0 - \sum_{i=1}^{n} w_i(x_i - l_i))^2$. We want to update $\vec{w}$ so as to reduce $\mathcal{E}$, and will use gradient descent to do it (recall Algorithm 1). Thus $\vec{w} \leftarrow \vec{w} - \alpha \nabla \mathcal{E}(\vec{w})$. This means that each w_i will be updated as $w_i \leftarrow w_i - \alpha \frac{\partial \mathcal{E}}{\partial w_i}$. Taking the derivative of $\mathcal{E}$ with respect to w_0 gets us $\frac{\partial \mathcal{E}}{\partial w_0} = (r - w_0 - \sum_{i=1}^{n} w_i(x_i - l_i))(-1) = -b$. Okay, that was weirdly easy. For any other w_j, $\frac{\partial \mathcal{E}}{\partial w_j} = (r - w_0 - \sum_{i=1}^{n} w_i(x_i - l_i))(-(x_j - l_j)) = -b(x_j - l_j)$. Since we're multiplying everything by $-\alpha$, thus $\vec{w} \leftarrow \vec{w} + \langle \alpha b, \alpha b(x_1 - l_1), ..., \alpha b(x_n - l_n) \rangle$. Ta da!

While the delta rule is easy to implement, much of the XCSF community has since moved to estimation using the more complex **recursive least squares**, as it's considered stabler. For more information, see Pier Luca Lanzi, Daniele Loiacono, Stewart W. Wilson, and David E. Goldberg, 2007, Generalization in the XCSF classifier system: Analysis, improvement, and extension, *Evolutionary Computation*, 15(2), 133–168.

transitions. Instead, XCSF just keeps a historical average estimate of the error b using the $1 - \alpha$ trick. We'll call this the "Prediction Error", but note that it's used identically to the old "Utility Error" in computing fitness via accuracy (in Algorithms 131 and 133).

$$\text{PredictionError}(M_i) \leftarrow (1 - \alpha) \times \text{PredictionError}(M_i) + \alpha ||b||$$

At this point the algorithm below should make more sense. Compare to Algorithm 131:

Algorithm 135 *XCSF Fitness Updating*
1:   $M \leftarrow$ match set
2:   $s \leftarrow$ input data point
3:   $r \leftarrow$ desired output for the input data point
4:   $\alpha \leftarrow$ learning rate   ▷ $0 < \alpha < 1$. Make it small.
5:   $\beta \leftarrow$ fitness adjustment parameter   ▷ $\beta > 1$
6:   $\delta \leftarrow$ fitness adjustment parameter   ▷ Presumably $0 \leq \delta \leq 1$. I'm guessing 1 is fine.

7:   $\vec{a} \leftarrow \langle a_1, ..., a_{||M||} \rangle$ vector of accuracies, one per rule in M
8:   **for** each rule $M_i \in M$ **do**
9:      $\langle x_1, ..., x_n \rangle \leftarrow$ the point $\vec{x}$ represented by s
10:     $\{\langle l_1, ..., l_n \rangle, \langle u_1, ..., u_n \rangle, \langle w_0, ..., w_n \rangle\} \leftarrow$ lower points, upper points, weights in M_i ▷ Note w_0
11:     $b \leftarrow r - (w_0 + \sum_{i=1}^{n} w_i(x_i - l_i))$ ▷ Error between correct value and prediction
12:     $\vec{w} \leftarrow \vec{w} + \langle \alpha b, \alpha b(x_1 - l_1), ..., \alpha b(x_n - l_n) \rangle$ ▷ Delta rule
13:     Revise M_i to new $\vec{w}$ values
14:     $\text{PredictionError}(M_i) \leftarrow (1 - \alpha) \times \text{PredictionError}(M_i) + \alpha \times ||b||$
15:     **if** $\text{PredictionError}(M_i) > e$ **then**   ▷ Convert error into "accuracy" (big error, low accuracy)
16:        $a_i \leftarrow \delta \left(\dfrac{e}{\text{PredictionError}(M_i)} \right)^{\beta}$
17:     **else**
18:        $a_i \leftarrow 1$
19:   **for** each rule $M_i \in M$ **do**
20:     $\text{Fitness}(M_i) \leftarrow (1 - \alpha) \text{Fitness}(M_i) + \alpha \dfrac{a_i}{\sum_{M_j \in M} a_j}$ ▷ Normalize the accuracies

Evolution Details   Selection, Crossover, and Mutation, are basically the same as in XCS. However you decide to represent your rules (as an array of numbers say), you'll want to take care that crossover and mutation don't produce invalid rule conditions. XCSF can also use XCS's fitness redistribution (Algorithm 132) though obviously "utility" doesn't exist any more, and "utility error" should be changed to "prediction error".

Initialization is more or less the same as in XCS or ZCS (see the text discussing Algorithm 127 for reminders), through XCSF usually initially generates populations by starting with an empty population rather than a fully randomly-generated one. Also, because the population starts out empty, XCSF usually adds new individuals in response to an uncovered state s. To do this, XCSF traditionally defines the box defining the condition of the rule as follows. Let's say that s is the point $\vec{x}$ in the space. For each dimension k of the box, XCSF creates two random numbers i_k and j_k, each between 0 and some maximum value q (which you have to define). Then the box is defined as running from the lower point $\langle x_0 - i_0, x_1 - i_1, ..., x_n - i_n \rangle$ to the upper point $\langle x_0 + j_0, x_1 + j_1, ..., x_n + j_n \rangle$.

Now we're ready to describe the main loop. It's basically ZCS, but with a slightly different inner loop because rather than dealing with action sets, actions, rewards, state transitions, and so on, XCSF picks a state s, determines the Match Set for it, computes and reports a collective predicted value, and then revises the rules and updates their fitnesses. There is no action set at all.

Here's the revised top-level algorithm. Notice the strong relationship with ZCS (Algorithm 127):

Algorithm 136 *The XCSF Algorithm*
1: $S \leftarrow \{s_1, ..., s_z\}$ input data points
2: $y(s) \leftarrow$ function which returns the desired output for input data point $s \in S$
3: *popsize* $\leftarrow$ desired population size
4: $f \leftarrow$ fitness value to be assigned to initial population members ▷ Can be whatever. Say, 1.
5: $n \leftarrow$ agent runs per evolutionary loop ▷ Make it large.
6: $c \leftarrow$ probability of crossover occurring ▷ Make it small.

7: $P \leftarrow$ Generate Initial Population, given f and *popsize*
8: **repeat**
9:     **for** n times **do**
10:         **for** each $s \in S$ **do** ▷ Do these in randomly shuffled order
11:             $M \subseteq P \leftarrow$ match set for state s ▷ That is, all $P_i \in P$ which cover s
12:             **if** M is empty **then** ▷ Oops, nothing's covering s, make something
13:                 $M \leftarrow \{$ Create New Individual Covering s $\}$ ▷ See Text
14:                 **if** $||P|| = popsize$ **then** ▷ We're full, delete someone
15:                     $P \leftarrow P - \{\text{SelectForDeath}(P)\}$
16:                 $P \leftarrow P \cup M$
17:             Report the collective prediction of s by the members of M
18:             $r \leftarrow y(s)$
19:             UpdateFitnesses with M, s, and r
20:     Parent $P_a \leftarrow$ SelectWithReplacement(P) ▷ And now we begin the breeding stage
21:     Parent $P_b \leftarrow$ SelectWithReplacement(P)
22:     Child $C_a \leftarrow$ Copy(P_a)
23:     Child $C_b \leftarrow$ Copy(P_b)
24:     **if** $c \geq$ random number chosen uniformly from 0.0 to 1.0 **then**
25:         $C_a, C_b \leftarrow$ Crossover(C_a, C_b)
26:         RedistributeFitnesses$(P_a, P_b, C_a, C_b, \text{true})$
27:     **else**
28:         RedistributeFitnesses$(P_a, P_b, C_a, C_b, \text{false})$
29:     $C_a \leftarrow$ Mutate(C_a)
30:     $C_b \leftarrow$ Mutate(C_b)
31:     **if** $||P|| = popsize$ **then** ▷ Make room for at least 2 new kids
32:         $P \leftarrow P - \{\text{SelectForDeath}(P)\}$
33:     **if** $||P|| + 1 = popsize$ **then**
34:         $P \leftarrow P - \{\text{SelectForDeath}(P)\}$
35:     $P \leftarrow P \cup \{C_a, C_b\}$
36: **until** we have run out of time
37: **return** P

10.6 Is this Genetic Programming?

Back to XCS and SAMUEL. In some important sense, policies are **programs** which control agents. These programs consist of *if*→*then* rules where the *if* side consists of the current state of the world. Even without control structures, this is often a lot more sophisticated than the lion's share of "programs" that tree-structured or machine-code genetic programming develops (see Sections 4.3 and 4.4). But is this sufficient to be called "programming"?

Well, in lots of environments, you need more than just the state of the world to decide what to do. You also need a **memory** where you store some form of information gleaned from the **history** of what's happened. That memory is typically called the **internal state** of the agent (as opposed to the world state, or **external state**).

Consider Figure 67 at right. The robot starts in room A and wants to go out the door. We would like to develop a policy that enables the robot to go to room C, flick the switch (which opens the door), return to A, and go out the door. The policy might be:

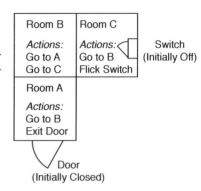

Figure 67 A robot world with three rooms, a door, and a switch. available actions for each room are shown. The robot can only exit if the door is opened. Flicking the switch opens the door.

In A and door closed → go to B
In B → go to C
In C and switch off → flick switch
In C and switch on → go to B
In B → **um....**
In A and door open → go out the door

The problem is that we already have a rule for B! Go to C. We need *two* rules for B: if I'm headed to flick the switch, go to C, but if I'm headed out the door, go to A. Trouble is, in room B we have nothing to go on, no external state information, which can help us distinguish these features. The two B situations are **aliased**: they require different actions but exhibit the same external state.

We need some memory: specifically, we need memory of whether we flicked the switch or not. Let's give the agent a single bit of memory. Initially the bit is 0. Now we might construct this policy:

In A and door closed → go to B
In B and memory bit is 0 → go to C
In C and switch off → flick switch and set memory bit to 1
In C and switch on → go to B
In B and memory bit is 1 → go to A
In A and door open → go out the door

Problem solved! Here's the thing: by adding a single bit of memory, we've potentially **doubled our state space**. A single bit isn't too bad, but several bits and we radically increase the complexity of our world. Techniques for handling these issues are fairly cutting-edge. I personally view policy optimization methods as the closest thing we have to successful "genetic programming" at present: but we're still a long ways from true automatic programming. Your job is safe.

11 Miscellany

Always the most interesting section of a book.[182]

11.1 Experimental Methodology

11.1.1 Random Number Generators, Replicability, and Duplicability

Random Number Generators Metaheuristics employ randomness to some degree. Like all stochastic techniques, the validity of your results may rely on the quality of your **random number generator**. Unfortunately, there are a lot of very *very* bad random number generators in common use. Many of the more infamous generators come from a family of **linear congruential random number generators**, where the next random number is a function of the previous one: $x_{t+1} = (ax_t + c)$ mod m. The values for a, c, and m must be very carefully chosen in order for this generator to be even adequate to use. But bad choices of these constants have led to some truly infamous results. The RANDU generator, for example, ruined experimental results as far back as the 1960s. A mistake in the ANSI C specification led to the propagation of a horrible generator in C and C++'s rand() function even to this day. And Java's java.util.Random produces such *non*-random results that there's an entire web page devoted to making fun of it.[183] When I examine new Java metaheuristics toolkits, the first thing I check is whether they're using java.util.Random or not.

The revelation of a poor generator has cast doubt on more than one research paper in the literature. You ought to pick a high-grade generator. My own personal choice is the **Mersenne Twister**, a highly respected generator with very good statistical properties and an ultra-long period (the amount of time before it starts repeating its sequence), but there are other very good ones out there as well.

Generators need to be seeded and used properly. Too many times have I seen beginners repeatedly instantiating a new java.util.Random instance, generating one integer from it, then throwing it away, seemingly blissfully unaware that this is grotesquely nonrandom. This awful approach gives you a sequence of numbers loosely following your computer's wall clock time. A good way to use a random number generator in your experiments is:

1. Choose a very high grade random number generator.

2. Pick a unique seed for each and every experimental run you do.

3. Seed your generator based on the seed you picked.

4. If you're using a language like Java in which generators are objects, create only one generator per experimental run and continue to use it throughout the run, never creating a new one.

Unless you know *exactly* what you're doing, it'd be wise **to not deviate from this procedure.**

Replicability When you perform your experiments and write them up for a conference or journal, you *must* strive for **replicability**. You should report your results in such a way that a competent coder could *replicate* your experiments, using a different programming language and operating

---

[182]Compare to Footnote 3, p. 11.
[183]"Sun Refines Randomness": http://alife.co.uk/nonrandom/

system, and still get *more or less* the same results. Otherwise, who's to know if you just didn't make this stuff up? To make replicable experiments you'll need to describe your algorithm and relevant parameters in sufficient detail. Pseudocode would be nice.

Even if you have described your algorithm in detail, if the algorithm is gigantic and absurdly complex, it's not considered replicable. You can't just thumb your nose at your readers and say "replicate this giant monster, *I dare you*." Instead, you'll probably need to provide actual code somewhere for your readers to access so they don't have to write it themselves. People are scared of providing code so others can examine it, mostly because they're ashamed of their code quality. Be brave.[184]

Duplicability If you are performing experiments and making claims, it's helpful to strive not just for replicability but for the higher standard of **duplicability**. Here you're enabling others to *exactly* duplicate your results, ideally in environments other than your particular computer. The difference between replicability and duplicability is fundamental when dealing with a stochastic system: replicable experiments can be *more or less* repeated, with results which are statistically equivalent. Duplicable experiments are *exactly the same* when run elsewhere. For example, a good metaheuristics toolkit should be able to enable you to move to a new operating system and a new CPU and repeat the identical experiment.[185] To get duplicability, you'll need to think about your language and environment choice.

Why is this important? Let's say you've published some experiments, and Person X approaches you telling you he can't replicate your results. Uh oh. "No problem", you say, and you hand him your code. Then he tries to run the code on his system and gets... a different result. How do you prove your claims are still valid? Could it be a bug in his operating system, compiler, or CPU? Or yours? Did you forget to give him the specific random number generator seeds that produce the given result? It's for these reasons that duplicability provides a bit of piece of mind. Replicability is crucial; duplicability would be nice. Consider it.

11.1.2 Comparing Techniques

By far the most common kind of experiment you'll find yourself doing in metaheuristics is comparing two different techniques. For example, let's say you want to show that, on some problem Foo, if you apply Particle Swarm Optimization with $\alpha = 0.9, \beta = 0.1, \gamma = 0.1, \delta = 0, \epsilon = 1$, and with a population of size 10, you'll get better results than if you use the $5 + 1$ Evolution Strategy using Gaussian Convolution with $\sigma^2 = 0.1$. How do you do this?

By What Yardstick Should We Compare our Techniques? This is the first question that needs to be answered. At the end of a run, you often are left with a single best solution (or at least one

---

[184]I must admit, I often am not. But I try to be.

[185]And now we come to the delicate point where I suggest that you may wish to consider a language other than C++: it's not a language which makes duplicability easy. C++ and C depend critically on the specifics of your CPU: how large is a long? How is cos performed? How about sqrt? Is your CPU big-endian, little-endian, or something else? Does compiling with certain floating-point optimizations turned on change the results? It can be frustrating to get results running on Machine A, only to recompile on Machine B and get something subtly, but importantly, different. Perhaps with everyone using the same Intel processors these days, it's less of a concern. But still, consider picking a "safe" language: Java in particular can provide precise duplicable results if you need it to.

which isn't worse than any of the others). The quality or fitness of this solution is known as the **best of run**. In most cases you'd like this best of run quality to be as good as possible.

For most metaheuristics comparisons your goal is to demonstrate that technique A in some sense performs *better* than technique B with regard to best of run quality. Nowadays evaluations are the primary cost in in metaheuristics, so most researchers tend to ask the following question: if you could do a *single run* with a fixed budget of m evaluations, and needed a solution of the highest quality possible, which technique should you pick? This is exactly the same thing as asking: which technique has the highest *expected* (or *mean*) best of run?[186]

An alternative question that has been asked before is: how many evaluations do I need to run before I reach some level q of quality? Often q is simply defined as "the optimum". Or: if I run my technique n times, how often do I reach this level? Such formulations have taken many guises in the past, but the most common one, found in the genetic programming world, is the so-called **computational effort** measure.

It is my opinion that this alternative question usually isn't a good question to ask. Metaheuristics are applied to hard problems. If you're gauging techniques by how quickly they solve a problem, then your problem is trivial and your claims are may be unhelpful for more realistic problems. Further, such measures are somewhat challenging to establish statistical significance for, and computational effort in particular may be less accurate than hoped for.[187]

A third question comes from the machine learning community: if I find a candidate solution which does well for some set T of **test cases**, how well is this solution likely to perform in the real world? This is a question of **generalizability**: we're asking how well technique A learns about the world from a small sample (T) of inputs. One simple approach to gauging this is to create two disjoint sets of test cases T and S. You can make T however large you like, but I'd make S relatively large, perhaps 100. T will be the test cases used to to develop our solution (commonly called the **training set**). Once we have a final solution, we gauge its quality by applying it to the test cases in S — which it has never seen before — and seeing how well it performs. S is called the **test set**. There exist more nuanced methods for doing train/test methodologies, such as **k-fold cross validation**, but the one described is very common.

Finally, multiobjective problems pose special difficulties, because the result of a multiobjective run is not a single solution but a whole set of solutions which lie along the Pareto front. As a result, there really is *no satisfactory way to compare multiobjective optimization techniques*. Still though,

---

[186]What if you could run a technique five times and take the best result of the five? Which is better then? It turns out, it's not necessarily A. If A had a mean of 5 but a variance of 0.01, while B had a mean of 4 (worse) but a variance of 20, you'd pick A if you ran just once, but you'd prefer B if you could run more than once and take the maximum of the runs.

[187]Liviu Panait and I wrote a paper attacking the philosophy behind computational effort and similar measures and noting its poor correlation with expected-quality measures: Sean Luke and Liviu Panait, 2002, Is the perfect the enemy of the good?, in W. B. Langdon, *et al.*, editors, *GECCO 2002: Proceedings of the Genetic and Evolutionary Computation Conference*, pages 820–828, Morgan Kaufmann Publishers, New York.

Steffan Christensen and Franz Oppacher have also been tough on the computational effort measure: they've established that it significantly underestimates the true effort: Steffen Christensen and Franz Oppacher, 2002, An analysis of Koza's computational effort statistic for genetic programming, in James A. Foster, *et al.*, editors, *Proceedings of the 5th European Conference on Genetic Programming (EuroGP 2002)*, pages 182–191, Springer.

Matthew Walker, Howard Edwards, and Chris Messom been establishing methods to compute statistical significance for the computational effort measure. If you're interested in going after the alternative question, you should definitely try to use a method like theirs to add some rigor to any claims. Their latest work is Matthew Walker, Howard Edwards, and Chris Messom, 2007, The reliability of confidence intervals for computational effort comparisons, in Dirk Thierens, *et al.*, editors, *GECCO '07: Proceedings of the 9th Annual Conference on Genetic and Evolutionary Computation*, volume 2, pages 1716–1723, ACM Press.

researchers have to do *something*. Eckart Zitzler, Kalyanmoy Deb, and Lothar Thiele proposed various measures for comparing techniques[188] which are still in wide use today. Many of these techniques assume that you know beforehand what the true Pareto front is: this probably will not be true for real problems. Much research is now turning towards comparing techniques based on which has the largest **hypervolume** — the volume of the multiobjective space dominated by the front discovered by the technique. Hypervolume is, unfortunately, nontrivial and expensive to compute.

Statistical Significance Okay so you've settled on a question to ask and a way of getting results out of your Particle Swarm Optimization and Evolution Strategy techniques. You run PSO once and get a 10.5. You run your Evolution Strategy once and get a 10.2. So PSO did better, right?

Nope. How do you know that your results aren't due to the random numbers you happened to get from your generator? What happens if you run a second time with a different random number generator seed? Will PSO still beat ES then or will it be the other way around? Keep in mind that this is a *stochastic* technique, not a deterministic one. To determine that PSO really is better than ES for problem Foo, you'll need to run some n times and take the average. To eliminate the possibility of randomness messing with your results, n needs to be large.

You could do this trivially by running your problems A and B, say, a billion times each, and comparing their means. But who has time to do a billion runs? We need a way to state with some definiteness that A is better than B after testing A and B each some smaller number of times: perhaps 50 or 100. To do this, we need a **hypothesis test**.

The literature on hypothesis tests is huge, and there are many options. Here my goal is to suggest a couple of approaches which I think will serve you well for the large majority of situations you may find yourself in. Before we get to hypothesis tests, let's begin with some strong suggestions:

- Unless you know what you're doing, always run each technique at *least* 30 times. I strongly suggest 50 or 100 times per technique. The more runs you do, the easier it is to prove that the techniques produce different expected results.

- Each run should be *independent* — there should be no relationship between the runs. In particular, each run should employ a unique random number seed.

- Be as conservative as you possibly can with regard to your claim. Don't just compare your newfangled Particle Swarm method against a specific Evolution Strategy. Instead, try Evolution Strategies with lots of different parameter settings to find the one which performs the best. Compare your new method against that best-performing one. Make it as hard as possible for your claim to succeed.

Okay, so you've done all these things. You now have 100 independent results for technique A and 100 independent results for technique B. The mean of the A results is better (let's say, higher) than the mean of the B results. What do you do now?

Your hypothesis is that A is better than B. The **null hypothesis** — your enemy — claims that there's no difference between the two, that is, the perceived difference is just due to your random numbers. You need to compute what the *probability* is that the null hypothesis is wrong. You want

---

[188]Eckart Zitzler, Kalyanmoy Deb, and Lothar Thiele, 2000, Comparison of multiobjective evolutionary algorithms: Empirical results, *Evolutionary Computation*, 8(2), 125–148

dof	\multicolumn{4}{c}{Desired Probability}	dof	\multicolumn{4}{c}{Desired Probability}	dof	\multicolumn{4}{c}{Desired Probability}
	95%	98%	99%	99.8%		95%	98%	99%	99.8%		95%	98%	99%	99.8%
1	12.706	31.821	63.657	318.313	35	2.030	2.438	2.724	3.340	69	1.995	2.382	2.649	3.213
2	4.303	6.965	9.925	22.327	36	2.028	2.434	2.719	3.333	70	1.994	2.381	2.648	3.211
3	3.182	4.541	5.841	10.215	37	2.026	2.431	2.715	3.326	71	1.994	2.380	2.647	3.209
4	2.776	3.747	4.604	7.173	38	2.024	2.429	2.712	3.319	72	1.993	2.379	2.646	3.207
5	2.571	3.365	4.032	5.893	39	2.023	2.426	2.708	3.313	73	1.993	2.379	2.645	3.206
6	2.447	3.143	3.707	5.208	40	2.021	2.423	2.704	3.307	74	1.993	2.378	2.644	3.204
7	2.365	2.998	3.499	4.782	41	2.020	2.421	2.701	3.301	75	1.992	2.377	2.643	3.202
8	2.306	2.896	3.355	4.499	42	2.018	2.418	2.698	3.296	76	1.992	2.376	2.642	3.201
9	2.262	2.821	3.250	4.296	43	2.017	2.416	2.695	3.291	77	1.991	2.376	2.641	3.199
10	2.228	2.764	3.169	4.143	44	2.015	2.414	2.692	3.286	78	1.991	2.375	2.640	3.198
11	2.201	2.718	3.106	4.024	45	2.014	2.412	2.690	3.281	79	1.990	2.374	2.640	3.197
12	2.179	2.681	3.055	3.929	46	2.013	2.410	2.687	3.277	80	1.990	2.374	2.639	3.195
13	2.160	2.650	3.012	3.852	47	2.012	2.408	2.685	3.273	81	1.990	2.373	2.638	3.194
14	2.145	2.624	2.977	3.787	48	2.011	2.407	2.682	3.269	82	1.989	2.373	2.637	3.193
15	2.131	2.602	2.947	3.733	49	2.010	2.405	2.680	3.265	83	1.989	2.372	2.636	3.191
16	2.120	2.583	2.921	3.686	50	2.009	2.403	2.678	3.261	84	1.989	2.372	2.636	3.190
17	2.110	2.567	2.898	3.646	51	2.008	2.402	2.676	3.258	85	1.988	2.371	2.635	3.189
18	2.101	2.552	2.878	3.610	52	2.007	2.400	2.674	3.255	86	1.988	2.370	2.634	3.188
19	2.093	2.539	2.861	3.579	53	2.006	2.399	2.672	3.251	87	1.988	2.370	2.634	3.187
20	2.086	2.528	2.845	3.552	54	2.005	2.397	2.670	3.248	88	1.987	2.369	2.633	3.185
21	2.080	2.518	2.831	3.527	55	2.004	2.396	2.668	3.245	89	1.987	2.369	2.632	3.184
22	2.074	2.508	2.819	3.505	56	2.003	2.395	2.667	3.242	90	1.987	2.368	2.632	3.183
23	2.069	2.500	2.807	3.485	57	2.002	2.394	2.665	3.239	91	1.986	2.368	2.631	3.182
24	2.064	2.492	2.797	3.467	58	2.002	2.392	2.663	3.237	92	1.986	2.368	2.630	3.181
25	2.060	2.485	2.787	3.450	59	2.001	2.391	2.662	3.234	93	1.986	2.367	2.630	3.180
26	2.056	2.479	2.779	3.435	60	2.000	2.390	2.660	3.232	94	1.986	2.367	2.629	3.179
27	2.052	2.473	2.771	3.421	61	2.000	2.389	2.659	3.229	95	1.985	2.366	2.629	3.178
28	2.048	2.467	2.763	3.408	62	1.999	2.388	2.657	3.227	96	1.985	2.366	2.628	3.177
29	2.045	2.462	2.756	3.396	63	1.998	2.387	2.656	3.225	97	1.985	2.365	2.627	3.176
30	2.042	2.457	2.750	3.385	64	1.998	2.386	2.655	3.223	98	1.984	2.365	2.627	3.175
31	2.040	2.453	2.744	3.375	65	1.997	2.385	2.654	3.220	99	1.984	2.365	2.626	3.175
32	2.037	2.449	2.738	3.365	66	1.997	2.384	2.652	3.218	100	1.984	2.364	2.626	3.174
33	2.035	2.445	2.733	3.356	67	1.996	2.383	2.651	3.216	∞	1.960	2.326	2.576	3.090
34	2.032	2.441	2.728	3.348	68	1.995	2.382	2.650	3.214					

Table 4 Table of t-values by degrees of freedom (*dof*) and desired probability that the Null Hypothesis is wrong (2-tailed t-tests only). To verify that the Null Hypothesis is wrong with the given probability, you need to have a t-value larger than the given value. If your degrees of freedom exceed 100, be conservative: use 100, unless they're huge, and so you can justifiably use ∞. 95% is generally an acceptable minimum probability, but higher probabilities are preferred.

that probability to be as high as possible. To be accepted in the research community, you usually need to achieve at least a 95% probability; and ideally a 99% or better probability.

A hypothesis test estimates this probability for you. Hypothesis tests come in various flavors: some more often claim that A is better than B when in fact there's no difference. Others will more conservatively claim that there's no difference between A and B when in fact there is a difference. You *always want to err on the side of conservatism*.

The most common hypothesis test, mostly because it's easy to do, is **Student's t-Test**.[189] Among the most conservative such t-Tests is one which doesn't presume that the results of A and B come from distributions with the same variance.[190] We'll use the "two-tailed" version of the test. To do the test, you first need to compute the means μ_A, μ_B, variances σ_A^2, σ_B^2, and number of results (n_A, n_B, in our example, $n_A = n_B = 100$) for technique A and technique B respectively. With these you determine the *t statistic* and the *degrees of freedom*.

$$t = \frac{|\mu_A - \mu_B|}{\sqrt{\frac{\sigma_A^2}{n_A} + \frac{\sigma_B^2}{n_B}}}$$

$$\textit{degrees of freedom} = \frac{\left(\frac{\sigma_A^2}{n_A} + \frac{\sigma_B^2}{n_B}\right)^2}{\left(\frac{\sigma_A^2}{n_A}\right)^2 / (n_A - 1) + \left(\frac{\sigma_B^2}{n_B}\right)^2 / (n_B - 1)}$$

Let's say your degrees of freedom came out to 100 and you have chosen 95% as your probability. From Table 4, we find that you must have a *t* value of 1.984 or greater. Imagine that that your *t* value came out as, oh, let's say, 0.523. This tells us that you have failed to disprove the Null Hypothesis with an adequate probability. Thus you have no evidence that PSO is actually better than ES for the Foo problem.

As you can see from the table, if you want to make it easier to pass the t-test, the way to do it is to increase your degrees of freedom. This translates into doing more runs (that is, increasing n_A and n_B). More runs is always good! But beware: if you need a *very* large number of runs to do this, it's likely the case that though your techniques are different, the difference is very small. Now you'll run up against the "so what?" question: so what if PSO eeks out just barely better results than ES on problem Foo? Thus what you usually want to be able to argue is both (1) that the difference between your two techniques **statistically significant**, that is, that a hypothesis test agrees with you that it actually exists; and (2) that the difference is also considerable and likely to be important.

The t-Test should be viewed as the **absolute minimum** you should do for published work. Anything less and you should be ashamed of yourself. The problem with the t-Test — and it's a *big* problem — is that it is parametric, that is, it relies solely on the mean, variance, and sample count of your results. This is because the t-Test makes a huge assumption: that the results produced by your techniques A and B are each drawn from a normal (Gaussian) distribution.

In metaheuristics scenarios, that's almost never true.

A great many metaheuristics problems produce results which are fairly skewed. Now the t-Test is pretty robust even with relatively skewed data. But if the data is too skewed, the t-Test starts being less accurate than it should. Also very bad for the t-Test is data with multiple peaks.

To compensate for this, there's a better approach: a **nonparametric hypothesis test**. This kind of test ignores the actual values of your data and only considers their rank ordering with respect to one another.[191] As a result, such tests are much less sensitive, but they are not fooled by assumptions about how your results are distributed. If you pass a non-parametric test, few can criticize you.

---

[189]It's called this because it's based on work by William Sealy Gosset around 1908, who worked at Guinness Brewery and secretly published under the pseudonym "Student". He did so because Guinness wouldn't allow its workers to publish anything out of fear of leaking trade secrets. The t-Test itself was, however, mostly derived by Ronald Aylmer Fisher, a famous statistician who conversed with Gosset and made his work popular.

[190]This t-Test variant is known as **Welch's t-Test**, after Bernard Lewis (B. L.) Welch, who developed it.

[191]Sound familiar? Think: fitness-proportionate selection versus tournament selection.

There are a various nonparametric tests, notably the **Mann-Whitney U Test**, but Mark Wineberg and Steffen Christensen[192] suggest a particularly simple and effective alternative :

1. Throw all the results of techniques A and B together into one vector.

2. Sort the vector by result value.

3. Replace the result values with their rank values (that is, their locations in the vector).

4. Results with the same value are assigned the average of their combined ranks.

5. Break the results back into the technique-A results and the technique-B results.

6. Using the rank values rather than the original result values, do a t-Test.

Let's do an example. Imagine that, against good judgement and the recommendations of this text, you have decided only to do five runs of each technique (PSO and ES). Your results were:

PSO: 0.1 0.5 0.8 0.9 0.9   ES: 0.2 0.3 0.5 0.7 0.9

We put them together into one vector and sort it.

| 0.1 | 0.2 | 0.3 | 0.5 | 0.5 | 0.7 | 0.8 | 0.9 | 0.9 | 0.9 |
| PSO | ES | ES | ES | PSO | ES | PSO | ES | PSO | PSO |

Next we include ranks.

1	2	3	4	5	6	7	8	9	10
0.1	0.2	0.3	0.5	0.5	0.7	0.8	0.9	0.9	0.9
PSO	ES	ES	ES	PSO	ES	PSO	ES	PSO	PSO

Next we average ranks for results with the same values.

1	2	3	4.5	4.5	6	7	9	9	9
0.1	0.2	0.3	0.5	0.5	0.7	0.8	0.9	0.9	0.9
PSO	ES	ES	ES	PSO	ES	PSO	ES	PSO	PSO

Next we replace the values with just the ranks.

| 1 | 2 | 3 | 4.5 | 4.5 | 6 | 7 | 9 | 9 | 9 |
| PSO | ES | ES | ES | PSO | ES | PSO | ES | PSO | PSO |

Finally, we break the results back out into their groups again. The ranks are all that are left.

PSO: 1 4.5 7 9 9   ES: 2 3 4.5 6 9

We can now do a plain-old t-Test on these revised values instead. Note that we're no longer testing whether the *means* of the two techniques are different from one another. Instead, since we're looking at rank orderings, it's somewhat closer to saying that the *medians* of the two techniques differ. It's still a better measure than a plain t-Test by a long shot.

---

[192]See the very last entry in Section 11.3.1 for pointers to their excellent lecture slides. A number of suggestions here were inspired from those slides.

Comparing More than Two Techniques   t-Tests only compare two techniques. Let's say you have five techniques, A, B, C, D, and E. You want to prove that A does better than the rest. How do you compare them? One approach is to compare A against B (with a hypothesis test), then A against C, then A against D, then A against E. If you do this, remember that it's critical that each time you compare A against another technique, you should do a **new set of independent runs** for A, with new random number generator seeds. Don't reuse your old runs. Or perhaps you want to compare each method against every other method: that is, A versus B, A versus C, A versus D, A versus E, B versus C, B versus D, B versus E, C versus D, C versus E, and finally D versus E. Phew! Again, remember that each comparison should use new, independent runs.

Doing individual pairwise hypothesis tests isn't sufficient though. Keep in mind that the point of a hypothesis test is to compute the *probability* that your claim is valid. If you do a single comparison (A versus B) at 95% probability, there is a 5% chance that your claim is false. But if you compare A against *four* other techniques (A versus B, A versus C, A versus D, A versus E), each at 95% probability, you have an approximately 20% chance that one of them is false. If you compared each method against the others, resulting in *ten* comparisons, you have an approximately 50% chance that one of them is false! It's pretty common that you'll do a lot of experiments in your paper. And so with a high probability one of your hypothesis tests will come up false.

It's better style to try to fix this probability, and ideally get it back up to 95% (or whatever value you had originally chosen). The simplest way to do this is to apply the **Bonferroni correction**. Specifically, if you have m comparisons to do, and the desired probability of one of them being wrong is p total, then revise each individual probability of being wrong to be p/m, and thus the probability of being right is $1 - p/m$. In our examples above, if we wish to compare A against the other techniques (four comparisons), and want to retain a 95% probability of being right—that is, a 1/20 chance of being wrong, then each of our comparisons should be done with a $\frac{1/20}{4} = 1/80$ probability of being wrong. That translates into using a $1 - 1/80 = 0.9875\%$ probability for each hypothesis test. Similarly, if you're comparing all the techniques (ten comparisons), you'll have $1 - 1/200 = 0.995\%$. Not easy to beat!

A much less extreme method, in terms of how high your probability has to go, is the **ANOVA**, a fairly complex method which compares m techniques at one time and tells you if *any one of them* is different from the others. Interestingly, the ANOVA doesn't tell you *which* techniques are different from which others: for that you apply a so-called *post-hoc comparison*, the most conservative of which (always be conservative!) is the *Tukey* comparison.[193] One difficulty with the ANOVA is that, like the original t-Test, it assumes that your distributions are normal. Which is rarely the case. There exist non-parametric ANOVA methods as well. The ANOVA (and related tests) are far too complex to describe here: consult a good statistics book.

One of the strange effects you'll get when comparing m techniques is nontransitivity among your results. For example, let's say that, looking at their means, $A > B > C > D > E$. But when you run the ANOVA, it tells you that A and B aren't statistically different, and B and C aren't statistically different, but A and C *are* statistically significantly different! Furthermore, D and E aren't statistically different, but A, B, and C are all statistically significantly different from D and E. Eesh. How do you report something like this? Usually, with overbars connecting groups with no significant difference among them: $\overline{A\ B}\ \overline{B\ C}\ \overline{D\ E}$ Be sure to notice the overlapping but unconnected overbars over A, B, and C.

---

[193]Named after the statistician John Tukey.

11.2 Simple Test Problems

The test problems below are common, and sometimes trivial, fitness or quality functions suitable for small experiments and projects. Problems are provided for fixed-length boolean and real-valued vectors, multiobjective scenarios, and Genetic Programming (and Grammatical Evolution).

Many of these problems have been overused in the field and are a bit dated: if you're working on a scientific research paper, you ought to spend some time examining the current benchmarks applied to techniques like yours. Also: if you're using test problems as benchmarks to compare techniques, be wary of the temptation to shop for benchmarks, that is, to hunt for that narrow set of benchmark problems that happens to make your technique look good. You can always find one, but what have you gained? Instead, try to understand how your technique performs on a wide range of well-understood problems from the literature, or on problems of strong interest to a specific community.[194]

11.2.1 Boolean Vector Problems

Max Ones Max Ones, sometimes called **OneMax**, is a trivial boolean problem: it's the total number of ones in your vector. This is the classic example of a **linear problem**, where there is *no linkage* between any of the vector values at all. Simple Hill-Climbing can solve this problem easily. Max Ones is due to David Ackley:[195]

$$f(\langle x_1, ..., x_n \rangle) = \sum_{i=1}^{n} x_i$$

Leading Ones This problem is also quite simple: it counts the number of ones in your vector, starting at the beginning, until a zero is encountered. Put another way, it returns the position of the first zero found in your vector (minus one). The equation below is a clever way of describing this mathwise, but you wouldn't implement it like that — too expensive. Just count the ones up to the first zero. Leading Ones is *not* a linear problem: the contribution of a slot x_i in the vector depends critically on the values of the slots $x_1, ..., x_{i-1}$. Nonetheless, it's pretty simple to solve.

$$f(\langle x_1, ..., x_n \rangle) = \sum_{i=1}^{n} \prod_{j=1}^{i} x_j$$

Leading Ones Blocks This variant of Leading Ones is somewhat more challenging. Given a value b, we count the number of strings of ones, each b long, until we see a zero. For example, if $b = 3$, then $f(\langle 1,1,0,0,0,1,1,0,1 \rangle) = 0$ because we don't have a string of 3 at the

---

[194]At this point it's worth bringing up the infamous **No Free Lunch Theorem**, or **NFL**, by David Wolpert and William Macready. The NFL stated that within certain constraints, over the space of *all possible problems*, every optimization technique will perform as well as every other one on average (including Random Search). That is, if there exists a set of problems P for which technique A beats technique B by a certain amount, there also exists an equal-sized set of problems P' for which the opposite is true. This is of considerable theoretical interest but, I think, of limited practical value, because the space of all possible problems likely includes many extremely unusual and pathological problems which are rarely if ever seen in practice. In my opinion, of more of interest is what kinds of techniques perform well on the *typical* problems faced by practitioners, and why. For more on the NFL, see David Wolpert and William Macready, 1997, No free lunch theorems for optimization, *IEEE Transactions on Evolutionary Computation*, 1(1), 67–82.

[195]David Ackley, 1987, *A Connectionist Machine for Genetic Hillclimbing*, Kluwer Academic Publishers.

beginning yet. But $f(\langle 1,1,1,0,0,0,1,0,1\rangle) = 1$. Furthermore, $f(\langle 1,1,1,1,0,1,1,0,1\rangle) = 1$ but $f(\langle 1,1,1,1,1,1,0,1,0\rangle) = 2$, and ultimately $f(\langle 1,1,1,1,1,1,1,1,1\rangle) = 3$. A simple way to do this is to do Leading Ones, then divide the result by b, and floor it to the nearest integer:

$$f(\langle x_1, ..., x_n\rangle) = \left\lfloor \frac{1}{b} \sum_{i=1}^{n} \prod_{j=1}^{i} x_j \right\rfloor$$

Trap The so-called Trap Problems are classic examples of deceptive functions.. Here's a simple one which is easily described: the fitness of your vector is the number of zeros in the vector, *unless* you have *no zeros at all*, in which case the fitness of the vector is the suddenly optimally high $(n+1)$. Thus this problem sets up a gradient to lead you gently *away* from the optimal all-ones (no zeros) case, and deep into the trap. For example, $f(\langle 0,0,0,0\rangle) = 4$, $f(\langle 0,0,1,0\rangle) = 3$, $f(\langle 1,0,1,0\rangle) = 2$, $f(\langle 1,0,1,1\rangle) = 1$, but boom, $f(\langle 1,1,1,1\rangle) = 5$. A clever math formulation of this has two terms: the sum part is the number of zeros in the vector. The product part only comes into play when you have all ones. Various trap functions were originally due to David Ackley.[196]

$$f(\langle x_1, ..., x_n\rangle) = \left(n - \sum_{i=1}^{n} x_i\right) + (n+1) \prod_{i=1}^{n} x_i$$

11.2.2 Real-Valued Vector Problems

Many classic real-valued vector problems are minimization problems rather than maximization ones. To convert them to a maximization problem, the simplest solution is to negate the result. If you're using Fitness Proportionate Selection or SUS, you'll also need to add a big enough number that there aren't any negative values. I'd use Tournament Selection instead.

Most of the problems described below are shown, in the trivial 2-dimensional case, in Figure 68.

Sum Sum is the trivial real-valued version of Max Ones. It's just the sum of your vector. As would be expected, Sum is a linear problem and so has no linkage.

$$f(\langle x_1, ..., x_n\rangle) = \sum_{i=1}^{n} x_i \qquad x_i \in [0.0, 1.0]$$

Linear Linear functions are the generalization of Sum, and again have no linkage at all. They're just the weighted sum of your vector, where each weight is given by a constant a_i. Given a vector of constants $\langle a_0, ..., a_n\rangle$, which you provide, we weight each element, then add them up:

$$f(\langle x_1, ..., x_n\rangle) = a_0 + \sum_{i=1}^{n} a_i x_i \qquad x_i \in [0.0, 1.0]$$

---

[196]As was Max Ones. See Footnote 195, p. 213.

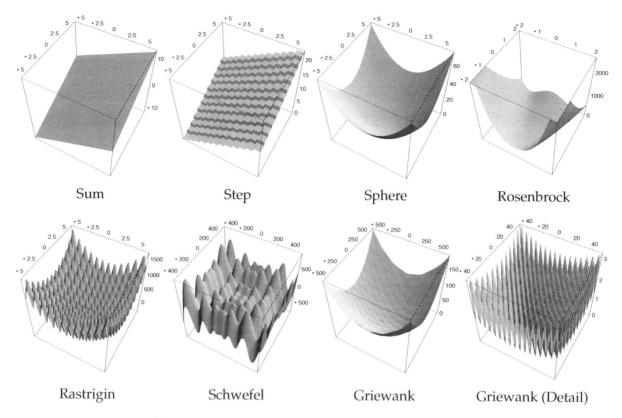

Figure 68 Real-valued problems in two dimensions ($\langle x_1, x_2 \rangle$).

Step Another no-linkage function, but this time it's got a wrinkle. Because it uses the floor function, there are regions where small mutations in any given floating point value don't change fitness at all. This function is part of a popular test suite by Ken De Jong,[197] and so has traditional bounds on the x_i values (between -5.12 and $+5.12$ inclusive). The function is usually minimized, though it doesn't matter much: you can search for the maximum too, it's about the same.

$$\text{(Minimize)} \quad f(\langle x_1, ..., x_n \rangle) = 6n + \sum_{i=1}^{n} \lfloor x_i \rfloor \qquad x_i \in [-5.12, 5.12]$$

Sphere Our last no-linkage problem, due to Ingo Rechenberg.[198] Here we're summing the *squares* of the individual elements. This is again a minimization problem, and is part of De Jong's test suite (note the bounds). Maximization is also interesting, as there are global maxima at the corners.

$$\text{(Minimize)} \quad f(\langle x_1, ..., x_n \rangle) = \sum_{i=1}^{n} x_i^2 \qquad x_i \in [-5.12, 5.12]$$

---

[197] Perhaps too popular. Ken De Jong has been waging a campaign to get people to *stop* using it! The test suite was proposed in De Jong's PhD thesis: Kenneth De Jong, 1975, *An Analysis of the Behaviour of a Class of Genetic Adaptive Systems*, Ph.D. thesis, University of Michigan. The thesis is available online at http://cs.gmu.edu/~eclab/kdj_thesis.html

[198] Ingo Rechenberg, 1973, *Evolutionsstrategie: Optimierung technischer Systeme nach Prinzipien der biologischen Evolution*, Fromman-Holzbook, Stuttgart, Germany.

Rosenbrock A classic optimization problem well predating the field, from Howard Rosenbrock.[199] In two dimensions, this function creates a little valley bent around a low hill, with large wings on each side. The minimum is at $\langle 1, 1, ..., 1 \rangle$, in the valley on one side of the low hill, and individuals often get stuck on the other side. The traditional bounds are shown. It's a minimization problem.

$$\text{(Minimize)} \qquad f(\langle x_1,...,x_n \rangle) = \sum_{i=1}^{n-1} (1 - x_i)^2 + 100(x_{i+1} - x_i^2)^2 \qquad x_i \in [-2.048, 2.048]$$

Rastrigin Originally proposed by Leonard Andreevich Rastrigin[200] in 1974 as a two-dimensional function, and later extended by Heinz Mühlenbein, M. Schomisch, and Joachim Born to more variables.[201] This function is essentially a large egg carton bent under a basketball: it's a combination of Sphere and a sine wave which creates a great many local optima. It's a minimization problem. Some literature has $x_i \in [-5.12, 5.12]$, following De Jong's tradition (that's what I'm doing here), but others use different bounds.

$$\text{(Minimize)} \qquad f(\langle x_1,...,x_n \rangle) = 10n + \sum_{i=1}^{n} x_i^2 - 10 \cos(2\pi x_i) \qquad x_i \in [-5.12, 5.12]$$

Schwefel This function, due to Hans-Paul Schwefel,[202] has many local optima like Rastrigin; but is organized so that the local optima are close to one another (and thus easier to jump to) the further you get from the global optima. It's thus described as a deceptive problem. Again, minimization. Notice the larger traditional bounds than we've seen so far.

$$\text{(Minimize)} \qquad f(\langle x_1,...,x_n \rangle) = \sum_{i=1}^{n} -x_i \sin\left(\sqrt{|x_i|}\right) \qquad x_i \in [-512.03, 511.97]$$

Some variations add $418.9829 \times n$ to the function to set the minimum to about 0.

Griewank Not to be outdone by Rastrigin, Andreas Griewank's similar function has a zillion local optima.[203] The function is minimized, and traditionally has bounds from -600 to $+600$, which creates massive numbers of local optima.

$$\text{(Minimize)} \qquad f(\langle x_1,...,x_n \rangle) = 1 + \frac{1}{4000} \left(\sum_{i=1}^{n} x_i^2 \right) + \prod_{i=1}^{n} \cos\left(\frac{x_i}{\sqrt{i}}\right) \qquad x_i \in [-600, 600]$$

---

[199]Howard Rosenbrock, 1960, An automatic method for finding the greatest or least value of a function, *The Computer Journal*, 3(3), 174–184.

[200]I believe this was from Leonard Andreevich Rastrigin, 1974, *Systems of Extremal Control*, Nauka, in Russian. Nearly impossible to get ahold of, so don't bother.

[201]Heinz Mühlenbein, D. Schomisch, and Joachim Born, 1991, The parallel genetic algorithm as function optimizer, in Richard Belew and Lashoon Booker, editors, *Proceedings of the Fourth International Conference on Genetic Algorithms*, pages 271–278.

[202]Hans-Paul Schwefel, 1977, *Numerische Optimierung von Computer-Modellen mittels der Evolutionsstrategie*, Birkhauser.

[203]Andreas Griewank, 1981, Generalized descent for global optimization, *Journal of Optimization Theory and Applications*, 34, 11–39.

Rotated Problems Many of the real-valued test problems described above consist of linear combinations of each of the variables. This often makes them susceptible to techniques which assume low linkage among genes, and so it's considered good practice to **rotate**[204] them by an orthonormal matrix M. If your original fitness function was $f(\vec{x})$, you'd instead use a new rotated fitness function $g(\vec{x}) = f(M\vec{x})$ (assuming that $\vec{x}$ is a column vector). This has the effect of creating linkages among variables which were previously largely unlinked, and thus making a more challenging problem for algorithms which assume low linkage.

Ideally you'd draw M randomly and uniformly from the space of rotations or reflections. If the problem is two-dimensional, it's easy to just do a rotation: choose a random value of θ from $[0, 2\pi)$, and set $M = \begin{bmatrix} \cos\theta & -\sin\theta \\ \sin\theta & \cos\theta \end{bmatrix}$. But that only works because there's a single possible rotation axis. For a dimensionality higher than two, doing this stuff quickly becomes non-obvious.

As it turns out, rotation in an n-dimensional space is more or less equivalent to choosing a new orthonormal basis in your vector space. The following algorithm uses the **Gram-Schmidt** process to transform a set of randomly chosen vectors into an orthonormal basis.

Algorithm 137 *Create a Uniform Orthonormal Matrix*
1: $n \leftarrow$ desired number of dimensions

2: $M \leftarrow n \times n$ matrix, all zeros
3: **for** i from 1 to n **do**
4:     **for** j from 1 to m **do**
5:         $M_{ij} \leftarrow$ random number chosen from the Normal distribution $N(\mu = 0, \sigma^2 = 1)$
6: **for** i from 1 to n **do**
7:     Row vector $\vec{M}_i = \vec{M}_i - \sum_{j=1}^{i-1} \langle \vec{M}_i \cdot \vec{M}_j \rangle \vec{M}_j$ ▷ Subtract out projections of previously built bases
8:     Row vector $\vec{M}_i = \frac{\vec{M}_i}{||\vec{M}_i||}$ ▷ Normalize

9: **return** M

As a reminder, $\langle \vec{M}_i \cdot \vec{M}_j \rangle$ is a dot product.

This algorithm is a very old method indeed, but the earliest adaptation to metaheuristics I am aware of is due to Nikolaus Hansen, Andreas Ostermeier, and Andreas Gawelczyk.[205] The algorithm above is based on their adaptation.

Important note: rotation will produce vectors $M\vec{x}$ which potentially lie outside your original bounds for $\vec{x}$: you'll need to make sure that $f(M\vec{x})$ can return rational quality assessments for these vectors, or otherwise change the original bounds for $\vec{x}$ to prevent this from happening.

---
[204]Okay, not quite rotate. Picking a new orthonormal basis will also add reflections. It's still good.

[205]Nikolaus Hansen, Andreas Ostermeier, and Andreas Gawelczyk, 1995, On the adaptation of arbitrary normal mutation distributions in evolution strategies: the generating set adaptation, in L. J. Eshelman, editor, *Proceedings of the Sixth International Conference on Genetic Algorithms*, pages 57–64, Morgan Kaufmann. A more straightforward description of the algorithm is in Nikolaus Hansen and Andreas Ostermeier, 2001, Completely derandomized self-adaptation in evolution strategies, *Evolutionary Computation*, 9(2), 159–195.

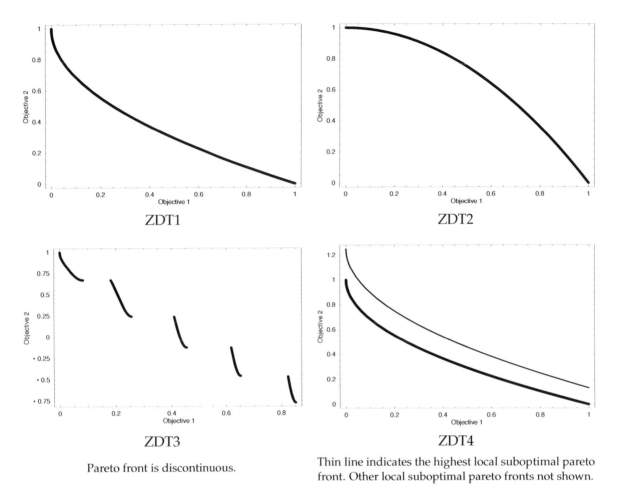

Figure 69 Pareto fronts of four multiobjective problems (ZDT1, ZDT2, ZDT3, and ZDT4) as described in Section 11.2.3. All four problems are minimization problems, so lower objective values are preferred.

11.2.3 Multiobjective Problems

The problems described below are all from a classic multiobjective comparison paper by Eckart Zitzler, Kalyanmoy Deb, and Lothar Thiele.[206] Like many multiobjective test problems, they're all set up for minimization: you can change this to maximization by negating (for example). All four problems have two objectives O_1 and O_2. The problems are all designed such that O_2 is a function of two auxillary functions g and h. The global Pareto fronts for all four problems, and in one case a strong local Pareto front, are all shown in Figure 69.

---

[206]Eckart Zitzler, Kalyanmoy Deb, and Lothar Thiele, 2000, Comparison of multiobjective evolutionary algorithms: Empirical results, *Evolutionary Computation*, 8(2), 125–148.

ZDT1 This is a basic multiobjective problem with a convex Pareto front for real-valued vector individuals $n = 30$ genes long. The problem has no local optima.

(Minimize) $O_1(\langle x_1, ..., x_n \rangle) = x_1$ $\qquad x_i \in [0, 1]$
$O_2(\langle x_1, ..., x_n \rangle) = g(\langle x_1, ..., x_n \rangle) \times h(\langle x_1, ..., x_n \rangle)$

$g(\langle x_1, ..., x_n \rangle) = 1 + \frac{9}{n-1} \sum_{i=2}^{n} x_i$

$h(\langle x_1, ..., x_n \rangle) = 1 - \sqrt{\frac{x_1}{g(\langle x_1, ..., x_n \rangle)}}$

ZDT2 This function is like ZDT1, but is concave. Again, $n = 30$. The problem has no local optima.

(Minimize) $O_1(\langle x_1, ..., x_n \rangle) = x_1$ $\qquad x_i \in [0, 1]$
$O_2(\langle x_1, ..., x_n \rangle) = g(\langle x_1, ..., x_n \rangle) \times h(\langle x_1, ..., x_n \rangle)$

$g(\langle x_1, ..., x_n \rangle) = 1 + \frac{9}{n-1} \sum_{i=2}^{n} x_i$

$h(\langle x_1, ..., x_n \rangle) = 1 - \left(\frac{x_1}{g(\langle x_1, ..., x_n \rangle)} \right)^2$

ZDT3 This function has a discontinuous Pareto front. Again, $n = 30$. The problem has no local optima.

(Minimize) $O_1(\langle x_1, ..., x_n \rangle) = x_1$ $\qquad x_i \in [0, 1]$
$O_2(\langle x_1, ..., x_n \rangle) = g(\langle x_1, ..., x_n \rangle) \times h(\langle x_1, ..., x_n \rangle)$

$g(\langle x_1, ..., x_n \rangle) = 1 + \frac{9}{n-1} \sum_{i=2}^{n} x_i$

$h(\langle x_1, ..., x_n \rangle) = 1 - \sqrt{\frac{x_1}{g(\langle x_1, ..., x_n \rangle)}} - \frac{x_1}{g(\langle x_1, ..., x_n \rangle)} \sin(10\pi x_1)$

ZDT4 This function has a convex Pareto front but has a many local suboptimal Pareto fronts to trap individuals, making this a moderately challenging problem. The problem is defined for a smaller value of n than the others: $n = 10$. The value x_1 ranges in $[0, 1]$, but the other x_i all range in $[-5, 5]$.

(Minimize) $O_1(\langle x_1, ..., x_n \rangle) = x_1$ $\qquad x_1 \in [0, 1], x_{i>1} \in [-5, 5]$
$O_2(\langle x_1, ..., x_n \rangle) = g(\langle x_1, ..., x_n \rangle) \times h(\langle x_1, ..., x_n \rangle)$

$g(\langle x_1, ..., x_n \rangle) = 1 + 10(n-1) + \sum_{i=2}^{n} x_i^2 - 10\cos(4\pi x_i)$

$h(\langle x_1, ..., x_n \rangle) = 1 - \sqrt{\frac{x_1}{g(\langle x_1, ..., x_n \rangle)}}$

11.2.4 Genetic Programming Problems

As they're optimizing small computer programs, genetic programming problems are somewhat more colorful, and detailed, than the mathematical functions we've seen so far. The problems described here aren't very complex: they're often tackled with a population of 1000 or so, run for 51 generations (including the initial generation). The problems described here are from John Koza.[207]

Symbolic Regression This is *the* canonical example problem for genetic programming, and is perhaps overused. The objective is to find a mathematical expression which best fits a set of data points of the form $\langle x, f(x) \rangle$ for some unknown (to the optimization algorithm) function f. The traditional function to fit is $f(x) = x^4 + x^3 + x^2 + x$, though Koza also suggested the functions $g(x) = x^5 - 2x^3 + x$ and $h(x) = x^6 - 2x^4 + x^2$. These functions are shown in Figure 70.

We begin by creating twenty random values $x_1, ..., x_{20}$, each between -1 and 1, which will be used throughout the duration of the run. An individual is assessed as follows. For each of the 20 x_i values, we set the leaf-node function x to return the value of x_i, then evaluate the individual's tree. The return value from the tree will be called, say, y_i. The fitness of the individual is how close those 20 y_i matched their expected $f(x_i)$, usually using simple distance. That is, the fitness is $\sum_{i=1}^{20} |f(x_i) - y_i|$.

Obviously this is a minimization problem. It's easily converted to maximization with $\frac{1}{1+\text{fitness}}$. An example ideal solution is: (+ (* x (* (+ x (* x x)) x)) (* (+ x (cos (- x x))) x))

Function	Arity	Description
(+ i j)	2	Returns $i + j$
(− i j)	2	Returns $i - j$
(* i j)	2	Returns $i \times j$
(% i j)	2	If j is 0, returns 1, else returns i/j
(sin i)	1	Returns $\sin(i)$
(cos i)	1	Returns $\cos(i)$
(exp i)	1	Returns e^i
(rlog i)	1	If j is 0, returns 0, else returns $\log(|i|)$
x	0	Returns the value of the independent variable (x).
ERCs	0	(*Optional*) Ephemeral random constants chosen from floating-point values from -1 to 1 inclusive.

Table 5 Symbolic Regression Function Set

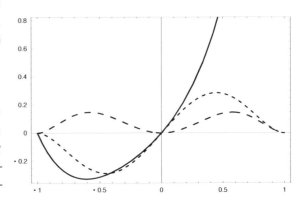

Figure 70 The functions $f(x)$: ———, $g(x)$: - - -, and $h(x)$: - - - - as discussed in the Symbolic Regression section. $f(1) = 4$.

11-bit Boolean Multiplexer The objective of the 11-bit Boolean Multiplexer problems is to find a boolean function which performs multiplexing over a 3-bit address. There are three boolean-valued address variables (A0, A1, and A2) and eight corresponding boolean-valued data variables (D0, D1, D2, D3, D4, D5, D6, D7). The 11-bit Boolean Multiplexer problem must return the value of the data variable at the address described by the binary values of A0, A1, and A2. For example, if A2 is false

---

[207] Adapted from John R. Koza, 1992, *Genetic Programming: On the Programming of Computers by Means of Natural Selection*, MIT Press and from John R. Koza, 1994, *Genetic Programming II: Automatic Discovery of Reusable Programs*, MIT Press.

and A1 is true and A0 is true, the address is 3 (binary 011), and so the optimal individual would return the value stored in D3. Since there are eleven boolean variables altogether, there are 2048 permutations of these variables and hence 2048 test cases. A trivial variant, the 6-bit Boolean Multiplexer, has two address variables (A0 and A1), four data variables (D0, D1, D2, D3), and 64 test cases.

A Multiplexer individual consists of a single tree. To assess the fitness of an individual, for each test case, the data and address variables are set to return that test case's permutation of boolean values, and the individual's tree is then evaluated. The fitness is the number of test cases for which the individual returned the correct value for the data variable expected, given the current setting of the address variables.

An example of an ideal 11-bit Boolean Multiplexer solution is:

Function	Arity	Description
(and i j)	2	Returns $i \cap j$
(or i j)	2	Returns $i \cup j$
(not i)	1	Returns $\neg i$
(if $test$ $then$ $else$)	3	If $test$ is true, then $then$ is returned, else $else$ is returned.
a0, a1, and a2	0	Return the values of variables A0, A1, and A2 respectively.
d0, d1, d2, d3, d4, d5, d6, and d7	0	Return the values of variables D0, D1, D2, D3, D4, D5, D6, and D7 respectively.

Table 6   11-bit Boolean Multiplexer Function Set

(if (not a0) (if (not a0) (if (not a1) (if a2 (if a2 d4 d6) d0) (if a2 d6 (if a2 d4 d2))) (if (or a2 a2) (if a1 (or (if (not (if a2 d5 d0)) (and (and d4 d0) (and a2 d5)) (or (and d7 d0) (not a1))) (if (not a1) (if (if d4 d1 d5) d0 d5) (or d6 (or (and (and d4 d0) (or (and d5 d1) (and d6 d6))) (and d7 (or (if a0 (or a2 a2) d4) (and d1 (and d5 a2)))))))) d5) (if a1 (or d3 (and d7 d0)) (if a0 d1 d0)))) (if (or a2 a2) (if a1 (if (not a1) (if (and d7 d0) (if a2 d5 d0) (if a2 d6 d3)) (and d7 (or (if a0 a2 (or d1 a1)) (not a1)))) d5) (if a1 (or (if (not a0) (if a2 d6 (if a2 d4 d2)) (if a1 d3 (or (or d3 (if a1 d3 d1)) (not a2)))) (not a1)) (if a0 d1 d0))))

Even N-Parity The Even N-Parity problems are, like 11-bit Boolean Multiplexer, also boolean problems over some n number of data variables. In the Even N-Parity problems, the objective is to return true if, for the current boolean settings of these variables, there is an even number of variables whose value is true. There are thus 2^n test cases. Fitness assessment is basically the same as 11-bit Boolean Multiplexer.

Even N-Parity varies in difficulty depending on N, due to the number of test cases. Bill Langdon notes that Parity doesn't have any building blocks.[208] An ideal Even 4-Parity solution:

Function	Arity	Description
(and i j)	2	Returns $i \cap j$
(or i j)	2	Returns $i \cup j$
(nand i j)	2	Returns $\neg(i \cap j)$
(nor i j)	2	Returns $\neg(i \cup j)$
d0, d1, d2, $etc.$	0	Return the values of variables D0, D1, D2, ... respectively. The number of dx nodes in the function set is the number of bits in the particular Parity problem being run.

Table 7   Even N-Parity Function Set

(nand (or (or (nor d3 d0) (nand (or d3 d1) (nor d2 d3))) d3) (nor (nor (and (or (and (or (or (nor d1 d2) (and d3 d0)) (and d1 d2)) (nand (and d0 d3) (nand (or d0 d1) (or d2 d1)))) (and (or d0 d2) (and d1 d1))) (nand (and (nor d3 d0) (and (and (nand (nand (nor d3 d3) (or (or d0 d0) (nor (and d3 d0) (nor d1 (nand d3 d2))))) d2) (nor d1 d1)) (or (or d0 d1) (nor d3 d2)))) (nand (or d0 d1) (nor d3 d3)))) (or (and (nand d1 d1) (and d1 d3)) (nor (nand (or d1 d2) (nor d3 d0)) d0)))) (and (or (or (or (and (nand d1 d1) (and d1 d3)) (nor (nand (or d1 d2) (nor d3 d0)) (and (nand d1 d3) (and d3 d0)))) (and d3 d0)) (and d3 d2)) (and (and d1 d2) (or (or d0 (nor (or d0 d0) (and d2 d3))) d0)))))

---

[208]William Langdon, 1999, Scaling of program tree fitness spaces, *Evolutionary Computation*, 7(4), 399–428.

Artificial Ant Artificial Ant is an oddly challenging problem[209] for genetic programming. The Artificial Ant problem attempts to find a simple robotic ant algorithm which will find and eat the most food pellets within 400 time steps.[210] The ant may move forward, turn left, and turn right. If when moving forward it chances across a pellet, it eats it. The ant can also sense if there is a pellet in the square directly in front of it. The grid world in which the Artificial Ant lives is shown in Figure 71. The pellet trail shown is known as the "Santa Fe Trail". The world is toroidal: walking off an edge moves the ant to the opposite edge.

Function	Arity	Description
(progn3 *a b c*)	3	*a*, *b*, then *c* are executed.
(progn2 *a b*)	2	*a*, then *b* are executed.
(if-food-ahead *then else*)	2	If food is immediately in front of the ant, *then* is executed, else *else* is executed.
move	0	Moves the ant forward one square, eating food if it is there.
left	0	Rotates the ant ninety degrees to the left.
right	0	Rotates the ant ninety degrees to the right.

Table 8   Artificial Ant Function Set

An Artificial Ant individual consists of a single tree. Fitness assessment works as follows. The ant starts on the upper-left corner cell, and facing right. The tree is executed: as each sensory or movement node is executed, the Ant senses or moves as told. When the tree has completed execution, it is re-executed again and again. Each movement counts as one time step. Assessment finishes when the Ant has eaten all the pellets in the world or when the 400 time steps have expired. The Ant's fitness is the number of pellets it ate.

The Artificial Ant problem is different from the Symbolic Regression and the boolean problems in that the return value of each tree node is ignored. The only thing that matters is each node's action in the world, that is, each node's side effect: moving the ant, turning it, etc. This means that in Artificial Ant, the order in which the nodes are executed determines the operation of the individual, whereas in the previous problems, it doesn't matter in what order subtrees are evaluated. A (highly parsimonious) example of an optimal Artificial Ant solution is: (progn3 (if-food-ahead move (progn2 left (progn2 (progn3 right right right) (if-food-ahead move right)))) move right).

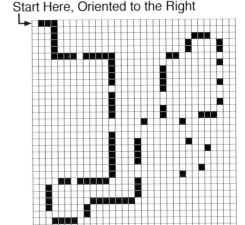

Figure 71   The Santa Fe Trail, a toroidal grid world. Black squares indicate pellet locations.

---

[209]One of my all-time favorite papers, mostly due to its Knuth-like excessive attention to detail, is exactly on this topic: W. B. Langdon and R. Poli, 1998, Why ants are hard, in John R. Koza, *et al.*, editors, *Genetic Programming 1998: Proceedings of the Third Annual Conference*, pages 193–201, Morgan Kaufmann.

[210]400 may be due to a misprint that has since established itself. John Koza is believed to have actually used 600.

Lawnmower In the Lawnmower problem, the individual directs a lawnmower to mow a toroidal grid lawn, much as the Artificial Ant domain directs an ant to move about its toroidal grid world. In the Lawnmower domain, an individual may turn left, mow forwards, or "hop" some $\langle x, y \rangle$ units away. Lawnmower has no sensor information: it must be hard-coded to mow the lawn blind. The standard lawn size is 8 by 8.

Koza proposed this domain originally to demonstrate the advantages of automatically defined functions (ADFs).[211] Lawnmower is difficult without ADFs but fairly trivial when using ADFs. When not using ADFs, a Lawnmower individual consists of a single tree, and the function set is shown in Table 9. When using ADFs, a Lawnmower individual consists of three trees: the main tree, an ADF1 tree and an ADF2 tree; and the function set is augmented as described in Table 10.

To assess fitness, the lawnmower is placed somewhere on the lawn, and the individual's tree is executed once. Each mow and frog command moves the lawnmower and mows the lawn in its new location. Once the tree has been executed, the fitness is the number of squares of lawn mown. An example optimal individual with ADFs:

Main Tree: (progn2 (progn2 (adf1 (progn2 (adf1 left) (v8a $\langle 7,0 \rangle$ $\langle 0,4 \rangle$))) (progn2 left $\langle 3,4 \rangle$)) (v8a (progn2 (adf1 (v8a left left)) (progn2 (frog mow) (adf1 adf2))) (adf1 (progn2 (v8a $\langle 6,7 \rangle$ adf2) (progn2 $\langle 1,1 \rangle$ mow)))))

ADF1: (v8a (v8a (v8a (progn2 (v8a adf2 mow) (v8a adf2 mow)) (frog (v8a mow arg1))) (v8a (v8a (frog arg1) (progn2 $\langle 1,4 \rangle$ $\langle 2,6 \rangle$)) (progn2 (v8a $\langle 1,5 \rangle$ adf2) (frog mow)))) (v8a (v8a (v8a (progn2 adf2 adf2) (v8a adf2 mow)) (v8a (progn2 arg1 adf2) (frog left))) (frog (v8a (v8a arg1 left) (v8a $\langle 7,0 \rangle$ mow)))))

ADF2: (progn2 (v8a (progn2 (v8a (v8a mow mow) (v8a mow $\langle 5,1 \rangle$)) (v8a (v8a mow left) (progn2 left mow))) (v8a (progn2 (v8a mow mow) (progn2 $\langle 1,3 \rangle$ $\langle 2,1 \rangle$)) (v8a (progn2 $\langle 3,6 \rangle$ mow) (progn2 v8a left $\langle 3,4 \rangle$)))) (v8a (progn2 (progn2 (v8a mow left) (v8a mow $\langle 7,7 \rangle$))) (progn2 (v8a (progn2 left left) (v8a mow left)) (v8a (progn2 left $\langle 2,1 \rangle$) (v8a $\langle 1,7 \rangle$ mow)))))

---

[211]I've reordered/renamed Koza's original ADFs.

Function	Arity	Description
(progn2 a b)	2	a, then b are executed. Returns the return value of b.
(v8a i j)	2	Evaluates i and j, adds the vectors they return, modulo 8, and returns the result.
(frog i)	1	Evaluates i. Let $\langle x, y \rangle$ be i's return value. Then frog moves $\langle x, y \rangle$ squares relative to its present rotation, where the positive X axis points in the present "forward" direction of the lawnmower, and the positive Y axis points in the present "heading left" direction. Returns $\langle x, y \rangle$.
mow	0	Moves the lawnmower forward one square, mowing that square of lawn if it is not already mown. Returns $\langle 0, 0 \rangle$.
left	0	Rotates the lawnmower ninety degrees to the left. Returns $\langle 0, 0 \rangle$.
ERCs	0	Ephemeral random constants of the form $\langle x, y \rangle$, where x is an integer chosen from the range $(0, ..., x_{max} - 1)$ and y is an integer chosen from the range $(0, ..., y_{max} - 1)$, where x_{max} and y_{max} are the width and height of the lawn in squares, respectively.

Table 9 Lawnmower Function Set.

Additional ADF functions for Main Tree

Function	Arity	Description
(adf1 arg1)	1	Automatically defined function which calls the ADF1 tree.
adf2	0	Automatically defined function which calls the ADF2 tree.

Additional ADF functions for ADF1 Tree

Function	Arity	Description
adf2	0	Automatically defined function which calls the ADF2 tree.
arg1	0	The value of argument *arg1* passed when the ADF1 tree is called.

Removed ADF functions for ADF2 Tree

Function	
(frog i)	*Removed from the ADF2 function set.*

Table 10 Additions to the Lawnmower Function Set when set up with two additional ADF trees (ADF1 and ADF2). All three trees have the same function set except where noted above.

Although this individual looks imposing, in fact with ADFs Lawnmower is fairly easy for genetic programming to solve. Much of this individual is junk. The reason ADFs work so much better in this domain is simple and unfair: a Lawnmower individual is executed only once, and has no iteration or recursion, and so within its tree must exist enough commands to move lawnmower to every spot of lawn. To do this for a single tree demands a big tree. But with when using ADF trees, the main tree can repeatedly call ADFs (and ADF1 can repeatedly call ADF2), so the total size of the individual can be much smaller and still take advantage of many more total moves.

Like Artificial Ant, Lawnmower operates via side-effects and so execution order is important.

11.3 Where to Go Next

This is a woefully inadequate collection of resources that I've personally found useful.

11.3.1 Bibliographies, Surveys, and Websites

It's an open secret that computer science researchers put a great many of their papers online, where they're often accessible from CiteSeer^x. Google Scholar is also useful, but usually points to documents behind publisher's firewalls.

http://citeseerx.ist.psu.edu
http://scholar.google.com

The *Hitchhiker's Guide to Evolutionary Computation* was the FAQ for the Usenet group comp.ai.genetic. It's fairly dated: for example its software collection doesn't include anything current. Still, there's a lot there, especially older work.

http://code.google.com/p/hhg2ec/

The single biggest bibliography in the field is the Genetic Programming Bibliography, by Bill Langdon, Steven Gustafson, and John Koza. I cannot overstate how useful this huge, immaculately maintained bibliography has been to me (much of my work has been in genetic programming).

http://www.cs.bham.ac.uk/~wbl/biblio/

Bill Langdon also maintains an extensive collection of bibliographies of EC conferences, etc.

http://www.cs.bham.ac.uk/~wbl/biblio/ec-bibs.html

Carlos Coello Coello maintains a very large collection of multiobjective optimization resources.

http://www.lania.mx/~ccoello/EMOO/

Tim Kovacs maintains a fairly complete bibliography on Learning Classifier Systems.

http://www.cs.bris.ac.uk/~kovacs/lcs/search.html

Jarmo Alander built a bibliography of practically all Genetic Algorithm publications up to 1993.

ftp://ftp.cs.bham.ac.uk/pub/Mirrors/ftp.de.uu.net/EC/refs/2500GArefs.ps.gz

Many other bibliographies can be found at the *Collection of Computer Science Bibliographies*. Look under the Artificial Intelligence, Neural Networks, and Parallel Processing subtopics.

http://liinwww.ira.uka.de/bibliography/

Liviu Panait and I wrote a large survey of cooperative multiagent learning, which includes a lot of stuff on coevolution and its relationships to other techniques (like multiagent Q-learning).

http://cs.gmu.edu/~eclab/papers/panait05cooperative.pdf

Liviu Panait and Sean Luke, 2005, Cooperative multi-agent learning: The state of the art, *Autonomous Agents and Multi-Agent Systems*, 11, 2005

A good Particle Swarm Optimization website, with lots of resources, is *Particle Swarm Central*.

http://www.particleswarm.info

Marco Dorigo maintains one of the best Ant Colony Optimization websites out there, including pointers to software, publications, and venues.

http://www.aco-metaheuristic.org

Paula Festa and Mauricio Rensede maintain an annotated bibliography of GRASP literature.

http://www.research.att.com/~mgcr/grasp/gannbib/gannbib.html

Lee Spector has a website on the Push language and publications.

http://hampshire.edu/lspector/push.html

Julian Miller runs a website on Cartesian Genetic Programming.

http://cartesiangp.co.uk/

Michael O'Neill maintains a website on Grammatical Evolution resources.

http://www.grammatical-evolution.org

Rainer Storn also maintains a website on Differential Evolution.

http://www.icsi.berkeley.edu/~storn/code.html

Various papers on Guided Local Search may be found at Edward Tsang's laboratory website:

http://www.bracil.net/CSP/gls-papers.html

Mark Wineberg and Steffen Christensen regularly do a lecture on statistics specifically for metaheuristics researchers. Mark keeps a PDF of the lecture slides on his home page.

http://www.cis.uoguelph.ca/~wineberg/publications/ECStat2004.pdf
http://www.cis.uoguelph.ca/~wineberg/

ACM SIGEvo is the ACM's special interest group on evolutionary computation. In addition to sponsoring various major conferences and journals, they also have a newsletter, *SIGEvolution*. The IEEE Computational Intelligence Society's Evolutionary Computation Technical Committee (IEEE-CIS-ECTC, phew) is the approximate equivalent for the IEEE.

http://www.sigevo.org
http://www.sigevolution.org
http://www.ieee-cis.org/technical/ectc/

11.3.2 Publications

Ready for *lots* more? Thomas Weise's 800-page, free open text *Global Optimization Algorithms: Theory and Application* goes in-depth in a number of the topics covered here. It's got a lot of formalism, with analysis and descriptive applications, and well over 2000 references. Did I mention it's free?

http://www.it-weise.de

As far as books go, I think the single best guide to the *craft* of stochastic optimization is *How to Solve It: Modern Heuristics*,[212] by Zbigniew Michalewicz and David Fogel. Fun to read, filled with stories and examples, and covering a very broad collection of issues and topics.

Zbigniew Michalewicz and David Fogel, 2004, *How to Solve It: Modern Heuristics*, Springer

The best book on Ant Colony Optimization is Marco Dorigo and Thomas Stützle's *Ant Colony Optimization*.

Marco Dorigo and Thomas Stützle, 2004, *Ant Colony Optimization*, MIT Press

If you are interested in genetic programming, check out *Genetic Programming: an Introduction* by Wolfgang Banzhaf, Peter Nordin, Robert Keller, and Frank Francone. It's aging but still good.

Wolfgang Banzhaf, Peter Nordin, Robert E. Keller, and Frank D. Francone, 1998, *Genetic Programming: An Introduction*, Morgan Kaufmann

A much newer Genetic Programming work is *A Field Guide to Genetic Programming* by Riccardo Poli, Bill Langdon, and Nick McPhee, which has the added benefit of being free online if you're too cheap to buy the print copy! (Buy the print copy.)

Riccardo Poli, William B. Langdon, and Nicholas Freitag McPhee, 2008, *A Field Guide to Genetic Programming*, Available in print from lulu.com
http://www.gp-field-guide.org.uk/

Kalyanmoy Deb's *Multi-Objective Optimization Using Evolutionary Algorithms* is a good text for multiobjective optimization, but it's expensive.

Kalyanmoy Deb, 2001, *Multi-Objective Optimization using Evolutionary Algorithms*, Wiley

---

[212]This book's name is adapted from a very famous book which revolutionized the use of algorithmic methods for solving complex problems: George Pólya, 1945, *How to Solve It*, Princeton University Press.

Kenneth Price, Rainer Storn, and Jouni Lampinen's *Differential Evolution* is likewise good but expensive.

> Kenneth Price, Rainer Storn, and Journi Lampinen, 2005, *Differential Evolution: A Practical Approach to Global Optimization*, Springer

James Kennedy, Russell Eberhart, and Yuhui Shi's seminal book on Particle Swarm Optimization is *Swarm Intelligence*. Unfortunately this was a very poor choice of name: there was already a *Swarm Intelligence*, published two years earlier, largely about Ant Colony Optimization. That one was by Eric Bonabeau, Marco Dorigo, and Guy Theraulaz.[213]

> James Kennedy, Russell Eberhart, and Yuhui Shi, 2001, *Swarm Intelligence*, Morgan Kaufmann

> Eric Bonabeau, Marco Dorigo, and Guy Theraulaz, 1999, *Swarm Intelligence: From Natural to Artificial Systems*, Oxford University Press

Though it is getting somewhat long in the tooth, Melanie Mitchell's *An Introduction to Genetic Algorithms* is still quite a good, well, introduction to genetic algorithms.

> Melanie Mitchell, 1996, *An Introduction to Genetic Algorithms*, MIT Press

David Fogel's *Blondie24* recounts the development of a one-population competitive coevolutionary algorithm to learn how to play checkers very strongly, and casts it in the context of artificial intelligence in general.

> David Fogel, 2001, *Blondie24: Playing at the Edge of AI*, Morgan Kauffman

Last, but far from least, Ken De Jong's *Evolutionary Computation: A Unified Approach* puts not only most of the population methods but a significant chunk of all of metaheuristics under one unifying framework. It covers a lot of what we don't cover here: the theory and analysis behind these topics.

> Kenneth De Jong, 2006, *Evolutionary Computation: A Unified Approach*, MIT Press

11.3.3 Tools

There's lots of stuff out there. Here's just a few:

So let's get the obvious one out of the way first. ECJ[214] is a popular population-based toolkit with facilities for parallel optimization, multiobjective optimization, and most representations, including genetic programming. ECJ is designed for large projects and so it has a somewhat steep learning curve. But its author is very responsive, and unusually handsome as well. If you meet this person in the street, you should give him a big hug. ECJ also dovetails with a multiagent simulation toolkit called MASON. Both are in Java. ECJ's web page points to a lot of other Java-based systems, if ECJ's too heavyweight for you.

> http://cs.gmu.edu/~eclab/projects/ecj/
> http://cs.gmu.edu/~eclab/projects/mason/

---

[213]Believe it or not, there's now *a third* book which has foolishly been titled *Swarm Intelligence!*

[214]ECJ doesn't actually stand for anything. Trust me on this. Though people have made up things like "Evolutionary Computation in Java" or whatnot.

If you prefer C++, here are two particularly good systems. EO is an evolutionary computation toolkit, and an extension, ParadisEO, adds single-state, parallel, and multiobjective optimization facilities. A competitor, Open BEAGLE, also provides good evolutionary and parallel tools.

http://eodev.sourceforge.net/
http://paradiseo.gforge.inria.fr
http://beagle.gel.ulaval.ca

If you're looking for more general purpose metaheuristics frameworks (single-state optimization, combinatorial optimization methods, etc.), you might consider the ones examined in a recent survey by José Antonio Parejo, Antonio Ruiz-Cortés, Sebastián Lozano, and Pablo Fernandez.[215] Besides some of the above frameworks (ECJ, EO/ParadiseEO), they looked at EasyLocal++, EvA2, FOM, HeuristicLab, JCLEC, MALLBA, OAT, and Opt4j.

http://tabu.diegm.uniud.it/EasyLocal++/
http://www.ra.cs.uni-tuebingen.de/software/EvA2/
http://www.isa.us.es/fom/
http://dev.heuristiclab.com
http://jclec.sourceforge.net
http://neo.lcc.uma.es/mallba/easy-mallba/
http://optalgtoolkit.sourceforge.net
http://opt4j.sourceforge.net

If you need a good XCS library, Martin Butz has an XCSF library in Java, and Pier Luca Lanzi has XCS implementations in C and C++.

http://www.wsi.uni-tuebingen.de/lehrstuehle/cognitive-modeling/code/
http://illigal.org/2003/10/01/xcs-tournament-selection-classifier-system-implementation-in-c-version-12/
http://illigal.org/2009/03/24/xcslib-the-xcs-classifier-system-library/

The Particle Swarm Optimization folks have coalesced around a single C file as a kind of reference standard. It's well written and documented. As of this printing, the latest was the SPSO-2011 version. You can find this and lots of other PSO systems here:

http://www.particleswarm.info/Programs.html

Genetic Programming Systems Because of its complexity, GP tends to encourage systems built just for it. ECJ, EO, and Open BEAGLE all have strong support for tree-style GP and, in some cases, variations like Grammatical Evolution or Push. They're popular tools if you're doing Java or C++. Besides these systems, you should also check out...

If you're looking to do GP in straight C, lil-gp is a bit long in the tooth nowadays but still handy.

http://garage.cse.msu.edu/software/lil-gp/

---

[215] José Antonio Parejo, Antonio Ruiz-Cortés, Sebastián Lozano, and Pablo Fernandez, 2012, Metaheuristics optimization frameworks: a survey and benchmarking, *Soft Computing*, 16, 527–561.

Likewise, if you'd like to do GP in MATLAB, check out Sara Silva's GPlab.

http://gplab.sourceforge.net/

Lee Spector maintains a list of Push implementations. The big one is Clojush, written in Clojure.

http://faculty.hampshire.edu/lspector/push.html

There are several Grammatical Evolution systems, all listed here, including the seminal libGE.

http://www.grammatical-evolution.org/software.html

The best-known implementation of Linear Genetic Programming is Discipulus. Note: it is not free.

http://www.rmltech.com/

Julian Miller's Cartesian Genetic Programming lists all the current CGP implementations.

http://cartesiangp.co.uk/resources.html

Eureqa is a well-regarded system for using Genetic Programming to analyze, visualize, and solve nontrivial Symbolic Regression problems.

http://creativemachines.cornell.edu/eureqa/

11.3.4 Conferences

The big kahuna is the *Genetic and Evolutionary Computation Conference*, or GECCO, run by ACM SIGEvo (http://www.sigevo.org). GECCO is the merging of the former GP and ICGA conferences. It's usually held in the United States, and has lots of smaller workshops attached to it.

If you're an **undergraduate student,** I highly recommend that you submit to the *GECCO Undergraduate Student Workshop*. It's a great venue to show off your stuff, and they're friendly and encouraging. If you're a **graduate student** and would like some tough feedback on your proposed thesis work, a great pick is the *GECCO Graduate Student Workshop*, where you present your work in front of a panel of luminaries who then critique it (and they're not nice!). This is a *good thing*: better to hear it in a friendly workshop than when you're doing your proposal or thesis defense! Both workshops are specially protected from the rest of the conference and run by people who really care about you as a student.

The primary European conference is the *International Conference on Parallel Problem Solving from Nature*, or PPSN. It's not historically been very large but of unusually high quality.

The third major conference is the *IEEE Congress on Evolutionary Computation*, or CEC, held in various spots around the world. It's often quite large.

The three conferences above are dominated by evolutionary computation techniques. An alternative conference for other methods is the *Metaheuristics International Conference* or MIC.

The oldest theory workshop, and almost certainly the most respected venue in the field,[216] is the venerable *Foundations of Genetic Algorithms* workshop, or FOGA, run by ACM SIGEvo, and usually in the United States. It's not just about the Genetic Algorithm any more, but rather about all kinds of metaheuristics theory: indeed, in 2009 there wasn't a *single Genetic Algorithm paper* in the whole workshop! FOGA is held every other year. The year that FOGA's not held, an alternative theory workshop has lately been hosted at Schloss Dagstuhl (http://www.dagstuhl.de) in Germany.

Europe is also host to the *European Conference on Genetic Programming*, or EuroGP, an alternative conference focused, not surprisingly, on genetic programming.

Not to be outdone, the invitation-only *Genetic Programming Theory and Practice* Workshop, or GPTP, is held each year at the University of Michigan.

Ant Colony Optimization also has its own conference apart from the big ones above: the *International Conference on Ant Colony Optimization and Swarm Intelligence* or ANTS.[217]

Particle Swarm Optimization and Ant Colony Optimization folks, among others, have also lately been attending the *IEEE Swarm Intelligence Symposium* or SIS.

The area of **Evolvable Hardware (EH)**[218] concerns itself with the optimization of hardware designs: circuits, antennas, and the like. This field often has a prominent showing at the *NASA/ESA Conference on Adaptive Hardware and Systems*.

I would be remiss in not mentioning conferences in **Artificial Life (ALife)**,[219] the simulation of abstract biological processes. ALife has long been strongly associated with metaheuristics, and particularly with evolutionary computation.[220] Major ALife conferences include the *International Conference on the Simulation and Synthesis of Living Systems* (or ALife), the *European Conference on Artificial Life* (or ECAL), and *From Animals to Animats: the International Conference on Simulation of Adaptive Behavior* (or SAB). ALife and ECAL are run by the International Society of Artificial Life (http://alife.org). SAB is run by the International Society for Adaptive Behavior (http://www.isab.org.uk).

---

[216] For example, I have twice chosen to publish at FOGA rather than in even our best journals. That's not atypical.

[217] Annoyingly, this is not an acronym.

[218] Evolvable Hardware is notable in that the fitness function is often done in real hardware. Here's a famous story. Adrian Thompson was an early Evolvable Hardware researcher who worked on optimizing computer circuits using evolutionary algorithms. Adrian had access to early releases of the Xilinx XC6216 FPGA, a chip which was capable of forming arbitrary circuits on-chip through the deft use of a grid of programmable gates. The evolutionary algorithm performed fitness assessment by actually programming the chip with the given circuit, then testing its performance on an oscilloscope. Problem is, when Adrian received the final optimized circuits, they were sometimes consisted of disconnected circuits with various vestigial sections that didn't do anything. But when he deleted these regions, the circuit stopped working on the chip! It turns out that the early Xilinx chips given to Adrian had bugs on them, and the evolutionary algorithm was finding solutions which *identified and took advantage of the bugs*. Not generalizable! See Adrian's homepage for various literature: http://www.informatics.sussex.ac.uk/users/adrianth/ade.html

[219] ALife lies at the intersection of computer scientists interested in stealing ideas from biology, and biologists interested in using computers for modeling. Since you're probably in the former camp, allow me to suggest a recent text which romps all over the area, everything from evolutionary neural networks to swarms to Lindenmayer systems: Dario Floreano and Claudio Mattiuissi, 2008, *Bio-Inspired Artificial Intelligence: Theories, Methods, and Technologies*, MIT Press.

[220] ALife is so strongly associated with evolutionary computation that the journal *Evolutionary Computation* has a sister journal, *Artificial Life*, which is among the primary journals in ALife.

11.3.5 Journals

At this point, I think the three primary journals in the field are all evolutionary computation journals: but they accept papers on all topics in metaheuristics (and indeed many of the seminal non-EC metaheuristics papers are in these journals).

The oldest and (I think) the most respected journal in the field is *Evolutionary Computation* (MIT Press), often nicknamed *ECJ*.[221] Originally founded by Ken De Jong, *Evolutionary Computation* has a long track record of strong theoretical publication and good empirical work.[222]
As artificial life and metaheuristics have long been closely associated, *Evolutionary Computation* has a sister journal, also by MIT press: *Artificial Life*.

IEEE Transactions on Evolutionary Computation (*IEEE TransEC*) is a first-rate, highly ranked journal which has a bit more of an application and technical emphasis. My first solo journal publication was in IEEE TransEC and it was a most pleasant publication experience. Because it's an IEEE journal, IEEE TransEC also benefits from a high Impact Factor, which isn't something to be dismissed!

Genetic Programming and Evolvable Machines (*GPEM*) is a newer journal which emphasizes genetic programming and evolvable hardware, but takes a wide range of papers. It's well regarded and is published by Springer.[223] The GPEM editor also maintains a blog, listed below.

http://gpemjournal.blogspot.com/

11.3.6 Email Lists

There are plenty of email lists, but let me single out three in particular.

EC-Digest is a long-running mailing list for announcements of interest to the metaheuristics community. It's moderated and low-bandwidth.

http://ec-digest.research.ucf.edu/

The Genetic Programming Mailing List is an active discussion list covering GP.

http://tech.groups.yahoo.com/group/genetic_programming/

The Ant Colony Optimization Mailing List is a relatively light discussion list mostly for announcements regarding ACO.

https://iridia.ulb.ac.be/cgi-bin/mailman/listinfo/aco-list
http://iridia.ulb.ac.be/~mdorigo/ACO/mailing-list.html

---

[221] I'm not sure if Ken De Jong has yet forgiven me giving my software the same acronym— I just didn't know that *Evolutionary Computation* sometimes had a *Journal* after it!
[222] Truth in advertising: I'm presently on the *Evolutionary Computation* editorial board.
[223] More truth in advertising: I'm on the editorial board of *Genetic Programming and Evolvable Machines*.

11.4 Example Course Syllabi for the Text

Weeks are numbered, and each week is assumed to be approximately four hours of lecture time. Topics are organized in approximate order of significance and dependency. Note that the Combinatorial Optimization, Coevolution, and Model Fitting sections make fleeting, nonessential reference to one another. Rough chapter dependencies are shown in the Table of Contents (page 1).

Simple Syllabus A lightweight one-semester course covering common algorithms and topics.

1. Introduction, Gradient-based Optimization (Sections 0, 1)
2. Single-State Methods (Sections 2–2.4)
3. Population Methods (Sections 3–3.2, 3.6)
4. Representation (Sections 4–4.1, 4.3–4.3.3)

Optional:

5. Multiobjective Optimization (Section 7)
6. Combinatorial Optimization (Sections 8.1–8.3)
7. Parallel Methods (Sections 5–5.3)
8. Coevolution (Sections 6–6.3)

Firehose Syllabus An intensive one-semester senior-level or masters' level course.

1. Introduction, Gradient-based Optimization (Sections 0, 1)
2. Single-State Methods (Section 2)
3. Population Methods (Section 3)
4. Representation (Sections 4–4.1, 4.3, and 4.4)
5. Representation (Sections 4.2, 4.5, and 4.6)
6. Multiobjective Optimization (Section 7)
7. Combinatorial Optimization (Section 8)
8. Parallel Methods (Section 5)
9. Coevolution (Section 6)
10. Model Fitting (Section 9)
11. Policy Optimization (Sections 10–10.2) *(presuming no prior knowledge of Q-Learning)*
12. Policy Optimization (Sections 10.3–10.5)

Index

ϵ-greedy action selection, 179, 196
$(\mu+\lambda)$, 34
$(\mu+1)$, 48
(μ, λ), 33
$(1+\lambda)$, 24
$(1+1)$, 23
$(1, \lambda)$, 24

Ackley, David, 39, 213, 214
action set, 192
actions, 174
activity level, 187
Agarwal, Sameer, 141
agent, 90, 173, 174
Agrawal, Samir, 23
Alander, Jarmo, 224
aliased states, 204
allele, 31
Alsing, Roger, 0
Alternating Optimization (AO), 123
Andre, David, 81
Angeline, Peter, 68
annealing, 26
ANOVA, 212
Ant Colony Optimization (ACO), 152
Ant Colony System (ACS), 156
Ant System (AS), 153
ant trails, 152
AQ, 162
arbitration scheme, 90, 182
archive, 126, 141
arity, 75
arms race, 122
arrays, 12
artificial immune systems, 129
Artificial Life (ALife), 230
Asada, Minoru, 175
assessment procedure, 17
Asynchronous Evolution, 106
automatically defined functions (ADFs), 79
automatically defined macros (ADMs), 80

Baker, James, 44
Baldwin Effect, 51
Baluja, Shumeet, 167
Banzhaf, Wolfgang, 84, 226
Baxter, John, 28
Bayes Network, 171
Bayesian Optimization Algorithm (BOA), 172
Bellman Equation, 177
Bellman, Richard, 177
Bennett, Forrest, 81
best of run, 207

biasing, 32, 62
bin packing, 147
black box optimization, 9
bloat, 87, 95
Blondie24, 112
Bonabeau, Eric, 227
Bonferroni correction, 212
bootstrapping, 178
Born, Joachim, 216
Box, George Edward Pelham, 24
Box-Muller-Marsaglia Polar Method, 24
breeding, 31
Brindle, Anne, 45
building blocks, 40, 221
Butz, Martin, 195, 228

candidate solution, see individual, 17
Cantú-Paz, Eric, 172
Cartesian Genetic Programming (CGP), 85
Caruana, Rich, 167
Cavicchio, Daniel Joseph Jr., 51, 130
Cellular Encoding, 81
Chellapilla, Kumar, 111, 112
child, 31
Chinook, 113
Christensen, Steffen, 211, 225
chromosome, 31
classification, 161, 182
closure, see operator, closed
co-adaptive, 110
Coello Coello, Carlos, 224
coevolution, 109
    N-Population Cooperative, 110, 122
    1-Population Competitive, 109, 111
    2-Population Competitive, 109, 117
        parallel, 119
        parallel previous, 120
        sequential, 118
        serial, 118
    compositional, 109
    test-based, 109
collections, 11
Collins, J. J., 84
combinatorial optimization problem, 147
Compact Genetic Algorithm (cGA), 168
compactness, 82
components, 147
computational effort, 207
cons cells, 83
convergence, 40
convergence time, 13
Copy, 17, 59
copy-forward, 103

233

cost, 148
covariance matrix, 166
cover, 182
Cramer, Nichael, 73
credit assignment, 126
crossover, 31, 33, 38
    Clustered, 190
    Intermediate Recombination, 42
        for Integers, 64
    Line Recombination, 41
        for Integers, 64
    Multi-Point, 39
    One-Point, 38
        for Lists, 87
    Subtree, 77
    Two-Point, 38
        for Lists, 87
    Uniform, 38
        among K Vectors, 41
Crowding, 130
    Deterministic, 130
cycles, 114

Dawkins, Richard, 50
De Jong, Kenneth, 48, 122, 124, 215, 227, 231
Deb, Kalyanmoy, 23, 139, 141, 208, 218, 226
deceptive functions, 22, 59, 214
decision trees, 161
decoding, 60
delta rule, 201
demes, 103, 109, 117
desirability, 155
Differential Evolution (DE), 54
diploid, 118
directed acyclic graph, 69
directed mutation, 31, 55
Discipulus, 84
distance measure, 128
distributions, 161
    bivariate, 171
    Gaussian, 23
    marginal, 161, 166
    normal, 23
    standard normal, 24
Diversity Maintenance, *see* niching
Dorigo, Marco, 152, 156, 225–227
duplicability, 206
dynamic programming, 178

Eberhart, Russell, 55, 227
Edge Encoding, 81
Edwards, Howard, 207
elites, 46
elitism, 156
encoding, 60
    developmental, 66, 82

direct, 66
    indirect, 66, 82, 84, 91
ephemeral random constant, 77
epistasis, 38, 40
Estimation of Distribution Algorithms (EDAs), 161, 164
    Multivariate, 171
    Univariate, 167
evaluation, 31
evaporation, 153
Evolution Strategies (ES), 33
Evolutionary Algorithm (EA), 31
Evolutionary Computation (EC), 31
Evolutionary Programming (EP), 36
Evolvable Hardware (EH), 230
Expectation Maximization (EM), 123, 171
explicit speciation, 127
Exploration versus Exploitation, 20, 22, 179
external state, 174, 204

Feature-based Tabu Search, 27, 158
Feo, Thomas, 151
Fernandez, Pablo, 228
Festa, Pauola, 225
Fisher, Ronald Aylmer, 210
fitness, *see* quality, 31
    absolute, 110
    baseline, 190
    external, 111
    internal, 111
    joint, 123
    relative, 110
fitness assessment, 31
    relative, 113
fitness functions, *see* problems
fitness landscape, 31
fitness scaling, 45
fitness sharing, 128
    implicit, 129
Floreano, Dario, 230
Fogel, David, 111, 112, 226
Fogel, Lawrence, 36, 111
forest, 79
Forrest, Stephanie, 129
FORTH, 82
Francone, Frank, 84, 226
full adjacency matrix, 67
Full algorithm, 75
function set, 75
functions, 12

Gambardella, Luca, 156
Gauss, Karl Friedrich, 23
Gawelczyk, Andreas, 217
Gelatt, Charles Daniel Jr., 25
gene, 31
generalizability, 207, 230

generation, 31
Generation Gap Algorithms, 48
generational, 31
generative models, 165
Genetic Algorithm (GA), 36
Genetic Programming (GP), 73, 204
GENITOR, 47, 48
genome, 31
genotype, 31, 59
Gibbs Sampling, 9
global optima, 14
global optimization algorithm, 15, 20
Glover, Fred, 26, 52
GNARL, 68
Goldberg, David, 128, 168, 172, 200, 201
Gosset, William Sealy, 210
Gradient Ascent, 10, 13
Gradient Ascent with Restarts, 15
Gradient Descent, 13
Gram-Schmidt process, 217
Grammatical Evolution (GE), 84
graphs, 66
Gray code, 61
Gray, Frank, 61
Greedy Randomized Adaptive Search Procedures (GRASP), 151
Grefenstette, John, 51, 186, 190
Griewank, Andreas, 216
Grow algorithm, 75
Guided Genetic Algorithm, 160
Guided Local Search (GLS), 158
Gustafson, Steven, 224

Hamming cliff, 60
Hamming distance, 128
Hansen, Nikolaus, 217
hard constraints, 149
Harik, Georges, 130, 168
Hessian, 14
heuristic, 148
Hierarchical Bayesian Optimization Algorithm (hBOA), 172
Hill-Climbing, 10, 17
Hill-Climbing with Random Restarts, 20
Hillis, Daniel, 118
history, 204
Holland, John, 36, 191
homologous, 40, 78
Hornby, Gregory, 92
hyperellipsoids, 201
Hyperheuristics, 51
hypervolume, 134, 208
hypothesis, *see* model
hypothesis test, 208
    nonparametric, 210

iCCEA, 126

illegal solutions, 147
incest prevention, 127
individual, *see* candidate solution, 31
induction, 161
infeasible solutions, 147
informant, 56
informative gradient, 22
initialization, 32, 59
    adaptive, 191
initialization procedure, 17
internal state, 204
introns, 86, 95
invalid solutions, 147
inverse problems, 10
inviable code, 95
island models, 103
    asynchronous, 104
    synchronous, 104
island topology, 103
    fully-connected, 103
    injection model, 103
    toroidal grid, 103
Iterated Local Search (ILS), 28, 148

Jaśkowski, Wojciech, 116
Join, 32
Jordan, Michael
    the basketball player, 126
    the professor, 182

k-fold cross validation, 207
k-Means Clustering, 123
k-Nearest-Neighbor (kNN), 161, 184
Kauth, Joan, 47, 48
kd-tree, 165
Keane, Martin, 81
Keijzer, Martin, 83
Keller, Robert, 84
Kennedy, James, 55, 227
kernelization, 185
Kirkpatrick, Scott, 25
Kitano, Hiroaki, 91
Klein, Jon, 83
Koch Curve, 92
Kovaks, Timothy, 224
Koza, John, 48, 73, 81, 220, 222, 224
Krawiec, Krzysztof, 116

L-Systems, *see* Lindenmayer Systems
Laguna, Manuel, 52
Lamarck, Jean-Baptiste, 50
Lamarckian Algorithms, 50
Lampinen, Jouni, 54, 227
Langdon, William, 221, 222, 224, 226
Lanzi, Pier Luca, 195, 196, 200, 201, 228
laziness, 126

Learnable Evolution Model (LEM), 51, 161
learning bias, 162
Learning Classifier Systems (LCS), 173, 183, 191
learning gradient, 111
learning rate, 156
Lindenmayer Systems, 92, 230
Lindenmayer, Aristid, 92
Linear Genetic Programming, 83
linear problem, 213
linkage, 38, 40, 213
lists, 73, 83
Lobo, Fernando, 168
local optima, 14
local optimization algorithm, 14, 20
Loiacono, Daniele, 200, 201
loss of gradient, 122
Lourenço, Helena, 28
Lozano, Sebastián, 228
Lucas, Simon, 96

machine learning, 161
Mahfoud, Samir, 130
Manhattan distance, 139
Manhattan Project, 25
Mann-Whitney U Test, 211
Markov Chain Monte Carlo (MCMC), 9
Markov, Andrey Andreyevich, 175
Markovian environment, 175
Marsaglia, George, 24
Martí, Rafael, 52
Martin, Olivier, 28
master-slave fitness assessment, 105
match score, 183
match set, 90, 186, 192
matrices, 12, 66, 73, 81
Mattiussi, Claudio, 230
maxima, 13
McPhee, Nicholas, 226
mean vector, 166
Memetic Algorithms, 50
memory, 204
Mercer, Robert Ernest, 51
Messom, Chris, 207
Meta-Genetic Algorithms, 51
Meta-Optimization, 51
metaheuristics, 9
metric distance, 128
Metropolis Algorithm, 25
Metropolis, Nicholas, 25
Meyarivan, T., 141
Michalewicz, Zbigniew, 148, 226
Michalski, Ryszard, 161
Michigan-Approach Learning Classifier Systems, 90, 173, 183, 191
microclassifiers, 198
Miikkulainen, Risto, 68, 113

Miller, Juian, 85
Miller, Julian, 225
minima, 13
miscoordination, 126
Mitchell, Melanie, 227
model, 12, 161
    discriminative, 162
    generative, 162
modification procedure, 17
modularity, 79, 82, 91
Mona Lisa, 0
Montana, David, 80
Monte Carlo Method, 25
Moscato, Pablo, 50
Mühlenbein, Heinz, 41, 168, 216
Muller, Mervin, 24
mutation, 31, 33
    Bit-Flip, 37
    Creep, 190
    Duplicate Removal, 89
    Gaussian Convolution, 23, 35
    Gaussian Convolution Respecting Zeros, 67
    Integer Randomization, 63
    Point, 63
    Polynomial, 23
    Random Walk, 63
    Subtree, 78
mutation rate, 35
    adaptive, 35

NEAT, 68, 113
Needle in a Haystack style functions, 22, 59
neighbors, 108
NERO, 113
neural networks, 161
Neural Programming (NP), 72
Newton's Method, 14
Newton, Sir Isaac, 14
Ng, Andrew, 182
niches, 110
niching, 110
No Free Lunch Theorem (NFL), 213
noisy functions, 21
Non-Dominated Sorting, 139
Non-Dominated Sorting Genetic Algorithm II (NSGA-II), 141
non-homologous, *see* homologous
Nordin, Peter, 84, 226
null hypothesis, 208

O'Neill, Michael, 84, 225
objective, 133
objective functions, *see* problems
One-Fifth Rule, 36
operator
    adaptive, 35

closed, 73, 84, 149
    self-adaptive, 35, 83, 191
Opportunistic Evolution, 106
Ostermeier, Andreas, 217
over-specification, 10, 90, 182

Pólya, George, 226
Panait, Liviu, 96, 126, 171, 207, 225
Parejo, José Antonio, 228
parent, 31
Pareto domination, 133
Pareto front, 133
    concave, 133
    convex, 133
    discontinuous, 134
    local, 134
    nonconvex, 134
Pareto Front Rank, 138
Pareto nondominated, 133
Pareto strength, 141
Pareto weakness, 142
Pareto wimpiness, 142
parse trees, 74
parsimony pressure, 96
    double tournament, 96
    lexicographic, 96
    linear, 96
    non-parametric, 96
Particle Filters, 44
Particle Swarm Optimization (PSO), 31, 55
particles, 56
Pelikan, Martin, 172
penalties, 159
Perelson, Alan, 129
phenotype, 31, 59
pheromone, 152
    higher-order, 158
piecewise linear function, 200
Pitt-Approach Rule Systems, 90, 173, 186
Poli, Riccardo, 222, 226
policy, 90, 173, 174
policy search, 182
Pollack, Jordan, 68
population, 31
    alternative, 117
    collaborating, 117
    foil, 117
    primary, 117
Population-Based Incremental Learning (PBIL), 167
PostScript, 82
Potter, Mitchell, 122, 124
Pratap, Amrit, 141
prediction, 195, 200
prediction error, 195
premature convergence, 34, 40
preselection, 130

Price, Kenneth, 54, 227
probability distributions, 12
problem, 17
problems
    11-bit Boolean Multiplexer, 220
    Artificial Ant, 74, 222
    De Jong test suite, 214–216
    Even N-Parity, 221
    Griewank, 216
    Knapsack, 147
    Lawnmower, 223
    Leading Ones, 213
    Leading Ones Blocks, 213
    Linear Problems, 214
    Max Ones, 213
    OneMax, 213
    Rastrigin, 216
    rotated, 216
    Schwefel, 216
    Sphere, 215
    Step, 214
    Sum, 214
    Symbolic Regression, 74, 75, 77, 80, 220
    Traveling Salesman (TSP), 27, 147
    ZDT1, 218
    ZDT2, 219
    ZDT3, 219
    ZDT4, 219
Prusinkiewicz, Przemyslaw, 92
PTC2, 76
Push, 83

Q-learning, 173, 175, 178
Q-table, 175
Q-value, 176
quadtree, 165
quality, *see* fitness, 17
queues, 12

Ramped Half-and-Half algorithm, 76
Ramsey, Connie, 186
random number generator, 205
    java.util.Random, 205
    linear congruential, 205
    Mersenne Twister, 205
    RANDU, 205
Random Search, 10, 20
random walk, 25
Rastrigin, Leonard Andreevich, 216
Rechenberg, Ingo, 33, 215
recombination, *see* crossover
recursive least squares, 201
REINFORCE, 182
reinforcement, 173
    negative, 174
    positive, 174

reinforcement learning, 173, 178
    multiagent, 126
relative overgeneralization, 126
Rensende, Mauricio, 225
replicability, 205
representation, 19, 59
resampling techniques, 31
Resende, Mauricio, 151
reward, *see* reinforcement
Richardson, Jon, 128
Robert Keller, 226
Robinson, Alan, 83
robustness, 111
Rosenbluth, Arianna and Marshall, 25
Rosenbrock, Howard, 216
Ruiz-Cortés, Antonio, 228
rule
    active, 187
    default, 90, 183
    production, 89
    state-action, 89, 90, 173
rule body, 89, 183
rule covering, 189
rule deletion, 189
rule generalization, 189
rule head, 89, 183
rule merging, 189
rule specialization, 189
rule strength, 187
Ryan, Conor, 84, 96

saddle points, 13
sample, 31
sample distributions, 164
sampling
    region-based, 163
    rejection, 162
    weighted rejection, 163
Sampson, Jeffrey R., 51
SAMUEL, 51, 186
Saunders, Gregory, 68
Scatter Search with Path Relinking, 52
schedule, 25
schema theory, 40
Schlierkamp-Voosen, Dirk, 41
Schoenauer, Marc, 148
Schomisch, M., 216
Schultz, Alan, 186
Schwefel, Hans-Paul, 33, 41, 42, 216
seeding, 32, 62
selection, 31
    Fitness-Proportionate, 43
    Fitnessless, 116
    non-parametric, 45
    parent, 32, 54
    Roulette, 43

Stochastic Universal Sampling, 44
    survival, 32, 54
    Tournament, 45
        Restricted, 130
    Truncation, 43
selection pressure, 24
selection procedure, 17
Shi, Yuhui, 227
Sigvardsson, Oskar, 0
Silva, Sara, 229
Simulated Annealing, 25
Skolicki, Zbigniew, 99, 145
Smith, Robert, 129
smoothness, 22, 59
Solkoll, 0
sorting networks, 118
sparsity, 139
spatially embedded models, 107
species, 110
specificity, 182
Spector, Lee, 80, 81, 83, 225
spread, 134
Srinvas, N., 139
Stützle, Thomas, 28, 152, 226
stack languages, 82, 84
Stanley, Kenneth, 68, 113
state space, 90
states, 174
statistically significant, 210
steady-state, 31, 47
Steepest Ascent Hill-Climbing, 18
Steepest Ascent Hill-Climbing with Replacement, 18
Stewart, Potter, 9
stochastic, 18
stochastic optimization, 9
stochastic processes, 175
stochastic search, 9
Storn, Rainer, 54, 225, 227
Strength Pareto Evolutionary Algorithm 2 (SPEA2), 142
strings, *see* lists
Student's t-Test, 210
subpopulations, 103, 109
subsolution, 123
subsumption, 199
subtree selection, 79
supervised learning, 183
Support Vector Machines (SVMs), 161, 185
swarm, 56
symbols, 93
    nonterminal, 91
    terminal, 91

tabu list, 26
Tabu Search, 26, 148
Teller, Augusta and Edward, 25
Teller, Eric (Astro), 25, 72

temperature, 26
test cases, 111, 117, 207
test problems, *see* problems
test set, 207
tests, 111
Theraulaz, Guy, 227
Thiele, Lothar, 208, 218
Thompson, Adrian, 230
threads, 101
Tinsley, Marion, 113
tournament size, 45
training set, 207
transition model, 174
Tree-Style Genetic Programming, 48
trees, 73
Truncation Selection, 33
Tsang, Edward, 158, 225
Tukey, John, 212
tuples, 12
Tweak, 17, 20, 59
type constraints, 80
typing
    atomic, 81
    polymorphic, 81
    set, 81

unbiased estimator, 170
under-specification, 10, 90, 183
unimodal functions, 21
Univariate Marginal Distribution Algorithm (UMDA), 168
utility, 174
utility error, 184
utility variance, 183, 187

value, 148, 174
Vecchi, Mario, 25
vector processor, 108
vectors, 12
Vo, Christopher, 171
Voronoi tessellation, 184
vote, 90
Voudouris, Chris, 158

Walker, Matthew, 207
weak methods, 9
weights, 148
Welch's t-Test, 210
Welch, Bernard Lewis, 210
Whitley, Darrell, 47, 48
Wiegand, Paul, 126
Wieloch, Bartosz, 116
Williams, Ronald, 182
Wilson, Stewart, 192, 200, 201
Wineberg, Mark, 211, 225

XCS, 195
XCSF, 200

Xilinx, 230

Zeroth Level Classifier System (ZCS), 192
Ziggurat Method, 24
Zitzler, Eckart, 208, 218

Made in the USA
Lexington, KY
02 November 2013